The Essential WILLIAM H. WHYTE

The Essential
WILLIAM H. WHYTE

Edited by Albert LaFarge

FORDHAM UNIVERSITY PRESS
New York
2000

Permissions Acknowledgments appear on page 373.

Library of Congress Cataloging-in-Publication Data
Whyte, William Hollingsworth.
     The essential William H. Whyte / William H. Whyte; edited by
   Albert LaFarge.
         p. cm.
   Includes bibliographical references and index
   ISBN 0-8232-2025-7 (hc.)--ISBN 0-8232-2026-5 (pbk.)
     1. Cities and towns. 2. Sociology, Urban. 3. Urban anthropology.
   I. LaFarge, Albert. II. Title.

HT151.W56 2000
307.76--dc21   99-056109

Printed in the United States of America
00 01 02 03 04   5 4 3 2 1
First Edition

Contents

Contents

Foreword

William H. Whyte, known to friends and family as Holly, was a prophet of common sense. He did not approach the city with a preconceived vision; he came to it as an observer, and he based his philosophy of open space, his prescription for the civilized way of making cities, on what he saw. He was in every way an urban anthropologist, and he had the objectivity of a great scientist, prepared to gather the evidence and be guided by it. He cared more than anything about how people used the spaces they were given, and he told us more than we had ever known about that. Where architects and planners had been designing by intuition, Holly Whyte gave them facts.

But that, as all of you know, was only the beginning. We might have admired Holly as much as we did had he been only a gatherer of facts, but that was not all he was trying to do. His facts were gathered for a purpose. His objective research on the city, on open space, on the way people use it, was set within what I think I must call a moral context. Holly believed with deep passion that there was such a thing as quality of life, and that the way we build cities, the way we make places, can have a profound effect on what kinds of lives are lived within those places. That is why, surely, Holly never set himself up as a high-powered consultant, though he probably could have made a fortune doing so. He never wanted to be beholden to rich real-estate developers, though many of them would certainly have been willing to pay high fees for the privilege of a Holly Whyte endorsement on their plazas. Selling himself like that would have destroyed the purity and integrity of his mission, and he knew it.

Holly, unlike so many people who work in urban design, was also never one to exaggerate the importance of physical form. He had no illusions that a well-designed street or plaza was the same as bread on the table or justice in the courtroom. But he was never inclined to minimize the value of physical form, either. Indeed, one of the greatest contributions he made was in putting all of this in perfect perspective, making it neither too important nor too unimportant in the scheme of things.

And how deeply he believed that the quality of life he valued was enhanced by the urban experience, by the street, by the notion of the public realm. In the last generation, we have seen what we might call the triumph of the private realm in this country, as malls and atriums and gated communities take over from streets and parks and squares. Holly would have none of this. He was our prophet of the public realm. He believed in the urban values of engagement and serendipity, and not the suburban values of disengagement and separation and unchanging order. He believed that the greatest achievement of the city is the street, and he complained in his book *City* that our urban planners and public officials were engaged in what he called "a holy war against the street." He was right. Holly knew that, as the architect Louis Kahn once said, "a street is a room by agreement," and he loved the conceptual notion of the agreement as much as the physical notion of the room itself, for Holly always believed that the greatest lesson the city has to offer us is the idea that we are all in it together, for better or for worse, and we have to make it work.

He put his facts where his heart was, and he put his heart where his facts were. Holly was the first to cut through the hypocrisy of the economic arguments companies often trumped up for leaving the city, and to point out that they were really just excuses for indulging in the suburban values of disengagement—not to mention excuses for allowing the boss an easy commute to home or golf course, since Holly was also the first to demonstrate that almost every company that left Manhattan departed for turf close to the chief executive's backyard.

To Holly, the selfishness of this gesture summed up a certain anti-urban attitude that he had committed himself to reversing. In his mind, cities were where community was to be found. And as Holly so deftly demolished the corporate rationale for leaving Manhattan, he cut right through another common hypocrisy of our time, the hypocrisy of architects who designed sterile, unpleasant, and hostile places, and pretended that they were esthetic experiences. Holly knew better. He had the empirical facts to prove it, and as usual, those empirical facts never hardened into a rigid esthetic viewpoint. His love of easy, casual human use, as exemplified in his insistence that there be movable chairs in Bryant Park, did not blind him to the virtues of the ultimate spare modernist plaza, the Seagram Building on Park Avenue, because he could see how well it worked. His visual sensibility worked the opposite from the way, say, an architectural magazine editor's does. Where the magazine wants only to look at places as objects, with its photographs devoid of people, Holly's mind's eye had every place filled with people. He only began to see things when the people were in them.

Every time I think I've had an idea about cities and streets and how they work, I look back and discover that Holly saw it first. He taught all of us, more than anything, to look, to look hard, with a clean, clear mind, and then to look again—and to believe in what you see. That is the first of his lessons, and the one that informs all the others. Believe in what you see, and believe in the fact that the people who use cities are often way ahead of the people who design them—that is what Holly Whyte taught us all, and what was central to his passion for civic engagement, for community, and for the enlightenment of urban life.

Paul Goldberger
October 1999

Preface and Acknowledgments

I had the immense good fortune to be drawn, quite by chance, to the work of William H. Whyte in 1993 while working as an editor at Henry Holt, the publishing house that had contracted to publish his memoirs. My involvement with Holly Whyte (as he was informally known) began after his deadline passed and a manuscript was not forthcoming. I was enlisted initially as a goad to Holly, who was quick to assure me his memoirs would be ready soon. But his pace was slowing under the weight of several disabilities, not least of which was poor eyesight, and before long I volunteered as his amanuensis at his home on East 94th Street, visiting twice a week for several months. The present volume is a by-product of that collaboration. (Sadly, Whyte's memoir was left unfinished at the time of his death, with the exception of a colorful account of his experience as a Marine intelligence officer on Guadalcanal during World War II. That story, completed with the help of his step-brother James Perry, is also published by Fordham University Press.)

In making the selections for the present volume, I have tried to demonstrate how Whyte's twin careers as *Organization Man* author and urban anthropologist were united by a distinct sensibility and a rare generosity of spirit. While *The Essential William H. Whyte* is designed to be useful to students of sociology, urban studies, architecture, anthropology, and related disciplines, as well as to professionals in these fields, it also promises to have a wide and enduring appeal among educated lay readers. Whyte began his writing career as a journalist for *Fortune* at the height of the magazine's popularity, and his writing is consistently direct, and jargon-free. (The opening words of his first book, *Is Anybody Listening?*—"This is a book for laymen by a layman"—set the tone for his subsequent writings.) For those who believe that common sense can be learned by example, Whyte's writing will provide inspiration and classic instruction.

In assembling this volume I have received crucial help from many outstanding people who deserve to be acknowledged here: David Dillon, Patrick Doran, Sandra Gayle, Brendan Gill, Paul Goldberger, Mary Haldi, Barbara Kerr, Jack Macrae, James Perry, the staff of the Project for Public Spaces (especially Eugenia Askren, Steve Davies, Fred Kent, Kathy Madden, Ann Nissen, Andy Schwartz, and Norma Smith), Paco Underhill, and Sandra Weiner. At Fordham University Press, I would like to thank first Saverio Procario, a true publisher *and* a gentleman, and also Jacky Philpotts, Anthony Chiffolo, Kristen Cerbone, and Loomis Mayer for their help in guiding this book into print. Durrett Wagner did, seemingly, the work of ten men in the copyediting stage, from his redoubts in Illinois and Colorado. And Karen White Doody did the superb jacket and text design and composition.

And of course my wife, Jeanne Toft, whose love and companionship sustain me.

This book is dedicated to the people who were dearest to Holly Whyte: his widow Jenny Bell, their daughter Alexandra Whyte, and granddaughters Madeleine and Grace Hollingsworth Sperber-Whyte.

Introduction

William Hollingsworth Whyte Jr. was born on October 1, 1917, and reared in the town of West Chester, in Pennsylvania's bucolic Brandywine Valley about 25 miles west of Philadelphia. He graduated cum laude from Princeton University in 1939. He joined the U.S. Marine Corps in 1941 as Intelligence Officer in the 1st Marine Division, served through the entire Guadalcanal campaign, and was discharged in 1945 with the rank of captain. He joined *Fortune* magazine the next year and quickly rose to Assistant Managing Editor. His first book, *Is Anybody Listening?*, on which he was listed as co-author with the editors of *Fortune*, was published in 1952 and carried the subtitle, *How and Why U.S. Business Fumbles When It Talks With Human Beings.*

Whyte's next book, which would make him internationally famous, grew out of a series of *Fortune* articles and was presented as "his attempt to trace the long-range shift American organization life is bringing about in Americans' personal values." Published in 1956, *The Organization Man* caused a sensation and went on to sell over two million copies in a dozen languages.

Whyte was an astute observer who reported how people actually behaved (rather than how we assume we behave). A charitable critic with a real moral bent, Whyte was cheerful by nature, ever the optimist; even if his observations about postwar American life were laced with warnings, some of them quite ominous, Whyte was always thinking positively, and he was clearly a patriot. His affable personality and the agreeableness of his prose permitted him to go further in his social criticism than was typical in the popular media of the day, and people listened.

The financial success of *The Organization Man* allowed Whyte to give up his big office and salary at *Fortune* and turn to the full-time study of how to preserve and improve the quality of America's rural open spaces. In 1959, he condensed his findings in a *Life* magazine article, "A Plan to Save Vanishing U.S. Countryside" (reprinted in *Reader's Digest*), and in a monograph entitled *Securing Open Space for Urban America: Conservation Easements*, published by Urban Land Institute in the same year.

It was around this time that Whyte began a lifelong association with Laurance S. Rockefeller, whom he had met and impressed during his years at *Fortune*. One of the first tasks they undertook together was a study for the Outdoor Recreation Resources Review Commission, which was created by Act of Congress in June 1958 and chaired by Rockefeller. Whyte served as an adviser to the commission and prepared its final report, which was presented to Congress and President Lyndon B. Johnson on January 31, 1962. Whyte subsequently served on President Johnson's Task Force on the Preservation of Natural Beauty, earning praise from the president for his role in a project that made a "major contribution toward the Great Society." Whyte was a trustee of the American Conservation Assocation, a non-profit organization founded by Rockefeller and devoted to "the preservation of nature and the enjoyment of its values by the public." Whyte's influential study entitled *Cluster Development* (1964) was published by the association and carried a foreword by Rockefeller. Whyte's research during this period culminated in *The Last Landscape* (1968), a classic primer on land use that criticized so-called regional plans and their visions of decentralized, suburban utopias.

Whyte's work on open space conservation led him progressively closer to the core of the city at a time when downtown areas were perceived by many as losing their attraction. The center, he argued, would always be a city's key asset. In 1969, he drafted the text of the Plan for New York City, a zoning proposal published by the Planning Commission and hailed by *The New York Times* for its clarity.

In 1971, after a year as Distinguished Professor of Urban Sociology at Hunter College in New York, Whyte organized the Street Life Project, a pioneering empirical study of the way people use the streets and spaces of the center city. Using time-lapse photography, he and his assistants charted such phenomena as schmoozing patterns, the rituals of street encounters, and why people flock to some public plazas and avoid others. As a result of this research, New York City adopted an unprecedented open-space zoning code revision in 1975 that was touted in a front-page Times story headlined, "Radical Midtown Zoning Overhaul Proposed, Giving Greater Diversity." Several other American cities soon followed with similar provisions.

Whyte's 1980 book, *The Social Life of Small Urban Spaces*, produced alongside a *Nova* television documentary narrated by Whyte and featuring his time-lapse film clips, was quickly adopted by planners as a standard text on making downtown spaces livelier. That year, Wolf von Eckhart of *The Washington Post* described Whyte as "one of a small band of generalists who twenty-two years ago began to arrest and reverse the horrendous damage specialists were doing to our cities."

In 1988, Whyte brought together the principal strands of his work into the widely acclaimed *City: Rediscovering the Center*, a ringing affirmation of the great assets of the city—and a richly empirical proof of the folly of trying to graft suburban plans and values onto urban centers.

Whyte received many awards in his long and distinguished career and was an honorary member of the American Institute of Certified Planners. In 1984, New York Mayor Ed Koch bestowed the Doris C. Freedman Award on Whyte in recognition of three decades of research "that greatly enriches the public environment" of the city. Brendan Gill of *The New Yorker* dubbed Whyte "the Thoreau of the streets," and *Smithsonian* considered him "our leading scholar of people and how they behave in urban environments."

An adoptive New Yorker since his early days at *Fortune*, Whyte became known as one of the city's greatest defenders. He and his wife, the fashion designer Jenny Bell, raised their daughter Alexandra in a townhouse on Manhattan's Upper East Side, in a neighborhood he appreciated as an "upper-middle-class bohemia." In a television interview in the early 1990s, Adam Smith asked Whyte to name his three favorite American cities, and he replied with a chuckle, "New York, New York, New York." But Whyte championed all cities—their density, their spontaneity, even their messiness—and his enthusiasm was nothing if not infectious.

THE RISE OF ORGANIZATION MAN

The Class of '49

Fortune, June 1949

This was the first in a series of *Fortune* articles which eventually grew into *The Organization Man* (1956), Whyte's controversial bestseller. The gist was aptly summarized in a banner on the article's opening spread: "Looking to big business for security, a cautious generation turns its back on venture." Whyte characterized the Class of '49, America's first generation of postwar college graduates, as "more reconciled than any other recent college generations to the place of big business." Where the members of his own Class of '39 had shown entrepreneurial drive, the new breed seemed willing to trade independence for the safety of a job at A.T.&T. In predicting that "if there ever was one, this will be a generation of managers," Whyte captured the essence of young America's ambitions in the aftermath of World War II.

During these next few weeks of June there will be graduated from some 1,200 campuses what may be the most significant class in our history. Few earlier classes have aroused such wide interest, or provoked such dissimilar conclusions. To most of those who have worked closely with it—from the professors and the placement directors to the recruiters for industry—'49 is the best class the country has ever produced. To a small, and worried, minority, it is the most portentous.

In most every respect, '49 is remarkable. It is one of the biggest classes of all time: some 150,000 (including midyear graduates) men—40,000 more than in the largest prewar class. It is the most mature: the average male senior is twenty-four, 70 percent are veterans, and 30 percent are married. It is the most responsible: where the men of the first postwar class—'46—were apt to be restless, hard to handle, and, later, job skippers, '49 has proved to be the most self-disciplined group the colleges have ever had. Mentally, it is admirably adjusted to the now tightened job market; employers, faced only a year ago with an "interest-me-if-you-dare" attitude, report that they have never seen a class more eager to make itself useful to business.

But it is in a different respect that the character of '49 is really extraordinary. For '49—and, in varying degrees, its companion classes of '48 and '50—has turned its back on what its elders automatically assume is—and *should* be—one of the most cherished prerogatives of youth. Forty-nine is taking no chances.

It is what they don't want rather than what they do that the men of '49 know best. And what they don't want is risk. Bulling about the future, the state of the economy, and their place in it, they seem, to a stranger from another generation, somehow curiously old before their time. Above everything else security has become the great goal.

Security, of course, can mean many things. In '49's case it is bound up in people. Spiritually, it means working *for* people, in the sense of service, of justifying one's place in the community. Materially, it is, simply, working *under* them. The class of '49 wants to work for somebody else—preferably somebody big. No longer is small business the promised land. As for the idea of going into business for oneself, the idea is so seldom expressed as to seem an anachronism. "I never saw a bunch that so wanted to make this free-enterprise system work," says a professor of business administration, "but they are interested in the system rather than the individual enterprise. They will be technicians—not owners."

The search for security is not new among college men—certainly the senior of the thirties dreamed far more cautiously than his brother of the twenties. But never has it been so overriding, or so obvious. Each campus has its peculiarities, but on the great question of security the U.S. college senior has become almost homogeneous. From the huge metropolitan universities to the small-town campuses the men of '49 everywhere seem haunted by the fear of a recession. "I know AT&T might not be very exciting," explains a senior, with a phraseology that has become almost standard on U.S. campuses, "but there'll always be an AT&T." The "always" is a key word, for the principal criterion of the job-seeking senior is now the question of longevity. How well protected is the firm with a cash reserve? Is its product depression-proof? On more than one campus the most popular reference book is not the dictionary, but Moody's.

For similar reasons the advanced degree is more sought after than ever before; this summer and fall, upwards of 35,000 members of '49 will go on to graduate schools—roughly half for degrees other than law, medicine, and dentistry. The G.I. Bill, of course, is greatly responsible, but so is the fact that postgraduate work offers a continuation, a chance to postpone the entry into the arena. The college man, moreover, is beginning to belittle the bachelor's degree. Since "everybody's going to college now," he wonders if the B.A. or B.S. of today has any better cash value than the high-school diploma of the twenties or thirties.

The role of the entrepreneur is not coveted, nor, for that matter, does it seem properly understood. In the colleges canvassed by *Fortune* an average of only 2 percent of the seniors have any intention of going into business for themselves; similarly, many shy from any line of work that, because of its demand for the entrepreneurial spirit, is generally associated with coronary thrombosis or high blood pressure. On this score American literature has performed a disservice; the entrepreneur as a young man has been made singularly unappealing and in the postwar dissections, particularly those detailing the big operator in New York, even he has so lost stomach for enterprise that he finds happiness only when he stops being an entrepreneur, chucks "21" and the boss's wife, and heads for the country. Citing *The Hucksters* as a definitive work, it is easy for the student to moralize on his distaste for economic battle; his heel quotient, he explains, simply isn't big enough. If '49 has a class bogey, it is ulcers.

This distaste might be written off as simple prudence—certainly '49 has been well schooled in the fact that the mortality rate of small business is due in large part to inexperience. There is little evidence, however, that any sizable number are joining big business with the idea of preparing themselves for a later fling on their own, or that they seek it as a temporary haven from the economic storm so many appear to expect. The relationship is to be for keeps; it is the floor, not the ceiling, that the men of '49 are concerned about.

Not so, however, in the Southwest; to judge from the seniors of two of its universities the region would appear to be the last great reservoir of the gambling spirit. At Texas A&M 75 percent of the senior class want to go into business for themselves. "Few expect to go in immediately," the university reports, "but many of the veterans have some money saved and expect to hold it for the day when they can go on their own. They have been bossed as long as they want to be." At the University of Tulsa, the figures are almost identical; of 109 seniors polled, 80 percent plan to go into business for themselves. And almost all of them want big money.

Forty-nines in the Southwest may talk of big money, but in less cocky regions they do not. One business recruiter has gone through 300 interviews without once hearing a senior mention salary, and the experience is not unusual. This in itself is not so surprising; it is evidence, among other things, of '49's frequently expressed faith that industry does not intend to exploit it. What is surprising is the almost complete absence of speculation among '49s as to how much money they may make twenty or thirty years hence—and the few figures that are mentioned rarely surpass $10,000. For the most part '49s simply will not talk of the future in terms of the dollar. In terms of the Good Life, however, they are most articulate.

This life is, first of all, calm and ordered; many a senior confesses a desire to teach, not that he likes teaching but that he likes the sort of life he associates with it—there is a touch of elms and quiet streets in the picture. Basically, he wants a good wife—and if he does not have one already he hopes to have one within the year; he wants a comfortable home, about three children, one, maybe two cars ("a little knockabout for the wife"), and later, perhaps, a summer cottage. True, one might have to stretch $10,000 a bit to do it, but the point is that, in seniors' plans at least, the figure is not even incidental.

This urge to sink roots has had the effect of making '49 in some ways one of the most immobile of classes. The great trek of ambitious college men to the East is over. For one thing, a great many don't particularly want to go there. For another, the economic pull has slackened; as industry has been branching out and decentralizing, so too have the job opportunities. For many areas the combination has been a blessing. Kentucky, for example, recently so concerned over the export of its youth that leading citizens had directed a stay-at-home campaign at the state's undergraduates, now reports a marked increase in the number of seniors who plan to stick there. Similarly, in other southern colleges an increasing majority of seniors plan to stay in their home state or in the Southeast rather than seek jobs in the traditionally higher-paying North.

The class of '49, patently, is a settling-down generation. And while it may seem ironical that the one generation perhaps most buttressed with economic security should hunger for it most, it could hardly have been otherwise. Looking back, the men of '49 see life compounded of insecurity. Born, for the most part, between 1924 and 1926, they went through the early thirties at the most impressionable time of youth; and in their adolescence through a period of civil ferment, which, by its very preoccupation with security, seems to '49 in retrospect a time of chaos. Then, finally, the war.

The armed services, so many predicted, would send back to civilian life a youth permanently impatient with authority. They did quite the opposite. The teen-ager in uniform may have chafed, but he was malleable, and in an organization in which conformity was emphasized and reward de-emphasized, he learned easily how to keep his nose clean. And he has not forgotten it. He is not afraid of bigness; where his brother of the twenties, fearful of anonymity, was repelled by hugeness in an organization, he is attracted.

To a '49 conditioned to organization, big business spells security. Of those seniors going into business on graduation (roughly one-half the class) about 15 percent expect to go into their father's business; except for them, however, only a few want to go into anything other than a large concern. In the majority view, the small firm is small mainly because it doesn't deserve to be large, and it suffers from nepotism, shaky finances, and a roll-top-desk philosophy of management. "Perhaps we in the colleges are a bit to blame," says the head of a department of business administration. "So much of our curriculum is in terms of the big corporation that the student doesn't appreciate the opportunities that there are in small business."

Even if small business does offer opportunities, '49 feels, it offers them too soon. The class of '49 is used to *formal* training and it is wary of stepping out without a good deal more. Big business, therefore, with its reassuringly institutionalized schools, sometimes complete with classrooms, dormitories, and graduating classes, is the ideal next step. To the senior of '49, the training program itself implies a high degree of security; it should make him more valuable not only as a technician but also as a company investment. The more the company spends on him, goes an increasingly popular line of thought, the less likely it is to let him go. Finally, the training program, like postgraduate work, offers the student a continuation of a comfortable role. To those worried because they don't yet know what they want to do, the prospect is sedative. "'You don't have to make up your mind,' we tell them, in effect," says one executive. "'Come with us and you will find out while you're in training.'"

Another cogent reason why college seniors prefer big business is the simple fact that the big companies go after them and the small ones don't. Of the 450,000-odd incorporated firms in the U.S., only about 1,000 actively recruit on the campuses, while roughly another 3,000 recruit by correspondence. And it is the active 1,000 firms that get the cream. Not all are "ten percenters"—some, indeed, will not take an "A" man for fear he might be antisocial; but by and large they manage to sign up the campus leaders. "I can see it on the recruiters' faces when they come in the door," says the dean of a school of commerce. "Will they be lucky enough to get one of the three or four of my top men? What does it mean? It means the top 10 percent of the class are automatically led to the big firms. An offer from one firm, a better one from another. They can't resist."

Backing up their great spring recruiting drives, the large firms direct a stream of brochures at the college man. These are more important documents than one would suspect, for often it is on the first impression created by them that the senior—and now, increasingly, the junior—will select the four or five firms he wishes to aim for. They are good brochures; where before the war they were prone to expound on the romance of the company, they now are meaty, straight-forward documents. Sales work is still prettied up a bit in the telling, but generally the text is without euphemism, and it bears down heavily on the appeals that count. Pointed references to the firm's sales growth during the last depression are frequent, and almost always underscored are the firm's low executive turnover, liberal pension and annuity plans, and its "family" aspect. ("After hours, G.E. men and women relax . . . enjoy the most up-to-date recreation facilities in all General Electric communities throughout the country.") To a class at once gregarious and security-minded, it is a persuasive package.

Small business, of course, could make some good sales points of its own; frequently it can offer equal security and, sometimes, a great deal more opportunity. College placement directors are well aware of this, but even when they do line up a small company with a position to offer they find the students apathetic. "Funny," says one placement director, echoing many another, "the only kind I can interest in the small-company job are the dynamic sort—the one type that's least likely to get lost in a big company. I'd sooner interest the other kind; I point out to the shy, diffident fellows that in a small outfit where they'd be something of a jack-of-all-trades they'd get a better chance to express themselves, to grow out of their shell. They still don't want it."

The new graduate can argue that this is plain horse sense, and that far from being afraid of taking chances, he is simply looking for the best place to take them in. Big business, the argument goes, has borrowed the tools of the classroom and the library and made them pay off. It has its laboratories, its market-research departments, and the time and patience to use them; small business does not. The odds, then, favor the men who join big business. "They wouldn't hesitate to risk adopting a new industrial technique or product," explains a proponent of this calculated-risk theory, "when in a position to do same—but only after they'd subjected it to tests of engineers, market researchers, and so on." With big business, in short, risk taking would be a cinch.

What kind of job do the seniors ask of Big Business? Merchandising is still the number one choice, but in the last few years a relatively new field, personnel, has been building up to a phenomenal—and illuminating—popularity. The field itself can be dismissed in a few words: it is one of the most overcrowded; the work is semiprofessional and it is rarely open to new recruits. Why, then, '49's enthusiasm? Wearily, recruiters report an explanation that, from campus to campus, varies by hardly a syllable: "Because I like people."

Forty-nine's concept of the job is a mirage, but it is a revealing one. In reality the job is connected more with time studies, Wonderlic tests, and stop watches than with being nice to people, but to '49 it seems to promise the agreeable role of a sort of combination Y.M.C.A. worker, office Solomon, and father confessor to the men at the lathes. Looking back on their military careers, whether they "handled" a squad or a company, '49s feel themselves admirably equipped for the work, and many, indeed, were confirmed in this belief by the Army and Navy's vocational counselors.

In many cases, the college curriculum has also been responsible. Increasingly, departments of economics and business administration have been expounding "human relations" in industry; today there is a wide selection of courses on the subject, many of them highly specialized, cutting across such fields as psychology and physical education. The colleges can put up an extremely good case for this new emphasis on industrial relations, but too frequently the result is a senior disillusioned by a seeming lack of comparable interest on the part of business. "In the field of personnel," says a professor at a large state university, "education is miles ahead of industry." Which, in at least one respect, it is.

Forty-nine's mirage of the personnel field—which, for all the recruiters' discouragement, many a senior is drawn to until the last interview—is especially enticing for another, if infrequently expressed, reason. Personnel work is somewhat out of the main stream; much like the service life, it seems to offer a certain freedom from competition. It is a technician's job, the job of one who *services* industry; and, rightly or wrongly, a large part of '49 equates that niche with security.

To '49, this security encompasses something more than mere safety. At a recent Temple University round table on the pursuit of happiness, one student put it this way: "People who are just selfish and wrapped up in themselves have the most trouble, and people who are interested in other people . . . are the type of person that is not too much concerned about security. Somehow the security is provided in the things they do and they are able to reach out beyond themselves."

On every campus the same theme is rephrased, and with an intensity that would astound the somewhat more mercenary senior of the thirties. Not infrequently the terms border on the mawkish—as if the goal was simply to defend the little people, in the fashion of a Frank Capra hero—but generally, they boil down to the question of doing something *worth while*. Worthwhileness, like security, is open to considerable definition, but to most '49s it seems to mean service to others. More extroverted than his predecessors, the average '49 has a highly developed sense of community; he is fascinated by human relationships, and the place of the individual in the group. He will tend, accordingly, to lubricate rather than to build, and thus to evaluate success less on the basis of concrete achievement than on services performed.

Certainly, this kind of thinking is to be welcomed. But to what degree is it a rationalization—a self-ennobling excuse for turning away from the more riskful life? One would assume that that most selfless of occupations, the ministry, was attracting an increasing number of college men. It is not; an average of less than 2 percent of the seniors in the colleges covered by *Fortune* planned to go into the ministry, and in some of the colleges this represents a decline from 1939. Nor is there any stampede to government service. "There is so little public spirit among our applicants," one state employment director reports of '49, "that we all comment on it when we find it." Politics is scarcely mentioned at all.

Perhaps the answer is that the class of '49, more reconciled than any other recent college generations to the place of big business, sees in it the most effective vehicle for community service; in the eyes of the senior the same attribute, efficiency, that makes the large cooperation appealing as a sanctuary from depression, also makes it, on a foot-pounds-of-energy basis, by far the best stage for being *useful* to other people. Thus, again, we are back to the personnel job, for here, then, is the optimum career. In '49's conception, not only does it promise economic security; it promises spiritual security as well. To a class intent on the happy mean, it resolves everything.

Thanks to the law of supply and demand, on the average, only about 10 percent of the seniors going into business—to judge from rough estimates gathered in April—persist in their quest for the personnel job, but the other preferences are in character. For 40 percent, the largest single category, sales and merchandising, has become the number one choice. It is, however, sales with a difference. Forty-nine's interest is less accumulative than administrative; "sales engineering," whatever that may be, is a favored term, and those few who want to sell in the old, vulgar sense of the word want to sell on salary, *not* commission. For this reason, insurance, favored by only 5 percent, has dropped in popularity. Actually the jobs offered are more often for home-office administrative work than for selling, but to the average senior insurance still appears to mean high pressure and low drawing accounts, and he wants no part of it.

Similarly, there is an almost complete disinterest in investment and brokerage work. Fifteen percent have marked down finance as their first preference, but here again, as in sales, the interest is administrative rather than accumulative. "Unlike the class of 1940," says John L. Munschauer, director of placement at Cornell, "no one mentions speculating or investing in stocks and bonds as a method of acquiring a fortune; nor have I heard them mention stocks and bonds as a method of saving and supplementing income. Those considering banking and finance are primarily interested in such things as credit, mortgage loan work, trust-and-estate work, and financial analysis." Elsewhere, the same is true.

In selecting a field, the senior of '49 has had to pay much more attention to the actual needs of industry than did the senior of last year. The seller's market in junior executive material is over, and no longer, as in '48, are corporations' recruiting staffs bidding against each other like so many fraternities in rushing season. The effect, as many a senior will admit, has been salutary for all concerned; and by comparison with prewar standards, the market is still quite healthy. From all estimates, the great majority of the seniors seeking jobs in business should be placed by midsummer.

Despite the slackened demand, starting salaries remain at an all-time high. With little variation from college to college, the average going rate for '49s ranges between $55 and $60 a week. Certainly the figures suggest none of the downgrading of the bachelor's degree so many college men complain of. In 1939, the average starting salary was about $25 a week; thus, even after allowing for the increased cost of living, the 1949 figure represents a considerable jump in real income. Has it been too great?

Most employers appear to think not, but there are a few dissenters. "We have done almost irreparable damage to the men we have so hired," says H. Paul Abbott, of the Insurance Co. of North America Companies. "They have gained a false sense of their values. . . . Many of these men will go through the rest of their business careers believing themselves to be underpaid. They have drunk of a heady brew . . . the hangover will soon be upon them."

What kind of student does business want? The engineer, of course, is in demand. So, presumably, should be the general student, for by far the largest single classification for which business seeks college men for non-engineering jobs is that of "general business trainee." But while on the one hand it asks for the well-rounded man, on the other it asks for the man who isn't so well-rounded after all, for it demands that he has been specialized at the same time. According to a survey of fifty-eight top U.S. firms made by The Johns Hopkins University, business' specifications are heavily loaded against the general student: out of every 100 solicitations, thirty-seven are for engineering students; twenty-four for other technical students; twenty-nine for business administration students; for liberal-arts men, ten.

The students have adapted themselves, and so have the colleges. Since 1939 the colleges have been setting up more and more of what might be called "content" and "how-to" courses; today a man can major in radio journalism, pictorial journalism, advertising, photography, industrial and labor relations, public relations, business management in the furniture industry, insect control, the fertilizer industry, real estate, ceramic engineering, airport management and operation—and many another specialty on which the dollar sign is equally visible. As a result, the emphasis on the humanities has declined far more drastically than most laymen suspect; in 1929, 27 percent of the students in the colleges surveyed by *Fortune* majored in either English, philosophy, the classics, modern languages, or history; ten years later the figure had dropped to 17; today, it is down to 10.

By any commercial standards, '49 should be an eminently "practical" class. Yet, for some businessmen, it is still not practical enough. In too many cases, as corporations have developed closer ties with the campus, often with grants and scholarships, they have come to regard the function of the U.S. college as little more than the preparation of students for industry's own schools. In one recent if somewhat extreme example of this attitude, an executive of the Ford Motor Co. proposed that colleges remedy a deficiency in their curriculums by setting up a course in "the psycho-socio dynamics of industrial organization." This, among other things, would instruct the pre-business student in the personality pattern of industry "into which he must merge his individual personality."

When this proposal was made at a conference of recruiters and placement directors, the latter with quite enough troubles already in selling the liberal-arts man, the response was an involuntary gasp of horror. For one of the most signal features of the conference had been the suggestion by the recruiters themselves that, for business' own sake, perhaps it was time business asked the colleges to bear down a little more heavily on the liberal arts—though not, of course, at the expense of business courses. Westinghouse Electric's Manager of University Relations, for one, proposed that the technical schools include more social science and humanities; their graduates, the company felt, were altogether too specialized and narrow in their thinking.

There are signs others are beginning to feel the same way. One firm, for example, which in the past has leaned heavily to engineering majors for its general trainees, has found that the engineers are inclined to treat every problem as an engineering problem; since many are not, the firm is now looking around for liberal-arts men. Similarly, a large Detroit advertising agency says it prefers men who have *not* specialized in advertising. "We can teach them advertising," it says. "We can't teach them how to use their minds."

Compounded with '49's natural gregariousness, this vocationalized schooling has produced a class that on the whole has little regard for the arts—either as spectators or participants. The work of the artist satisfies few of '49's criteria for spiritual security; the artist is "too much wrapped up in himself" and his contribution to the community too obscure. Even for the intellectual of the class the creative role seems unrewarding. "Culturally," writes Elliot E. Cohen, the editor of *Commentary*, in a penetrating sketch of today's young intellectual, "he feels himself the survivor of a long series of routs and massacres. Insecurity is his portion, and doom and death are to him familiar neighbors. . . . There is very little in him of that lust for life and experience, of the joy of living for its own sake, of a sense of wide horizons, or worlds to conquer, or much of that early curiosity that drove his older brother expansively over the realms of knowledge."

As in everything else, so in business '49's energies promise to be analytical rather than creative; if ever there was one, this will be a generation of managers. What will be its impact on business? On a few points at least, the indications are clear. Competence, certainly, '49 will supply in abundant measure, and never has there been a class so absorbed with the techniques—and the desirability—of making business more efficient. Its approach augurs well indeed for the future of industrial relations, and not merely in the narrow sense of management's relations with labor, but of its relations with government and the community as well. In every application of business '49s should make good neighbors.

Too good? Here lie the more unanswerable questions. Will this community-conscious group furnish any quota of free-swinging s.o.b.'s we seem to need for leavening the economy? Or will it be so intent on achieving a superlubricated, integrated private enterprise—a sort of socialization by big business instead of government—that it will prefer a static, and thus more manageable, economy to a dynamic one? Will '49s, in short, be so tractable and harmonious as to be incapable, twenty or thirty years hence, of making provocative decisions? The answers will be a long time in coming.

The Transients

Fortune, May 1953

Whyte coined the term Management Man to describe a new breed of migratory young executives-in-training who willingly moved from one "Levittown-like suburb" to the next in pursuit of promotion in large corporations. He predicted that "these unostentatious, salaried nomads" were the heralds of a new era in American business—and America's social landscape.

For a quick twinge of superiority there is nothing quite like driving past one of the new Levittown-like suburbs. To visitors from older communities, the sight of rank after rank of little boxes stretching off to infinity, one hardly distinguishable from the other, is weird, and if they drive along the streets at dusk, when the little blue lights of the television sets begin to shine out of the picture windows, they can speculate that if they were to blink their eyes in proper rhythm the scene flashing by would freeze into one motionless picture. Appalling! If this is progress, God help us . . . 1984. But, onlookers are also likely to conclude, one must be sympathetic too; after all, it is a step up in life for the people who live there, and one should not begrudge them the opiate of TV; here, obviously, is a group of anonymous beings submerged in a system they do not understand.

The onlooker had better wipe the sympathy off his face. Underneath the television aerials lies a revolution. What he has seen is not the home of little cogs and drones. What he has seen is the dormitory of the next managerial class.

The most important single group in these communities is what has been variously called business bureaucrats, industrial civil servants, technicians of society—the junior executives, research workers, young corporation lawyers, engineers, salesmen. The bond they share is that they are (1) between twenty-five and thirty-five, (2) organization men, and (3) all on the move. It is significant enough that there are now so many of them; more significant, it is these unostentatious, salaried nomads who will be running our business society twenty years from now.

Many future managers, of course, do not live in such places; and many work for companies that don't require them to move. Nevertheless, it may be the new suburban communities that provide the sharpest picture of tomorrow's management. Not only are managerial transients concentrated here, they are concentrated almost totally free of the pressures of older traditions and older people that would affect them elsewhere. In such propinquity, they bring out in each other—perhaps at times caricature—tendencies latent elsewhere, and one sees in bold relief what might be almost invisible in more conventional environments. To an older eye, perhaps the picture is abnormal, but what may be abnormal today is very likely to be normal tomorrow.

For some months *Fortune* has been making an intensive study of four of the new suburbs. As we will report in succeeding issues, there is a remarkable similarity, in attitudes toward politics, education, economics, sex, religion, from suburb to suburb. Almost a new way of life is in the making in these communities, and it is not a synthetic way of life "sold" by mass producers of suburbs; it is the expression of the younger people's need and wants.

Before looking under the TV aerials, however, there are some immediate questions to take up: How has this new mobility been brought to pass? Is it likely to decline or increase? Does it signal the rise of a new and eventually inbred caste? To attempt a definitive answer to any of these would be presumptuous. But on one thing at least the evidence is clear: America's social structure is going through a shake-up the full effects of which are yet to be felt.

Thirty years ago the notion that the U.S. had a fairly fluid society would not have been particularity controversial—"classless" America, indeed, was almost a universal cliché. Today, however, the dominant school of thought on American society maintains that the country's pride in "classlessness" and in the idea that a good man can always rise is illusion. After two centuries, some social students hold, the American system is finally shaking down into a fixed, stable hierarchy.

As interpreted in terms of the six ranks of anthropologist Lloyd Warner (whose "upper upper," lower upper," etc., classification of Newburyport, Massachusetts, was handled so roughly by ex-Newburyporter John P.

Marquand in *Point of No Return*), American society is a traditional community in which the Hill, local business ties, and interlocking family relationships firmly fix the individual's position, from which he can move upward (from the Elks, say, to the Rotary) only by sanction of the next-upper group. Furthermore, other studies indicate, what with the unionization of labor and the professionalization of management, the way up the ladder is growing tougher. The solution, it has been argued, lies not in the individual's cherishing illusions that he's going to go up but in adjusting to the realities of his home environments.

We do not agree. Such studies have done a service in sensitizing Americans to class and status factors they like to pretend don't exist. Their very emphasis on what is static, however, has obscured what is dynamic. What about the people who *leave* home?

It is the thesis of this article that the man who leaves home is not the exception in American society, but the key to it. Almost by definition, the management man is a man who left home, and like the man who went from the Midwest to Harvard, kept on going. There have always been, of course, people who left home, but the number of them has increased—and so vastly that those who stay put are as affected by the emigration as those who leave.

The growing importance of the transients has been obscured by a sort of economic time lag; organization people don't make the big money, and they are making less real income than they did ten years ago. But though it may be the automobile dealer and the owner of the local bottling franchise who drive the Cadillacs, it is the organization man who now makes the decisions that most affect the lives of others. "Those fat cats around here are falling all over themselves entertaining Charlie," says the wife of a plant engineer. "They could buy and sell us twice over, but he's going to decide the location of the new chemical plant." The story has endless variations; from the man in the investment division of an insurance company whose brief may decide a whole industry's future to the new-product engineer. Organization Man is becoming dominant.

Even if part of the American Dream is still true, one big chunk of it is dead, finished, kaput. For the future will be determined not by the independent entrepreneur or the "rugged individualist" whom our folklore so venerates; the future will be determined by Organization Man. It is not occasion for cheer; but neither is it occasion for pessimism. It is, however, occasion for reflection. Wherever it is we are going, we are going there very, very fast.

After the war, one thing looked sure. Americans had had their bellyful of moving; now, everybody agreed, they were going to settle down and stop this damned traipsing around. Here is the way things worked out:

Americans are moving more than ever before: Never have long-distance movers had it so good; according to figures provided by the five leading firms, moving is now at a rate even higher than in wartime. And compared with prewar, the five firms are all moving at least three times as many families, and one is moving ten times as many. Furthermore, not only are more families moving, those who move move more frequently; one out of every seven of its customers, Allied Van Lines reports, will *within a year* pick up stakes and move again to a new state, and seven out of ten will be "repeaters" within the next five years.

This is not just a matter of moving from one part of town to another; in 1951, 7 percent of all male adults moved away from their county, and of these roughly half moved out of the state entirely. Concentrate on the twenty-five to thirty-five-year-old group and the figure goes up sharply; in 1951 roughly 12 percent of men twenty-five to thirty-five years old moved outside of their county, and 6 percent moved to a new state.

Moving Day, Park Forest, Illinois, 1953. (*Photo by Dan Wiener*)

The more education, the more mobility: If a man goes to college now, the chances are almost even that he won't work in his home state. Recent census figures and *Time*'s study, *They Went to College*, indicate that the educational level is higher among migrants than among nonmigrants, and the higher the educational level, the more intensive the migration. In the twenty-five to thirty-five-year-old group, to extrapolate from census figures, about sixteen out of every hundred men who have only a high-school education have been interstate migrants, versus 29 percent of those who have had at least one year of college. Of men who complete college, 46 percent move. Of those who worked their way through in a college outside their home state, about 70 percent don't go back. And for all college men, incidentally, the higher the grades, the more likely they are to go to work elsewhere than their home states.

Organization people move the most: To judge from studies by direct-mail experts of *Time*, *Life*, *Fortune*, and McGraw-Hill, the greatest amount of address changing occurs among managerial people. Similarly, records of long-distance movers show that the greatest single group among their customers, upwards of 40 percent, consists of corporation people being transferred from one post to another (with the employer usually footing the bill). If to this group are added government, Army, and Navy people, and men joining new companies, over 70 percent of all moves are accounted for by members of large institutions.

The impact of this transiency on U.S. society is incalculable. The small town, for example, has long exported some of its youth; but what was once a stream has become a flood. It is no longer a case of the special boy who had to get out of town to cross the tracks or find an outlet for his energies; now as many as three-quarters of the town's young college men may be in the same position. Where are they to go after college? Back home? Lawyers and doctors can, and the majority do; they are in the happy position of being able to go home, to keep professionally alert, and to make a good bit of money at the same time. But for the others, opportunity seems to be elsewhere—not just for the delivery boy who became an Air Force lieutenant, but for the young man on the Hill who's gone off to join du Pont.

In terms of status it is difficult to say whether the migrants have gone up or down. But they moved more than geographically; what is taking place is a horizontal movement in which the transients have come together in a new kind of group that fits none of the old social categories.

And they will never go back. Once the cord is broken, a return carries overtones of failure. "I'm fed up with New York," says one executive, "but if I went back to Taylorston I know damned well they'd think my tail was between my legs." The point is that he probably would think so too; one of the great tacit bonds the transients share is a feeling, justifiable or not, that by moving they acquire an intellectual sophistication that will forever widen the gap between them and their home towns. "Dave and I thought often about going back to East Wells," a successful young executive's wife explains. "It is a beautiful old New England town and we both had such happy times there. But all the people who had anything on the ball seem to have left. There are a few who took over their fathers' businesses, but the rest—well, I hate to sound so snobbish, but dammit, I *do* feel superior to them."

It is curious how much the transients think about the home town. A majority of the people interviewed by *Fortune* spontaneously brought it up, and the phrase "No, I'll never go back" was repeated almost verbatim scores of times. Many transients left a lot behind them or at least in retrospect it seems so to them; most came from reasonably prosperous families and when they look back they recall the kinfolk and friends about, and the reassuring feeling that they were in that fortunate group who counted. But local prestige, they now well know, is not for export. "This is quite a conflict today," says anthropologist Lloyd Warner. "John Marquand shows this very well. Why does Charles Gray in *Point of No Return* go back to visit Newburyport? Why does John, for that matter? That's something all of us want to do, to keep the old image of our position."

Even if by chance the company sends the transients back, they can never really go home. As one puts it, "Because of this last transfer I'm back here, almost by accident, where I was born. It ought to be a setup; frankly, my family is as old guard around here as they come. Well, it's a lot of crap, sure, but I must say I get a good bit of pleasure knowing that I can join the City Club and my boss can't. But it's damned privately I think about it. If I am going to go ahead in this organization, the people I've got to get along with are the office crowd, and don't think I wouldn't get the business if they started reading about me in the social columns." Says another, "It's odd. Here I've got a social position a lot of people would give a fortune to get, but the minute I joined the corporation I had to turn my back on it. We're sort of declassed, and, as far as Amy and I are concerned, it is as if we weren't born here at all."

But the most important reason they can't go home is that they won't find it there if they do. In the rapid growth of the metropolitan areas, once self-contained market towns have been transformed into suburbs, and more important yet, the plant expansion of U.S. industry has turned others into industrial towns. In many towns, as a result, the migration of the young people has been offset by such an influx of newcomers that those who have stayed put are in the position of being abroad at home.

For some towns the tensions have been near explosive. Even though the influx swells local coffers, the townspeople, in somewhat the way natives view the "summer people," view with apprehension the people moving into the developments nearby, and the fact that many of the "new people" have no intention of staying long doesn't make them easier to take. And the townspeople's attitude is reciprocated enough so that the developments going up around the town often form a ring of animosity. A study by New York University's Dr. Marie Jahoda reveals that over 45 percent of the people in Fairless Hills, in lower Bucks County, Pennsylvania, believe that the county people dislike them. They are probably right; citizens of the older communities know something has hit them, and though they're not exactly sure just what it is, they sense, correctly, that those "horrid developments" despoiling the old so-and-so place are the symbol of it.

The "new people" and the corporation that brought them have not only upset the historic wage structure of the small town; more abrading, they have upset the whole local hierarchy. Locally blue as the blood of some townspeople may be, the general manager of the corporation plant, simply by virtue of his position, wields key power, and they know it. It is little wonder that corporations think long and hard about the tact of the proconsuls—and proconsular wives—they send to the small town.

In different degree the same process has been going on in the great metropolitan centers. Considering the greater number of opportunities available, why should young people leave the big cities? One might assume that the city would find enough of its own home-grown talent to staff the managerial echelons. Even here, however, the natives have been outnumbered. Philadelphia, for example, has long been considered somewhat inbred, yet a study by sociologist Digby Baltzell reveals that as early as 1940, 64 percent of the Philadelphia business and professional leaders listed in *Who's Who* were born outside of the Philadelphia area. Today the proportion is even higher and so it is in many other cities. As the seats of economic power have shifted from local institutions to national organizations, membership in the elite of any city or town is being determined more and more by current functional rank. Not only are national institutions sending in new people, native institutions are being opened to outsiders more than ever before. The urban elite, in short, has become an ex officio elite.

The shift to organization power that has brought so much of this about has been in the making a long time. As sociologist Max Weber long ago noted, before the turn of the century the trend to a "bureaucratic" organization of society was already in high motion. Since then the trend has been steadily accentuated, until today most college men almost automatically see their future in terms of the salaried life of an organization.

The reasons are obvious enough. While there is an undue assumption by many young men that entrepreneurship equals insecurity, if the young man has no independent income or capital what is he to do? The big organization wants him; wants more of him, in fact, than are available. Its recruiters go to him before he graduates from college, and they promise good starting salaries (currently: $275 to $335 a month), good extra training, and a secure future. To join up seems not only the line of least resistance but the logical course as well.

Clearly, the big organization is now the prime vehicle for a career, and in more institutions than the corporations. At their present size, the armed forces, a great institutional career in themselves, are in effect a great training ground for indoctrinating each new age group in the organization way. So are the government bureaus. Even in the professions the emphasis has switched to the organization; of the professional men who graduated in the last decade, only about one in five is working for himself; the bulk are to be found in group clinics, law factories, AEC labs, corporation staff departments, and the like. Academic life has been similarly affected; what with the growth of foundations and huge government research grants, academics now find it's easier to obtain $200,000 for a group project than a few thousand for somebody doing something all by himself—if the businessman were to eavesdrop on some of the grant-raising shoptalk of the academics he wouldn't throw the term "ivory tower" around so loosely.

In the wake of this shift to the big organization is the moving van. Certainly the recruit does not join up because he *wants* to move a lot, and it is often in spite of it. But moving, he knows, has become part of the bargain, and unsettling as transfer might be, even more unsettling are the implication of not being asked to transfer. "We never plan to transfer," as one company president explains, a bit dryly, "and we never make a man move. Of course, he kills his career if he doesn't. But we never *make* him do it." The fact is well understood; it is with a smile that the recruit moves—and keeps on moving, year after year; until, perhaps, that distant day when he is summoned back to Rome.

It is not just more moves per man. Even companies reporting no increase in the number of times each individual moves report an increase in the sheer number of men being moved. G.E. has compared a cross section of its forty-five-year-old executives with one of its thirty-five-year-olds; in the ten years after they were twenty-five, 42 percent of the older group had moved at least once; during the same age period, 58 percent of the younger had moved.

Corporations never planned it quite that way. Decentralization and expansion, rather than deliberate personnel policy, have determined the pattern. Companies have systematized it, to be sure; moves are settling into more of a rhythm, almost invariably they are sweetened with a raise, and in some companies, sweetened by special departments that handle all the housekeeping fuss of the trip. By and large, however, the question of the man's personal development—however emphasized when the boss breaks the news to him—has been secondary to the day-to-day necessity of filling vacancies out in the empire.

That is, up until now. Periodic transfer, some companies are coming to believe, is a positive good in itself; and even where no immediate functional reason exists, it might often be important to move the man anyway. What better way, they ask, to produce the well-rounded executive?

Instead of leaving transfer to be determined haphazardly by different departments, some companies, like G.E., have made such decisions part of a systematic managerial program. By thus making a man's "permanent" assignment (i.e., one lasting at least three years) part of a deliberate rotation policy, the man is given "more choices in life to make," and the company, as a result, is given a pool of seasoned talent. Other companies agree; by deliberately exposing a man to a succession of environments, they best obtain that necessity of the large organization—the man who can fit in anywhere. "The training," as an I.B.M. executive succinctly puts it, "makes our men interchangeable."

For all the training, it should be noted, there are still a number of environments in which executives don't fit in—and some in which they fit in all too well. A good many companies have belatedly realized they have lost some of their best men by carelessly assigning them to San Francisco or Los Angeles for a spell. Even mouth-watering salary boosts often fail to achieve repatriation; once tasted, the California way of life dulls such appetites—a fact that has found its way into the West Coast salary structure, generally lower than in the East. When Shell Chemical moved its head office to New York from San Francisco some of its management group resigned rather than go along, and several who did go along eventually decided to go back. Another company recently located a lab on the coast in spite of "economic" consideration, they privately admit, to hang on to talent they might otherwise lose.

On the other hand, there are some kinds of environments many people can't be tempted into trying at all. This has been particularly evident in the postwar moves of entire headquarters to the hinterlands. Making a small town a way station on the executive route is one thing; making it Mecca, another. An organization's creative and professional people, recent incidents indicate, will move permanently to a small town only if it is in striking distance of a large city and the professional contacts it affords. Similarly, almost any executive is likely to balk-for a while at least—if the town is so small that the influx of the company threatens a resurgence of the paternalistic company town.

But these obstacles are residues of the past, not portents of the future. For there is a momentum to mobility that, in a sort of chicken-and-egg sequence, goes something like this: the more people move about, the more similar the American environments become; and the more similar they become, the easier still it is to move about.

Increasingly, the young couple who move do so only physically; with each transfer the decor and the architecture may change, the faces and the names may change; but the people, the conversation, and the values do not, and sometimes the decor and the architecture don't either. If there are no company people to help the newcomers break the ice, there are almost bound to be some fellow transients nearby, and the chances are pretty good that some of them will be couples that the most recent arrivals have run into somewhere else in this great new freemasonry of transients. "I just jump to read the new-arrivals list in the local paper," says a typical transient. "We've already run up against a couple from our Cambridge days at the Business School, and we're sure that some from Park Fairfax or Fresh Meadows will be along soon too." It is, as transients like to observe, a small world.

The rate at which mobility will continue to increase will depend greatly, of course, on the amount of plant expansion that will take place in the years ahead. But turnover is not just a function of industrial expansion. Turnover begets turnover; as some companies' attitudes indicate, the necessity of movement has a way of becoming a virtue, and this applies to the individual as well as the company. The emotions with which transients look on moving are highly mixed; they don't want to move, and yet in a way they do—and the thought can become father to the wish. "I swear to myself I hate it," one young transient explains, " yet I know I'll be moving, and, well, that affects me. You know, we went right close by the Grand Canyon and we didn't go out of our way to see it. Why? Because we knew we'd be by there again, and—I know it's hard to understand—but some-how we wouldn't like it if we didn't feel that way."

In the midst of this constant movement the problem of personal stabil-ity, of a meaningful continuity in his life, becomes pressing for the individ-ual. For this reason some people prophesy that the transients will identify themselves more completely with the Organization. With the new empha-sis on human relations, college-to-grave security, extracurricular benefits, and the like, the ideal of an organization so beneficent that it provokes the total allegiance of its member has become more than a possibility; it is, in the eyes of some, the constant the individual must have to keep himself on keel in a world changing so fast.

Leaving aside the question of whether or not such fealty is desirable, is it coming to pass? Here we must look at all age brackets of management, and look at their loyalties in terms of actual behavior. Are the younger brackets showing more desire than their elders for one lifetime job?

A good index is the amount of movement from one company to another. To judge by the figures *Fortune* has gathered, the facts are quite the opposite of what is generally assumed. There seems to be *more*, not less, job switch-ing, and the figures indicate that the trend is likely to continue.

According to a new study by the management-consultant firm Booz, Allen & Hamilton, there are now twenty-nine more personnel changes per hundred management jobs than before the war, and a great part of the increase is caused by switches from one company to another. An analysis of the alumni records of several colleges reveals the same trend. Of the men who graduated in the late thirties, the number who have worked for only one corporation are in a minority (between 20 and 35 percent). A hefty majority have changed jobs two or three times; among men fifteen years and more out of college the men who have worked for four or more corpo-rations are likely to outnumber those who have worked for only one. Similarly, a great many men are shifting out of their original fields entirely. In twenty-five years four out of every ten Harvard '26ers have switched fields; in only ten years three out of ten '39ers have switched.

Are job changers the unsuccessful, the "floaters"? Some of them are, of course, but many of the job changers are among the most obviously successful of their age group. A *Fortune* study of older executives ("The Nine Hundred," November 1952) reveals that while a third of America's leading corporation executives are in the same firm they started with, 43 percent of the chief executives were hired directly into their present positions from another com-pany—and for many of these men this was only one of a long series of moves.

As the growing number of business-school graduates go up the ranks, furthermore, top management may become even more fluid. The Harvard Business School has made available to *Fortune* the preliminary returns from an exhaustive study of alumni of selected classes since 1911; making allowances for the different time lapse for each class and the disruption of the war, the record of job changes indicates that the professional manager is shifting companies—and fields—with increasing facility. The class of '36 is typical of the developing pattern; only 22 percent have stuck with one company since graduation, 26 percent have worked for two, 24 percent for three, and 28 percent for four or more. Later classes haven't had as much chance to move, but they seem to anticipate that they will; of the 137 members of the class of 1951, only 28 percent said they expected to stay with their present companies.

But what of the corporations' pension and benefit programs? Do they not lead, as it is now fashionable to complain, to a certain entrapment? To a degree, yes, but for the simple reason that most large organizations have remarkably similar programs, this adhesive factor tends to wash out. It is true, of course, that the longer a man stays, the more equity in the form of company-paid annuities and deferred profit sharing he builds up, and he cannot take all this with him. But how all important to him, really, is this kind of security?

The research department of Booz, Allen & Hamilton has been analyzing the attitudes of some 422 executives who have made the jump. The findings appear to come together on one vital point: in the majority of cases the primary reason for switching was not money, increased security or location. The executives switched most often because advancement was blocked. With executives checking only one reason for switching, the order was (1) bigger job, more responsibility; (2) don't like present management policies; (3) advancement in company uncertain; (4) change of activity desired. In seventh place: increased income. It is clear between the lines that the great motivating factor was the sense of a ceiling, psychological or actual, in one job and the need for more self-expression through another. Security is rarely mentioned.

The executive's own dissatisfactions are not the only factors stimulating switching. Though the executive may not know it, if he has been doing a notably good job his name is very probably in the card files of one or more of the management-consultant firms. And the files are active; if an executive is getting restless the intelligence has a way of reaching the consultants, and even if he isn't restless they might approach him anyway. To a degree not commonly recognized, a great proportion of consultants' work consists of matching such men with clients dissatisfied with some of their own people—and the secret talent hunt that has resulted is not abating. "More than they used to," one consultant says, "corporations seem to feel that around the corner is the dream boy."

The fact is not unnoticed within companies. Since so many corporations do look elsewhere for their top executives, many men shy at committing their psyche wholly to the company because they know that when the time comes for their crack at a particular spot the company is as likely as not to go out and hire a banker or a lawyer or some other outsider to fill it. The result is a good bit of almost premature restlessness. "I have to battle with my clients to keep them from changing jobs too much," says a veteran of a big placement agency. "My boys see this going on all around them and they get restless. There is one top man who made five different connections in eight years, each time being lured away by another of the consultants at a bigger salary."

Ironically, it is the corporation itself that taught the executives how to fly. Because it has exposed its young men to a succession of environments and new contacts, cutting old roots has not the terrors for them that it does for those who have never moved. Yet for the corporation as well as the individual, the individual's ability to move is profoundly necessary.

The fact that ties are increasingly easy to sever acts as a counterforce against the tendency for an organization to inbreed itself into a static, encompassing bureaucracy. As long as corporations have any life in them, they will always be productive of conflicts and tensions, and thus mobility, or the prospect of it, is a necessary safety valve. Complete allegiance is a snare; for all the injunctions to "get along" with people, it is important for the organization that the executive know that there are times when he damn well ought *not* to get along. And to be able to dissent, to champion the unpopular view, he must be able to move. He may not move—but the knowledge that he can, that he is psychologically capable of it, is the guarantee that he can maintain his independence.

The fact that managers circulate so easily does inhibit the growth of total fealty to the company; conceivably, however, it could stimulate another kind of fealty. Might not this freemasonry of organization men evolve into a circulating national elite more and more closed to outsiders? Some observers so fear. We would like to note several developments, however, that suggest that such an elite may never have a chance to jell.

Back in 1932 Taussig and Joslyn in their notable study of executives forecast that by the mid-century more than two-thirds of the top businessmen in the U.S. would be the sons of business owners and executives. Their prophecy has been almost on the nose. Of the 900 top executives in the U.S. today, roughly 62 percent are the sons of businessmen; and the figure in even higher, 68 percent, for executives under fifty. Out of all proportion, it might appear, a small group in our country will be supplying a majority of the executives of the future.

An inbred elite, however, has not been the result. *If* the rest of the population had stood still, yes; but it has not. As the new generation of management has been maturing, whole groups, not merely individuals, have moved into the middle class. The fact, for example, that a declining number of businessmen come from farm homes is not due to oligarchy so much as to the decrease in the proportion of farmers in the U.S. population.

Few men, to be sure, are rising directly from the shop into management, but we tend to exaggerate the number who ever did. If we go back to 1870, we find, contrary to American mythology, that very few of the business leaders of that time had been laborers or even laborers' sons. As a study by Gregory and Neu shows, the business leaders of that day were overwhelmingly of middle- or upper-class background, and more, not less, of them were sons of heads of companies than today.[1]

As the middle class has expanded, the hereditary advantages of the upper strata have declined drastically. The spread of American education, the growing accessibility to culture, have so ironed out regional and social differences that a vastly greater number of Americans can now compete on even terms in what might be called a national society. And not only are more people available for the managerial group; the prestige and income differences between it and other groups have been greatly lessened. Joining it now is hardly cause for exultation or a sense of special caste; so many people have been moving up that what might seem to be advancement for a particular individual may be nothing more than keeping even with great numbers of other people. From farmer's son to $8,000-a-year management man may once have been quite a contrast; today, as a drive through the Indiana farm country might call to mind, it is something less than spectacular. Who's advanced over whom?

But the fact that the managerial group is open to all comers does not in itself dispel the specter of an inbred elite. What of the question of values? Might not management people share a common outlook to such an extent that they will cohere without consciously planning the matter at all? Already, as they so frequently put it, they feel "in the same boat," and the more their transiency mixes them together, the more they are likely to feel so.

But they have no collective sense of direction. They have none because their organizations have none: owing to essential differences in functions and goals and, not unimportant, the American inability to put things together into a tidy world view, our many different hierarchies are not so compatible as might appear. Like the union man who becomes an industrial-relations executive, the ex-government lawyer turned corporation counsel, the erstwhile blue blood who becomes a sales trainee, many organization men have a conflict in loyalties they must resolve. The men who move are not vouchsafed a common, all-purpose religion.

It is in the development of their professional techniques, not in ideology, that they find continuity—and this, perhaps, is one more reason why managerial people have not coalesced into a ruling class. "They have not taken over the governing functions," Max Lerner recently reassured an academic audience, "nor is there any sign that they want to or can. They have concentrated on the fact of their skills rather than on the uses to which their skills are put. The question of the *cui bono* the technician regards as beyond his technical competence." If they are to be an elite, in short, they will be an elite in spite of themselves.

For the individual, this lack of fixed guideposts often produces a keen sense of temporariness. "One of the hazards of the kind of life we lead," says a man now poised at the threshold of the top management of our largest corporation, "is the loss of well-defined objectives. What is the purpose? What is the end? I was deeply a part of my job in the chemical division. My wife and I were deeply part of the community; I was contributing and was effective. Then they asked me to come to New York—the V.P. in charge told me that by coming here I'd have a box seat in the 'Big Time.' If his guess has been bad, it's a terrible waste. I hope the company isn't playing checkers with me. I feel a lack. I don't know what I'm being groomed for. I don't know what contacts to keep alive. A sales manager knows he should keep his customer contacts, but in the broad management philosophy you can't do this. You have to guess. I felt I had trained for twenty years for a tremendous job that had plenty of challenge, and I was in it for only nine months. Somehow I feel this move is out of my pattern—whatever that is. I'd hate to lose all that's behind me because somebody is playing checkers with me."

Younger executives have yet to recognize that there ever will be such dilemmas to face. The great expansion of our economy has created so many new slots to be filled that the young man of moderate ability has appeared to be rising vertically for a fairly long while. The succession of salary raises stimulated by inflation has further confirmed the illusion. The corporation organization, of course, remains a pyramid; but if one were to draft an organization chart based on some junior-executive bull sessions, the chart would look strangely like a series of parallel lines, the lines going up and up until they disappear into a sort of mist.

"I get so depressed listening to the hot shots on the 8:06," says one somewhat disenchanted executive. "Very few of them are really destined for top management. But they don't see it that way. They don't know about the pyramid yet. I don't think the colleges have got this across to them."

What has already happened to the salaried transient suggests that if mobility continues to increase it may produce a rootlessness that can have far-reaching consequences. What, in the years to come, will be the effect on the younger members of management, on their children—and on the organizations some will one day head-of a way of life so much more nomadic than that of their elders? The development of new values in the transients' suburban villages indicates that the effect will be profound.

How much to the good, or bad, this change will be is a question we must defer. There is no virtue, certainty, in change per se; whether or not it is to be for the good depends on what the change is to. But for the moment at least, there is one hopeful conclusion we can draw. If the sheer fact of change is true, the picture of a society gradually stratifying is wrong. Those are mistaken who hold that the routes of mobility are being closed; that we are finally shaking down into a stable system; that we are, at last, on a plateau. Quite the opposite; the evidence indicates that our society has never been more dynamic—and the best thing about our system, perhaps, is that there isn't too much of it. Not just yet, anyway.

How the New Suburbia Socializes

Fortune, August 1953

Whyte's fascination with the complex interplay of landscape and psyche is evident in this closely observed study of Park Forest, Illinois, a community founded in 1948 and therefore among the newest of America's burgeoning suburbs. The surprise, Whyte reported, was that where Americans formerly "hated to concede that their behavior was determined by anything except their own free will," the new suburbanites were "fully aware of the pervading power of the environment over them" and willingly accepted "the way things are." Based on his findings, Whyte predicted that architects and planners would have a role in shaping American social life.

What will the American's social life be like ten or twenty years from now? A good place to look is the great labyrinth of ranch-type houses and garden-apartment villages going up outside the major cities. Contrary to what elders like to believe, these new package suburbs are not artificial communities somehow outside the main stream of U.S. life. They are a response to some new facts; with the growth of the great institution, in particular the corporation, a key part of the population has become transient, and in their journeys from post to post the next generation of executives have found the new suburb an ideal home away from home. Thanks to the great expansion of the middle class, the new suburbs have also become a mecca for thousands of young people moving up and out of city wards. Here, in short, is the second melting pot, and the values that are being formed in it may become dominant in the America of not so many years from now.

Friendship, for example. The most striking phenomenon in the new suburbs is that people's friendships, even their most intimate ones, seem predetermined; less on individual personality do friendships depend than on such seemingly inconsequential matters as the placement of a sidewalk, the view out of a picture window, the height of a fence, or the width of a street.

Propinquity, of course, has always been a factor in friendship; after all, you do have to come in contact with people before you can like them. In the new suburbs, however, it has become so powerful a factor that merely by observing certain physical clues of an area a visitor can come amazingly close to predicting who is friends with whom and who isn't.

It is not a simple case of conformity. Within these suburbs there is a great deal of diversity. The people in them come from every part of the country, and they are of every religion. The transient junior executive is found most frequently, but among his neighbors will be mechanics, professors, lawyers, research scientists, traveling salesmen, white-collar workers—indeed, almost the whole spectrum of American occupations. There are, as the case of the burlesque stripper will demonstrate, some interesting frictions. It is the accommodation of people with each other, however, that is more significant. That people can find so much in common with one another that most of them need go no further, literally, than a stone's throw for their friendships is, to be sure, not altogether cheering; it is, however, a striking demonstration of how very deeply mass media and education have ironed out the regional and religious differences and prejudices that have separated people.

Equally significant is a subtle change that seems to be taking place in the American's attitude toward his environment. Once people hated to concede that their behavior was determined by anything except their own free will. Not so with the new suburbanites; they are fully aware of the all-pervading power of the environment over them. As a matter of fact, there are few subjects they like so much to talk about; and with the increasing lay curiosity about psychology, psychiatry, and sociology, they discuss their social life in surprisingly clinical terms. But they have no sense of Plight; this, they seem to say, is the way things are, and the trick is not to fight it but to understand it.

As the residents themselves often point out, Park Forest, Illinois, the prototype of the new suburbia, is almost a "laboratory experiment" in social relationships. In designing the rental courts and the homes-for-sale "superblocks" at Park Forest, the architects happened on a basic design that has proved to be highly functional in shaping people's lives. Just what makes it functional, furthermore, is not too difficult to determine. In designing the 105 rental courts the architects staggered the buildings in different fashion in each court; similarly, no two superblocks are laid out exactly alike. By comparing these differences in design with any differences in social activity among areas, one can discover a cause-and-effect relationship.

No two areas have quite the same "character." Some courts have so little *esprit de corps* that the residents get together only occasionally; and in some, feuding and cussedness are chronic. Other courts are notably "outgoing," and though the moving van is constantly bringing in new people and taking out the old ones, the partying, the kaffeeklatsching, and the group activity continue undiminished.

The same is true in the curving superbocks for sale (price: around $13,000). "We're very lucky here," goes a typical diagnosis. "At the beginning we were so neighborly that your friends knew more about your private life than you did yourself. It's not quite that active now, but it's real friendly—even our dogs and cats are friendly with each other. The street behind us is nowhere near as friendly. They knock on doors over there."

The chance of who happened to land in what block is, of course, important. One of the most habitual mistakes in studying people in groups, let it be conceded, is to forget that they are also individuals, and to treat them instead almost as robots, doing what they do simply because of the external influences of the world around them. But no matter how hard you investigate the effect of individual differences, they fail to explain the social patterns.

Take, for example, a particular group—the forty or forty-five families, say, that live in a cluster of buildings centered around a parking court. Look into the religion of each, their family background, where they were born, how much education they've had, their taste in books and TV, whether or not they drink, what games they like to play. You will find that each of these considerations somehow affects their friendships. Yet when you try to correlate these factors with the way groups shape up, almost by elimination you are left with only one basic explanation: what really counts is the effect of the physical layout.

The way physical design influences social traffic is sometimes capricious; some people, as we will see later, are so ambiguously located that they can never quite be sure who they should be friends with. By and large, however, the social traffic follows a logical pattern.

It begins with the children. The new suburbs are matriarchies, yet the children are in effect so dictatorial that a term like *filiarchy* would not be entirely facetious. It is the children who set the basic design; their friendships are translated into the mother's friendships, and these, in turn, to the family's. Fathers just tag along.

Kaffeeklatsch, Park Forest, 1953. (*Photo by Dan Weiner*)

Play areas: Since children have a way of playing where *they* feel like playing, their congregating areas have not turned out to be exactly where elders
planned them to be; in the homes area the backyards would seem ideal, and
communal play areas have been built in some of them. But the children will
have none of them; they can't use their toy vehicles there and so they play
on the lawn and pavements out front. In the court areas the children have
amenably played in and around the interior parking bay out of traffic's way;
the courts' enclosed "tot yards," however, haven't turned out to be as functional as was expected; in many courts the older children use them as a barricade to keep the younger children *out*.

It is the flow of wheeled juvenile traffic, then, that determines which is
to be the functional door; i.e., in the homes, the front door; in the courts,
the back door. It determines, further, the route one takes from the functional door; for when wives go visiting with neighbors they gravitate toward
the houses within sight and hearing of their children and the telephone.
This crystallizes into the court "checkerboard movement" (i.e., the regular
kaffeeklatsch route) and this forms the basis of adult friendships.

Placement of driveways and stoops: The adjoining back porches in the
courts and the area around adjacent driveways of homes for sale make a natural sitting, baby-watching, and gossip center. So strong is the adhesive
power of such adjacent facilities that people sharing them tend to become

close friends even though equidistant neighbors on the other side may have much more in common with them.

Lawns: The front lawn is the thing on which homeowners expend most time, and the sharing of tools, energies, and advice that the lawns provoke tends to make the family friendships go along and across the street rather than over the backyards.

Centrality: The location of one's home in relation to the others not only determines your closest friends; it also virtually determines how popular you will be. As the chart indicates, the more central one's location, the more social contacts one has. In the streets containing rental apartments there is a constant turnover; yet no matter who moves in or out, the center of activity remains in mid-block, with the people at the ends generally included only in the larger gatherings.[1]

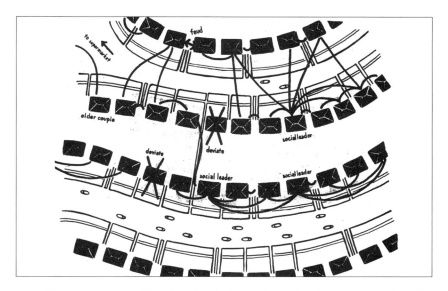

How Homeowners Get Together: (1) Individuals tend to become most friendly with neighbors whose driveways adjoin theirs. (2) Deviates or feuding neighbors tend to become boundaries of the gang. (3) People in the most central positions make the greatest number of social contacts. (4) Street width and traffic determine whether or not people make friends across the street. (5) People make friends with those in back of them only where some physical feature creates traffic—such as the short-cut pavement one woman on the lower street uses on her way to the supermarket.

Chronology of construction: Since a social pattern once established tends to perpetuate itself, the order and direction in which an area is built is an enduring factor. If one side of the street is built first rather than both sides simultaneously, the group tends to organize along rather than across the street. This also helps explain why so little backyard socializing develops; by the time the backyard gets fixed up, the front-lawn pattern has already jelled.

Limitations on size: One reason it's so important to be centrally placed is that an active group can contain only so many members. By plotting each gathering along any block one discovers that there is usually an inner core of about four to six regulars. Partly because of the size of the living rooms (twenty by fifteen), the full group rarely swells beyond twelve couples, and only in the big functions such as a block picnic are the people on the edges included.

From this one might gather that the rules of the game are fairly simple. They are not. Where, as social leaders chronically complain, do you draw the line?

Physical barriers can provide a sort of limiting point. Streets, for example, are functional for more than traffic; if it is a large street with heavy traffic, mothers will forbid their children to cross it, and by common consent the street becomes a boundary for the adult group. Because of the need for a social line, the effect of even the smallest barrier is multiplied. In courts where the parking bays have two exits, fences have been placed across the middle to block through traffic; only a few feet high, they are as socially impervious as a giant brick wall.

Similarly, the grouping of apartment buildings into wings of a court provides a natural unit whose limits everyone understands. All in all, it seems, the "happiest" groups are those in which no home is isolated from the others—or so sited as to introduce a conflict in the social allegiance of its residents.

Ambiguity is the one thing the group cannot abide. If there is no line, the group will invent one. They may settle on an imaginary line along the long axis of the court or, in the homes area, a "barrier" family (of which more later) will provide a convenient line.

There is common sense behind it. If it's about time you threw a party for your neighbors, the line solves many of your problems for you. Friends of yours who live on the other side understand why they were not invited, and there is no hard feeling.

People are not yet such pawns of their environment, of course, that physical, objective factors are all that determine their social lives. Such

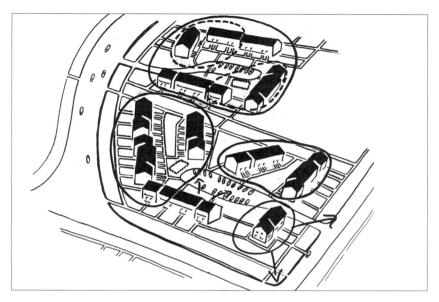

What Makes a Court Clique: In the rental courts formed around parking bays, social life is oriented inward. In the large court at the bottom, for example, wings whose back doors face each other form natural social units. Buildings sited somewhat ambiguously tend to split the allegiance of their inhabitants, or else, like the lonely apartment unit at the lower right, isolate them. Smaller courts like the one at the top are usually more cohesive; and though there may be subgroupings, court people often get together as a unit.

characteristics as age have influence. Since most Park Forest couples are in their early thirties, couples much over forty are often so far removed in taste and interests that they do not mesh with the group. Teenagers are also likely to be lonely.

Whether one drinks or not can be critical; in some courts the groups split along drinking and non-drinking lines, as well as along the usual geographic ones. Bridge playing is another factor; and when those who play bridge a lot speak of neighbors who are more given to pinochle, they often speak with a trace of condescension.

But the remarkable aspect of friendship in the new suburbia is how much it transcends such personal characteristics. Despite the great number of occupational and company ties, closest friendships generally have not crystallized this way; after dark, even the car pool loses its pull.

The fact that these different kinds of people can mix so easily is due largely to the great spread of American middle-class values. But it is also due to an active effort the people make to meet one another halfway. Just as the Bunco player may put his mind to mastering bridge, so the Ph.D.'s wife learns to have fun at a coffee; just as the Fundamentalist learns to unbend with a tentative risqué story and beer now and then, so his neighbors tone down their own stories.

This denominator-seeking is abundantly illustrated in the many commercial "parties" so popular at Park Forest (Linda Lee clothes demonstrations, the Beauty Counselor, etc.). Stanley Home products demonstrators, for example, ask the hostess to serve only two refreshments, preferably coffee and doughnuts. If the choice is left to her, she may so overdo that others will fear to be hostesses lest their own offerings suffer in comparison. Similar care marks the games that precede the product demonstration. "The best kind of thing to start with," says one Park Forest housewife who has demonstrated Stanley products, "is something like the waistline game. That's where you lay a piece of rope on the floor and start making an ever bigger circle; one by one the girls tell you when they think it's as big as their waistline. They always overestimate, because your waistline is oblong and not a circle. They get a big charge out of that. But if you do anything that shows up people's intelligence, it's tricky. With a spelling game or naming states—you'd be surprised how many people can't name ten states—they just get uncomfortable."[2]

This seeking of common values applies markedly to religion. The neighborhood friendship patterns would be impossible unless religious beliefs had lost much of their segregating effect. Indeed, the tolerance has become an almost active one. Several people of other faiths, for example, have joined the National Council of Jewish Women; they like its discussion programs (e.g., the current one on mental health), and they feel no conflict with their own beliefs. The tolerance pervades day-to-day life. "When Will and Ada had to dash East last month—they're devout Catholics—I took care of little Johnny for them," recalls one non-Catholic. "It really tickled me. Here I was picking Johnny up at St. Irenaeus school every afternoon and seeing to it that he said his Rosary every night before he went to bed." Park Forest abounds with such stories, and the good will implicit in them is real.

The social millennium, of course, is still some way off. The recent unresolved controversy over admitting Negroes to Park Forest has stirred up a great deal of bad feeling. It is important to note, however, that much of the feeling was not rooted in racial ill will so much as in economic and social fears. For the couple who had just moved to Park Forest from, say, a deteriorating ward in Chicago, the sudden introduction of the Negro issue seemed to them a threat to everything they had been striving for. But a dynamic is at work; as it may be years before the issue can be handled equably, the feeling of social vulnerability that contributed to the tension will not remain the same.

It is in the more subtle field of family background that one finds the most energetic kind of tolerance. Park Foresters are egalitarian, but not unconsciously so. They miss few of the clues of family background provided by slips in speech or peculiarities of taste, and in almost every block there is someone—to use a favored euphemism—that the others say "has not had all the advantages some people have had."

Such a person is not snubbed. Quite the opposite; the others will go out of their way to make him feel at home and through a sort of osmosis educate him in the values of the group. There are, of course, failures; some newcomers are so shy, so sensitive about their background that they rebuff advances, and occasionally they see no reason to acclimate themselves at all. One court was thoroughly confounded by the arrival of a housewife who was an ex-burlesque stripper and, worse yet, volubly proud of the fact. She never learned, and the collision between her breezy outlook and the family mores of the court was near catastrophic. "They're just jealous because I'm theatrical folk," she told an observer as she prepared to depart with her husband in a cloud of smoke. "All those wives think I want their husbands. What a laugh. I don't even want my own. The bitches." The court has never been quite the same since.

But such instances are singular. Given half a chance, the group will endure a good many rebuffs before they give up. Similarly, when misfortune strikes a neighbor, they are not only remarkably generous, but remarkably tactful. If, say, the child of a couple in straits accidentally breaks someone's windshield, the group may not only chip in to pay for the damage, but will try to conceal the fact that they have done so. The response of those in trouble is often irrationally antagonistic. But no matter; they may have "a personality problem," and there is nothing so challenging to the others as its diagnosis and therapy.

The tolerance goes downward. It does not, however, go *upward* very far. The leveling process is just that, leveling, and those financially above the norm who let the fact be visible are risking trouble. Though neighbors speak kindly of someone who "had not had all the advantages," the phrase "they are more . . . fortunate than the rest of us" is likely to be spoken with a real bite.

Just how much bite depends on how happy the group is. The more happiness, the more bite. For the more vigorous is the search for common denominators, the stronger the pressure to alikeness. Sometimes this extends even to house design. The architects have tried to vary the façades of each house and one might assume that in putting up aluminum awnings, making alterations, repainting and the like, residents would try hard to enlarge the differences. This is not always so; in some areas residents have apparently agreed to unify the block with a common design and color scheme for garages and such.

In such blocks an otherwise minor variation becomes a blatant deviance; a man who paints his garage fire-engine red in a block where the rest of the garages are white has literally and psychologically made himself a marked man. So with fences; if they are obviously designed to keep the children safe eyebrows are not raised. But if the height or elaborateness of the fence indicates other motives, there will be feeling.

Lawns are another good clue. A lawn notably less manicured than the others in a block is a strong indication that all is not well between its owner and the others. It is not merely that the state of the lawn itself has provoked feeling. The lawn is an effect as well as a cause, and in talking to owners of neglected lawns one gets the suspicion that they have subconsciously used them as a weapon to tell the others where they can head in. "I suppose I should do more about it," says one resident, waving to a rather weedy expanse outside, "but my wife and I think there are other things more important in life."

Such "barrier" families, incidentally, can be of service to the group, for they furnish a line of social demarcation that the layout and geography do not supply. So functional is the barrier family in this respect that even if they move out and those who replace them are middling-normal, the line will remain in the same place.

Who are the deviates? Basically there are four categories of residents. First are the members of the group—the great majority. Second are those whose friendships, through community-wide activities, tend to cut across the whole community rather than to be concentrated in one geographic area. Third are those intrinsically antisocial people who wouldn't get along with anybody anywhere. Fourth are those who are almost pathetically eager to be members of the group, but who somehow bring out all the bullying instincts in those about them.

If the deviate is at the end of a block or is otherwise isolated physically, he may remain ignorant of what he is missing. In a more central and thereby exposed position the result will be different. "Estelle is a case," says one resident of a highly active block. "She was dying to get in with the gang when she moved in. She is a very warmhearted gal and is always trying to help people, but she's well—sort of elaborate about it. One day she decided to win over everybody by giving an afternoon party for the gals. Poor thing, she did it all wrong. The girls turned up in their bathing suits and slacks, as usual, and here she had little doilies and silver and everything spread around. Ever since then it's been a planned campaign to keep her out of things. Even her two-year-old daughter gets kept out of kids' parties. It's really pitiful. She sits there in her beach chair out front just dying for someone to come and kaffee-klatsch with her, and right across the street four or five of the girls and their kids will be yakking away. Every time they suddenly all laugh at some joke she thinks that they are laughing at her. She came over here yesterday and cried all afternoon. She told me that she and her husband are thinking about moving somewhere else so they can make a fresh start."

The community-leader types who make friends across the community have less friction with the group than might be imagined. This is the more curious because they are visibly different. Members of the League of Women Voters—which includes a large proportion of the residents most given to intellectual and cultural interests—are apt to be somewhat absent-minded about their clothes and their housekeeping. "Most of us League gals are thin," says one. "We're so busy, and we don't have time for coffee and doughnuts." Such people, nevertheless, cannot be regarded as isolates. For one thing, they do not give the group much of a chance to isolate them; for another, although they may draw a firm line at intimacy, they are good about baby-sitting, returning borrowed lawn mowers, and the other neighborly graces.

One moral that might be drawn from all this is that a more socially conscious architecture could eliminate the friction. Given the growing homogeneity of the American people and given the information now available about layout, it should theoretically be possible to design an optimum "happy" block.

But one question obtrudes. How good is the happiness? The more we know about the social effects of planning, of course, the more intelligently we can plan. It does not follow, however, that a socially benevolent design would be a blessing. One does not have to damn the cohesive group to point out that it carries a price. The more social the block, the rougher it is on those who can't make the grade, and in some cases it is questionable if the *Gemütlichkeit* of the gang compensates for the misery of the deviate.

Even more important is the effect of cohesion on the members of the group themselves. There is evidence that the closer the ties to the neighborhood group the less likely one is to express other yearnings. Upon charting the location of the people most active in the community's seventy-odd civic organizations, it appears that the courts that produce an above-average share of leaders usually are not the courts the best known for congeniality and partying.

In the great problem of expending leisure time there are some people who can keep their own interests and the group's in proper, if occasionally uneasy, balance. Then at the other extreme are those for whom complete absorption in the group is a fulfilling experience. But what of those in the middle? Many sense that by their immersion in the group they are frustrating other urges, yet they feel that responding to the group mores is akin to a moral duty— and so they continue, hesitant and unsure, imprisoned in brotherhood.

"Every once in a while I wonder," says one transient in an almost furtive moment of contemplation. "I don't want to do anything to offend the people here; they're kind and decent, and I'm proud we've been able to get along with each other—with all our differences— so well. But then, once in a while, I think of myself and my husband and what we are not doing, and I get depressed. Is it just enough not to be bad?"

The Fallacies of "Personality" Testing

Fortune, September 1954

Whyte's exposé of corporate personnel policies described a troubling trend in corporate culture: the so-called personality tests, which allowed corporations to measure
individual profiles against an ideal "master" template of conformity, were being used
not merely to screen unfit candidates out of the organization but also to check up on
employees who had found their way in. Whyte argued that "almost by definition the
dynamic person is an exception—and where aptitude tests reward, personality tests
often punish him." Whyte warned of vengeful, if unintended, long-term consequences
of the systematic enforcement of conformity in organization life. Moreover, he contested the organization's claim to employees' psyches: "The bill of rights should not
stop at the corporation's edge." The article ends with a famous (and brilliant) decod-
ing of the cryptic tests and some advice on how to cheat personnel officers at their
own Orwellian game.

Business is being tantalized by a fascinating possibility. After a long experi-
mentation period with school children, college students, and inmates of
institutions, applied psychologists are becoming more and more confident
that with "personality" tests they can come close to answering the hitherto
elusive question of who will succeed and who won't. As a matter of routine,
of course, most managements have been screening job applicants with tests
of aptitude and intelligence, but while these have been useful in eliminating the obviously unfit, they have not been able to predict performance, for
they tell nothing of a man's motivation and all those intangibles that can
make the difference between success and mediocrity. Now, however, psychologists have tests by which they attempt to measure a man for almost
any personality trait, and plot with precision his standing compared to the
rest of the population.

At first there were only rough measures—such as how introverted and neurotic a man is—but there are now in regular business use tests that tell a man's superiors his degree of radicalism versus conservatism, his practical judgment, social judgment, degree of perseverance, stability, contentment, hostility to society, and latent homosexuality. Some psychologists are tinkering with a test of sense of humor. To probe even deeper, testers are also applying the "projective" techniques like the Rorschach Ink Blot Test, which lead the subject into x-raying himself for latent feelings and psychoses.

Probing adults is not the same thing as probing school children, of course, and the fact that some of the former balk at exposing themselves might appear an important obstacle. But this has not been the case. Testers have learned to attach great significance to the way people respond to the idea of the tests: if a man refuses to answer certain questions, psychologists believe they can deduce suppressed anxieties almost as well as if he had answered the questions.

America's secondary-school educators were the first to seize upon these tests, but business is catching up very quickly indeed. Two years ago only about a third of U.S. corporations used personality testing; since then the proportion has been climbing—of the sixty-three corporations checked by *Fortune*, 60 percent are using personality tests, and these include such bellwether firms as Sears, General Electric, and Westinghouse. While there are still some executives vigorously opposed to personality testing, all the signs point to a further increase.

The most widespread use of tests has been for the fairly mundane job of screening applicants. Even in companies not notably enthusiastic about personality tests, it is now part of standard operating procedure to add several personality tests to the battery of checks on the job applicant. If business declines, tests may also be applied to cut down the work force. "For trimming inefficiency in the company operation," Industrial Psychology Inc. (Tuscon, Arizona) advises clients, "there is no better place to direct the ax than in the worker category." And there is no better way to do this, it adds, than to run the force through tests.

But the really significant development in personality testing lies in another direction. In perhaps 25 percent of the country's corporations the tests are used not merely to help screen out those who shouldn't get into the organization but to check up on people who are already in it. And the people being checked on, furthermore, are not workers so much as management itself. Some of these companies don't bother to give personality tests to workers at all; aside from the fact that testing can be very expensive, they feel that the limited number of psychologists available should concentrate on the more crucial questions.

Should Jones be promoted or put on the shelf? Just about the time an executive reaches forty-five or fifty and begins to get butterflies in his stomach wondering what it has all added up to and whether the long-sought prize is to be his after all, the company is probably wondering too. Where once the man's superiors would have threshed this out among themselves, in some companies they now check first with the psychologists to find out what the tests say. At Sears, for example, for the last ten years no one has been promoted in the upper brackets until the board chairman has consulted the tests. At Sears, as elsewhere, the formal decision is of course based on other factors also, but the weight now being given test reports makes it clear that for many a potential executive the most critical day he spends in his life will be the one he spends taking tests.

One result has been the rise of a considerable industry. In the last five years, the number of test blanks sold has risen 300 percent. The growth of psychological consulting firms has paralleled the rise; in addition to such established firms as the Psychological Corp., literally hundreds of consultants are setting up shop. Science Research Associates of Chicago, a leading test supplier, reports that within the last twelve months *seven hundred* new consultants have asked to be put on its approved list of customers. Colleges are also getting into the business; through research centers like Rensselaer Polytechnic's Personnel Testing Laboratory, they have become directly competitive with leading commercial firms.

The types of service offered vary greatly. Some firms will do the entire operation by mail; for example, the Klein Institute for Aptitude Testing, Inc., of New York, within forty-eight hours of getting the completed test back will have an analysis on its way to the company. Usually, however, the job is done on the premises. Sometimes the consultant group, like the Activity Vector Analysts, will process the entire management group at one crack. More usually the analysts, very often a group of professors in mufti, will come in and study the organization in order to find the personality "profiles" best suited for particular jobs. They will then tailor a battery of tests and master profiles. Though the analysts may help out with the machinery of testing, the company's personnel department generally handles the rest of the job.

A dynamic would appear to be at work. The more people that are tested, the more test results there are to correlate, and the more correlations, the surer are many testers of predicting success or failure, and thus the more reason there is for more organizations to test more and more people. At Westinghouse Electric, for example, 10,000 management men have already been coded onto I.B.M. cards that contain, in addition to vital statistics and work records, the men's personality-test ratings. What with the schools already doing much the same thing, with electronics making mass testing increasingly easy, there seems no barrier to the building of such inventories for every organization.

Except common sense. For a large question remains: leaving aside for the moment the matter of invasion of privacy, have the tests themselves been really tested?

In an effort to find out, *Fortune* did some extensive testing of its own. What was under investigation, let it be made plain, was not the use of tests as guides in clinical work, or their use in counseling when the individual himself seeks the counseling. Neither was it the problem of ethics raised by the work of some practitioners in the field, interesting as this bypath is. What we have addressed ourselves to is the validity of "personality" tests as a standardized way of rating and slotting people. Question: do the tests really discriminate the man of promise from the run of the mill—or do they discriminate *against* him?

What would happen if the presidents of our largest corporations took the same tests that future executives are being judged by? What would happen if the tests were applied to a group of scientists, not just average scientists, but a group of the most productive ones in the world? Would they be rated as good risks? Would their scores jibe with their achievements? By actually giving tests to sixty exceptional persons, we found out. Conclusion: if the tests were rigorously applied across the board today, half of the most dynamic men in business would be out walking the streets for a job.

The effects of the day-to-day use of tests are less spectacular, but they are nonetheless far reaching. For the tests, *Fortune* submits, do not do what they are supposed to do. They do not do what they are supposed to do because, for one thing, they are not scientific. Neither in the questions nor in the evaluation are they neutral; they are, instead, loaded with debatable assumptions and questions of values. The result, deliberate or not, is a set of yardsticks that reward the conformist, the pedestrian, the unimaginative— at the expense of the exceptional individual whom management most needs to attract.

The reader will have a chance to estimate how he himself might fare. On page 56 is a selection of questions from seven personality tests now in use. When the reader has tried his hand at answering them, he can then score himself by turning to page 62, where he will find what the layman rarely sees: the "right" answers that are not supposed to exist, and the weights attached to them. Since the questions are only a sampling of the full tests, the reader's scores cannot be directly equated with those he would get if he took them in full, but he may find them illuminating nonetheless. One further caution: he should not be unnerved if he flunks some; that, as we hope to demonstrate, is an inevitable consequence of frankness, or intelligence, or both.

To a large degree the growing acceptance of personality tests rests on prestige by association, for these tests at first glance seem no more than an extension of the established methods of aptitude testing. The difference, however, is crucial. What is being measured in aptitude and intelligence testing are responses that can be rated objectively—such as the correctness of an answer to 2+2 or the number of triangles in a bisected rectangle. The conclusions drawn from these aptitude and intelligence scores are, furthermore, limited to the relatively modest prediction of a man's minimum ability to do *the same sort of thing he is asked to do on the tests.* If the tests indicate that a man has only 5,000 words in his vocabulary, it is a reasonable assumption that he won't do particularly well in a job requiring 50,000 words. If he is all thumbs when he puts wiggly blocks together, he won't be very good at a job requiring enough manual dexterity to put things like wiggly blocks together.

To jump from aptitude testing to personality testing, however, is to jump from the measurable to the immeasurable. What the personality testers are trying to do is convert abstract traits into a concrete measure that can be placed on a linear scale, and it is on the assumption that this is a true application of the scientific method that the whole mathematical edifice rests. But merely defining a trait is immensely difficult, let alone determining whether it can be measured as the opposite of another. Can you be 59 percent "emotional," for example, and if so, is "emotionalism" the precise statistical opposite of "steadiness"? People are daily being fitted onto linear scales for such qualities, and if their dimensions don't fit they are punished, like those on Procrustes' bed, for their deviance.

But what is "personality"? The surface facets of a man—the way he smiles, the way he talks? Obviously not; we must go much deeper, the psychologists tell us. But how much deeper? Few testers would dream of claiming that one can isolate personality from the whole man, yet logic tells us that to be able statistically to predict behavior we would have to do just this.

The mathematics is impeccable—and thus entrapping. Because "percentiles" and "coefficients" and "standard deviations" are of themselves neutral (and impressive sounding), the sheer methodology of using them can convince people that they are translating uncertainty into certainty, the subjective into the objective, and eliminating utterly the bugbear of value judgments. But the mathematics does *not* eliminate values, it only obscures them. No matter how objective testers try to be, even in the phrasing of their questions they are inevitably influenced by the customs and values of their particular world.

Questions designed to find your degree of sociability are an example. In some groups the reading of a book is an unsocial act, and the person who confesses he has at times preferred books to companions might be quite introverted to do such a thing. But the question is relative; applied to someone in a climate where reading is normal—indeed, the source of much social talk—the hidden "value judgment" built into the test can give a totally unobjective result. People are not always social in the same terms; a person who would earn himself an unsocial score by saying he would prefer bridge to bowling with the gang is not necessarily unsocial and he might even be a strong extrovert. It could be that he just doesn't like bowling.

If the layman gags at the phrasing of a question, testers reply, sometimes with a chuckle, this is merely a matter of "face validity." They concede that it is better if the questions seem to make sense, but they claim that the question itself is not so important as the way large numbers of people have answered it over a period of time. To put it in another way, if a hundred contented supervisors overwhelmingly answer a particular question in a certain way, this means something, and thus no matter whether the question is nonsensical or not, it has produced a meaningful correlation coefficient.

Meaning what? This is not the place to go into a lengthy dissertation on statistics, but two points should be made about the impressive test charts and tables that so often paralyze executives' common sense. A large proportion of the mathematics is purely internal; that is, different parts of the tests are compared with each other rather than with external evidence. Second, the external evidence used in many "validation" studies will be found on closer examination to consist of the scores persons made on similar personality tests rather than such untidy matters as how they actually performed on the job. That there should be a correlation between test scores is hardly surprising; test authors are forever borrowing questions from each other (some questions have been reincarcerated in as many as ten or twelve different tests) and what the correlations largely prove is how incestuous tests can be.

But how much have scores been related to individual behavior? Among themselves psychologists raise the same question, and for muted savagery there is nothing to match the critiques they make of each other's tests. The Bernreuter Personality Inventory is a particular case in point. This is by far the most widely used test in business (1953 sales by Stanford University Press, one of several distributors: one million copies). Yet a reading of the professional journals shows a long succession of negative results; when psychologists independently checked Bernreuter scores against other, more objective evidence of what the people tested were like, they found no significant relationships, and sometimes reverse correlations.

As top psychologists point out, a really rigorous validation would demand that a firm hire all comers for a period of time, test them, seal away the tests so the scores would not prejudice superiors, and then, several years later, unseal the scores and match them against the actual performance of the individuals involved. This has rarely been even attempted. To be sure, a good bit of work on the performance of *groups* has been done; for example, a group considered more productive has an average score on a test higher than another group. The average of a group, however, tells us very little about the *individuals* involved, for some of the "best" people will have lower test scores than some of the "poor" ones.

Testers evade this abyss by relying on a whole battery of tests rather than on just one or two. But no matter how many variables you add you cannot make a constant of them. If a man has a high "contentment index" and at the same time a very high "irritability index," does the one good cancel the other bad? Frequently the tester finds himself right back where he started from. If he is a perceptive man he may make a very accurate prognosis, but when, several years later, the prognosis turns out to be true, this is adduced as evidence of the amazing accuracy of test scores.

As an example of how values get entwined in testing, let's watch as a Worthington Personal History is constructed. This technique is a "projective" one; it is so projective, indeed, that the tester doesn't even have to bother seeing the man at all. The client company has the applicant fill out what seems to be an innocuous vital-statistics blank and then mails it to Worthington Associates. There an analyst studies it for such clues as whether the man used check marks or underlinings, how he designated his relatives, what part of his name he gives by initials, what by the full word.

Let the reader match his diagnostic skill against the testers. In a hypothetical example given in the *Personnel Psychology* journal, we are told that the applicant, one Jonathan Jasper Jones Jr., writes down that he is twenty-six, that the date of his marriage was November 1951, that he has only one dependent, his wife, that her given name is Bernardine Butterfield, her age twenty-eight, and that she works as a nurse receptionist in a doctor's office.

Enigma? Carefully, the analyst writes that these clues alone indicate that Jones "may not take his general obligations very seriously, may have a tendency to self-importance, wishful thinking, may be reluctant to assume general adult responsibilities; may be inclined to be passive-dependant, i.e., reliant on others for direction and guidance, in his general work relationships; may be inclined to take pleasure in unearned status or reflected glory."

How in the world did he deduce all this? Let us peek into the laboratory. The name was the first clue. It told the analyst that Jones was narcissistic. Whenever a man writes out his name in full, the tester notes in his chart that he is "narcissistic." Two initials, last name— "hypomanic." First initial, middle and last name: "narcissistic, histrionic." Any erasure or retracing: "anxious, tense." Characteristically, the applicant gets the short end of every assumption; even if he adopts the customary alternative—first name, middle initial, last name—he is put down as "mildly compulsive."

Deeper and deeper the analyst goes:

Spouse's age: twenty-eight.

Fact: married a girl two years older than himself.

Empirical observation—the majority of men marry women younger than themselves.

Primary deduction—may have been influenced in marrying her by unconsciously considering her as a mother surrogate.

Tentative inference—may like to have an older woman, or people, take care of him.

Provisional extension—may be inclined to be passive-dependent, i.e., reliant on others for direction and guidance, in his general work relationships.

And so on.

Analysts, of course, have just as much right to read between the lines as the next man; what makes their posture interesting is the claim that this is the scientific method. There are all the inevitable tables (the biserial correlation for tenure on Worthington cutoff is 0.34) in which the accuracy of the internal mathematics is confused with the accuracy of the premises. There is the usual spurious humility: the authors caution that no single deduction is necessarily correct; it is only when all the deductions are fitted into a "formal quantitative scoring procedure based on an organized system of psychodynamic factors" that they become correct. Add up enough wrongs, in short, and you get a right.

The analysis of J. J. Jones is a rather extreme example but it leads us to a defect characteristic of all tests. Against what specification is the man being measured? Assuming for the moment that we are able to diagram Jonathan Jones exactly, how are we to know the kind of work the diagram indicates he is suited for? There is not much point in testing people to find out if they will make good salesmen or executives unless we know what it is that makes the good ones good.

And thus we come to the "profile." Testers collate in chart form personality scores for groups of people in different occupations to show how they compare with other adults on several personality traits. This is generally expressed as a "percentile" rating; if thirty salesclerks' sociability scores average somewhere around the 80th percentile, for example, this indicates that the average salesclerk is more sociable than 79 out of 100 adults. Thus a man being considered for a particular kind of job can be matched against the master profile of the group. If the shoe fits, he is Cinderella.

Profiles are also worked up for jobs in individual companies. At Sears, Roebuck there are charts that diagram the optimum balance of qualities required. Here is the one on executive values:

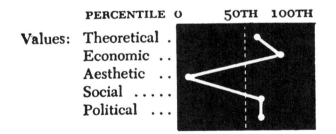

A man does not have to match this profile exactly, but it won't help him at all if his line zigs where the chart zags. Take a man who scores considerably higher than the 10th percentile on aesthetic values, for example; such people, Sears notes, "accept artistic beauty and taste as a fundamental standard of life. This is *not* a factor which makes for executive success. . . . Generally, cultural considerations are not important to Sears executives, and there is evidence that such interests are detrimental to success."

Sears has every right to de-emphasize certain qualities and emphasize others; and in hewing to this type, it should be noted, Sears has built up one of the most alert management groups in the country. But the profile is not to be confused with science. When they are used as selection devices, tests are not a neutral tool; *they become a large factor in the equation they purport to solve*. For one thing, the tests tend to screen out—or repel—those who would upset the correlation. If a man can't get into the company in the first place because he isn't the company type, he can't very well get to be an executive in it and be tested in a study to find out what kind of profile subsequent executives should match. Long before personality tests were invented, of course, plenty of companies had proved that if you hire people only of a certain type then all your successful men will be people of that type. But no one confused this with the immutable laws of science.

Bias, in short, is no longer personalized; now it's institutionalized. For the profile is self-confirming. When it doesn't screen out those who fail to match it, it will mask the amount of deviance in the people who do pass. Few test takers can believe the flagrantly silly statement in the preamble to many tests that there are "no right or wrong answers." There wouldn't be much point in the company's giving the test if some answers weren't regarded as better than others. "Do you daydream frequently?" In many companies a man either so honest or stupid as to answer "yes" would be well advised to look elsewhere for employment.

Even when the man who should have looked elsewhere slips through, the profile will be self-confirming. For the profile molds as well as chooses; it is, as Sears puts it, a statement of "the kind of behavior we have found to be desirable." Several years of give and take, and the organization will smooth the man out. Thus when the psychologists do their "validating," or rechecking, later he will score near enough to the median to show them how right they were all along.

Up to a point the company "type" has some virtue; any first-rate organization must have an *esprit de corps* and this implies a certain degree of homogeneity. But the pitfalls are many, for while a self-confirming profile makes for a comfortable organization, it eventually can make for a static one. Even the largest corporations must respond to changes in the environment; a settled company may have its very existence threatened by technological advances unless it makes a bold shift to a new type of market. What, then, of the pruning and molding that adapted it so beautifully to its original environment? The dinosaur was a formidable animal.

The profile can be self-confirming for the individual too. For tests intensify a mutual deception we practice on one another. Who is "normal"? All of us to some degree have a built-in urge to adjust to what we conceive as the norm, and in our search we can come to feel that in the vast ocean of normality that surrounds us only we are different. We are the victims of each other's façades.

And now, with the norm formally enshrined in figures, we are more vulnerable than ever to this tyrant. "Science" seems its ally, and thus, faulty or not, the diagnosis can provoke a sense of guilt or inadequacy; for we can forget that the norm is often the result of the instinctive striving of previous test takers to answer as they think everyone else would answer.

If the organization man escapes the danger of self-tyranny he faces another. At first superiors may scoff at the diagnosis, but if they have been putting reliance on testing they have a stake themselves in its correctness. Suspicion, unfortunately, demands proof, and sometimes it so counterbalances judgment that unconsciously a management will punish the man so that faith in the tests may be confirmed. One large midwestern company was about to promote a man when it decided to have him take a test. The report that the consultant firm mailed back to the company was freighted by the analyst with warnings about the man's stability. The company was puzzled. The man had consistently done a fine job. Still . . . The more the company mused, the more worried it became; at last it decided to tell the man the promotion he had expected so long was going to someone else. Six months later, the company reports, the man had a nervous breakdown. As in all such stories, the company says this proves how accurate the test was.

Are the people who don't score well necessarily the misfits? Almost by definition the dynamic person is an exception—and where aptitude tests reward, personality tests often punish him. Look at profiles and test scoring keys, and you will find that you will come closer to a high score if you observe two rules:

(1) When asked for word associations or comments about the world, give the most conventional, run-of-the mill, pedestrian answer possible.

(2) When in doubt about the most beneficial answer to any question, repeat to yourself:

I loved my father and my mother, but my father a little bit more.

I was a happy, normal American boy and everybody liked me.

I like things pretty much the way they are.

I never worry about anything.

I love my wife and children.

I don't let them get in the way of company work.

I don't care for books or music much.

The sheer mechanics of the tests also punish the exceptional man. A test with prefabricated answers is precisely the kind of test that people with superior intelligence find hardest to answer. How *big* was that fire in the basement of the theater? This is not a quibble; it is the kind of question that occurs to the intelligent mind, and the ability to see shadings, to posit alternatives, is virtually indispensable to judgment, practical or otherwise.

Which brings us to *Fortune*'s experiment. With the stipulation by *Fortune* that their individual scores should not be identified, fourteen corporation presidents and board chairmen agreed to take a battery of tests including Personal Audit, Thurstone Temperament, and the Test of Practical Judgment. Next, twelve of the country's most brilliant scientists agreed to do the same. As a further check, twenty-nine rising middle-management men who had been picked to attend an advanced-management school took the Thurstone and Practical Judgment tests.

Here are the highlights of the test results.

(1) Not one corporation president had a profile that fell completely within the usual "acceptable" range, and two failed to meet the minimum profile for foremen. On the "How Supervise" questions, presidents on the average got only *half* the answers right, thus putting them well down in the lower percentiles. They did particularly badly on the questions (15–20 on page 56–7) concerning company employee-relations policies. Only three presidents answered more than half of these questions correctly.

(2) The scientists' Personal Audit profiles were more even than the presidents'—if anything, they scored as *too* contented, firm, and consistent. They did, however, show up as extremely misanthropic, over half falling under the 20th percentile for sociability.

(3) The middle-management executives scored well on stability and sociability, but on practical judgment only three were at or over the mean indicated for executive work.

(4) The range of scores was so great as to make a median figure relatively meaningless. On the Thurstone "S" score for sociability, for example, only eight of the forty-three management men fell between the 40th and 60th percentiles, the remainder being grouped at either extreme.

(5) Internally, the scores were highly contradictory. Many of the same people who got high "steadiness" scores on the Personal Audit scored very badly for "stability" on the Thurstone test. Similarly, many who scored high on "contentment" had very low "tranquility" scores.

One explanation for this great variance between results and the standard norms would be that the men in the sample were answering frankly and thus their scores could not be properly compared with the standard norms given. But if this is true, then we must conclude that *the norms themselves embody slanted answers.* Another explanation of their showing would be that they scored low because they were in fact neurotic or maladjusted, as the tests said. But this leaves us with a further anomaly. If people with an outstanding record of achievement show up as less well "adjusted" than the run of the mill, then how important a yardstick is adjustment? *Fortune*'s sample, of course, is small. So is the supply of outstandingly talented people.

The study of a man's past performance, the gauging of him in the personal interview, are uncertain guides; executives are right to use them with humility. But they are still the key, and the need is not to displace them but to become more skilled with them. The question of who will be best in a critical situation cannot be determined scientifically before the event. No matter how much information we may amass, we must rely on judgment, on intuition, on the particulars of the situation—and the more crucial the situation the less certain we can be of prediction. It is an immensely difficult task, perhaps the most difficult one that any management faces. But the question cannot be fed into a computer nor can it be turned over by proxy for someone else to decide, and any management that so evades its most vital function needs some analysis of its own.

And doesn't the individual have some rights in this matter too? Our society has taught him to submit to many things; thousands of civilians who went into the military meekly stood naked in long lines waiting for their numbered turn in the mass physical examinations. Many civilians who have been asked to work on government projects have submitted to being fingerprinted and to the certainty that government agents would soon be puzzling their friends and neighbors with questions about their backgrounds. In these cases a man can console himself that there is a reason; that if he is to enjoy the benefits of collective efforts he must also pay some price.

But there is a line. How much must a man testify against himself? The bill of rights should not stop at the corporation's edge. In return for the salary the organization gives the individual, it can ask for superlative work from him, but it should not ask for his psyche as well. Here and there, we are happy to report, some declarations of independence have been made. Last year the executives of a large and well-known New England corporation were subjected by the management to psychological examination by an outside consultant. Whether it was because of the consultant's manner or because of the New England character, the executives at length revolted. Let them be judged, they said, for their work. As for their inner feelings—that, as one man said who was almost fired for saying so, that was no one's damn business but their own.

How Maladjusted Are *You*?

Here is a series of questions taken from various leading personality tests now being used by business, not only to screen candidates but also to analyze executives. No single test has been reproduced in full, but the sampling is enough to give you some idea as to the diagnosis each would make of you. When you are finished answering the questions, turn to page 62 and you will find a table by which you can estimate your scores. From these you can plot how your personality jibes with the testers' norms.

A. Items from "The Personality Inventory"

Circle either "Yes," "No," *or* "?"

1. Yes No ? Do you day-dream frequently?
2. Yes No ? Can you stand criticism without feeling hurt?
3. Yes No ? Do you often feel just miserable?
4. Yes No ? Do you usually object when a person steps in front of you in a line of people?
5. Yes No ? Are you troubled with shyness?
6. Yes No ? Do you ever heckle or question a public speaker?
7. Yes No ? Do you worry too long over humiliating experiences?
8. Yes No ? Have books been more entertaining to you than companions?
9. Yes No ? Are your feelings easily hurt?
10. Yes No ? Are you greatly embarrassed if you have greeted a stranger whom you have mistaken for an acquaintance?
11. Yes No ? Does some particularly useless thought keep coming into your mind to bother you?
12. Yes No ? Do your feelings alternate between happiness and sadness without apparent reason?
13. Yes No ? Do you worry over possible misfortunes?
14. Yes No ? Do you keep in the background at social functions?

B. Items from "How Supervise?" test

Here are some methods used by different companies in handling their relations with employees. Circle either D *(desirable),* ? *(uncertain), or* U *(undesirable).*

15. Establishing "worker courts" operated by workers to try and punish workers for violation of safety rules   D   ?   U

16.	Putting plates on the base of each important piece of equipment showing its value and cost of operation	D ? U
17.	Requiring department heads to spend at least one week of the year visiting other up-to-date plants	D ? U
18.	Having the employees choose one worker from each department to attend regular meetings of the departmental supervisors	D ? U
19.	Giving supervisors longer vacations than those enjoyed by the average worker	D ? U
20.	Setting up a system for making loans to workers at very low interest rates	D ? U

Check A (agree), DA (disagree), or ? (uncertain) to indicate how you feel about each item.

21.	What the worker thinks is unimportant so long as he is doing his job well	A ? DA
22.	What the worker does during his "off hours" should be of no concern to his employer	A ? DA
23.	The usefulness of the product he is making is of little concern to the average employee	A ? DA
24.	The best way to make sure that rules will be obeyed is to put plenty of teeth in them	A ? DA
25.	Ability to handle workers is inborn, not learned	A ? DA
26.	When a new supervisor is chosen, the duties of his job should be readjusted to fit his best abilities	A ? DA
27.	Knowing a great deal about an individual's home life is a great help in selecting the right person for a responsible job	A ? DA
28.	Gripes about things other workers do are more likely to be true than gripes about working conditions	A ? DA

C. Items from "Test of Practical Judgment"

Check best answer:

29. If you were in the basement of a theater and discovered a fire, would you
  a. Call the fire department
  b Notify the management
  c Ask the audience to leave quietly
  d. Endeavor to extinguish it

30. Why was the Civil Service established?
    a. As a sound political move
    b. As a source of qualified workers
    c. To increase the number of government bureaus
    d. To make jobs for highly trained technicians

On all the following, indicate which would be your first, second, and third choices:
31. What would you do if you saw someone breaking into and entering into your employer's store?
    a. Telephone your employer
    b. Notify the police
    c. Try to scare him away
    d. Try to apprehend him
32. What is the purpose of a store window display?
    a. To display merchandise
    b. To bring customers into the store
    c. To attract a crowd
    d. To arouse favorable comment
33. Suppose you are working as a junior clerk and your employer enters your department while you are reading a newspaper, would you
    a. Continue reading and show no embarrassment
    b. Fold it up and return to your duties
    c. Appear that you are making news clippings relative to your work
    d. Try to interest the boss by reading aloud an interesting headline
34. Why is it safest to fly an airplane rapidly and at a high altitude?
    a. It can be maneuvered more easily
    b. Visibility is better
    c. There are fewer air-pockets
    d. The motor operates better
35. If you were bored by the conversation of an acquaintance, would you
    a. Listen with polite but bored attention
    b. Listen with feigned interest
    c. Frankly state that the subject doesn't interest you
    d. Show signs of impatience

D. Items from the "A–S Reaction Study"
36. A salesman in a men's shop takes great trouble to show you a quantity of merchandise; you are not entirely suited; do you find it difficult to leave without making a purchase?
    Frequently   Sometimes   Not at all

37. If you are asked to solicit funds for a cause in which you are genuinely interested, do you feel reluctant to do such soliciting?

    Yes   No

38. You have heard indirectly that an acquaintance has been gossiping about you in a way which, though not likely to be serious in consequence, is nevertheless uncalled for and distinctly uncomplimentary. The acquaintance is an equal of yours in every way. Do you usually

    Let it pass without feeling

    "Have it out" with the person

    Feel disturbed but let it pass

    Take revenge indirectly

39. A man tries to push ahead of you in line before a ticket window. You have been waiting for some time and can't wait much longer. Do you usually

    Remonstrate with the intruder

    Give the intruder a "dirty look" or make audible comments to your neighbor

    Decide not to wait and go away

    Do nothing

40. Are you embarrassed if you have greeted a stranger whom you have mistaken for an acquaintance?

    Very much   Somewhat   Not at all

41. If you feel irritated or antagonistic on account of the "bossy" manner in which a chairman conducts a meeting, do you usually take the initiative in opposing him?

    Occasionally   Usually   Never

42. Have you largely on your own initiative in the past five years taken the lead in organizing clubs, teams, committees, Sunday school or education classes, or other groups?

    More than three   One to three   None

43. You are dining with someone whom you are trying to impress. The waiter presents a bill which is slightly larger than you expect it to be. Do you check or verify the bill before paying it?

    Openly   Secretly   Not at all

E. Items from "The Personal Audit"

Each word in capitals is followed by four words. Draw a circle around the word that seems to you to go most naturally with the word in capitals. There are no right or wrong answers. <u>*Work rapidly.*</u>

44.	PAST	yesterday	forget	sorrow	hidden
45.	LEG	limb	walk	shapely	stocking
46.	PURPLE	lavender	royal	wine	crimson
47.	IMMORAL	vulgar	person	vile	criminal
48.	SMOOTH	level	soft	flat	touch
49.	FILTHY	dirty	disgusting	mind	body
50.	DREAM	vision	night	trance	romance
51.	LOVE	adore	esteem	worship	yearn
52.	SEDATE	dignified	calm	refined	modest
53.	YELLOW	golden	cowardly	skin	sheet
54.	DAY	light	sunny	work	dark
55.	NUDE	naked	unclothed	immodest	shameless
56.	REVOLTING	repulsive	repugnant	loathsome	degrading
57.	DEBT	obligation	weight	necessary	nightmare
58.	RAPE	attack	assault	ruin	temptation

Below is a list of activities or things. If you feel about the same way toward them now that you did three or four years ago, draw a circle around "S." If you have partly changed your feelings, draw a circle around "P." If your feeling now is considerably different, draw a circle around "D."

59. S P D   More stringent enforcement of international law.
60. S P D   Raising the standard of living.
61. S P D   Governmental attitude toward labor unions.
62. S P D   Propaganda in politics.
63. S P D   Old-age pensions.
64. S P D   Social and educational equality of different races and creeds.
65. S P D   Lowering the retirement age from 65/70 to 60/65.
66. S P D   Getting regular amount of sleep.
67. S P D   Relative advantages of cultural vs. technical education.
68. S P D   Likelihood of war in the near future.
69. S P D   The use of applied psychology in business.
70. S P D   Being finger-printed for governmental identification.
71. S P D   Salaries earned by corporation presidents and other executives.

F. Items from "Thurstone Temperament Schedule"

72. Is your mood easily influenced by people? around you ?	Yes	?	No
73. Can you relax in a noisy room?	Yes	?	No
74. Do you often see so many alternatives that a decision is difficult?	Yes	?	No
75. Do you remain calm when a friend is in pain?	Yes	?	No
76. Can you study with the radio on?	Yes	?	No
77. Do you often alternate between happiness and sadness?	Yes	?	No
78. Do you tend to become hungry quickly with a sudden pang?	Yes	?	No
79. Are you usually cool and composed in dangerous situation?	Yes	?	No
80. Can you work under distraction?	Yes	?	No
81. Do you often fret about the little daily chores?	Yes	?	No
82. Are you annoyed to leave a task unfinished?	Yes	?	No
83. When you are emotionally upset, do you tend to lose your appetite?	Yes	?	No
84. Does it irritate you to be interrupted when you are concentrating?	Yes	?	No
85. Can you return to work easily?	Yes	?	No
86. Does it bother you to have to finish a job by a deadline?	Yes	?	No
87. Do you often feel impatient?	Yes	?	No
88. Does it take a long time in the morning before you are fully awake?	Yes	?	No
89. Are you generally regarded as optimistic?	Yes	?	No
90. Are you often annoyed to have to leave your work?	Yes	?	No
91. Are your hands and feet often cold?	Yes	?	No

G. Items from the "Minnesota Multiphasic Personality Inventory"
 Indicate "true," "false," *or* "uncertain":

92. There is something wrong with my mind.

93. Once a week or oftener I feel suddenly hot all over, without apparent cause.

94. I dream frequently about things that are best kept to myself.

95. I have used alcohol extensively.

96. Once in a while I feel hate toward members of my family whom I usually love.
97. My mother was a good woman.
98. My sex life is satisfactory.
99. I believe there is a Devil and a Hell in afterlife.
100. No one seems to understand me.
101. I daydream very little.
102. I brood a great deal.
103. I have not lived the right kind of life.
104. I believe I am being followed.
105. I have strange and peculiar thoughts.
106. Someone has been trying to poison me.
107. Evil spirits possess me at times.
108. I have no fear of spiders.
109. I am afraid of losing my mind.
110. Horses that don't pull should be beaten or kicked.
111. At times I think I am no good at all.
112. I like mannish women.
113. My table manners are not quite as good at home as when I am out in company.

How to Cheat on Personality Tests

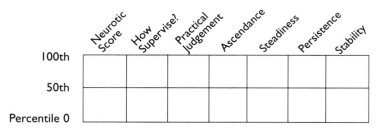

Assuming you have answered the above questions honestly, the first step is to find what kind of score honesty gives you. To do this, first find your percentile rating for each sub-test in the scoring tables below and then mark them on the chart above. Since the questions are only a sampling, the percentile ratings indicated below are only a rough approximation of the more precise ratings supplied with the full tests. Without feeling too guilty, therefore, you can give yourself some benefit of the doubt in interpolating your position.

A. "The Personality Inventory" (R.G. Bernreuter)
Add up the weights for each of the answers you checked.

1. Yes (5)	No (-4)	? (-2)	8. Yes (3)	No (-2)	?(-1)
2. Yes (-6)	No (5)	? (2)	9. Yes (7)	No (-7)	? (2)
3. Yes (7)	No (-7)	? (0)	10. Yes (4)	No (-4)	? (-1)
4. Yes (-1)	No (1)	? (-1)	11. Yes (7)	No (-7)	? (1)
5. Yes (6)	No (-7)	? (1)	12. Yes (7)	No (-7)	? (0)
6. Yes (1)	No (-1)	? (-1)	13. Yes (6)	No (-5)	? (-3)
7. Yes (5)	No (-7)	? (2)	14. Yes (4)	No (-2)	? (-1)

Your score on these weights is for the B1-N "Neurotic Tendency Scale": the higher your score, the more neurotic you are presumed to be. While percentile ratings given for the full test can't be directly applied to this subtest, if your score was +27 or over, you would very likely fall around the 99th percentile—i.e., psychiatric treatment indicated. A score under -40 would indicate you to be exceedingly, even excessively, adjusted.

The beginner should be warned against trying to get *too* normal a score. If he gives himself the benefit of the doubt on every question, he is likely to go right off the chart and thus expose himself as a liar. Which brings us to the first lesson: the nub of the matter is consistency. Since you probably will take two or three tests at a time, don't answer too much out of character. If you are an introvert, don't pass yourself off as a back-slapper, but try rather to close the gap between yourself and the median.

B. "How Supervise?" (Q. W. File and H. H. Remmers)
Correct answers:

		21. DA	25. DA
15. D	18. D	22. DA	26. DA
16. D	19. U	23. DA	27. A
17. D	20. D	24. DA	28. DA

Your score is the number of right answers less the number of wrong answers. Question marks don't count. By rough interpolation from the norms of the complete test, a score of 13 should put you in the 99th percentile of higher-level supervisors; 9 would put you in the 50th percentile; 4 in the 1st percentile. (Only three of the twelve presidents tested by *Fortune* passed this one.)

C. "Test of Practical Judgment" (A. J. Cardall)
Here are the correct answers, with point values:

29. b. +2	32. a. +3	34. a. +3
30. b. +3	b. +3	b. +3
31. b. +3 (1st)	d. +3	c. +1
d. +1 (2d)	33. b. +3	35. b. +3
a. +1 (3d)	a. +3	a. +3
	d. +3	d. +3

A score of 36 or over should put you in the 100th percentile; 24 at about the 50th percentile; 15 in the 1st percentile. To be a good executive, you should score near the 85th percentile.

D. "A–S Reaction Study" (G. W. Allport and F. H. Allport; revised by R. O. Beckman)
From the table below, find the weights given the answers you checked.

36. Frequently -2; Sometimes -1; Not at all +1
37. Yes -2; No +1
38. Let it pass without feeling 0
    "Have it out" with the person +2
    Feel disturbed but let it pass -1
    Take revenge indirectly -1
39. Remonstrate with the intruder +2
    Give the intruder a "dirty look" or make audible comments to your
        neighbor -2
    Decide not to wait and go away -4
    Do nothing -3
40. Very much -3; Somewhat -2; Not at all +2
41. Occasionally +1; Usually +2; Never -2
42. More than three +3; One to three +1; None -3
43. Openly +1; Secretly 0; Not at all -1

The higher your total, the more dominant you are presumed to be. A score between +14 and +6 should put you between the 90th and 100th percentile of ascendance. A score between -15 and -5 would place you under the 10th percentile—i.e., extremely submissive.

E. "The Personal Audit" (C. R. Adams and W. M. Lepley)
Questions 44 to 58 are designed to find where you stand on the steadiness-

emotionality scale. Each word circled in the column at extreme right counts 3 points; in the third column, 2 points, in the second column, 1 point. The score is the sum of these points.

A score of 0 should put you in about the 99th percentile; 9 in the 50th; 18 in the 1st. "High percentile scores indicate normal ways of thinking. Low percentile scores indicate that the individual is atypical. Unusually sensitive, feelings are volatile and deep-seated. Intense and usually not too well-adjusted, marriage may not prove too satisfactory. Repression and sexual conflicts are not uncommon."

Questions 59 to 71 are designed to test your degree of persistence. D's count two points; P's one point. The S's are scored zero. The sum of these products is the score. A score of 0 would put you at about the 99th percentile, or extremely persistent; 9 at about the 50th percentile; and 19 in the 1st percentile, or extremely fluctuating. "High percentile scores indicate stable attitudes and interests with little likelihood of pronounced changes occurring after age twenty-five. Mature people tend to score at this level."

F. "Thurstone Temperament Schedule" (L. L. Thurstone)
Correct answers:

72. No	76. Yes	80. Yes	84. No	88. No
73. Yes	77. No	81. No	85. Yes	89. Yes
74. No	78. No	82. No	86. No	90. No
75. Yes	79. Yes	83. No	87. No	91. No

If you have nineteen or twenty correct, rate yourself in the 100th percentile for stability. Ten to eleven correct, between the 60th and 40th percentiles; six to seven correct, between the 20th and 10th percentiles. "If you have a high stable percentile score you probably remain calm in a crisis, can disregard distractions while working, and are not irritated if interrupted when concentrating."

G. "Minnesota Multiphasic Personality Inventory" (S. R. Hathaway and J. C. McKinley)

Since there are 528 other questions in the full test, any ratings would be meaningless in this sample. The very questions, however, show what is being probed for. There are deep waters here, and *unless the test is preliminary to a full diagnosis by a trained psychologist*, your self-interest is served by answering as if you were very much like what everybody else is supposed to be like. Since an L (lie) score is built into the test, in this case you should be reasonably consistent in your answers. A few mild neuroses conceded here and there will help give you a good L score and won't push you up too far in the other scales.

"Give the Devils No Mercy"

Fortune, December 1955

Whyte was a "graduate" of corporate management training, as is evident in this color-ful memoir of his experiences in the Vick Chemical Company's School of Applied Merchandising. "It was a gladiators' school," a grueling, eleven-month program of sell-ing VapoRub and other remedies to small-town pharmacists. Whyte's apprenticeship came at "the end of the heroic years" of American commerce, when the customer was the acknowledged enemy to be conquered and only the fittest predators survived. In the intervening decade, Whyte noted wistfully, even the Vick School had "changed with the times"—into a euphemistic "Executive Development Program."

Over the last several years I have had occasion to talk with several groups of college seniors about business life, and invariably they ask about junior-executive training programs. Well, it so happens, I explain, that I was a graduate of one of the pioneer training schools, that of Vick Chemical Co., maker of such cold remedies as VapoRub chest salve and Va-tro-nol nose drops. I proceed to tell them of my own experiences and dwell with some relish on the sales techniques taught us by that hardheaded company.

The seniors begin to grin broadly. Plainly, they don't believe me, or if they do believe me, they look shocked. Was business really like that? As I describe the "double clincher," the "sign trick," and other such skills, the seniors imply clearly that I ought to be ashamed of myself. I begin to feel like a relic from some dark age of commercial depravity. My experience hadn't been so very long ago—1939, to be exact—but to judge from the incredulous faces before me it might as well have been 1890.

For what historical interest it may hold, accordingly, I shall set down some brief notes on what it was like to be a trainee in one company back in the 1930s. I intend to draw no great moral. True enough, when measured against managerial practices that young men now consider progressive, the Vick experience illustrates the direct opposite. But the comparisons need not be invidious.

As veterans of other organizations will recall, the basic approach used by Vick's was by no means peculiar to that company. Even our little alumni group, furthermore, is of two minds about the experience. We shudder at the recollection of some of the things we had to do, yet we feel grateful for having been given so concentrated a dose of reality so early. They really separated the men from the boys in those days, we assure each other; yes, indeed, they don't make them like us any more.

Back in 1939, when corporations, and not college seniors, were in the drivers' seats, a chance to join Vick's was something special. It wasn't just a job we were going off to; it was a *school*—the Vick School of Applied Merchandising. Out of hundreds of applicants, we explained to our less fortunate classmates, some thirty men from different colleges were going to be rewarded with a year's postgraduate training under a farseeing and enlightened management. There would be classroom work in New York, a continuing course in advertising, and then eleven months of field study under veteran practitioners of merchandising and distribution. True, the work was connected with sales, and then as now, seniors were apprehensive lest they be required to do something so vulgar as direct selling. At Vick's, however, we would not be selling so much as learning merchandising, which, of course, would be quite different.

Furthermore, we would be paid for all this. By all rights, we actually should pay tuition for this training, for though we would do some work in connection with our studies, the company let us understand that the incidental services we would perform would be far outweighed by the heavy investment in us. Nevertheless, the company was going to pay us $75 a month and traveling expenses. In addition, it was going to credit us with an extra $25 a month that, for reasons we were soon to appreciate, would be paid only if we stuck to the end of the year.

In the summer of 1939, about thirty of us—brisk, well-groomed, confident, egos unbruised—gathered in New York and the schooling began. We were indoctrinated in the history of the company, told of Lunsford Richardson's discovery of VapoRub, and we spent a day at the Philadelphia plant watching VapoRub being mixed.

One thing became quickly apparent: we were not being trained to be executives. Vick did assert that the program would help produce the leaders of tomorrow, and very prominent in many Vick offices was a framed picture of a sea captain at the wheel, beneath which was a signed statement by the chairman of the company, Mr. H. S. Richardson, that the foremost duty of management was to bring along younger men. At the same time, it was made clear that the question whether any of us would one day be executives could easily be deferred a long time.

Our training was what would now be called job-centered. We were required to memorize list prices, sales spiels, rebuttals to possible objections, and the prices and techniques of Plough, Inc., whose Penetro line was frequently to give us trouble. There was no talk that I can remember about the social responsibilities of business, and I am sure the term "human relations" never came up at all.

But the company did have a philosophy, and it was put to us with considerable force. Shortly before the month in New York ended, Mr. Richardson assembled us for lunch at the Cloud Club atop the Chrysler Building. Through the windows of this executive eyrie, we saw stretched out before us the spires of the Graybar Building, the Chanin Building, and a magnificent sweep of Park Avenue. Certainly, here was Golconda. Were we up to it? Some would make it. Some would not. The race would be to the swiftest.

Over coffee Mr. Richardson drove home to us the kind of philosophy that might get some of us back up to the Cloud Club for keeps. He posed a hypothetical problem. Suppose, he said, that you are a manufacturer and for years a small firm has been making paper cartons for your product. This supplier has specialized so much to service you that he has become utterly dependent on your business. But one day another man walks in and says he will make the boxes for you cheaper. What do you do? He bade each one of us in turn to answer.

But *how much* cheaper, we asked? How much time could we give the old supplier to match the new bid? Mr. Richardson became impatient. Either you were a businessman or you were not a businessman. The new man, obviously, should get the contract. Mr. Richardson advised us strongly against letting sentimentality obscure fundamentals. Business was survival of the fittest, he indicated, and we would soon learn the fact.

He was as good as his word. The Vick School was just that—survival of the fittest. Of the thirty who sat there in the Cloud Club, the rules of the game dictated that only six or seven would be asked to stay with Vick's. The rest would "graduate" to make way for another batch.

Within a few days of our glimpse of the Cloud Club, we were deployed through the hinterland—in my case, the mountain counties of eastern

Kentucky. We were each given a panel truck, a load of signs, a ladder, a stock of cough-drop and nose-drop samples, and an order pad. After a few days under the eye of a senior salesman, we were on our own.

To take a typical day of any one of us, we would rise at six or six-thirty in some bleak boardinghouse or broken-down hotel and, after a greasy breakfast, set out to squeeze in some advertising study. This consisted of stapling a supply of large fiber signs on barns and clamping smaller metal ones to telephone poles and trees. By eight we would have arrived at a general store for our first exercise in merchandising. Our assignment was to persuade the dealer to order a year's supply of Vick goods all at once, or preferable, more than a year's supply. After the sale, or no sale, we would turn to market research—i.e., count the storekeeper's shelf stock, estimate his annual sales of Vick's and competitive lines. Next we would do some introductory work on new products. Nose drops being unknown in the mountains, we would suddenly instruct the dealer to tilt his head back and, before he could recover his senses, squirt up his nostrils a whopping dropperful of Va-tro-nol. Wiping the tears from his eyes, the dealer would delightedly tell the loungers by the stove to let the Vick drummer shoot some of that stuff up their noses. After this messy job was done, we plastered the place with cardboard signs, and left. Then, some more signposting in the barnyards, and ten or twelve miles of mud road to the next call. So, on through the day, the routine was repeated until at length, long after dark, we would get back to our lodgings in time for dinner—and two hours' work on our report forms.

The acquisition of a proper frame of mind toward all this was a slow process. The faded yellow second sheets of our daily report book tell the story. At first, utter demoralization. Day after day, the number of calls would be a skimpy eight or nine, and the number of sales sometimes zero. But it was never our fault. In the large space left for explanations, we would affect a cheerful humor—the gay adventurer in the provinces—but this pathetic bravado could not mask a recurrent note of despair. I quote some entries from my own daily report forms:

"They use 'dry' creek beds for roads in this county. 'Dry!' Ha! Ha! . . . Sorry about making only four calls today, but I had to go over to Ervine to pick up a drop shipment of $3/4$ tins and my clutch broke down. . . . Everybody's on WPA in this county. Met only one dealer who sold more than a couple dozen VR a year. Ah, well, it's all in the game! . . . Bostitched my left thumb to a barn this morning and couldn't pick up my first call until after lunch. . . . The local brick plant here is shut down and nobody's buying anything . . . Five, count 'em, *five* absent dealers in a row. Seems they're having a fishing derby in these parts today. Could I wring Isaac Walton's neck! . . . Sorry about the $20.85 but the clutch broke down again. . . . The Penetro man was through here last week and are the dealers loaded! . . . They use railroad tracks for roads in this county!"

By all these bids for sympathy, the people in the home office were unmoved; they let us understand it was *they* who were being put upon. The weekly letter written to each trainee would start with some perfunctory remarks that it was too bad about the clutch breaking down, the hurt thumb, and so on. But this spurious sympathy was only a prelude to some sharp comments on the torpor, lack of aggressiveness, and slipshod work revealed between the lines of our daily reports. We too are sorry about those absent dealers, the office would say, but we note that in the very same area McClure, Youst, and Coyle don't seem to be running into this trouble. Perhaps if you got up earlier in the morning?

But it was the *attitude* of the student that concerned the home-office people most. As they sensed quite correctly from my daily reports, I was growing sorry for myself; I used to read timetables at night, and often in the evening I would somehow find myself by the C.&O. tracks when the east-bound George Washington swept by, its shining windows a fleeting reminder of civilization left behind. I was also sorry for many of the country storekeepers, most of whom existed on a precarious credit relationship with wholesalers, and as a consequence I sold them very little of anything.

The company sent its head training supervisor to see if anything could be salvaged. After several days with me, this old veteran of the road told me he knew what was the matter. It wasn't so much my routine, wretched as this was; it was my state of mind. "Fella," he told me, "you will never sell anybody anything until you learn one simple thing. The man on the other side of the counter is the *enemy*."

It was a gladiators' school we were in. Selling may be no less competitive now, but in the Vick program, strife was honored far more openly than today's climate would permit. Combat was the ideal—combat with the dealer, combat with the "chiseling competitors" (characteristically, the company had an entry blank on its daily report forms for "chiseling competitors" but no blank for any other kind), and combat with each other. There was some talk about "the team," but it was highly abstract. Our success depended on beating our fellow students.

Slowly, as our sales-to-calls ratios crept up, we gained in rapacity. Somewhere along the line, by accident or skill, each of us finally manipulated a person into doing what we wanted him to do. Innocence was lost, and by the end of six months, with the pack down to about twenty-three men, we were fairly ravening for the homestretch back to the Cloud Club. At this point, our motivations brought to peak strength, we were taken off general-store and grocery work and turned loose on the rich drugstore territory.

The advice of the old salesman now became invaluable. While he had a distaste for any kind of dealer, with druggists he was implacably combative. He was one of the most decent and kindly men I have ever met, but when he gave us pep talks about this enemy ahead of us, he spoke with great intensity. Some druggists were good enough fellows, he told us (i.e., big, successful ones who bought big deals), but the tough ones were a mean, servile crew; they would insult you, keep you waiting while they pretended to fill prescriptions, lie to you about their inventory, whine at anything less than a 300 percent markup, and switch their customers to chiseling competitors.

The old salesman would bring us together in batches, like Fagin's brood, for several days of demonstration. It was a tremendous experience for us, for though he seemed outwardly a phlegmatic man, we knew him for the artist he was. Outside the store he was apt to be jumpy and nervous, but once inside, he was composed to the point of apparent boredom. He rarely smiled, and almost never opened up with a joke. His demeanor seemed to say, I am a busy man and you are damn lucky I have stopped by your miserable store. Sometimes, if the druggist was unusually insolent, he would blow cigar smoke at his face. "Can't sell it if you don't have it," he would say condescendingly, and then, rather pleased with himself, glance back at us, loitering in the wings, to see if we had marked that.

Only old pros like himself could get away with that, he told us in the postmortem sessions, but there were lots of little tricks we could pick up. As we gathered around him, he would demonstrate how to watch for the victim's shoulders to relax before throwing the clincher; how to pick up the one-size jar of a competitive line that had an especially thick glass bottom and chuckle knowingly; how to feign suppressed worry that maybe the deal was too big for "the smaller druggist like yourself" to take; how to disarm the nervous druggist by fumbling and dropping a pencil. No mercy, he would tell us; give the devils no mercy.

Now came the acid test of our gall. One of the gauges by which we were next to be judged was the number of drugstores in which we managed to erect "flange" signs. By all the standards of the trade this signposting should have been an impossible task. Almost every chiseling competitor would give the druggist at least $5 to let him put up a sign; we could not offer this druggist a nickel. Our signs, furthermore, were not the usual cardboard kind the druggist could throw away after we had left. They were hideous plates of metal, and they were screwed to the druggists' cherished oak cabinets.

The trick was in the timing. When we were in peak form the procedure went like this. Just after the druggist had signed the order, his shoulders would subside, and this would signal a momentary period of mutual bonhomie. "New fella, aren't you?" The druggist was likely to say, relaxing. This was his mistake. As soon as we judged the good will to be at full flood, we would ask him if he had a ladder. (There was a ladder out in the car, but the fuss of fetching it would have broken the mood.) The druggist's train of thought would not at that moment connect the request with what was to follow, and he would good-naturedly dispatch someone to bring out a ladder. After another moment of chatter, we would make way for the waiting customer who would soon engage the druggist's attention. Then, forthrightly, we would slap the ladder up against a spot we had previously reconnoitered. "Just going to get this sign up for you," we would say, as if doing him the greatest favor in the world. A few quick turns of the awl, place the bracket in position, and then the automatic screwdriver. Bang! Bang! On with the sign. Then down with the ladder, shift it over to the second spot, and up again.

About this time the druggist would start looking up a little unhappily, but he was constrained from action. He didn't want to hurt our feelings. Ineffectually, he would mumble something about not being keen on the signs. We would hold up the second one. It bore a picture of a woman getting a nose dropper in position. We would leer fatuously at it. "Just going to lay this blonde on the top of the cabinet for you, Mr. Jones," we would say, winking.

I shudder to tell the rest. We were beyond shame now, and in our final month in Brooklyn, in the very shadow of the Cloud Club, we were knocking over some 95 percent of the stores—with what jokes and techniques I shall not describe.

But this was the end of the heroic years. No longer is there a Vick School of Applied Merchandising. Several classes followed us in much the same fashion, but Vick's has changed with the times, too. Trainees are no longer eliminated by "graduation"; they are exposed to many more aspects of management, and they don't have to badger dealers with metal signs. They are enrolled in the Vick "Executive Development Program."

From *The Organization Man* (1956)

Encapsulating Whyte's "continuing exploration of American organization life," as the book jacket advertised it, *The Organization Man* was about "the clash between the individualistic beliefs he is supposed to follow and the collective life he actually lives—and his search for a faith to bridge the gap." The book, by a self-confessed organization man (a proud veteran of the U.S. Marine Corps, "graduate" of the Vick School of Applied Merchandising, and Assistant Managing Editor of *Fortune*), stirred a national debate which resonated around the world, and the book was eventually translated into a dozen languages.

Whyte detailed many of the ways in which postwar America was adapting to—and in a sense willingly creating—a new way of life based on a belief in the group as the source of creativity, and belongingness as the individual's ultimate need. Whyte warned that an almost utopian faith in what he called a Social Ethic took little—quite possibly too little—account of the long-range effects of this sea change in the national character. "Not that they don't care but rather that they tend to assume that the ends of organization and morality coincide, and on such matters of welfare they give their proxy to the organization."

The defects of the organization—whether it was a corporation, a scientific or religious institution, or academia (a word coined by Whyte, according to the Second edition of the *Oxford English Dictionary*)—were made all the more difficult to assail by its very benevolence. "It is easy to fight tyranny," Whyte admonished, "but less so benevolence, and where the old authoritarian wanted your sweat, the new administrator wants your soul."

Whyte's exhortation to resist the pressures of the organization—in short, to fight it—was based on the optimistic premise that "individualism is as possible in our times as in others. I speak of individualism within organizational life."

INTRODUCTION

This book is about the organization man. If the term is vague, it is because I can think of no other way to describe the people I am talking about. They are not the workers, nor are they the white-collar people in the usual, clerk sense of the word. These people only work for The Organization. The ones I am talking about *belong* to it as well. They are the ones of our middle class who have left home, spiritually as well as physically, to take the vows of organization life, and it is they who are the mind and soul of our great self-perpetuating institutions. Only a few are top managers or ever will be. In a system that makes such hazy terminology as "junior executive" psychologically necessary, they are of the staff as much as the line, and most are destined to live poised in a middle area that still awaits a satisfactory euphemism. But they are the dominant members of our society nonetheless. They have not joined together into a recognizable elite—our country does not stand still long enough for that—but it is from their ranks that are coming most of the first and second echelons of our leadership, and it is their values which will set the American temper.

The corporation man is the most conspicuous example, but he is only one, for the collectivization so visible in the corporation has affected almost every field of work. Blood brother to the business trainee off to join Du Pont is the seminary student who will end up in the church hierarchy, the doctor headed for the corporate clinic, the physics Ph.D. in a government laboratory, the intellectual on the foundation-sponsored team project, the engineering graduate in the huge drafting room at Lockheed, the young apprentice in a Wall Street law factory.

They are all, as they so often put it, in the same boat. Listen to them talk to each other over the front lawns of their suburbia and you cannot help but be struck by how well they grasp the common denominators which bind them. Whatever the difference in their organization ties, it is the common problems of collective work that dominate their attentions, and when the Du Pont man talks to the research chemist or the chemist to the army man, it is these problems that are uppermost. The word *collective* most of them can't bring themselves to use—except to describe foreign countries or organizations they don't work for—but they are keenly aware of how much more deeply beholden they are to organization than were their elders. They are wry about it, to be sure; they talk of the "treadmill," the "rat race," of the inability to control one's direction. But they have no great sense of plight; between themselves and organization they believe they see an ultimate harmony and, more than most elders recognize, they are building an ideology that will vouchsafe this trust.

It is the growth of this ideology, and its practical effects, that is the thread I wish to follow in this book. America has paid much attention to the economic and political consequences of big organization—the concentration of power in large corporations, for example, the political power of the civil-service bureaucracies, the possible emergence of a managerial hierarchy that might dominate the rest of us. These are proper concerns, but no less important is the principal impact that organization life has had on the individuals within it. A collision has been taking place—indeed, hundreds of thousands of them, and in the aggregate they have been producing what I believe is a major shift in American ideology.

Officially, we are a people who hold to the Protestant Ethic. Because of the denominational implications of the term many would deny its relevance to them, but let them eulogize the American Dream, however, and they virtually define the Protestant Ethic. Whatever the embroidery, there is almost always the thought that pursuit of individual salvation through hard work, thrift, and competitive struggle is the heart of the American achievement.

But the harsh facts of organization life simply do not jibe with these precepts. This conflict is certainly not a peculiarly American development. In their own countries such Europeans as Max Weber and Durkheim many years ago foretold the change, and though Europeans now like to see their troubles as an American export, the problems they speak of stem from a bureaucratization of society that has affected every Western country.

It is in America, however, that the contrast between the old ethic and current reality has been apparent—and most poignant. Of all peoples it is we who have led in the public worship of individualism. One hundred years ago de Tocqueville was noting that though our special genius—and failing—lay in cooperative action, we talked more than others of personal independence and freedom. We kept on, and as late as the twenties, when big organization was long since a fact, affirmed the old faith as if nothing had really changed at all.

Today many still try, and it is the members of the kind of organization most responsible for the change, the corporation, who try the hardest. It is the corporation man whose institutional ads protest so much that Americans speak up in town meeting, that Americans are the best inventors because Americans don't care that other people scoff, that Americans are the best soldiers because they have so much initiative and ingenuity, that the boy selling papers on the street corner is the prototype of our business society. Collectivism? He abhors it, and when he makes his ritualistic attack on Welfare Statism, it is in terms of a Protestant Ethic undefiled by change—the sacredness of property, the enervating effect of security, the virtues of thrift, of hard work and independence. Thanks be, he says, that there are some people left—e.g., businessmen—to defend the American Dream.

He is not being hypocritical, only compulsive. He honestly wants to believe he follows the tenets he extols, and if he extols them so frequently it is, perhaps, to shut out a nagging suspicion that he, too, the last defender of the faith, is no longer pure. Only by using the language of individualism to describe the collective can he stave off the thought that he himself is in a collective as pervading as any ever dreamed of by the reformers, the intellectuals, and the utopian visionaries he so regularly warns against.

The older generation may still convince themselves; the younger generation does not. When a young man says that to make a living these days you must do what somebody else wants you to do, he states it not only as a fact of life that must be accepted but as an inherently good proposition. If the American Dream deprecates this for him, it is the American Dream that is going to have to give, whatever its more elderly guardians may think. People grow restive with a mythology that is too distant from the way things actually are, and as more and more lives have been encompassed by the organization way of life, the pressures for an accompanying ideological shift have been mounting. The pressures of the group, the frustrations of individual creativity, the anonymity of achievement: are these defects to struggle against—or are they virtues in disguise? The organization man seeks a redefinition of his place on earth—a faith that will satisfy him that what he must endure has a deeper meaning than appears on the surface. He needs, in short, something that will do for him what the Protestant Ethic did once. And slowly, almost imperceptibly, a body of thought has been coalescing that does that.

I am going to call it a Social Ethic. With reason it could be called an organization ethic, or a bureaucratic ethic; more than anything else, it rationalizes the organization's demands for fealty and gives those who offer it wholeheartedly a sense of dedication in doing so—*in extremis*, you might say, it converts what would seem in other times a bill of no rights into a restatement of individualism.

But there is a real moral imperative behind it, and whether one inclines to its beliefs or not he must acknowledge that this moral basis, not mere expediency, is the source of its power. Nor is it simply an opiate for those who must work in big organizations. The search for a secular faith that it represents can be found throughout our society—and among those who swear they would never set foot in a corporation or government bureau. Though it has its greatest applicability to the organization man, its ideological underpinnings have been provided not by the organization man but by intellectuals he knows little of and toward whom, indeed, he tends to be rather suspicious.

Any groove of abstraction, Whitehead once remarked, is bound to be an inadequate way of describing reality, and so with the concept of the Social Ethic. It is an attempt to illustrate an underlying consistency in what in actually is by no means an orderly system of thought. No one says, "I believe in the social ethic," and though many would subscribe wholeheartedly to the separate ideas that make it up, these ideas have yet to be put together in the final, harmonious synthesis. But the unity is there.

In looking at what might seem dissimilar aspects of organization society, it is this unity I wish to underscore. The "professionalization" of the manager, for example, and the drive for a more practical education are parts of the same phenomenon; just as the student now feels technique more vital than content, so the trainee believes managing an end in itself, an *expertise* relatively independent of the content of what is being managed. And the reasons are the same. So too in other sectors of our society; for all the differences in particulars, dominant is a growing accommodation to the needs of society—and a growing urge to justify it.

Let me now define my terms. By Social Ethic I mean that contemporary body of thought which makes morally legitimate the pressures of society against the individual. Its major propositions are three: a belief in the group as a source of creativity; a belief in "belongingness" as the ultimate need of the individual; and a belief in the application of science to achieve the belongingness.

The gist can be paraphrased thus: Man exists as a unit of society. Of himself, he is isolated, meaningless; only as he collaborates with others does he become worth while, for by sublimating himself in the group, he helps produce a whole that is greater than the sum of its parts. There should be, then, no conflict between man and society. What we think are conflicts are misunderstandings, breakdowns in communication. By applying the methods of science to human relations we can eliminate these obstacles to consensus and create an equilibrium in which society's needs and the needs of the individual are one and the same.

Essentially, it is a utopian faith. Superficially, it seems dedicated to the practical problems of organization life, and its proponents often use the word *hard* (versus *soft*) to describe their approach. But it is the long-range promise that animates its followers, for it relates techniques to the vision of a finite, achievable harmony. It is quite reminiscent of the beliefs of utopian communities of the 1840s. As in the Owen communities, there is the same idea that man's character is decided, almost irretrievably, by his environment. As in the Fourier communities, there is the same faith that there need be no conflict between the individual's aspirations and the community's wishes, because it is the natural order of things that the two be synonymous.

Like the utopian communities, it interprets society in a fairly narrow, immediate sense. One can believe man has a social obligation and that the individual must ultimately contribute to the community without believing that group harmony is the test of it. In the Social Ethic I am describing, however, man's obligation is in the here and now; his duty is not so much to the community in a broad sense but to the actual, physical one about him, and the idea that in isolation from it—or active rebellion against it—he might eventually discharge the greater service is little considered. In practice, those who most eagerly subscribe to the Social Ethic worry very little over the long-range problems of society. It is not that they don't care but rather that they tend to assume that the ends of organization and morality coincide, and on such matters as social welfare they give their proxy to the organization.

It is possible that I am attaching too much weight to what, after all, is something of a mythology. Those more sanguine than I have argued that this faith is betrayed by reality in some key respects and that because it cannot long hide from organization man that life is still essentially competitive the faith must fall of its own weight. They also maintain that the Social Ethic is only one trend in a society which is a prolific breeder of countertrends. The farther the pendulum swings, they believe, the more it must eventually swing back.

I am not persuaded. We are indeed a flexible people, but society is not a clock and to stake so much on countertrends is to put a rather heavy burden on providence. Let me get ahead of my story a bit with two examples of trend versus countertrend. One is the long-term swing to the highly vocational business-administration courses. Each year for seven years I have collected all the speeches by businessmen, educators, and others on the subject, and invariably each year the gist of them is that this particular pendulum has swung much too far and that there will shortly be a reversal. Similarly sanguine, many academic people have been announcing that they discern the beginnings of a popular swing back to the humanities. Another index is the growth of personality testing. Regularly year after year many social scientists have assured me that this bowdlerization of psychology is a contemporary aberration soon to be laughed out of court.

Meanwhile, the organization world grinds on. Each year the number of business-administration majors has increased over the last year—until, in 1954, they together made up the largest single field of undergraduate instruction outside of the field of education itself. Personality testing? Again, each year the number of people subjected to it has grown, and the criticism has served mainly to make organization more adept in sugar-coating their purpose. No one can say whether these trends will continue to out-pace the counter-trends, but neither can we trust that an equilibrium-minded providence will see to it that excesses will cancel each other out. Countertrends there are. There have always been, and in the sweep of ideas ineffectual many have proved to be.

It is also true that the Social Ethic is something of a mythology, and there is a great difference between mythology and practice. An individual-ism as stringent, as selfish as that often preached in the name of the Protestant Ethic would never have been tolerated, and in reality our prede-cessors cooperated with one another far more skillfully than nineteenth-century oratory would suggest. Something of the obverse is true of the Social Ethic; so complete a denial of individual will won't work either, and even the most willing believers in the group harbor some secret misgivings, some latent antagonism toward the pressures they seek to deify.

But the Social Ethic is no less powerful for that, and though it can never produce the peace of mind it seems to offer, it will help shape the nature of the quest in the years to come. The old dogma of individualism betrayed real-ity too, yet few would argue, I dare say, that it was not an immensely powerful influence in the time of its dominance. So I argue of the Social Ethic; call it mythology, if you will, but it is becoming the dominant one. [. . .]

A GENERATION OF BUREAUCRATS

When I was a college senior in 1939, we used to sing a plaintive song about going out into the "cold, cold world." It wasn't really so very cold then, but we did enjoy meditating on the fraughtness of it all. It was a big break we were facing, we told ourselves, and those of us who were going to try our luck in the commercial world could be patronizing toward those who were going on to graduate work or academic life. We were taking the leap.

Seniors still sing the song, but somehow the old note of portent is gone. There is no leap left to take. The union between the world of organization and the college has been so cemented that today's seniors can see a continuity between the college and the life thereafter that we never did. Come graduation, they do not go outside to a hostile world; they transfer.

For the senior who is headed for the corporation it is almost as if it were part of a master scheme. The locale shifts; the training continues, for at the same time that the colleges have been changing their curriculum to suit the corporation, the corporation has responded by setting up its own campuses and classrooms. By now the two have been so well molded that it's difficult to tell where one leaves off and the other begins.

The descent, every spring, of the corporations' recruiters has now become a built-in feature of campus life. If the college is large and its placement director efficient, the processing operation is visibly impressive. I have never been able to erase from my mind the memory of an ordinary day at Purdue's placement center. It is probably the largest and most effective placement operation in the country, yet, much as in a well-run group clinic, there seemed hardly any activity. In the main room some students were quietly studying company literature arranged on the tables for them; others were checking the interview timetables to find what recruiter they would see and to which cubicle he was assigned; at the central filing desk college employees were sorting the hundreds of names of men who had registered for placement. Except for a murmur from the row of cubicles there was little to indicate that the scores of young men were, every hour on the half hour, making the decisions that would determine their whole future life.

Someone from a less organized era might conclude that the standardization of this machinery—and the standardized future it portends—would repel students. It does not. For the median senior this is the optimum future; it meshes so closely with his own aspirations that it is almost as if the corporation was planned in response to an attitude poll.

Because they are the largest single group, the corporation-bound seniors are the most visible manifestation of their generation's values. But in essentials their contemporaries headed for other occupations respond to the same urges. The lawyers, the doctors, the scientists—their occupations are also subject to the same centralization, the same trend to group work and to bureaucratization. And so are the young men who will enter them. Whatever their many differences, in one great respect they are all of a piece: more than any generation in memory, theirs will be a generation of bureaucrats.

They are, above all, conservative. Their inclination to accept the status quo does not necessarily mean that in the historic sweep of ideas they are conservative—in the more classical sense of conservatism, it could be argued that the seniors will be, in effect if not by design, agents of revolution. But this is a matter we must leave to later historians. For the immediate present, at any rate, what ideological ferment college men exhibit is not in the direction of basic change.

This shows most clearly in their attitude toward politics. It used to be axiomatic that young men moved to the left end of the spectrum in revolt against their fathers and then, as the years went on, moved slowly to the right. A lot of people still believe this is true, and many businessmen fear that twenty years of the New Deal hopelessly corrupted our youth into radicalism. After the election of 1952 businessmen became somewhat more cheerful, but many are still apprehensive, and whenever a poll indicates that students don't realize that business makes only about 6 percent profit, there is a flurry of demands for some new crusade to rescue our youth from socialistic tendencies.

If the seniors do any moving, however, it will be from dead center. Liberal groups have almost disappeared from the campus, and what few remain are anemic. There has been no noticeable activity at the other end of the spectrum either. When William Buckley Jr. produced *God and Man at Yale*, some people thought this signaled the emergence of a strong right-wing movement among the young men. The militancy, however, has not proved particularly contagious; when the McCarthy issue roused and divided their elders, undergraduates seemed somewhat bored with it all.

Their conservatism is passive. No cause seizes them. [. . .] There are Democrats and Republicans, and at election time there is the usual flurry of rallies, but in comparison with the agitation of the thirties no one seems to care too much one way or the other. There has been personal unrest—the suspense over the prospect of military service assures this—but it rarely gets resolved into a thought-out protest. Come spring and students may start whacking each other over the head or roughing up the townees and thereby cause a rush of concern over the wild younger generation. But there is no real revolution in them, and the next day they likely as not will be found with their feet firmly on the ground in the recruiters' cubicles. [. . .] In judging a college generation, one usually bases his judgment on how much it varies from one's own, and presumably superior, class, and I must confess that I find myself tempted to do so. Yet I do not think my generation has any license to damn the acquiescence of seniors as a weakening of intellectual fiber. It is easy for us to forget that if earlier generations were less content with society, there was a great deal less to be contented about. In the intervening years the economy has changed enormously, and even in retrospect the senior can hardly be expected to share former discontents. Society is not out of joint for him, and if he acquiesces it is not out of fear that he does so. He does not want to rebel against the status quo because he really likes it—and his elders, it might be added, are not suggesting anything bold and new to rebel *for*.

Perhaps contemporaryism would be a better word than conservatism to describe their posture. The present, more than the past, is their model; while they share the characteristic American faith in the future also, they see it as more of same. As they paraphrase what they are now reading about America, they argue that at last we have got it. The big questions are all settled; we know the direction, and while many minor details remain to be cleared up, we can be pretty sure of enjoying a wonderful upward rise.

While the degree of their optimism is peculiarly American, the spirit of acquiescence, it should be noted, is by no means confined to the youth of this country. In an Oxford magazine, called, aptly enough, *Couth*, one student writes this of his generation:

> It is true that over the last thirty years it has been elementary good manners to be depressed. . . . But . . . we are not, really, in the least worried by our impending, and other people's present, disasters. This is not the Age of Anxiety. What distinguishes the comfortable young men of today from the uncomfortable young men of the last hundred years . . . is that for once the younger generation is not in revolt against anything. . . . We don't want to rebel against our elders. They are much too nice to be rebellable-against. Old revolutionaries as they are, they get rather cross with us and tell us we are stuffy and prudish, but even this can't provoke us into hostility. . . . Our fathers . . . brought us up to see them not as the representatives of ancient authority and unalterable law but as rebels against our grandfathers. So naturally we have grown up to be on their side, even if we feel on occasion that they were a wee bit hard on their fathers, or even a little naïve.[1]

More than before, there is a tremendous interest in techniques. Having no quarrels with society, they prefer to table the subject of ends and concentrate instead on means. Not what or why but *how* interests them, and any evangelical strain they have they can sublimate; once they have equated the common weal with organization—a task the curriculum makes easy—they will let the organization worry about goals. "These men do not question the system," an economics professor says of them approvingly. "They want to get in there and lubricate and make them run better. They will be technicians of the society, not innovators." . . .

While the trust in organization is very strong among the majority group of college seniors headed for a business career, it is less so with a smaller group who say, at least, that they prefer a small firm. In the course of sessions during the past few years I have had with different undergraduate groups, to get the discussion rolling I have asked the students to answer several hypothetical questions on the "ideal" relationship between an individual and the demands of organization. I attach no great statistical significance to the actual figures, but I have kept the terms the same with each group, and I have noticed that consistently there is a difference between the answers of those headed for big organization and those not. As is brought out more forcefully by the kind of questions that the students themselves later asked, the big-corporation men are more inclined to the group way than the others.

Here is how a total of 127 men answered two chief questions: on the question of whether research scientists should be predominantly the team player type, 56 percent of the mean headed for a big corporation said yes, versus 46 percent of the small-business men. On the question of whether the key executive should be basically an "administrator" or a "bold leader," 54 percent of the big-corporation men voted for the administrator, versus only 45 percent of the small-business men. Needless to say, the weightings varied from college to college, and often the influence of a particular teacher was manifest—in one class the students complained that they probably seemed so chary of big business because they had been "brainwashed" by a liberal instructor. Whatever the absolute figures, however, there was generally the same relative difference between the big-business and the small-business men.

These differences raise an interesting question. It is possible that the majority group might be less significant than the minority—that is to say, the more venturesome may become the more dominant members of our society by virtue of their very disinclination to the group way. As a frankly rapacious young salesman put it to me, the more contented his run-of-the-mill contemporaries, the freer the field for the likes of him.

While this can only be a matter of opinion at this date, I doubt that our society, as it is now evolving, will suffer such a double standard. The corporation-bound man may be an exaggeration of his generation's tendencies but only in degree, not in character. Other occupations call for different emphases, but on the central problem of collective versus individual work, young men going into other fields, such as teaching or law or journalism, show the same basic outlook.

Seniors do not deny that the lone researcher or entrepreneur can also serve others. But neither do they think much about it. Their impulses, their training, the whole climate of the times, incline them to work that is tangibly social. Whether as a member of a corporation, a group medicine clinic, or a law factory, they see the collective as the best vehicle for service.

To a degree, of course, this is a self-ennobling apologia for seeking the comfortable life—and were they thoroughly consistent they would more actively recognize that public service is social too. But it is not mere rationalization; the senior is quite genuine in believing that while all collective effort may be worth while, some kinds are more so. The organization-bound senior can argue that he is going to the main tent, the place where each foot pound of his energy will go farthest in helping people. Like the young man of the Middle Ages who went off to join holy orders, he is off for the center of society. [. . .]

THE FIGHT AGAINST GENIUS

It is to be expected that industry should spend far less of its time on fundamental research than the universities, and for the same reason it is to be expected that the most outstanding men would tend to stay in the universities. But when all of this is said and done, the fact remains today that industry has a disproportionately small share of top men.

Why? The failure to recognize the virtue of purposelessness is the starting point of industry's problem. To the managers and engineers who set the dominant tone in industry, purposelessness is anathema, and all their impulses incline them to highly planned, systematized development in which the problem is clearly defined. This has its values. If researchers want to make a practical application of previous discovery—if a group at GM's Technical Center want a better oil for a high-compression engine, for example—they do best by addressing themselves to the stipulated task. In pure research, however, half the trick is in finding out *that there is a problem*—that there is something to explain. The culture dish remained sterile when it shouldn't have. The two chemicals reacted differently this time than before. Something has happened and you don't know why it happened—or if you did, what earthly use it would be.

By its very nature, discovery has an accidental quality. Methodical as one can be in following up a question, the all-important question itself is likely to be a sort of chance distraction of the work at hand. At this moment you neither know what practical use the question could lead to nor should you worry the point. There will be time enough later for that; and in retrospect, it will be easy to show how well planned and systematized the discovery was all along.

Rationalize curiosity too early, however, and you kill it. In the case of the scientist it is not merely that he finds it difficult to foresee what it will prove at the cash register; the sheer act of having to address himself to this or, as management would put it, the $64 question, dampens his original curiosity—and the expectation that the company will ask him to do it is just as dampening as the actual demand. The result is a net loss, not postponement, for if the scientist is inhibited from seizing the idle question at the time, it is not easily recaptured later. Like the nice gestures we so often think of and so often forget to do, many a question that would have led to discoveries has died as quickly as it was born; the man was too busy to pause for it.

If ever there were proof of the virtues of free research, General Electric and Bell Labs provide it. Consider three facts about them: (1) of all corporation research groups these two have been the two outstandingly profitable ones; (2) of all corporation research groups these two have consistently attracted the most brilliant men. Why? The third fact explains the other two. *Of all corporation research groups these two are precisely the two that believe in "idle curiosity."* In them the usual chronology is often reversed; instead of demanding of the scientists that they apply themselves to a practical problem, they let the scientists follow the basic problems they want to follow. If the scientists come up with something they then look around to see what practical problem the finding might apply to. The patience is rewarded. The work of GE's Irving Langmuir in heated solids, for example, eventually led to a new kind of incandescent lamp; similarly, the recent, and highly abstract, work of Bell Labs' Claude Shannon in communication theory is already proving to be a mine of highly practical applications.

The few notable successes elsewhere follow the same pattern. The succession of synthetic fibers that have made so much money for the Du Pont Company sprang from the curiosity of one man—Wallace Hume Carothers. Carothers did not start out to make nylon. When Du Pont ran across him he was working on molecular structure at Harvard. While the result was eminently practical for Du Pont, for Carothers it was essentially a by-product of the experimental work he had started at Harvard rather than an end in itself. The company's interest was the final product, but it got it only because Carothers had the freedom to pursue what would today seem to many mere scientific boondoggling.

These successes are disheartening. There is nothing at all new in the research philosophy that led to them; both GE and Bell Labs established their basic procedures several generations ago, and their pre-eminence has been commercially apparent for as long. Yet with these models before them, U.S. industry has not only failed to draw any lessons, it has been moving further and further in the opposite direction.

By their own statements of policy the majority of corporations make it plain that they wish to keep their researchers' eyes focused closely on the cash register. Unlike GE or Bell Labs, they discourage their scientists, sometimes forbid them, from publishing the results of their work in the learned journals or communicating them in any way to scientists outside the company preserve. More inhibiting, most corporations do not let their scientists devote more than a fraction of their time following up problems of their own choosing, and this fraction is treated more as a sort of indulgence than an activity worth while in its own right. "It is our policy," one research director says, "to permit our men to have *as much as* 5 to 10 percent of their time to work on anything they feel would be of interest." (Italics are mine.)

Even this pitiably small fraction is begrudged. Lest scientists interpret "free" work too freely, company directives imply strongly that it would be very fine if what the scientist is curious about during this recess coincides with what the organization is curious about. In "Research: The Long View," Standard Oil of New Jersey explains its policy thus:

> The researchers, as a matter of long-range policy, are encouraged, when circumstances permit, to give something like 10 percent of their time to "free research"—that is, work not currently part of a formal project. [The company] finds, however, that when its research people are kept well informed about the broad areas in which the company's needs and interests lie, a man's independent as well as his closely directed work both tend to have the same objectives. (*The Lamp*, June 1954)

To some management people the desire to do "free" work is a downright defect—a symptom of maladjustment that demands cure, not coddling. When a man wants to follow his own hunch, they believe, this is a warning that he is not "company-oriented." The solution? Indoctrination. In "Personnel Practices in Industrial Laboratories" (*Personnel*, May 1953) Lowell Steele puts the issue squarely. "Unless the firm wants to subsidize idle curiosity on the part of its scientists," he says, "it must aid them in becoming 'company-conscious.'" Company loyalty, in other words, is not only more important than idle curiosity; it helps *prevent* idle curiosity.

The administrators are perfectly correct. If they get scientists to be good company men like other normal people, they won't be bothered much by scientists' following their curiosity. The policy will keep out that kind of scientist. For what is the dominant characteristic of the outstanding scientist? Every study has shown that it is a fierce independence.

In her study of eminent scientists, psychologist Anne Roe found that what decided them on their career almost invariably was a college project in which they were given free rein to find things out for themselves, without direction, and once the joys of freedom were tasted, they never lost the appetite. The most important single factor in the making of a scientist, she concludes, is "the need and ability to develop personal independence to a high degree. The independence factor is emphasized by many other findings: the subjects' preference for teachers who let them alone, their attitudes toward religion . . . their satisfaction in a career in which, for the most part, they follow their own interests without direction or interference." (*Scientific American*, November 1952)

In the outstanding scientist, in short, we have almost the direct antithesis of the company-oriented man. If the company wants a first-rate man it must recognize that his allegiance must always be to his work. For him, organization can be only a vehicle. What he asks of it is not big money—significantly, Bell Labs and GE have not had to pay higher salaries than other research organizations to attract talent. Nor is it companionship, or belongingness. What he asks is the freedom to do what he wants to do.

For its part, The Organization can ask only so much in return. The Organization and he have come together because its long-range interests happen to run parallel with what he wants to do. It is in this, his work, that The Organization's equity in him lies. Only one *quid pro quo* can it properly ask for the money that it gives him. It can ask that he work magnificently. It cannot ask that he love The Organization as well.

And what difference would it make if he did? The management man is confusing his own role with that of the scientist. To the management man such things as The Organization and human relations are at the heart of his job, and in unconscious analogy he assumes that the same thing applies to the scientist, if perhaps in lesser degree. These things are irrelevant to the scientist—he works *in* an organization rather than for it. But this the administrator cannot conceive; he cannot understand that a man can dislike the company—perhaps even leave in disgust after several years—and still have made a net contribution to the company cash register infinitely greater than all of his better-adjusted colleagues put together.

Thus, searching for their own image, management men look for the "well-rounded" scientists. They don't expect them to be quite as "well rounded" as junior-executive trainees; they generally note that scientists are "different." They do it, however, in a patronizing way that implies that the difference is nothing that a good indoctrination program won't fix up. Customarily, whenever the word *brilliant* is used, it either precedes the word *but* (cf. "We are all for brilliance, but . . .") or is coupled with such words as *erratic, eccentric, introvert, screwball,* etc. To quote Mr. Steele again, "While industry does not ignore the brilliant but erratic genius, in general it prefers its men to have 'normal' personalities. As one research executive explained, 'These fellows will be having contact with other people in the organization and it helps if they make a good impression. They participate in the task of "selling" research.'"

By insisting on this definition of well-roundedness, management makes two serious errors. For one thing, it seems to assume that the pool of brilliant scientists is so large that it can afford to consider only those in the pool who are well-rounded. There is, of course, no such over-supply; even if there were, furthermore, no such pat division could be made. For brilliance and the kind of well-roundedness management asks are a contradiction in terms. Some brilliant scientists are gregarious, to be sure, and some are not—but gregariousness is incidental to the harmony management is so intent upon. A brilliant scientist can enjoy playing on the company bowling team and still do brilliant and satisfying work. But there is no causal relationship. If the company makes him drop what he wants to do for something he doesn't, he may still enjoy playing on the company softball team, may even lead it to victory in the interurban championships. But at the same time he is doing it he may be pondering how exactly to word his resignation. The extracurricular will not have sublimated his frustration; and for all his natural amiability, in the place where it counts—the laboratory—his behavior will very quickly show it. Quite truly, he has become maladjusted.

He couldn't do otherwise. Management has tried to adjust the scientist to The Organization rather than The Organization to the scientist. It can do this with the mediocre and still have a harmonious group. It cannot do it with the brilliant; only freedom will make them harmonious. Most corporations sense this, but unfortunately, the moral they draw from it is something else again. A well-known corporation recently passed up the opportunity to hire one of the most brilliant chemists in the country. They wanted his brilliance, but they were afraid that he might "disrupt our organization." Commenting on this, a fellow scientist said, "He certainly would disrupt the organization. He is a man who would want to follow his own inclinations. In a laboratory which understood fundamental research, he wouldn't disrupt the organization because they would want him to follow his own inclinations. But not in this one."

Even when companies recognize that they are making a choice between brilliance and mediocrity, it is remarkable how excruciating they find the choice. Several years ago my colleagues and I listened to the management of an electronics company hold a post-mortem on a difficult decision they had just made. The company had been infiltrated by genius. Into their laboratory three years before had come a very young, brilliant man. He did magnificent work and the company looked for even greater things in the future. But, though he was a likable fellow, he was imaginative and he had begun to chafe at the supervision of the research director. The director, the management said, was a rather run-of-the-mill sort, though he had worked loyally and congenially for the company. Who would have to be sacrificed? Reluctantly, the company made its decision. The brilliant man would have to go. The management was unhappy about the decision but they argued that harmonious group thinking (this was the actual word they used) was the company's prime aim, and if they had promoted the brilliant man it would have upset the whole chain of company interpersonal relationships. What else, they asked plaintively, could they have done?

Listening to some of industry's pronouncements, one would gather that it is doing everything possible to ward off the kind of brilliant people who would force such a choice. Here, in this excerpt from a Socony-Vacuum Oil Company booklet on broad company policy, is a typical warning:

No Room for Virtuosos

Except in certain research assignments, few specialists in a large company ever work alone. There is little room for virtuoso performances. Business is so complex, even in its non-technical aspects, that no one man can master all of it; to do his job, therefore, he must be able to work with other people.

The thought is put even more forcibly in a documentary film made for the Monsanto Chemical Company. The film, which was made to inspire young men to go into chemistry, starts off in the old vein. You see young boys dreaming of adventure in faraway places as they stand by the station in a small town and watch the trains roll by. Eventually the film takes us to Monsanto's laboratories. We see three young men in white coats talking to one another. The voice on the sound track rings out: "No geniuses here; just a bunch of average Americans working together."

There was no mere slip of the script writer's pencil. I had a chance later to ask a Monsanto executive why the company felt impelled to claim to the world that its brainwork was carried on by just average Americans. The executive explained that Monsanto had thought about the point and wanted to deter young men from the idea that industrial chemistry was for genius types.

At the very moment when genius types couldn't agree more, the timing hardly seems felicitous. It could be argued, of course, that since the most brilliant stay in the universities anyway, management's barriers against genius would be at worst unnecessary. But it is not this clear-cut; whether or not they have geniuses, companies like Monsanto do not have their research work carried on by just average Americans, and if they did the stockholders would do well to complain. As Bell Labs and General Electric prove, there are many brilliant men who will, given the right circumstances, find industrial research highly absorbing. For company self-interest, let alone society's, a management policy that repels the few is a highly questionable one.

Society would not be the loser if the only effect of management policy were to make the most brilliant stay in the university. This screening effect, however, is only one consequence of management's policy. What concerns all of us, just as much as industry, is the fact that management also has a very powerful molding effect on the people it does get. They may not all be geniuses, but many are highly capable men, and in the right climate they could make great contributions.

That management is not only repelling talent but smothering it as well is told by management's own complaints. Privately, many of the same companies which stress team play criticize their young Ph.D.'s for not being interested enough in creative work—or, to put it in another way, are a bunch of just good average Americans working together. "Practically all who are now Ph.D.'s want to be told what to do," one research leader has complained. "They seem to be scared to death to think up problems of their own." Another research leader said that when his firm decided to let its chemists spend up to 25 percent of their time on "free" work, to the company's surprise hardly any of the men took up the offer.

But it shouldn't be surprising. A company cannot bring in young men and spend several years trying to make them into one kind of person, and then expect them, on signal, to be another kind. Cram courses in "brainstorming" and applied creativity won't change them. If the company indoctrinates them in the bureaucratic skills and asks them to keep their minds on the practical, it cannot suddenly stage a sort of creative play period and then, on signal, expect them to be like somebody else.

In any person a native ability cannot remain very long dormant without atrophying, but this is particularly true in the case of the scientist. Compared to people in other fields, scientists characteristically reach their peak very early in their careers. If the climate is stultifying the young scientist will rarely be vouchsafed a chance later to make up for the sterility of his early years. "It is the effect on the few first-rate men you find in industrial labs that is noticeable," says Burleigh Gardner, of Social Research, Inc. "The most able men generally rise to the top. But how high up the top is depends so much on the environment you put them in. In the average kind of corporation laboratory we have studied, the force of the majority opinion makes them divert their energies to a critical degree. I doubt if any of them could ever break through the group pressures to get up to the blue sky, where the great discoveries are made."

In a perverse way there is one small advantage to society in the big corporation's research policy. If corporation policy inhibits the scientist, it inhibits the flow of really good ideas that will aggrandize the corporation, and this lack may eventually prove a deterrent to overcentralization.

Those who see the growing concentration of technology in Big Business as irrevocable argue that advances are no longer possible except with the huge laboratories and equipment which only the big corporations can afford. But this is not true. For some scientific ends elaborate facilities—cyclotrons for physicists, ships for oceanographers—are necessary means. But this is only part of the picture; historically, almost every great advance has been made by one man with a minimum of equipment—sometimes just paper and pencil—and though this is more true of fundamental research, it is true of applied research as well. Go down the list of commercial inventions over the last thirty years: *with very few exceptions the advances did not come from a corporation laboratory.* Kodachrome, for example, was perfected in Eastman's huge laboratories but was invented by two musicians in a bathroom. The jet engine is an even clearer case in point. As Launcelot Law Whyte points out, none of the five earliest turbo-jet developments of Germany, Britain, and the United States was initiated within an established aircraft firm. "It is usually the relatively isolated outsider," Whyte says, "who produces the greatest novelties. It is a platitude, but it is often neglected."

Because it is small, the small firm has one potential advantage over the big one. It can't afford big research teams to administrate or interlocking committees to work up programs, and it doesn't have a crystallized company "family" to adjust to. Because it hasn't caught up yet with modern management, to put it another way, it provides an absence of the controls that make the scientist restive. Few small corporations have seized the opportunity at the time of this writing [...], but the opportunity is there.

CONCLUSION

If, as I believe, the people I have been examining in this book are representative of the main stream of organization life, one thing seems clear. If ever there was a generation of technicians, theirs is it. No generation has been so well equipped, psychologically as well as technically, to cope with the intricacies of vast organizations; none has been so well equipped to lead a meaningful community life; and none probably will be so adaptable to the constant shifts in environment that organization life is so increasingly demanding of them. In the better sense of the word, they are becoming the interchangeables of our society and they accept the role with understanding. They are all, as they say, in the same boat.

But where is the boat going? No one seems to have the faintest idea; nor, for that matter, do they see much point in even raising the question. Once people liked to think, at least, that they were in control of their destinies, but few of the younger organization people cherish such notions. Most see themselves as objects more acted upon than acting—and their future, therefore, determined as much by the system as by themselves.

In a word, they *accept*, and if we do not find this comforting at least we should recognize that it would be odd if they did not feel this confidence. For them society has in fact been good—very, very good—for there has been a succession of fairly beneficent environments: college, the paternalistic, if not always pleasant, military life, then, perhaps, graduate work through the G.I. Bill of Rights, a corporation apprenticeship during a period of industrial expansion and high prosperity, and, for some, the camaraderie of communities like Park Forest. The system, they instinctively conclude, is essentially benevolent.

No one should begrudge them the prosperity that has helped make them feel this way. If we have to have problems, after all, the adversities of good times are as worthy as any to have to worry about. Nor should we regard the emphasis on co-operation as a reversal of our national character. When the suburbanites speak of re-establishing the spirit of the frontier communities, there is a truth in their analogy. Our country was born as a series of highly communal enterprises, and though the individualist may have opened the frontier, it was the cooperative who settled it. So throughout our history. Our national genius has always lain in our adaptability, in our distrust of dogma and doctrine, in our regard for the opinion of others, and in this respect the organization people are true products of the American past. "The more equal social conditions become," de Tocqueville, no friend of conformity, presciently observed, "the more men display this reciprocal disposition to oblige each other."

And there is the crux. When de Tocqueville wrote this a century ago it was the double-edged nature of this disposition that haunted him. He understood its virtue; he was an aristocrat and he confessed that he missed the excellence of the few in the good of many, but he saw clearly that our egalitarianism and our ease of social cooperation were the great fruits of democracy. We could not sustain these virtues without suffering their defects. But could we keep them in a balance? De Tocqueville made a prophecy. If America ever destroyed its genius it would be by intensifying the social virtues at the expense of others, by making the individual come to regard himself as a hostage to prevailing opinion, by creating, in sum, a tyranny of the majority.

And this is what the organization man is doing. He is doing it for what he feels are good reasons, but this only makes the tyranny more powerful, not less. At the very time when the pressures of our highly organized society make so stringent a demand on the individual, he is himself compounding the impact. He is not only other-directed, to borrow David Riesman's concept, he is articulating a philosophy which tells him it is right to be that way.

My charge against the Social Ethic, then, is on precisely the grounds of contemporary usefulness it so venerates. It is not, I submit, suited to the needs of "modern man," but is instead reinforcing precisely that which least needs to be emphasized, and at the expense of that which does. Here is my bill of particulars.

It is redundant. In some societies, individualism has been carried to such extremes as to endanger the society itself, and there exist today examples of individualism corrupted into a narrow egoism which prevents effective cooperation. This is a danger, there is no question of that. But is it today as pressing a danger as the obverse—a climate which inhibits individual initiative and imagination, and the courage to exercise it against group opinion? Society is itself an education in the extrovert values, and I think it can be rightfully argued that rarely has there been a society which has preached them so hard. No man is an island unto himself, but how John Donne would writhe to hear how often, and for what reasons, the thought is so tiresomely repeated.

It is premature. To preach technique before content, the skills of getting along isolated from why and to what end the getting along is for, does not produce maturity. It produces a sort of permanent prematurity, and this is true not only of the child being taught life adjustment but of the organization man being taught well-roundedness. This is a sterile concept, and those who believe that they have mastered human relations can blind themselves to the true bases of cooperation. People don't cooperate just to cooperate; they cooperate for substantive reasons, to achieve certain goals, and unless these are comprehended the little manipulations for morale, team spirit, and such are fruitless.

And they can be worse than fruitless. Held up as the end-all of organization leadership, the skills of human relations easily tempt the new administrator into the practice of a tyranny more subtle and more pervasive than that which he means to supplant. No one wants to see the old authoritarian return, but at least it could be said of him that what he wanted primarily from you was your sweat. The new man wants your soul.

It is delusory. It is easy to fight obvious tyranny; it is not easy to fight benevolence, and few things are more calculated to rob the individual of his defenses than the idea that his interests and those of society can be wholly compatible. The good society is the one in which they are most compatible, but they can never be completely so, and one who lets The Organization be the judge ultimately sacrifices himself. Like the good society, the good organization encourages individual expression, and many have done so. But there always remains some conflict between the individual and The Organization. Is The Organization to be the arbiter? The Organization will look to its own interests, but it will look to the individual's *only as The Organization interprets them.*

It is static. Organization of itself has no dynamic. The dynamic is in the individual and thus he must not only question how The Organization interprets his interests, he must question how it interprets its own. The bold new plan he feels is necessary, for example. He cannot trust that The

Organization can recognize this. Most probably, it will not. It is the nature of a new idea to confound current consensus—even the mildly new idea. It might be patently in order, but, unfortunately, the group has a vested interest in its miseries as well as pleasures, and irrational as this may be, many a member of organization life can recall instances where the group clung to known disadvantages rather than risk the anarchies of change.

It is self-destructive. The quest for normalcy, as we have seen in suburbia, is one of the great breeders of neuroses, and the Social Ethic only serves to exacerbate them. What is normalcy? We practice a great mutual deception. Everyone knows that they themselves are different—that they are shy in company, perhaps, or dislike many things most people seem to like—but they are not sure that other people are different too. Like the norms of personality testing, they see about them the sum of efforts of people like themselves to seem as normal as others and possibly a little more so. It is hard enough to learn to live with our inadequacies, and we need not make ourselves more miserable by a spurious ideal of middle-class adjustment. Adjustment to what? Nobody really knows—and the tragedy is that they don't realize that the so-confident-seeming other people don't know either. [. . .]

But what is the *"solution"?* many ask. There is no solution. The conflict between individual and society has always involved dilemma; it always will, and it is intellectual arrogance to think a program would solve it. Certainly the current experience does suggest a few steps we can profitably take, and I would like to suggest several. Common to all, however, must be a fundamental shift of emphasis, and if this is evaded, any change will exist largely on the level of language. The organization man has a tremendous affinity for vogue words by which the status quo can be described as dynamic advance, and "individualism," alas, is such a word. Let us beware, then, the hard-sell, twelve-point program. Many have been touted as in the name of individual expression, but as those suppressed by them will sense, they are usually organization-serving loyalty devices that fool only those who administrate them.

This caveat made, let me suggest several areas where constructive proposals are in order. First, "human relations." We need by all means to continue to experiment and study. Whatever we call human relations, they are central to the problem of The Organization and the individual, and the more we find out about the effect of the one on the other the better we can find more living room for the individual. But it's not going to be done if many of those who propagate the doctrine cling to self-proving assumptions about the over-riding importance of equilibrium, integration, and adjustment. The side of the coin they have been staring at so intently is a perfectly good one, but there is another side and it should not be too heretical at least to have a peek at it. Thousands of studies and case histories have dwelled on fitting the individual to the group, but what about fitting the group to the person? What about *individual* dynamics? The tyranny of the happy work team? The adverse effects of high morale?

One does not have to be in favor of unhappiness to explore such hypotheses, and now, encouragingly, a few whose good will is unquestionable are showing more disposition to do so. The Harvard Business School, which almost grew old with human relations, has been using the word *administrator* less, the word *leader* more, and lately its best research seems directed at the matter of individual initiative more than of group happiness. Rensis Likert, the leader of the "group dynamics" school, has announced that recent studies of organization are leading him and his colleagues to question their earlier conclusions that good morale necessarily produces high productivity. They still believe that the work group should be supervised as a group rather than on a man-to-man basis, but they do warn that the supervisor who concentrates on making the group happy may produce belongingness but not very much else.

Another fruitful approach would be a drastic re-examination of the now orthodox view that the individual should be given less of the complete task, the team more of it. For a century we have been breaking down tasks into the components and sub-components, each to be performed by a different cell member, and this assembly-line mentality has affected almost everything that men do for a living, including the arts. We can grant that to a degree the benefits of compartmentalized work have surpassed the disadvantages. But do we have to grant that progress demands more of same? That the monotony, the sacrifice of individual accomplishment are inevitable? On the assembly line itself, where specialization would seem most necessary, some companies have found that a reversal of emphasis can actually lead to more productivity. Instead of trying to offset the monotony of a task with externals, such as bowling alleys and "economic education," they have enlarged the task itself. By giving the worker more of the total job to do—asking him to wire the whole set, for example, instead of just one relay—they have given him that wonderful thing that is challenge, and he has responded with more effort, more skill, more *self-respect*.

Is there not a moral here for all organization life? If we truly believe the individual is more creative than the group, just in day-to-day routine there is something eminently practical we can do about it. Cut down the amount of time the individual has to spend in conferences and meetings and team play. This would be a somewhat mechanical approach to what is ultimately a philosophical problem, but if organization people would take a hard look at the different types of meetings inertia has accumulated for The Organization, they might find that the ostensibly negative act of cutting out many of them would lead to some very positive benefits over and above the time saved. Thrown more on their own resources, those who have nothing to offer but the skills of compromising other people's efforts might feel bereft, but for the others the climate might be invigorating. Of itself such a surface change in working conditions would not give them more freedom, but it would halt a bad momentum, it would force organization to distinguish between what are legitimate functions of the group and what are not, and even if it yielded only a few more hours, this would be no small blessing. Once enjoyed, room to move around in is sweet indeed, and men partially liberated might be tantalized into demanding more.

In fighting the incubus of team work, we need to look more understandingly at the frustrations of those involved. Let's go back a moment to the situation of the professional employee. Studies have now convinced organization people that engineers and scientists in industry make up its most disaffected group, and that something should be done about it. The diagnosis is valuable. But how does organization interpret it? Organization people have concluded that the trouble is that the professional tends to be career-oriented rather than company-oriented. What The Organization must do, they believe, is to direct its efforts at integrating him by giving him more company status, indoctrinating him more effectively in the "big picture," by making him, in short, a company man.

How futile, how destructive is this solution! Why should the scientist be company-oriented? Is he to be called maladjusted because he does not fit the administrator's Procrustean bed? And of what profit would be his integration? It is not to his self-interest, neither is it to that of The Organization. Leave him his other allegiance. It is his work that must be paramount, and efforts to divert him into contentment are the efforts best calculated to bridle the curiosity that makes him productive.

Is it so practical? There is a magnificent piece of evidence that it is anything but. In the great slough of mediocrity that is most corporation research, what two laboratories are conspicuous exceptions in the rate of discovery? They are General Electric's research department and Bell Labs:

exactly the two laboratories most famous for their encouragement of individualism—the most tolerant of individual differences, the most patient with off-tangent ideas, the least given to the immediate, closely supervised team project. By all accounts, the scientists in them get along quite well, but they do not make a business of it, and neither do the people who run the labs. They care not a whit if scientists' eyes fail to grow moist at company anthems; it is enough that the scientists do superbly well what they want to do, for though the consequences of profit for The Organization are secondary to the scientist, eventually there are these consequences, and as long as the interests of the group and the individual touch at this vital point, such questions as belongingness are irrelevant. Hard-boiled? No, tough-minded—and what more moral basis, it can be asked, for people working together, scientists or others?

It is not just for the scientist, not just for the brilliant, that the moral should be drawn, and this brings us to what ultimately is the single greatest vehicle for constructive change—education. The many points against the social adjustment emphases now prevailing are being vigorously sounded, and it is right that they should be, but one point needs to be made much more emphatically. The case for a rigorously fundamental schooling can be made on the utilitarians' own grounds: social usefulness. There are better reasons for the development of the individual, but until this point is made more clearly we seem by default to leave the debate on the either/or grounds of "democratic education" versus a highly trained elite. This is false antithesis. The great bulk of people will face organization pressures as inhibiting for them as for the few, and they need, as much if not more, to have the best that is within them demanded early. Is it "democratic" to hold that the humanities can have no meaning for them? They do not have to be taught to shake hands with other people; society will attend to this lesson. They have to be taught to reach. All of them. Some will be outstanding, some not, but the few will never flourish where the values of the many are against them.

I have been speaking of measures organizations can take. But ultimately any real change will be up to the individual himself, and this is why his education is so central to the problem. For he must look to his discontents with different eye. It has been said that dominance of the group is the wave of the future and that, lament it or not, he might as well accept it. But this is contemporaryism at its worst; things are not as they are because there is some good reason they are. Nor is the reverse true. It may one day prove true, as some prophets argue, that we are in a great and dismal tide of history that cannot be reversed, but if we accept the view we will only prove it.

Whatever kind of future suburbia may foreshadow, it will show that at least we have the choices to make. The organization man is not in the grip of vast social forces about which it is impossible for him to do anything; the options are there, and with wisdom and foresight he can turn the future away from the dehumanized collective that so haunts our thoughts. He may not. But he can.

He must *fight* The Organization. Not stupidly, or selfishly, for the defects of individual self-regard are no more to be venerated than the defects of cooperation. But fight he must, for the demands for his surrender are constant and powerful, and the more he has come to like the life of organization the more difficult does he find it to resist these demands, or even to recognize them. It is wretched, dispiriting advice to hold before him the dream that ideally there need be no conflict between him and society. There always is; there always must be. Ideology cannot wish it away; the peace of mind offered by organization remains a surrender, and no less so for being offered in benevolence. That is the problem.

The Case for the Universal Card

Fortune, April 1954

The notion advanced in this satirical piece may seem less ludicrous in the twenty-first century than it did in 1954, when it first ran in *Fortune.* Whyte would have preferred to remain anonymous as the author but was overruled by his superiors, who published the article under the suitably pompous pseudonym of Otis Binet Stanford and added a brief disclaimer identifying Whyte for any readers who failed to recognize the obvious joke. Even so, the British humor magazine *Punch* took it seriously enough to publish a high-minded (if satirical) rebuttal.

I am glad to have this opportunity to clear up the misunderstanding over the Universal Card development. For one thing, my own part in it. I have been much flattered by the praise my modest contribution has attracted; at the outset, however, I must make plain that it is really my colleagues in corporation personnel work who deserve the credit. All I have done, essentially, is to bring together the techniques that they are already using and extend them to their logical development.

The very boldness of the plan has disturbed some people. In American business, unfortunately, there are still many personnel men who have a laissez-faire attitude toward human relations, who argue that there is a large part of the employee's life and personality that is not of concern to the corporation. (This is an attitude, if it is not too ungracious for me to say so, that often marks the pages of *Fortune.*) These gentlemen, I am afraid, are guilty of a semantic error. The Universal Card system is just as "democratic," for example, as the managerial selection and training programs now in use in business. I intend no criticism by this; of necessity corporations have had to screen from their cadres non-college men and those whom psychological tests show to be unfitted for corporation life. But progress will be better served, I think, if, rather than gloss over these facts, we acknowledge them openly and thereby build more wisely for the future. The Universal Card plan may be bold, but there is no sloppy sentimentality about it.

The seminal idea hit me, not unlike Newton's apple, through an apparently humdrum incident. I was returning from Washington in a Pennsylvania Railroad diner. Having just left a very stimulating personnel workshop, I was mulling over our unsolved problems when the waiter presented the check. Finding myself low in funds, I called the steward and, with a view to cashing a check, began showing him all the cards in my wallet.

I had never before realized quite how many I carried. As I took them out one by one, the inventory mounted. There was (1) operator's license, (2) car-registration certificate, (3) company identification card, with my laminated picture, (4) social-security card, (5) air-travel card, (6) automobile insurance policy card, (7) A.A.A. bail-bond certificate, (8) Kirkeby Hotels credit card, (9) Hilton Hotels credit card, (10) Sheraton Hotels credit card, (11) United Medical Service card, (12) blood donor's card.

Nonetheless I was in a fix. The steward's courtesy was up to the same high standard as the food, but he had to explain to me that no card I had with me would do. None meshed with the Pennsylvania's accounting system. At that instant the idea hit. Why not *one master, all-purpose card?*

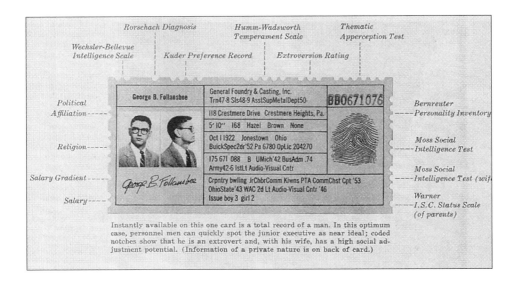

Instantly available on this one card is a total record of a man. In this optimum case, personnel men can quickly spot the junior executive as near ideal; coded notches show that he is an extrovert and, with his wife, has a high social adjustment potential. (Information of a private nature is on back of card.)

Everything began to fall into place. For the more I thought, the more I came to realize that the least of the card's advantages would be its convenience to the individual. The real promise lay in another direction. In one fell stroke the Universal Card could solve all the major unfinished problems of organization life.

Consider, for example, the tremendous duplication of records. From adolescence on, each of us leaves a trail of dossiers behind him as one organization after the other tests and retests and evaluates him. After all this effort, what happens? In a miscellany of file cabinets scattered all over, the records lie dormant and unused. Furthermore, *even if* they were brought together, the diversity of testing methods now used would keep the records from being interchangeable. Valuable as each method may be as a peephole into an applicant's character, the lack of standardization means each succeeding organization has to start on the man all over again.

As soon as I was home I dashed off a quick overview on the Universal Card solution to my colleagues. Their response was immediate—it was, many said, the greatest development in personnel work since the invention of the buzz session. Soon they were deep in action-research to help me "iron out the bugs." Let me again salute them; without their insights the final plan would have been impossible—it is, in the truest sense of the word, an example of cross-fertilization.

The opening wedge in our plan is to agree on a common battery of tests, so that every person being processed into a company will be tested by precisely the same criteria. Tentatively we have settled on an optimum battery that will include such proved tests as the Bernreuter Personality Inventory, the Wechsler-Bellevue I.Q. Scale, and the Kuder Preference Record. Similarly we are standardizing the Rorschach Ink Blot Test and the Thematic Apperception Test. Today, as we know all to well, each company is likely to use a different ink blot for the Rorschach and in the Thematic Apperception Test give the applicant any of several pictures to compose a story about. We have chosen one ink-blot design and one basic picture.[1]

With this unified personnel "vocabulary" we will have rendered the vital statistics about a man in a form instantly understandable throughout the member corporations. On the card would be the man's age, height, weight, fingerprints, blood type, birth date, introvert-extrovert percentile rating, parents' background and status rating, home-life situation, and all the many other things that are so necessary for the corporation to concern itself with.

Great economies would ensue. Since corporations would be all using the same testing methods they could begin to centralize the whole processing function. Instead of each one making the same heavy investment in staff psychologists, I.B.M. machines, and the like, a selected few would do this for the rest (charges would be levied on a pro rata basis). If the Du Pont company were to join the plan, for example, it could be asked to service the member corporations in the Delaware-Maryland area; similarly, General Electric in the New York area, and so on. Binding all of them together would be a central secretariat responsible for maintaining duplicate cards of the entire roster.

The employee, too, will enjoy some benefits. I do not refer merely to the convenience of the card as an all-purpose credit card, but rather to the solution of a problem of far more importance. Previous techniques have failed to give the employee the sense of belongingness to the corporation that means emotional security. To be sure, the corporation has provided him with pensions, medical benefits, housing, travel, and so many social services that he can fulfill all his felt wants and needs within the boundaries of the corporate family. Despite this, however, there is still so much sub-surface aggressiveness that some men tell the company to "chuck it," and an even larger number are psychologically capable of it. Rootless, restless, with no sense of direction to life save their own, such people are forever in danger of becoming lone-persons.

Under the Universal Card system, however, they could not cut the cord with the organization. Physically, they might move to other jobs—I see no way to prohibit the movement—but wherever they went the card and its accumulation of years of scrutiny and testing would follow them and condition their attitudes in the new work situation. No longer, then, would people have to be loyal in the old-fashioned sense of being loyal to "the" organization. They would be loyal to organization itself.

Now there are several objections that I must, in all conscience, take up. To get the least important one out of the way, let's look at the question of privacy. Many people, otherwise enthusiastic about the idea, have told me that they would hesitate to present a Universal Card to the gaze of waiters and hotel clerks.[2] But the solution is simple: the information about the discrete factors would not be written out but, as the reader can observe in the illustration, it would be coded and notched on the outer edge of the card. While the purpose of this, needless to say, is for ease in sorting and culling the cards with business machines, the byproduct would be a measure of privacy for the individual.

Some critics have hazarded the thought that because so many people would be Universal Card holders, in time quite possibly they could "catch on" to the code, and spot, on someone else's card, for example, that two long punches and one short one in the upper lefthand corner meant a bad sibling rivalry. Every six months, however, we would recode the cards. This would not only keep the code fresh, it would also lessen the temptation for someone to counterfeit a card and notch himself a better rating than he had.

It would also overcome the objection that a man would be irretrievably marked. Just because a man has exhibited symptoms of maladjustment does not mean he may not in time successfully adjust, and the periodic retesting will stimulate him to do just that. Conversely, a man who has been just coasting along because he initially was rated as an outgoing personality would be reminded that he must develop further if he is to keep his card.

This brings up the question of what is a "good" or "bad" rating. This is not so troublesome as it appears. As many followers of applied psychology will realize, value judgments do not enter into testing. Over the years the matching of Universal Card scores and subsequent performances will allow us to arrive *inductively* at the ideal "models," and thus dispense with the human factor. A constantly rotating board of experts would be in charge of the master matrixes and they would constantly revise and refine them as circumstances dictated. When a vacancy occurs in a corporation for, say, a comptroller, the secretariat at central headquarters would pull out the master matrix for this position. It would be a card notched for the optimum balance of characteristics for the slot. This would be put into an I.B.M. machine and then—very much as the F.B.I. does in searching for criminals in its fingerprint files—we would run through the entire stack of cards until we found the handful that came closest to the specifications.

So far I have been talking in terms of the corporation, but the card would apply just as logically to any of the other big organizations that have become the basic vehicles in our society. The government, the church, the whole field of education, the Atomic Energy Commission, the foundations—these organizations have quite similar problems of recruitment and training, promotion and transfer, and so on, and one by one they would inevitably see the logic of joining the central organization.

I should think they would very well have to. The Universal Card system would very quickly siphon off the cream of our young talent. Already on the campus we see all the basic rudiments of the system; students aim early for the big-corporation training program, and this fact, along with the activities of the recruiting agents that corporations regularly send to the colleges, has created a smoothly functioning pipeline. With only a few extra refinements, changes in filing procedures, etc., the campuses would be quickly incorporated into the Universal Card system. That done, all corporations would soon be knit together and in only a matter of years our society would at last be coherently organized. There would be only two kinds of people—people who have a Universal Card and people who do not have a Universal Card.

It would still be an "open" society. Cards would not be hereditary, except in the sense that cardholders would be in a better position to expose their children to the kind of environment that leads to cardholding. But others would have their chance too. Merely by continuing the yeoman work of America's professional educators, we would spot likely material by increased testing at the kindergarten level, and direct the curriculum ever more to vocational and group-centered training. As a result of this surveillance, and such encouragement as probationary fellowships, we would ensure a constantly replenishing reservoir of potential cardholders. Thus even though a parent might not be a cardholder himself, he could cherish the dream that one day one of his children could become one.

At the same time we were bringing newcomers in we would be pruning the current membership. There would be nothing static about the system, and if a man fell beneath an acceptable rating, we would revoke his card. This would be hard on the people concerned, but they would be the lone-persons, the mystics, the intellectual agitators—which is to say, the kind of people that the modern organization doesn't really want anyway. Today lone-persons frequently slip in because our processing isn't rigorous enough to pierce the simulated appearance of the well-adjusted extrovert that such people often cleverly role-play. With the Universal Card system they would be found out in short order, and then diverted to occupations out of the main stream.

Do not misunderstand me. I am not averse to "fresh thinking" and "imagination," and when used for poetry, painting, etc., they do no great harm. But at the same time to keep the ship going on an even keel we must shield the well-rounded people from individualists who are constantly needling them and questioning the system. Certainly the great mass of junior executives would welcome this freedom from unorthodox influences.

The greatest benefit of all is for society itself. More than anything else, the Universal Card system would protect us from authoritarianism. Those who are working with me do not relish 1984 and the prospect of Big Brother and dictators like him taking over. That is one of the reasons why we are so enthusiastic about the Universal Card. People like Big Brother can succeed only where they find society fragmented, unorganized, and leaderless. But if the Universal Card is adopted, Big Brother and his henchmen could not get into the position of authority. We would be there already.

You, Too, Can Write the Casual Style

Harper's, October 1953

Like "The Case for the Universal Card," this light piece is pie-in-the-face social criticism. Here the satirical pie is directed at pompous writers and the codification of their literary affectations.

A revolution has taken place in American prose. No longer the short huffs and puffs, the unqualified word, the crude gusto of the declarative sentence. Today the fashion is to write casually.

The Casual Style is not exactly new. Originated in the early twenties, it has been refined and improved and refined again by a relatively small band of writers, principally for *The New Yorker*, until now their mannerisms have become standards of sophistication. Everybody is trying to join the club. Newspaper columnists have forsaken the beloved metaphors of the sports page for the Casual Style, and one of the quickest ways for an ad man to snag an award from other ad men is to give his copy the low-key, casual pitch; the copy shouldn't sing these days—it should whisper. Even Dr. Rudolf Flesch, who has been doing so much to teach people how to write like other people, is counseling his followers to use the Casual Style. Everywhere the ideal seems the same: be casual.

But how? There is very little down-to-earth advice. We hear about the rapier-like handling of the bromide, the keen eye for sham and pretension, the exquisite sense of nuance, the unerring ear for the vulgate. But not much about actual technique. The layman, as a consequence, is apt to look on the Casual Style as a mandarin dialect which he fears he could never master.

Nonsense. The Casual Style is within everyone's grasp. It has now become so perfected by constant polishing that its devices may readily be identified, and they change so little that their use need be no more difficult for the novice than for the expert. (That's not quite all there is to it, of course. Some apparently casual writers, Thurber and E. B. White, among others, rarely use the devices.)

The subject matter, in the first place, is not to be ignored. Generally speaking, the more uneventful it is, or the more pallid the writer's reaction to it, the better do form and content marry. Take, for example, the cocktail party at which the writer can show how bored everyone is with everyone else, and how utterly fatuous they all are anyway. Since a non-casual statement—e.g., "The party was a bore"—would destroy the reason for writing about it at all, the Casual Style here is not only desirable but mandatory.

Whatever the subject, however, twelve devices are the rock on which all else is built. I will present them one by one, illustrating them with examples from such leading casual stylists as Wolcott Gibbs, John Crosby, John McCarten, and (on occasion) this magazine's "Mr. Harper." If the reader will digest what follows, he should be able to dash off a paragraph undistinguished from the best casual writing being done today.

(1) *Heightened Understanding.* Where the old-style writer would say, "I don't like it," "It is not good," or something equally banal, the casual writer says it is "*something less than* good." He avoids direct statement and strong words—except, as we will note, where he is setting them up to have something to knock down. In any event, he qualifies. "Somewhat" and "rather," the bread-and-butter words of the casual writer, should become habitual with you; similarly with such phrases as "I suppose," "it seems to me," "I guess," or "I'm afraid." "Elusive" or "elude" are good, too, and if you see the word "charm" in a casual sentence you can be pretty sure that "eludes me," or "I find elusive," will not be far behind.

(2) *The Multiple Hedge.* Set up an ostensibly strong statement, and then, with your qualifiers, shoot a series of alternately negative and positive charges into the sentence until finally you neutralize the whole thing. Let's take, for example, the clause, "certain names have a guaranteed nostalgic magic." Challenge enough here; the names not only have magic, they have guaranteed magic. A double hedge reverses the charges. "Names which have, *I suppose* (hedge 1), a guaranteed nostalgic magic, *though there are times that I doubt it* (hedge 2). . . ."

We didn't have to say they were guaranteed in the first place, of course, but without such straw phrases we wouldn't have anything to construct a hedge on and, frequently, nothing to write at all. The virtue of the hedge is that by its very negating effect it makes any sentence infinitely expandable.

Even if you have so torn down your original statement with one or two hedges that you seem to have come to the end of the line, you have only to slip in an anti-hedge, a strengthening word (e.g., "definitely," "unqualified," etc.), and begin the process all over again. Witness the following quadruple hedge: "I found Mr. Home entertaining *from time to time* (hedge 1) on the ground, *I guess* (hedge 2), that the singular idiom and unearthly detachment of the British upper classes have *always* (anti-hedge) seemed *reasonably* (hedge 3) droll to me, *at least in moderation* (hedge 4)." The art of plain talk, as has been pointed out, does not entail undue brevity.

If you've pulled hedge on hedge and the effect still remains too vigorous, simply wipe the slate clean with a cancellation clause at the end. "It was all exactly as foolish as it sounds," says Wolcott Gibbs, winding up some 570 casual words on a subject, "and I wouldn't give it another thought."

(3) *Narcissizing Your Prose.* The casual style is nothing if not personal; indeed, you will usually find in it as many references to the writer as to what he's supposed to be talking about. For you do not talk about the subject: you talk about its impact on you. With the reader peering over your shoulder, you look into the mirror and observe your own responses as you run the entire range of the causal writer's emotions. You may reveal yourself as, in turn, listless ("The audience seemed not to share my boredom"); insouciant ("I was really quite happy with it"); irritated ("The whole thing left me tired and cross"); comparatively gracious ("Being in a comparatively gracious mood, I won't go into the details I didn't like"); or hesitant ("I wish I could say that I could accept his hypothesis").

(4) *Preparation for the Witticism.* When the casual writer hits upon a clever turn of phrase or a nice conceit, he uses this device to insure that his conceit will not pass unnoticed. Suppose, for example, you have thought of something to say that is pretty damn good if you say so yourself. The device, in effect, is to say so yourself. If you want to devastate a certain work as "a study of vulgarity in high places," don't say this flat out. Earlier in the sentence prepare the reader for the drollery ahead with something like "what I am tempted to call" or "what could best be described as" or "if it had to be defined in a sentence, it might well be called . . ."

Every writer his own claque.

(5) *Deciphered Notes Device, or Cute Things-I-Have-Said.* In this one you are your own stooge as well. You feed yourself lines. By means of the slender fiction that you have written something on the back of an envelope or the margin of a program, you catch yourself good-humoredly trying to decipher these shrewd, if cryptic, little jotting. *Viz.:* "Their diagnoses are not nearly

as crisp as those I find in my notes"; ". . . sounds like an inadequate description, but it's all I have on my notes, and it may conceivably be very high compliment."

(6) *The Kicker*. An echo effect. "My reactions [included] an irritable feeling that eleven o'clock was past Miss Keim's bedtime,"— and now the Kicker—"*not to mention my own.*" This type of thing practically writes itself. "She returns home. She should never have left home in the first place. __ _____ _____ _." ("And neither should I.")

(7) *Wit of Omission*. By calling attention to the fact that you are not going to say it, you suggest that there is something very funny you could say if only you wanted to. "A thought occurred to me at this point," you may say, when otherwise stymied, "but I think we had better not go into *that*."

(8) *The Planned Colloquialism*. The casual writer savors colloquialisms. This is not ordinary colloquial talk—nobody is more quickly provoked than the casual writer by ordinary usage. It is, rather, a playful descent into the vulgate. Phrases like "darn," "awfully," "as all getout," "mighty," and other folksy idioms are ideal. The less you would be likely to use the word normally yourself the more pointed the effect. Contrast is what you are after, for it is the facetious interplay of language levels—blending, as it were, of the East Fifties and the Sticks—that gives the Casual Style its offhand charm.

(9) *Feigned Forgetfulness*. Conversation gropes; it is full of "what I really meant was" and "maybe I should have added," backings and fillings and second thoughts of one kind or another. Writing is different; theoretically, ironing out second thoughts beforehand is one of the things writers are paid to do. In the Casual Style, however, it is exactly this exposure of the writer composing in public that makes it so casual. For the professional touch, then, ramble, rebuke yourself in print ("what I really meant, I guess"), and if you have something you feel you should have said earlier, don't say it earlier, but say later that you guess you should have said it earlier.

(10) *The Subject-Apologizer, or Pardon-Me-for-Living*. The Casual Stylist must always allow for the possibility that his subject is just as boring to the reader as it is to him. He may forestall this by seeming to have stumbled on it by accident, or by using phrases like: "If this is as much news to you as it is to me," or "This, in case you've been living in a cave lately, is . . ."

(11) *The Omitted Word*. This all began modestly enough the day a *New Yorker* writer dropped the articles "the" and "a" from the initial sentence of an anecdote (e.g., "Man we know told us"; "Fellow name of Brown"). Now even such resolutely lowbrow writers as Robert Ruark affect it, and they

are applying it to any part of speech anywhere in the sentence. You can drop a pronoun ("Says they're shaped like pyramids"); verb ("You been away from soap opera the last couple of weeks?"); or preposition ("Far as glamour goes . . .").

(12) *The Right Word.* In the lexicon of the casual writer there are a dozen or so adjectives which in any context have, to borrow a phrase, a guaranteed charm. Attrition is high-"brittle," "febrile," "confected," for example, are at the end of the run. Ten, however, defy obsolescence: *antic, arch, blurred, chaste, chill, crisp, churlish, disheveled, dim, disembodied.*

They are good singly, but they are even better when used in tandem; *cf.,* "In an arch, antic sort of way"; "In an arch, blurred sort of way"; "In an arch, crisp sort of way." And so on.

Finally, the most multipurpose word of them all: "altogether." Frequently it is the companion of "charming" and "delightful," and in this coupling is indispensable to any kind of drama criticism. It can also modify the writer himself (e.g., "Altogether, I think . . ."). Used best, however, it just floats, unbeholden to any other part of the sentence.

Once you have mastered these twelve devices, you too should be able to write as casually as all getout. At least it seems to me, though I may be wrong, that they convey an elusive archness which the crisp literary craftsman, in his own dim sort of way, should altogether cultivate these days. Come to think of it, the charm of the Casual Style is something less than clear to me, but we needn't go into *that.* Fellow I know from another magazine says this point of view best described as churlish. Not, of course, that it matters.

How To Back into a *Fortune* Story

From *Writing for* Fortune: *Nineteen Authors Remember Life on the Staff of a Remarkable Magazine* (1980)

Whyte was among a distinguished group of writers for *Fortune* in its heyday. Many of these, including James Agee, Archibald MacLeish, and John Kenneth Galbraith, might never have found their way to a so-called business magazine were it not for *Fortune*'s founding editor-in-chief, Henry Luce, who made the magazine great by filling its pages with what he touted as "a literature of business." Whyte credited his success at *Fortune* to Luce's recognition that (in Luce's words) "it is easier to turn poets into business journalists than to turn bookkeepers into writers." In a similar vein, Galbraith reflected on the views of the legendary Luce in *Writing for* Fortune, published by Time, Inc. in celebration of *Fortune*'s fiftieth anniversary in 1980:

> Luce was conservative, Republican, establishmentarian, romantically chauvinist, and given strongly to the belief that making (as distinct from having) money was a firm measure of worth. But all this was second to the Luce curiosity. He believed that liberals, even socialists, if they could write, were better for reporting on business and economic affairs than conservatives, who were tedious or semiliterate or both.

The fact that the first issue of *Fortune* had been published into the teeth of the Great Depression in 1930 surely had something to do with the magazine's rapid evolution from a lavish testament to Luce's capitalist religion into a vehicle for serious social observation. But Luce earned lasting credit for creating a stimulating environment for serious writers to do their work, and giving them rein. Whyte was in some ways the exemplary *Fortune* writer—a quick study with a direct, punchy prose style and a keen eye for both the telling detail and the "big picture"—and with the help of a team of researchers and other staffers, he was a prolific contributor. In the essay that follows, written two decades after his departure from the magazine, Whyte recaptured some of the mystery and magic of the *Fortune* editorial process.

I am going to set down some thoughts on the kind of story that is more or less unique to *Fortune*. Physically, it is a big story: lots and lots of words, sometimes in three or more installments, or as part of a single-subject issue. The subject is pre-emptively embracing—new markets emerging, a broad social change—and not so much about what has happened as about what might or might not happen. Such a story is not the result of routine queries but of original, unexpected questions—the result, in short, of creative legwork.

But not much has ever been proposed in the way of guidelines for producing such stories; as a matter of fact, the day-to-day operation of the magazine has often been at cross-purposes with the nurturing of just such stories. I think I know why. Through a series of lucky events, I was backed into writing some of these stories, and I have been brooding over the lesson I've learned. There are about five, and they may be summed up by the words inadvertence, paranoia, messiness, time, and benign neglect.

I was lucky, because in my first years I was the junior writer on the staff and generally conceded to be the worst. I was so bad that I was not fired, but kept on as a kind of exhibit. Working with me was a catharsis. My weakness for clichés was the despair of Bill Furth and drove him to some of his best marginal essays on style. Bill Harris, then assistant managing editor, was awed by my complete lack of business sophistication. The rest of the staff, God knows, lacked it, too, but not the way I lacked it. ("The market interest. What's the market interest? Can't you get that through your head?") Herb Solow, who detested ornamentation and the elaborate metaphors and analogies I delighted in, thought my leads were models of bad writing. As if suspicious even of adjectives and adverbs, he would prune my leads of everything save a few verbs and nouns.

I wasn't really all that bad. Most of the time, I was working on an ill-begotten department called Shorts and Faces. No writer could do good work with these things. They were short pieces of about a thousand words on subjects too marginal for the middle of the book. Being thin, they required a lot of research to find reasons for anybody to read them, and considerable ingenuity in story construction to mask the lack of such reasons. No wonder I went in for metaphors and involved leads.

I was lucky to have had good researchers. Since the editors felt I needed a strong hand, that is just what I got. I was assigned some of the best, certainly the most assertive of the researchers (yes, Doris, Sara, and Marion, nicely assertive, but assertive). They bullied and badgered me; they disputed all my assumptions; they upstaged me in interviews. At length, I began to react like a *Fortune* writer. I bullied and badgered them back. Where are your notes? Would it be too much to get them before the story's printed? If you are so right about the story line, why don't you write the damn thing yourself?

As weeks of research went by, a curious thing would happen. The two of us would be drawn together, bound in mutual paranoia. No matter how violent our disagreements over the story, at least we were both interested in it; indeed, downright obsessed with it. But hardly anyone else would be. The editor would be interested later, but he was paid to be. Other people, mired in the parochialism of their own narrow interests, would avoid you in the halls, fearful you might buttonhole them and talk your story at them. The unfairness of it: here the two of us were onto a truly significant piece. But only a miserable slot for it in the book. The art department would completely misjudge the heft of it and play it like a light piece. It was splendid training. Since then, I've always been armored by the knowledge that they—editors, art people, the whole lot—can screw everything up. Alas, you lose this fine suspicion when you turn to editing.

I was lucky in another respect: mostly, I was assigned cats and dogs, rejects, stories "for the bank" (i.e., never to be run). What I didn't get were stories of obvious importance, on clear-cut topics, and with an inherent structure. But there is a nice thing about cats and dogs—they are far more of a challenge than the sound kind, and when a good one comes along, it can be very, very good.

One day, Managing Editor Del Paine called me in. Would I like to do a story on the current college seniors? Someone at Yale had told him they were the best crop in years—wonderful for business. But nobody on the staff was interested, and Del was somewhat miffed. Would I take a crack at it?

Off I went. As I traveled from campus to campus, I was struck by the force of one refrain. It was not at all what we had expected. Get ready, the seniors were saying, for catastrophe. They were headed for business all right, but not because they liked the idea. They wanted a storm cellar for the great depression ahead. And so, on the verge of the greatest peacetime boom in history, the class of 1949 girded for the future, looking to big business for security. It was a big story, and it was ours for the asking. Readers were delightedly appalled; so were newspaper editorial writers. My generation was appalled, too; we went with big organizations but at least we talked individualism in our bull sessions.

I learned a lesson from this story. A good hypothesis is vital in a broad inquiry, but it does not matter if the hypothesis is wrong. In many instances, you have an even better story. The test of a hypothesis is not truth, but convenience. It helps you make some order out of a wealth of material, gets you a little closer to a truth that will always remain elusive. I belabor the point because I have found that it is the one younger research people tend to get hung up on. They seek the truth too much, and so display an unconscious arrogance. They nurse specific hypotheses when they should be ruthlessly abandoning them for others. As they will learn in time, good research is a trail of busted hypotheses.

Let me turn now to messiness. I learned the virtues of this from Gil Burck. I had admired the strong structure of his pieces, but I could not reconcile this with his working methods or his office. They were chaos: notes strewn over chairs, desk, and, floor. He did seem to know where everything was, however, and would fish out of a stack of papers in this corner or that just the right thing he wanted you to see. Gil liked to quote de Maupassant on style as the arrangement of relevancies, but he did not explain how his messiness was transmuted into such order.

In retrospect one learns that messiness is an absolute must in the early stages of a story, especially the broad kind in which the structure or line is very much up in the air. In some kinds of stories, particularly corporation stories, the structure often suggests itself. But in a story that sprawls over a large field, you must create the structure yourself. To do this you must amass huge amounts of material—interview notes, books, articles, morgue clippings, and stringers' reports. You cannot easily sort it out and file it, for you do not yet know what the relevancies are. The point is to *wallow* in the material, go back and forth over it, untidily, with speed, and with no inhibitions about structure and order. Time enough for that later. This early period is the creative one, and the faster and looser you go over your material, the more stimulated you will be. This is the time when you will be most fecund with ideas, when you will be scribbling notes to yourself, when you will see connections, or think you do, that stolid analysis would never suggest. Most will be wrong, to be sure, but one to two that are right can be the making of a story.

So stay loose. Before long, you won't be able to. As deadlines impend, you will be tightening up. As you approach the miserable task of writing, you will necessarily become more analytical, more critical, more concerned with pruning that accumulation. In the earlier stage, you were building up intellectual capital; now you are mining it. The two approaches are somewhat antithetical and you should keep this in mind. Some writers claim they do their best thinking when they are writing—that writing, after all, is rewriting. Maybe so, but I've found that if you're not in control of your material in the first draft, you probably never will be.

You do not need order so much as the appearance of order. I achieved this by filing the material in sets of folders with colored labels. (*Viz.*, Research Plan; Phase 1 exposition, and so on.) I usually refile all this constantly—it's one of those therapies so useful in delaying writing—and the show of system is a bit spurious. But it works.

A word about time. *Fortune* usually allowed extra time; but even so, it was to the writer's interest to use every stratagem to gain still more time. In primary research, you often don't see the real story until very late in the game; forced to deliver early, you'll go for the conventional. I remember a story I was doing on the new suburbia. At the end of some six weeks I was still floundering around and the only story I could have come up with then was one about an eastern development run along the lines of a cruise ship. It would have been amusing and informative, and that would have been about it. Luckily, I found I had been away from the office for so long that I wasn't missed. So I stayed away two more months, and ended up in a new town near Chicago that brought together a lot of strands and was the framework for a four-part series.

During the gestation period, it is important to stay away from the editor—for the editor's sake, too. Until a writer is sure of his material, the talking out will distress the editor, and it won't help the writer. When he was editor, Eric Hodgins recalls in his *A Trolley to the Moon*, he never encouraged a writer to talk much about the story when he returned from the field. "I actively discouraged it," he said, "unless there was an important problem to discuss. [I discouraged it] on the grounds that every time the writer described his story yet unwritten, he leaked some creative steam out of his own boiler. He also killed any sense of surprise in the editor."

Messiness and its kindred virtues are vital in determining what stories to undertake. If my recollection is correct, the best stories were rarely initiated by schedule meetings. The meetings were pleasant sessions, fine for the exchange of information, progress reports, and gossip. For incubation of half-formed ideas, they were very poor. Proposals that led to some of our best stories were repeatedly shelved by schedule meetings.

When such stories got done, it was often for secondary reasons—to humor a writer for example, and let him get some pet obsession out of his system. It was not for nothing that many *Fortune* writers developed powerful neuroses, nor that editors developed considerable deftness in handling them. The neuroses were occupationally useful and could usually be cleared up by letting the writers do what they had wanted to do. Thus, many a story was seemingly self-scheduled, a regular assignment being loosely enough framed to permit the writer to put the telescope to the wrong eye and go off on his own tack. *Fortune* apocrypha are full of such tales.

The best stories come out of curiosity, and the exercise of it is particularly important in the development of series and single-subject issues. So is patience. The tendency of a schedule committee is to plan them all at once: to choose the topics, cast the writers, figure which niches might be filled by commissioning outside pieces. This is all very logical. It is all very logical for other magazines, too, and that is why so many cover stories are so alike.

The way to go about a series is to do the legwork before scheduling, a big chunk of it at least, and see where the trails lead. They are bound to turn up ideas no conference could ever anticipate. Here is the competitive edge. Nobody else is likely to be out looking, so if you go out and look, you will see something of value. Messiness, inadvertence, paranoia, time, benign neglect. They are the soundest path.

THE EXPLODING METROPOLIS

A farm in Pennsylvania's bucolic Brandywine Valley, 1957. In the background the subdivision of Foxcroft spreads outward from the city of Downingtown. (H. Landshoff, courtesy *Fortune*)

Urban Sprawl

Fortune, January 1958

One of Whyte's final contributions to *Fortune,* "Urban Sprawl" was reprinted in *The Exploding Metropolis* (1958), a collection of six *Fortune* articles about the American city and its possible futures. Whyte described the book, which he edited, as "a book by people who like cities." (One of those people was Jane Jacobs, whose article "Downtown is For People" evolved into her classic 1961 best-seller *The Death and Life of Great American Cities.* Jacobs inscribed a copy of her book, "To Holly Whyte, who had more to do with this book at a crucial stage than he probably realizes, but which I, at least, will always remember with gratitude.")

"Urban Sprawl" was, like so much of Whyte's writing, vigorously forward-looking. In Whyte's view, America faced pressing choices about decency, and "not to act now is to make a decision." In particular, he was concerned about the Federal Highway Act of 1956, whose frankly stated objective—"to disperse our factories, our stores, our people; in short, to create a revolution in living habits," in the words of its sponsors— prompted Whyte to remark that "the communities affected have little to say about the revolution." His warnings seem oracular in hindsight.

The phrase *urban sprawl* has since become part of the language, and the issues addressed in this article returned to national prominence on the cusp of the millennium. In 1999, Vice President Al Gore made it known that anti-sprawl initiatives such as open space preservation and reduction of traffic congestion would form an important part of his platform in the 2000 presidential race. At first, Gore's critics derided him for pursuing "local" issues in a national forum, but the statistics suggest otherwise, as is clear from a U.S. Department of Agriculture report, cited in *Harper's* magazine in June 1999, which estimated that the U.S. had lost an average of one million rural acres to urban sprawl every year since 1970.

In the next three or four years Americans will have a chance to decide how decent a place this country will be to live in, and for generations to come. Already huge patches of once green countryside have been turned into vast, smog-filled deserts that are neither city, suburb, nor country, and each day—at a rate of some 3,000 acres a day—more countryside is being bull-dozed under. You can't stop the progress, they say, yet much more of this kind of progress and we shall have the paradox of prosperity lowering our real standard of living.

With characteristic optimism, most Americans still assume that there will be plenty of green space on the other side of the fence. But this time there won't be. It is not merely that the countryside is ever receding; in the great expansion of the metropolitan areas the subdivisions of one city are beginning to meet up with the subdivisions of another. Flying from Los Angeles to San Bernardino—an unnerving lesson in man's infinite capac-ity to mess up his environment—the traveler can see a legion of bulldozers gnawing into the last remaining tract of green between the two cities, and from San Bernardino another legion of bulldozers gnawing westward. High over New Jersey, midway between New York and Philadelphia, the air traveler has a fleeting illusion of green space, but most of it has already been bought up, and outlying supermarkets and drive-in theaters are omens of what is to come. On the outer edge of the present Philadelphia metropolitan area, where there will be one million new people in the ten years ending 1960, some of the loveliest countryside in the world is being irretrievably fouled, and the main body of the suburbanites has yet to arrive.

The problem, of course, is not an absolute shortage of land. Even with the 60-million increase in population expected in the next two decades, America's 1.9 billion acres of land will be quite enough to house people, and very comfortably. It will not be enough, however, if land is squandered. It is in the metropolitan area that most people are going to be living, and the fact that there will remain thousands of acres of, say, empty land in Wyoming is not going to help the man living in Teaneck, New Jersey.

The problem is the pattern of growth—or rather, the lack of one. Because of the leapfrog nature of urban growth, even within the limits of most big cities there is to this day a surprising amount of empty land. But it is scattered; a vacant lot here, a dump there—no one parcel big enough to be of much use. And it is with this same kind of sprawl that we are ruining the whole metropolitan area of the future. In the townships just beyond today's suburbia there is little planning, and development is being left almost entirely in the hands of the speculative builder. Understandably, he follows the line of least resistance and in his wake is left a hit-or-miss pattern of development.

Aesthetically, the result is a mess. It takes remarkably little blight to color a whole area; let the reader travel along a stretch of road he is fond of, and he will notice how a small portion of open land has given amenity to the area. But it takes only a few badly designed developments or billboards or hot-dogs stands to ruin it, and though only a little bit of the land is used, the place will *look* filled up.

Sprawl is bad aesthetics; it is bad economics. Five acres are being made to do the work of one, and do it very poorly. This is bad for the farmers, it is bad for communities, it is bad for industry, it is bad for utilities, it is bad for the railroads, it is bad for the recreation groups, it is bad even for the developers.

And it is unnecessary. In many suburbs the opportunity has vanished, but it is not too late to lay down sensible guidelines for the communities of the future. Most important of all, it is not too late to reserve open space while there is still some left—lands for parks, for landscaped industrial districts, and for just plain scenery and breathing space.

The obstacles? There are many local efforts by private and public groups to control sprawl and save open space. But each group is going at the problem from its special point of view, indeed without even finding out what the other groups are up to. Watershed groups, for example, have not made common cause with the recreation people or utilities; farmers and urban planners have a joint interest in open space, but act more as antagonists than as allies—and all go down to piecemeal defeat.

It is going to take a political fight to bring these groups to focus on the problem, and the sooner begun the better. Many planners feel they should work first for a master government to deal with all the problems of the metropolitan area—or, at the very least, a master plan—educate the people into supporting it, then apply it to such particulars as land use. This is very orderly and logical; the trouble is the land may be gone before it works.

The proposal to be presented here is based on a more pragmatic approach. It is to look at each of the different self-interests involved—such as those of the farmers, the utilities, the communities—and see what kind of plan would best unify them. Such a program will involve compromises, but it can produce action—and action that may well galvanize the whole regional planning movement.

•

The farmers are in the pivotal position: not only do they own most of the desirable open land left in and near the metropolitan areas, they happen to have a disproportionately strong voice in the legislatures of even the most urban of states. They are, furthermore, themselves beginning to get interested in some sort of open-space plan, and while very few of them lie awake nights worrying over how it might benefit their city cousins, there is a real possibility that for once the rural bias of state legislatures may work out to the good of the cities.

Consider Santa Clara County, California. Nowhere has the collision between farm and city been so visible, and ultimately constructive. In 1945 it was a farm county, one of the richest in the nation, and in its fertile valley floor was 70 percent of the Class I farmland in the whole Bay area. From San Francisco, some thirty miles north, only a few homeseekers had come down, and urban development, as the map indicates, was concentrated in a few compact communities, notably San Jose.

Then, slowly at first, the new suburbanites began pushing down, and as the easy-to-develop sites in San Mateo County to the northeast were filled up, speculative builders began moving in on the valley floor. The pickings were excellent; the orchards had to be cut down, but the flat land was easy to bulldoze, and the farmers, dazzled by the prices offered—$3,000 to $4,000 an acre then—began selling off parcels quite readily.

The builders had no stringent zoning rules to contend with in the farm areas, and while FHA loan requirements made them follow tight specification for the houses themselves, they were not required to provide for park areas or school sites. And most didn't. For services, the developments looked to the nearest incorporated town, and with what to the farmers seemed infamous vigor, the towns began "strip-annexing" down county roads so that they could take in the subdivisions, send out the sewer lines, and, presumably, draw back a good tax return.

Retribution came fast. To their dismay, the farmers found that the tax assessor was raising the value of their land. The millage was going up too; the new families were mostly young people with lots of children to educate and not much money to do it with. Because of the checkered pattern of development, the land that remained was becoming more difficult to farm effectively. Much of the natural cover had been replaced by the roofs and pavements of the intervening subdivisions, and the storm runoff spilled onto the farmland. Worse yet, the suburbanites felt *they* were the injured parties; they didn't like to be wakened by tractors early in the morning and they objected vigorously to the use of sprays and

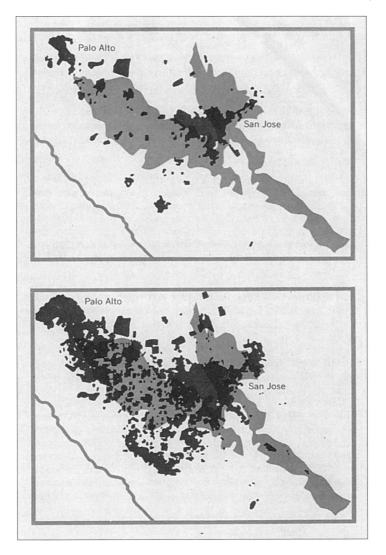

California Sprawl. Classic case of sprawl is shown in these maps of Santa Clara County, California. Top map shows urban development (dark) as it was in 1945. Lighter shaded areas indicate Class I agricultural land. By the end of 1956 (bottom map), developments were scattered all over it. Thanks to county action, however, one big patch of land was saved. This is the Berryessa agricultural zone just north of San Jose. The area, part of which is shown in the photograph, remains forbidden to developers.

smudge pots. Meanwhile, the water table of the valley was going down.

And the place looked like hell. "What happened to the land of heart's delight?" headlined the *Valley Farmer*. In a maze of signs and neon lights, the unspoiled country had almost disappeared. Some wealthy people picked up and moved farther away—with the speculative builders on their heels.

Being farmers, Santa Clara's farmers are strong-minded individualists, but as time went on they began taking an unusually keen interest in county planning. Fortunately, the county had a very able and vigorous planning director, Karl Belser; with the local Farm Bureau he and his staff conceived the idea of an exclusive agricultural zone in which developers could not set foot. The county supervisors approved the idea; and in 1954, at the petition of a group of pear growers, the first zone was set aside.

The municipalities remained a threat; they liked to annex and the county couldn't stop them. (In the dairy section southeast of Los Angeles, the farmers beat the municipalities at their own game. They incorporated themselves. Today there are three farm towns in the section—Dairyland, Dairy Valley, and Dairy City, now named Cypress. Though none has a main street to speak of, they have effectively zoned against subdivision and lighted signs; for services, they contract with the county.) Belser and the farmers went to see the state legislature at Sacramento, and in this friendly atmosphere persuaded the legislators to pass an interim law forbidding municipalities to poach. Today, looking down from the foothills, one can see several large areas of inviolate green—in all, some fifty square miles.

But zoning, as Belser notes, can only be a stopgap. While the farmer continues to pay relatively low taxes, the surrounding land keeps soaring in value, and so, potentially, does his own. What will happen when the land goes to $15,000 to $20,000 an acre? Farmers got the zoning approved; they can get it disapproved. The local Farm Bureau is quick to admit it, and now feels additional means must be sought to preserve farmland.

So, increasingly, do leaders of farm groups in other urban areas. They feel that more than self-interest is involved. Their argument, basically, is that the future food supply of the country is jeopardized by sprawl. Of 465 million acres of cropland in the U.S., only 72 million are in Class I land—and over half of this highly fertile Class I acreage is in urban areas. More U.S land can be converted to cropland, but it will not be so fertile—and it will certainly not be so close to the big city markets.

The argument is a good one, but the farmers will probably not get very far with it. Rightly or wrongly, many people believe that increasing farm productivity will ensure a plentiful food supply, and however strong the farmers' case, taxpayers are not likely to find it compelling. Coupled with other reasons for open space, however, the farmers' case can be quite effective. For then he doesn't have to push his argument so far; indeed, if the farmer does no more than demonstrate that it is not economically *harmful* to keep urban land in farming, he may provide the clincher to an open-space program.

The communities that have been annexing the farmers' land so voraciously suffer even more from sprawl. Where the new developments are scattered at random in the outlying areas, the costs of providing services become excruciating. There is not only the cost of running sewers and water mains and storm drains out to Happy Acres, but much more road, per family served, has to be paved and maintained.

Who foots the bill for the extra cost of services? Not the new people. Conventional tax practice spreads the load so that those who require the least services have to make up the difference. Where it will cost about $30 per household to furnish homes in town with water, it will cost about $80 to provide water to the outlying developments; since the water rate will be uniform, the townspeople have to make up most of the added cost.

For such communities industry could be a big help. Aesthetically, the campus-like industrial park is much more of an asset to a community than the usual tract development, and economically the advantage is greater yet. Fair Lawn, New Jersey, is a case in point. When the planners of Fair Lawn Industrial Park first broached the idea to the townspeople, a lot of them felt it would be much better to keep the area open for tract development. The 170 acres to be used for the tract would have accommodated 500 homes. These would pay about $350 a year each in taxes—and would require approximately $510 per year in municipal services and schools. Today the Fair Lawn Industrial District's fourteen plants return the community more than $450,000 a year in taxes and provide most of their own services. They look nice, too.

In most communities, however, zoning practices give industry the dirty end of the stick: the most suitable land is forbidden to it, and under the usual "cumulative" zoning, what land is left to industry means anything else *and* industry—with the frequent result that others come in first and spoil it for any company that may want to come in later.

Industry has far less freedom of choice than developers, for the site needs of an industrial district are fairly precise—access to railroads and highways, plentiful water, good utility service, and good drainage. Industry also has an equity in the whole environment of the community: more and more, plant-location people are thinking of what kind of place the community will be for employees, and the same sprawl that blights a community as a place to work blights it as a place to live in.

The utilities and the railroads suffer too. Sprawl has been nibbling away at so many industrial sites that some railroads and utilities have started advance land acquisition programs of their own: Cleveland Electric Illuminating Co., for example, has bought 2,000 acres on the outskirts of the metropolitan area and is holding it for future industrial use.

Sprawl also means low-volume utility operation for the amount of instal-lation involved. A square mile can accommodate, quite nicely, 2,000 dwellings and accompanying schools, churches, and neighborhood shop-ping facilities. Because of hit-or-miss development, however, a mile will more usually contain only about 200 small homes—and one-twentieth of the power demand.

The developer himself is hurt by sprawl. So long as there is no open-space plan, there is little assurance that Happy Acres is going to retain the ameni-ties the developers feature in their sales pitch. This may not be important for the hit-and-run builder, but it is very important for the big one. His rev-enue comes not merely from the sale of homes but from the prosperity of the shopping center, and he has a vested interest in the permanent charac-ter of the community. The huge suburb village of Park Forest, thirty miles south of Chicago, is a good case in point. Not only did the original plan leave provision for plenty of open space in the village; more to the point, the village was located on the edge of one of the Cook County Forest Preserves, and as developer Philip Klutznick points out, this has been one of the big plus values of the community.

A good open-space plan would undoubtedly preempt most of the easy-to-develop sites, and in many areas would force the developers to the hill-sides. Recent improvements in earth-moving equipment, however, have made hillside tracts more economical than once they were. Of necessity, Los Angeles builders have had to take to the canyons and the hills, and one of the most spectacular sights in the country is the way they are literally moving hills and terracing canyonsides for sites. This kind of development leaves some land in the valley worth looking at, and gives residents a much better place to look *from*.

Enlightened real-estate men are coming to feel that the old concept of "highest and best use" is outmoded. As generally used by realtors and appraisers, it means that the land has its highest and best use in terms of immediate dollars. Says Boyd Barnard, Philadelphia real-estate man: "Perhaps we may need to redefine 'highest and best use' in terms of suitability in the overall economic scheme of things, rather than the use which will produce the highest monetary return. A qualitative concept would preserve and create parks; the value of amenities for future generations resulting from proper planning in and around our growing metropolitan areas cannot now be measured."

Recreation groups cannot invoke the economic rationale, but their case for an open-space plan hardly needs it. The resort areas that once seemed such a change of scene to the city dweller are being enveloped by the metropolis. The banks of our rivers—assuming one would now want to swim from them—have been despoiled and our shorelines are going fast. In the whole stretch of Ohio's shoreline along Lake Erie, for example, practically no beach areas have been saved for the people. Along the Atlantic coast little free beach remains and the sewage outfalls gurgle ever more fetidly. Back in 1935 the National Park Service pinpointed twelve stretches that could be bought fairly cheap by the government. Only one stretch was bought; the National Park Service had no authority to buy land for new parks, and the legislation necessary for acquisition depends pretty much on local initiative.

On Cape Cod a magnificent stretch of open beach sweeps south from Provincetown some thirty miles to Eastham. It remains almost as it was when Thoreau walked along its dunes, and to many a New Yorker or Bostonian jaded by summer in the city, the sight of it is a wonderfully exhilarating experience. But it too will go. The National Park Service has made some gestures toward acquiring it, but all the effort seems to have accomplished is to stimulate local cupidities. At Highland Light, on the moors of Truro, the subdivision billboards are already up, and the old view will soon be gone. "And what pictures," Thoreau said of it, "will you substitute for that, upon your walls?"

The need for groups to join in common cause would be pressing in any event; what makes it truly urgent is the new highway program. Under the provisions of the Federal Highway Act of 1956, some 41,000 miles of new highway are going to be laid down, and the effect, as the planners of the act have frankly declared, will be "to disperse our factories, our stores, our people; in short, to create a revolution in living habits."

The communities affected, however, have little to say about the revolution; the act puts the program entirely in the hands of state engineers, and though they are supposed to hold public hearings, there is no provision that they must take any heed of what people say in the hearings. New rights-of-way, for example, will eat up a million acres of land. Yet the highway engineers are likely to favor precisely the land that planners would most like to keep untouched—park land in the built-up areas, flat or gently rolling land in the country.

Santa Clara County is again a case in point. No sooner had the agricultural zoning been put though than the local people found that the state highway engineers were planning to lay a new highway right in the middle of the narrow floor in the southern part of the county. The county people pleaded with the highway department to put the route on the edge of the foothills; this would add a little more mileage to the route but it would save the valley for both agriculture and amenity's sake, and it would also make for a much more scenic route. The highway engineers are thinking it over.

But perhaps the most important feature of the new highway program will be the location of the interchanges, for these will be to the community of the future what river junctions and railroad division points were in the past. The interchanges become the node of new developments, and whatever ideas planners may have had for the area, the pressure of land prices can be an almost irresistible force for hit-or-miss development.

But there can be coordination between the engineers and city planners, and if there is, the highway program will be a positive force for good land use. Through "excess condemnation," rights-of-way can be made broad enough to conserve large areas of open space. The spacing of interchanges can also help preserve open space. At the very least the highway program has provided a deadline. The highways are going through whether the communities like it or not; there will be no chance of controlling their location unless the communities get together to secure a pattern of open space and orderly development.

What should the program be? Ironically, for the fundamentals of a workable plan, the best guide is not what is being done now but what was done. For there have been open-space programs in the past—brilliant ones—and unique as each may have been, together they provide several valuable lessons.

New York's Central Park. In 1844, William Cullen Bryant took a walk over the hilly countryside north of the city. It struck him that a large tract should be bought for a "central reservation" while land was still cheap, for eventually it would be surrounded by the growing city. He started to agitate for it. Ridiculous, said the *Journal of Commerce*: there is plenty of countryside for people to go out and see, so why pay for it? But the populace liked the idea; the politicians declared for it, and in 1856 it became a reality.

Cook County Forest Preserve. In the early 1900s a group of Chicago citizens conceived the idea of buying up large tracts of land in the country around Chicago for the enjoyment of present and future generations. In short order they lined up public support, and after several rebuffs in the courts, the Forest Preserve was finally established. Promptly it started buying land. Today there are 44,000 acres in the preserve, valued at $150 million, and Superintendent Charles Sauers is still buying land—at a rate of 1,000 acres a year. (Because there are few places left these days where young couples can be alone, the thoughtful Sauers keeps the preserve open until eleven at night. Park rangers see to it the couples are not molested.)

Cleveland Park System. William Stinchcomb, father of Cleveland's superb park system (which embraces some 14,000 acres of natural woodland), delighted in horrifying visiting planners by telling them how be planned the system. He got the idea one weekend, sketched it out on a piece of paper—then spent the next thirty years filling in the purchases.

Westchester County Park System. Back about 1900 a private citizen named V. Everett Macy took a horseback ride along the Bronx River Valley and was appalled by the maze of shanties he saw. A group of millionaires had just built a private road on Long Island, and it occurred to Macy that it would be a good idea if a scenic road bordered by trees and meadows were built along the Bronx River. After some badgering, the state legislature set up a commission to acquire the land (New York City was to foot 75 percent of the bill, Westchester County the rest). The parkway was put through, and though a few towns along the route chiseled some of the parkway's land, it remains a delight.

A little later, political boss William Ward, who seems to have run Westchester County on lines drawn up by the Pharaohs, was sitting on a park bench—one of Stinchcomb's parks in Cleveland, it so happened. He spied a "Keep Off the Grass" sign. This annoyed him. He began to ponder how little grass there would be for Westchester County people to enjoy if a lot of land wasn't bought up quickly. On his return, he set up the Westchester County Park Commission, and instructed it to buy up waste land. As to how it would be used, he said, they could worry about that later. Eighteen thousand acres were picked up this way, and today they constitute, save for golf courses, about the only open space in the most populated section of the county.

Ohio Conservancy District. After the great flood of 1913, businessmen of Dayton, Ohio, decided something ought to be done. With their own money, they brought in consultant Arthur Morgan. Morgan concluded that the flooding problem couldn't be solved by local reservoirs or channels; instead, he proposed that a district be set up covering the whole watershed area. Its powers would include taxation, eminent domain, and the right to issue bonds. The businessmen got the enabling legislation passed by the legislature in 1914. With no funds from the state, the group built five dams and started acquiring land for flood control and recreation purposes. Before long, similar districts were set up throughout the state. The district form still has some legal bugs in it, but there are a score of lakes that never existed before, and thanks to the land-acquisition program, plenty of recreation land around them for people to enjoy.

The Boston Metropolitan Park System. Under the leadership of Charles Eliot, landscape architect, the cities and towns around Boston got together in 1893 to establish "reservations" on the outskirts of the built-up area— the Blue Hills Reservation and Middlesex Fells Reservation were acquired, but urban sprawl has now extended around and beyond them. A year ago the Massachusetts General Court approved a new project for "The Bay Circuit"—a belt of open spaces some twenty miles from the State House, with proposed reservations, forests, and parks separating metropolitan Boston from Lawrence, Lowell, Worcester, and Providence. The state has been authorized to proceed.

There seem to be four clear lessons. (1) Getting something done is primarily a matter of leadership, rather than research. (2) Bold vision, tied to some concrete benefit, can get popular support fairly quickly. (3) The most effective policy is to get the land first and rationalize the acquisition later. (4) Action itself is the best of all research tools to find what works and what doesn't.

There is no reason why there cannot be action now. Recently, *Fortune* and *Architectural Forum* brought together a group of nineteen experts for a two-day conference on urban sprawl.[1]

They came to agreement on the elements of a program that is simple, economic, and politically workable. It uses existing legislative devices, including one rather ingenious one that costs remarkably little. It would not demand the creation of a new level of metropolitan or regional government, and it could be in operation in one year. Here are its provisions:

First, land must be bought and it must be bought by an agency with the power and the funds to do it. This means the state government. The state could pass on its powers—to a metropolitan agency, for example—but it is a going concern and the process of setting up a special district "authority," however desirable it might be later, is not prerequisite. Nor is it necessary to set up a new department in the state government. In some states, it might be preferable to set up a specific land agency, but in most states it probably makes more political sense to use whatever department already has the most *de facto* powers, or to merge several agencies.

So far as funds are concerned, the state is the logical source. Since the open spaces are for the use of the people in the whole metropolitan area as well as the immediate locality, the fact that the funds will be coming out of general revenue means a more equitable assessment of costs. The state, furthermore, can often tap special funds; in California, up to $12 million of the state's income from offshore gas and oil leases can be earmarked for the purchase of recreation areas; similarly, in Pennsylvania all the revenues from oil and gas leases on state-owned land, now about $4 million a year, is allocated to the Secretary for Forest and Waters for reclamation and conservation purposes.

Most states already have the necessary machinery for acquiring the land. The No. 1 tool, of course, is outright purchase, with the right of eminent domain available when needed. Outright purchase is obviously appropriate for land that is desirable for an immediate, specific need, such as park space or beaches, and where funds are ready to develop it. For the more outlying areas, the state could do as it has done for the future highway rights-of-way: through "advance land acquisition" it can buy areas and then lease them until they are needed.

What may be an even more useful tool, however, is the purchase of development rights. The state doesn't buy the land but merely buys from the owner an easement—that is, the right to put up developments of any type or billboards. By not exercising the right, the state keeps the land open. The farmland remains in cultivation, and quite aside from the food produced, this is important to the suburbanite. Valuable as landscaped park land may be, the kind of surroundings that most delight many suburbanites are the less antiseptic kind afforded by well-run farms—meadows, cornfields, pastures, well-contoured hillsides, and those disappearing sights, the brook and the spring.

Though the state can use eminent domain to acquire the rights, the landowners should get quite a fair price; in exercising their right to have the price determined by condemnation proceedings they may get, if anything, too much—particularly in areas where developers are already waving dollars bills at the farmers. In outlying areas, however, the rights should be much less dear; and the farmer should find an immediate payment now more attractive than waiting ten years—and paying taxes ten years—for a killing that may or may not materialize. (In California the Navy has been purchasing development rights around airfields in farm country for $15 an acre.)

Another kind of land ideal for purchase of development rights is the golf course. Because of the pressure of land values on local taxes, many golf courses have been plowed under by subdivisions, whereupon local residents realize that though they never used it themselves, the golf course made a nice part of their scenery. If a golf club were able to sell its development rights, the money would remove the immediate pressures on the golf club to sell the land, and if the club is given adequate tax protection, the long-run pressures should be removed as well.

While purchase must be the core of an open-space program, a surprising amount of land, or the development rights to it, can be got free. There are people who love their land, and because they do they would like others to enjoy it when they have gone. Given some sort of machinery—and a little salesmanship—many a landowner can be persuaded to deed his estate to the community, or give it now with the proviso that he can stay on it as long as he lives.

A good example of what can be accomplished by vigorous solicitation is provided by the Massachusetts Trustees of Reservations. In 1891 a group of spirited citizens, with enough foresight to be alarmed even then, put on a vigorous campaign of persuasion, and got many people to donate tracts. Today it has 4,330 acres in thirty different areas, including many historic sites that otherwise would have been long since overrun.

Supplementing all of these acquisition measures, there should be revision of conventional tax practice. If a man keeps his land open by giving his development rights to the community, or selling them (and paying a capital-gains tax), it is patently unfair to tax him at the going rate for developed land. Since property taxes are usually based on market value of the acreage, there would have to be a change in tax-assessment policy. Those who have given up their development rights should have their land assessed at a lower rate than those who have not. In the long run this should involve no loss to the community; the open space afforded would make the surrounding land more valuable, and in time the community's total tax base should thereby be increased.

The state agency should have a first-rate planning staff of its own, but it should work as closely as possible with the local communities; though few have open-space plans, the existence of a state program should be quite a prod. The open-space program should also spur interstate planning groups in the metropolitan areas that cover two or more states. The many federal activities that affect open space—such as the military's voracious land-purchase program, the National Park Service's weak one—will probably never be coordinated, but a strong state agency could help see to it that the activities fit together somewhat better than they now do.

The selection of the land should not be unduly time-consuming. Obviously, some sort of master plan for the region is necessary, but this doesn't have to be set up in great detail before land is purchased. In urban areas relevant data—on drainage, soil classification, and such—already exist, and if past efforts are any criteria, some good energetic walking can accomplish wonders. For $10,000, estimates Henry Fagin, planning director of the Regional Plan Association of New York, the major open-space needs of the New York metropolitan region could be drafted in two months (though it might cost an extra $50,000, he adds, for a detailed study to prove it to the skeptical).

Time is a critical factor; if purchase of development rights is started now, considerable tracts of land can be preempted for open space at a fraction of the price that would be asked later. Only a relatively small acreage, furthermore, is needed for an effective open-space plan.

In Montgomery County, Maryland, for example, on the fringe of the Baltimore-Washington metropolitan area, 330 of the county's 494 square miles remain open farmland. The farmland now sells for about $500 per acre. If action were taken today, the framework of an open-space program could be established with the purchase of a few strategic stream valleys and hillsides totaling about eight square miles, or less than 2 percent of the county. Cost: about $2,500,000. (Minimum cost of building two miles of expressway: $2 million to $2,500,000.)

•

Bargain or no bargain, the program is going to take money. Some people are tempted by the idea that an open-space program could be painlessly achieved by relying entirely on the use of the community's police power—such as zoning or the "official map." Both measures have usefulness, of course, but strong local commercial or political pressures can break them down and, more to the point, they can be quite inequitable. Without having to put up any money, for example, the local government can, in theory, prevent a landowner from further development of his land by marking it on an official map as a future park or recreation area. But unless the community buys the land within several years—and gives the owner tax relief until then—property rights will have been undermined. Potential buyers become wary, and, in effect, the owner suffers condemnation without compensation. If an open-space program is to succeed, it must be made clear that it is essentially conservative; that its basic purpose is not to destroy property rights but to enhance their ultimate value.

Open spaces, of course, are only one part of a decent pattern of metropolitan land use; just as important is what happens to the land in between, and complementing any open-space program must be a strong effort to make development orderly in the unopen spaces. There must be, for one thing, tighter control over subdivision. At present, most of the communities on the fringe leave things pretty much up to the developer, and the result is often a crazy patchwork of street layout without any provision for parks or school sites.

Minimum-lot zoning, useful as it may be for a particular neighborhood, provides no real defense against sprawl. The great bulk of new inhabitants pressing outward from the city are middle-income people who can't afford half-acre and one-acre lots, and the U.S. has made so many of them they simply can't be dammed up. The mass developers leapfrog over pockets of resistance, and instead of an orderly, compact growth outward from a community, the entire buffer area of woods and farms that people took for granted becomes spattered with tract housing. The community does not get penetrated; it gets enveloped.

The problem is how to achieve an economically high density in developed acres and at the same time more amenable surroundings for the people in them. More control over the *location* of subdivisions is needed, and this means more coordination between the public agencies, such as the sanitary boards, whose permits are needed for development. Utilities would have good reason for cooperating in such a program.

Nor need the layout within new developments be left entirely to the whim of the builder. As Philadelphia has demonstrated, the community government can benefit both the builder and the home owner if it demands a configuration of streets that is at once comely and easy to service, and demands that open spaces for school and park sites be provided. Does the idea sound too advanced? Turn to the fifth chapter of Isaiah, written some twenty-six hundred years ago: "Woe unto them that join house to house, that lay field to field, till there be no place, that they may be placed alone in the midst of the earth!"

Of first importance, however, is the job of preempting open space, for the opportunity is a fleeting one. Before very long the millions born in the post-war baby boom will be coming of age, and as they swell the ranks of home-seekers, suburbia will expand as never before. By that time it may be too late; just in the next few years the highway program will be opening up hundreds of square miles to development, and land that now can be had for $500 an acre will come dear—if it is available at all. Yet the highway program also furnishes a great, if fleeting, opportunity; its new rights-of-way and interchanges will set the basic structure of the metropolitan areas of the future, and whether those areas will be livable will depend on the foresight of the communities involved as much as it will depend on the engineers. If the communities agree now on a rough idea of what kinds of areas they would like them to be, the highway program can become as asset instead of a hazard.

In any kind of general planning, there are pitfalls. The open-space proposal presented here, although essentially a conservative one, can raise the specter of a small group of central planners laying down antiseptic green belts and deciding where people ought to live whether or not they like the idea. But it would never work this way; an open-space program is not itself a plan, but a tool by which communities can do together what they cannot do individually; a state agency will be needed to give coordination—and money—but no plan will succeed unless it expresses the wishes of the communities and the people who lead them.

Certainly there are plenty of civic organizations whose energies can be harnessed—watershed councils, the Isaak Walton League, the Audubon groups, Chambers of Commerce, the League of Women Voters, the garden clubs. They have not yet been persuaded of their mutual interests, but once they are they will become a pressure group of great effectiveness.

The critical factor, to repeat, is time. We have an option, but it is a forced option: *not* to act now is to make a decision, and we cannot, as William James remarked, wait for the coercive evidence. Planners can help, so can more studies. But citizens must not merely acquiesce; it is they who must seize the initiative. Their boldness and vision will determine the issue.

From *Securing Open Space for Urban America: Conservation Easements* (1959)

This so-called technical bulletin of the Urban Land Institute was the fruit of Whyte's year-long leave of absence from *Fortune* (to which he did not return). Some general results of his findings in this study found a national readership in *Life* magazine ("A Plan to Save Vanishing U.S. Countryside") and again in *Reader's Digest*. A less technical discussion of easements can be found in the chapter from *The Last Landscape*, which follows on page 159.

FOREWORD

The purpose of this report is to be of some help to those who want action to save open space. There is in it no exposition on urban sprawl, why it is bad and why we should do something about it. Nor is there full treatment of the best known tools for achieving open space, such as the out-right purchase of land, for example. These tools may not be used as well as they should be, but their availability hardly needs belaboring.

There is one tool, however, which may be of considerable usefulness, but which is not well known, and it is on this tool that the report concentrates. It is the purchase by a public agency of rights in land from private owners to insure the continued integrity of key open areas. Essentially, it is nothing more than the adaptation of the ancient common law device of easements, and in several areas legislation is already in existence authorizing the purchase of easements for open space purposes. So far, the tool has yet to be applied on any scale for the control of urban sprawl. Few officials realize that such a tool exists, and partly because of this there are many questions which cannot be answered—the reaction of the tax assessor, for example, is one that can be answered satisfactorily only when there is an actual program for him to react to.

Study of what we've learned so far, however, can at least take us part of the way. Thus this report. In it we have attempted an inventory of the most relevant precedents and have also attempted an inventory of the knottiest questions for the future, for there must be no blinking the fact that there are some knotty questions indeed.

The first version of this report was completed in August 1958. Since then many planners, officials, and legal experts have helped greatly with criticisms and suggestions. I have also profited by the further chance to talk with more landowners, civic groups, developers, and special interest groups of one kind or another, and to follow the trials and errors of a number of promising open space programs.

What I have learned convinces me that there is one overriding consideration for any open space program. It is, simply, that open space must be sought as a positive *benefit*. Open space is not the absence of something harmful; it is a public benefit in its own right, now, and should be primarily justified on this basis. Some may argue that I am merely concentrating on one side of the coin, and that the other would do as well. I do not believe so; the concept of a benefit has important legal and tax aspects, and it is critical to the problem of rousing real public support.

It is for this reason that we must look carefully to the law of eminent domain, and it should be stressed at the outset that the tool under discussion is an extension of eminent domain rather than the police power. This is not to deprecate the latter, which is tremendously important in any open space plan. But while the two powers complement each other, there is a fundamental distinction between them; the failure to see the limits of the police power, I submit, is the greatest ideological obstacle to successful action.

In many cases the community can properly use its police power to conserve open spaces—through the zoning of flood plains against development, for example. If the police power were the main tool, however, this would be to a large degree a negative way of securing open space; that is, the community would have to maintain that it is harmful to the public interest for development to take place in particular areas—so clearly harmful that the community has no obligation to compensate the owner for the rights taken away from him.

This is placing an intolerable burden on common sense, let alone the law—and the feelings of landowners. For if it is a benefit we are getting—if we want to keep a stream valley open because we *like* it—the law is very clear. We've got to pay for it.

We may buy the whole property. We may buy only one or more rights in it, as with an easement. In either event, and whether or not condemnation is used, the law of eminent domain applies. We must do it for a public purpose, and we must offer the owner fair compensation for what he is giving up.

Those who have been working for open space don't need to be told it's a valid public purpose. But will the courts? Will the public? We must go on faith a bit, but it will help if we also hammer at the positive with as much force as we can. It is for this reason, I am now persuaded, that "Development Rights," the working title of the original report, is not the best one. Several planners had argued that it would tend to confuse people and I now think they were right. Among other confusions, the term has suggested the procedure which the English have now abandoned as unworkable—that is, the purchase of development rights to whole areas rather than specific open spaces, and the use of the sale-back of rights to specify where development could take place.

More important, however, the term stresses what is to be avoided, rather than what is to be gained. What we're really after is conservation of things we value, and thus I have been trying the term "conservation easement." Another term may well prove better, but "conservation easement" has a certain unifying value: It does not rest the case on one single benefit—as does "scenic easement"—but on the whole constellation of benefits: drainage, air pollution, soil conservation, historic significance, control of sprawl, and the like.

Let me sketch briefly how the kind of open space program envisioned can achieve several important benefits at one and the same time. To conserve key portions of the countryside of an area—such as the heart of a stream valley—the public agency purchases away from landowners their right to develop it into a subdivision or splatter it with billboards. Except for the open space restrictions, the owner keeps full title to the land. The amount of land involved will probably be only a small fraction of the total; the idea is not to prevent development of an area, but to channel it; there will be plenty of room left for subdivisions—and the people in them will enjoy a better environment than otherwise would be the case.

The purchase of easements in fringe areas should be considerably less expensive than acquisition in fee. The land, furthermore, will be kept alive—in securing the land against subdivision, more than a negative thing is secured: not only can land be kept in productive farming, for example, but maintained as a scenic asset; by keeping the land in cultivation, furthermore, the easement tool can be of material help in any program of watershed control. Indeed, upon this latter need one could rest the major justification.

The purchase of "conservation easements" also can have a great pre-emptive value. There is, of course, no substitute for outright acquisition of land in fee simple for parks and other kinds of property the public is going to need. At the same time, however, easements can provide future options. Even though the community might not know now what its precise land use needs will be in twenty years or so, by the conserving of key open spaces it insures that it will have choices to make, and that the developer's bulldozer will not have gotten there first. As I will note later, however, this is a minor reason for securing easements: the main justification must be *present* benefits.

Easements may also break certain ideological blocks. They are ancient, they respect property rights, and are far less "socialistic" than many pro-grams which conservatives now sanction.

Why not go a step further, buy the land outright and then lease it back to the owner, or a new owner, subject to open space restrictions? In many cases, this procedure might be in order and it is notable that the California Easement Act (see appendix A) has a provision for sale and leaseback. The writer's opinion is that the easement is a more promising device for large scale conservation. Those who decry it as too limited a tool have many arguments on their side but when they demand public ownership of open space as the only real solution, I feel they are flying from current reality. If easements prove faulty, the effort will have taught us something but at least it is an effort that can be made: Now let's not ask for Utopia or bust.

Some people believe emphasis on any specific tool is premature; they argue that first priority must be given to the study and development of a regional plan and regional planning instrumentalities—only then, they contend, does discussion of specific ways and means become pertinent. It is true that we must have regional planning if any long range program is going to succeed. It is also true that the easement tool is only one of many—and possibly it will be of less importance twenty or thirty years hence than sale and leaseback, the use of subdivision controls, control of sewage and water lines, etc., to achieve the most economic and amenable pattern of development.

Yet the easement tool may prove an important catalyst. As an abstrac-tion, regional planning simply doesn't connect with most citizens. They know what is happening to the countryside, but so long as they see no prac-tical way of coping with it—and most of them don't—they will turn their eyes to the host of other problems pressing for their attention. But show them that there is a way—a practical one, in the here and now—and their attitude changes. They ask questions, sharp ones. They do care about what's happening, and once they see a real chance to do something effective, a support that otherwise would lie dormant can become aroused.

This report does not go into the technical details of land selection. It does not go into them because no research is needed to establish the ways and means that can be used. Indeed, there have already been a plethora of studies on open space needs, and with monotonous regularity these studies time and again identify certain key areas. (In the Southeastern Pennsylvania area, William Wilcox of the Greater Philadelphia Movement has pointed out, there have been since 1932 nine studies on land needs, seven of them on recreation and open space needs.) To be sure, not all of the plans have been well conceived for today's situation, but they do at least illustrate that there shouldn't be any great difficulty in figuring out which areas deserve top priority. For the long haul, there should be the kind of comprehensive planning which will make of open space selections, not isolated bits and pieces, but a framework which supports such other elements as industrial development, highways, and the like. This, certainly, will require a lot of work, and constant work too, for years to come. But let us not await the millennium. It will be extremely difficult to commit the sin of choosing too much open space in getting started (or at almost any other time, for that matter), and any planner who can't think now of some land worth saving ought to get into another line of work.

We need long range planning, but we need a little retroactive planning, too: let's save the best land as soon as we can, and then, at our leisure, rationalize with further studies how right we were to have done it. [. . .]

THE PRECEDENTS

Basically, the principle of eminent domain is simple. The public can acquire property if it will serve a public purpose and if the owner is given just compensation.[1] In acquiring property, the public does not have to buy all of it, but that element of it that will serve the public purpose. We are talking, then, about property *rights*. They are plural; economists and lawyers are now agreed that we should think of "property" not as the tangible thing owned, but as a composite bundle of rights—the right of the man to sell his property, to encumber it, to have his wife and children inherit it, to build upon it and to develop it.

The public can acquire these rights in land by gift, purchase by voluntary agreement, or by condemnation. It may buy the whole bundle of rights—that is, acquire the land in fee simple—or it may acquire less than the full bundle.

It is this latter aspect that we are concerned with, and in the form of easements it has been common practice for generations;[2] though the particular purpose for which the public acquires the easements has shifted, the basic principle involved has remained the same. Today, we have channel-change easements, slope and drainage easements, scenic easements for highway and parkway purposes, highway development rights, air rights, sight-distance easements, easements of view, building protective easements, and many others; whatever the variation, they are essentially a purchase from a landowner of one or more of his rights in land so that the public interest may be served without having to purchase the entire bundle. Such easements have had a statutory basis for many years and have been upheld by the courts as a valid exercise of governmental power in the public interest.

While in many states there already exists a statutory basis for purchasing easements for the purpose of securing open space, the urban sprawl problem is so new—or at least, seems to be so new—that there are few cases directly bearing on this kind of use. The Massachusetts legislature authorized the Boston Metropolitan Park Commission to acquire rights in land in the basic act of 1893, and in 1898 additional powers were granted "to acquire by agreement or otherwise, the right forever or for such period of time as said board may deem expedient, to plant, care for, maintain or remove trees, shrubs and growth of any kind within said regulated spaces [along or near rivers and ponds]." (Chapter 463, Act of 1898)

Back in the 1920s, a study for the park needs of the Washington, D.C., area recommended six methods for "withdrawing land from urban occupation"; one of them was the acquisition of rights in land, or easements, as well as outright purchase. In the Federal Rights in Land Act of 1928 (40 USC, Section 72A), Congress gave the National Capital Park and Planning Commission authority for such acquisition, and in the Capper-Crampton Act of 1930 authorized the spending of $32,500,000 for three kinds of parks and open space projects. In 1956, in the act establishing the Bay Circuit surrounding metropolitan Boston, the Massachusetts legislature authorized acquisition of a variety of rights in land in order to preserve open spaces.

But though the authority has existed, up until now park officials have not sought recourse to it, and have concentrated on the acquisition of land for parks. Since 1894, the tool of rights in land has been exercised only once in Massachusetts; this was by the Metropolitan District Commission to protect land lying along the Charles River Basin in Waltham (no shrubs may be removed or planted, nor may any physical changes be made in this area without the approval and consent of the Metropolitan District Commission). The Metropolitan Parks Commission has received a great many gifts in fee and in private lands from landowners, but to date has not used its power of eminent domain for this purpose. The National Capital Planning Commission has been studying several proposals that envision development rights purchase but have been concerned primarily with the task of park and parkway acquisition.

There is, accordingly, no case law bearing directly on development rights. There do not appear to be any judicial decisions construing the Federal Rights in Land Act of 1928; and nothing directly in point in the cases construing the various Massachusetts park laws (Chapter 463, Acts of 1898, found in Chapter 92, Section 79 of the annotated laws of Massachusetts).

At this point in time, then, it is to analogy we must look for the most relevant precedents. Here are some of the principal kinds of easements for which a successful body of experience exists:

(a) *"Scenic Easements" for Park Purposes.* Since 1933, the State of California, through its Department of Natural Resources (Division of Beaches and Parks) has from time to time acquired scenic easements from landowners immediately adjacent to state park units. The easement is a fairly standard one; the landowner grants to the state the scenic easement deed (see Appendix B for the form of agreement), by which he gives up the right to put up any buildings on the land without state approval, erect billboards, and the like.

While the state has not extended this easement principle to the acquisition of future park sites, the powers given are fairly broad. Under Section 5006 of the state's public resources statute, "The State Park Commission, through the consent of the Department of Finance, may acquire by purchase or by condemnation proceedings, brought in the name of the people of the State of California, title to or any interest in real and personal property which the Commission deems necessary or proper for the extension, improvement, or development of the State park system."

Somewhat similarly, the New York State Division of Parks has in a few cases acquired easements by appropriation (Section 676-A of the Conservation Law), to prevent the construction of commercial facilities opposite the entrance to state parks. (Since Section 675 of the Conservation Law prohibits use of signs and advertising structures within 500 feet of the border of any state park or parkway, scenic easements have not been necessary.)

(b) *"Scenic Easements" for Parkways.* In the building of our national parkways, notably the Blue Ridge Parkway and the Natchez Trace Parkway, scenic easements have been used to conserve sections of natural landscape along the rights of way. These are defined as "a servitude devised to permit land to remain in private ownership for its normal agricultural or residential use and at the same time placing a control over the future use of the land to maintain its scenic value for the parkway."[3] The National Park Service does not itself purchase the easements; this is done by the highway departments of the various states involved, but the Park Service, which eventually receives the deeds, does lay down the general standards to be followed. Currently, it asks a minimum right of way averaging 125 acres per mile in fee simple, supplemented by scenic easements where appropriate.

The device not only insures a natural landscape, it saves money on maintenance costs. Along the Blue Ridge Parkway there are some 177 scenic easements totaling 1,468 acres, most in grassland. Maintaining the grassland within the regular right of way costs the Park Service about $4.50 a year per acre; on the land covered by easements the farmers do it by continuing to farm, thus saving the Park Service some $6,100 a year. (To save more money yet, the Park Service is now applying a sort of reverse gambit also; for right of way it owns, it often gives a "special use permit" so neighboring farmers can use it for grazing or crops or such—they pay a small fee for the privilege, as well as relieve the Park Service of the $4.50 per acre maintenance cost.[4])

The Great River Road proposed by the states bordering the Mississippi is to make considerable use of easements. Instead of a continuous, and somewhat antiseptic, strip park, it will be a "living landscape of our life and industry—the vast wheat and cotton fields; the waving sugar cane and the pumpkins among the corn shucks; the cattle grazing in pastures; the hay stalks and corn cribs readied for winter, and always the ever-changing panorama of the mighty river."[5] (See diagram by National Park Service of a typical stretch of the Great River Road, showing complementary uses of fee simple and easements.)

(c) *"Scenic Easements" for Highways.* In New York State, to cite one example, it is the present policy of the State Department of Public Works to acquire easements restricting the erection of billboards on all controlled access state highways. (In the past such easements have had a width of 750

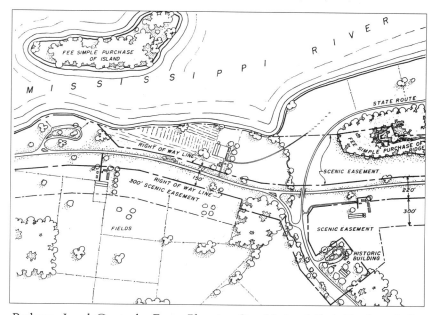

Parkway Land Controls. From *Planning Our National Park Roads and Our National Parkways* by Dudley C. Bayliss. Department of the Interior, National Park Service, 1957.

feet from the edge of the actual roadway. This policy is now going to be altered to take advantage of the new federal aid highway bill which the President signed April 16, 1958; this provides a financial incentive for states to acquire rights in strips 660 feet from the edge of the highway right of way.)

The New York State Thruway Authority, whose enabling legislation has a provision similar to Section 676-A of the N.Y. Conservation Law, has protected its right of way through a combination of police power and easements. Up to 500 feet from the edge of the roadway, signs are prohibited by the state's police power. Beyond this point the Thruway Authority has purchased in scattered areas 1000-feet easements from property owners to prohibit billboards. These were acquired at the same time as the rights of way.

(d) *"Right-of-Way Easements."* In addition to securing easements for billboard control, several states have also used them to conserve future rights of way at relatively low cost. In Wisconsin, such authority is to be found specifically in Section 84.105, Wisconsin statutes. Ohio, which has made considerable use of "reservation agreements" to protect rights of way, has no specific enabling legislation but has presumed the authority to exist in the general authority of the Department of Highways; since in specific statutes the department already has the power to acquire the entire bundle of property rights, it is presumed any lesser interest may also be acquired. Texas, which has used the easement devise under the name of "highway development rights," has a specific statute to this effect. California makes heavy use of easements both to prevent destruction of view and for the actual highway right of way; several thousands of California highways have been built on easements, and legally and economically it has worked out very satisfactorily.

(e) *"Airport Easements."* Another type of easement, for which a considerable body of experience exists, is the acquisition of rights in land from nearby landowners to assure an unobstructed path for landings on airfields. Under the federal airport program, all participating airports must provide for control over the "clear zone area" up to 2,700 feet by 1,000 feet. (Federal Airport Act, Public Law 377, 79th Congress, 1946)

(f) *"Easements for Water Control."* Many kinds of easements are used for this purpose. To conserve the sponge-like qualities of flood plains, for example, easements can be acquired to prevent building on them and, thus, a higher rate of run-off. By easements the public can also purchase the right to flood an area, or to discharge sewage effluent on it. Rates of compensation vary widely, depending to a great extent on the enjoyment of the land left to the owner.

THE PUBLIC PURPOSE

The precedents, then, are many. More than that, in different variants, the easement tool has been on the books for some time. We don't have to start from scratch; even without further legislation, much more use of the easement device could be made than now is the case; and while it is right to talk about new tools, it wouldn't hurt us to spend more time rediscovering what has already been given us.

That said and done, let us note that there are some definite advantages in tackling the problem the hard way. For if there is to be any really major program, it must be established for the public that open space is a benefit in its own right and not merely as an adjunct of some other established public program, as is the case with most present easements. Upon this proposition all else rests; it is not just a question of "selling"—for legal and tax reasons the case must be firmly documented, and the more homework done now, the less chance of critical setbacks later.

The best way to clear the easy hurdles may be to address ourselves to the toughest: justifying the use of condemnation. Some might wonder why so much stress is put on this contingency; gifts and negotiated purchase may well gain the bulk of the open space we want saved, and condemnation should be used very sparingly indeed, certainly so at the beginning of the program.

But eminent domain is an excellent discipline. We must prove that we have justification for using it; otherwise our lesser measures will be in jeopardy. This is so because the law of eminent domain applies to public purchases whether the owner wants to sell or not; whether it is by gift, or voluntary purchase, or by condemnation, when an agency of the public acquires a property, the purpose must be public. To put it another way, if we cannot establish that open space conservation is a public enough purpose to justify condemning an easement, we're going to have trouble justifying the public's paying money for it in any event. Even a gift of an easement does not allow us to sidetrack the issue; if a public agency is involved, it's got to be able to prove that a public purpose is being served. Sooner or later there will be a taxpayers' suit, and it is not difficult to imagine someone complaining that the public agency has no business accepting easements, let alone paying good money for them, since the whole idea is merely to help landowners dodge taxes.

How, then, do we define the public purpose? The law of eminent domain holds that the purpose of securing a property or a right in it must be public, and not primarily for a private interest only incidental to the public.[6] This does not mean that there is anything wrong if the landowner happens to benefit also; there is nothing in U.S. law that says someone has to suffer if the public is to gain.[7] Nor does it mean that the public has to have physical access to the property. In the past, some courts have taken a narrow view of what constitutes "use," but it is now generally held that the public can enjoy a benefit from the property without physically going on it.[8] To be on the safe side, however, it is important that we do not beg the question by failing to stress the positive benefits the public enjoys without access; the establishment of these—as is so admirably done in the opening section of the California bill—is the best way to avoid unnecessary troubles over "use." (Later I will take up the possibility of combining easements with provisions for limited physical use by the public, the right to fish in a stream, for example, that runs through a man's property. Suffice it to say now that the two benefits must be considered as separate, and not contin-gent. One thing at a time—the public gets a fair bargain when it gets a man to agree to keep his land open; if it wants to fish in his stream as well, that is another matter and it can't demand both benefits at the price of one.)

Who's to say what is a public use? The law is what common sense would indicate; in essence, it holds that something serves a public purpose if the public thinks so. This, in practice, means what the legislature says the pub-lic wants, and though the two are not always synonymous, the courts tend to go along; if the public through its elected representatives designates a public purpose to be served, the courts reason, this justifies exercise of the public's powers, so long as other constitutional requirements are met.

The courts' adjustment to new public needs may not be instantaneous, but they have shown much more flexibility than most laymen realize, and this is particularly true in connection with problems of urban growth. Compared to other extensions of eminent domain courts have approved, open space easements are relatively mild, if not antique. Consider, by con-trast, what public agencies have been doing under Title I of the Housing Act. They can take a man's property—all of it—and then resell it to some-body else, and at cheaper price, too. Not so many years ago the very idea would have been thought outrageous, unconstitutional, communistic; and so, indeed, it was. Now it's part of the status quo, for the public has real-ized the overriding need for such action if the larger community purpose is to be served.

It has been a far more drastic exercise of eminent domain than anything envisioned in open space conservation, but most courts have upheld it.[9] The most notable decision of all has been *Berman v. Parker*, 348 U.S. 26, 75 Sup. Ct. 98 (1954), in which the owner of a store, Samuel Berman, con-tended that the District of Columbia Redevelopment Land Agency was depriving him of his rights under the Fifth Amendment; his store wasn't hurting anybody, and here they were forcing him sell it so they could tear it down and sell the land to somebody else. On November 22, 1954, the Supreme Court upheld the Redevelopment Agency and the enabling act of 1945.

In delivering the majority opinion, Justice Douglas hauled off and took a resounding crack at the constricted view of the public welfare. He wrote:

The concept of the public welfare is broad and inclusive. The values it rep-resents are spiritual as well as physical, aesthetic as well as monetary. It is within the power of the legislature to determine that the community should be beautiful as well as healthy, spacious as well as clean, well-balanced as well as carefully patrolled. In the present case the congress and its authorized agencies have made determinations that take into account a wide variety of values. It is not for us to reappraise them. If those who govern the District of Columbia decide that the nation's capital should be beautiful as well as sanitary, there is nothing in the Fifth Amendment that stands in the way.

Let us now turn to the public benefits from open space. In a sense, they are indivisible, for an open space that serves one public purpose well will usually serve a number of others too. The aesthetic will probably be the basic motivating force, and thanks to the trend in court decisions, we need not be the slightest bit shy in affirming them. But solid economic and social benefits must be established also, and the more we go into them the more we realize how intertwined they are with the aesthetic. Let us run down the list briefly.

Water. Quite aside from any of the other benefits produced by an open space plan, it could be justified on the basis of watershed protection alone. In practice, a great proportion of the key areas that most people would agree should be conserved are likely to be stream valleys. Many people would not be thinking of the drainage and flood control aspect—but of the fishing and the swimming in the streams, or the beauty of the meadows, or the excellence of the farming, the contoured slopes that seem to go so well with the stream valleys.

Yet for the reasons these valleys are beautiful, they are tremendously useful. Like a great sponge, their flood plains temper the flow of the water downstream; the good soil practices of the farmers help keep down the silt that can be such a problem for communities and industries further downstream; because they have not been covered with asphalt, their runoff is much less; and when there is heavy rainfall, the streams and the creeks that flow into a natural storm sewer system are far better than anything constructed by man.

Agricultural land conservation. Closely related to watershed control is the problem of our declining supply of prime agricultural land. A heavy proportion of Class I land is located in the metropolitan areas. It is not the marginal farms that are sought after; it is the best kind of land that is most attractive to developers. Some farm people feel the argument for agricultural land conservation so compelling that they believe an open space program could be justified solely on this basis.

They have an impressive case, but in the writer's opinion farm groups are not going to get too far with the general public if they continue to go it alone. If my talks with non-farm people are any indication, the farmers' argument is not a persuasive one to lead off with; rightly or wrongly, many people think the farmers are getting away with murder as it is, and they have a vague idea that increasing mechanization, chemical farming, and such can easily compensate for the loss of acreage. They wouldn't be so sanguine if they studied the statistics thoroughly, but this is a chore they are not likely to undertake.

In making this qualification, I am not deprecating the cropland argument: I am merely suggesting that it does not become truly effective until the citizen sees his own equity in open space. Once he does, however, he can become quite receptive to the cropland argument. He now *wants* to believe it. For one thing, it helps neutralize his pessimistic assumption that maybe subdivision and commercial development is the "highest and best use" and that to think of saving farms in suburbia's path is being retrogressive and sentimental. He still may not really care about the farmers' problem, but their case now helps him prove to himself, and others, the economic soundness which his instincts impel him to. It's not necessary for him to agree completely with the cropland argument; what makes it important to him is its assurance that it won't be uneconomic to save farmland.

I have been speaking primarily of the citizens of the metropolitan areas, where the bulk of our population lives. When we turn to the citizens of our rural areas, however, the agricultural argument can be immediately compelling; and more to the point, in their hands it has a tremendous leverage. Urban planners have long lamented the lopsided way our legislatures overrepresent the rural interests, but as far as open space is concerned, this is not without some advantages.[10] If rural legislators perceive how an easement program can help their constituents, they won't have to be thoroughly sold on its benefits to the city; as a matter of fact, they're likely to see it as a defense *against* the city. If this sharpens their enthusiasm, so much the better.

Recreation. There can be no substitute for outright purchase of park lands, but easements can greatly complement—and protect—parkland, and they provide some definite recreation benefits of their own. Even if the public doesn't go onto the land itself, it can enjoy the fact of it; the drive through the countryside is enjoyable because there *is* countryside.

The existence of countryside—*some* countryside, at least—has considerable effect on any regional park system. Big parks are not so dependent on their surroundings, but smaller ones are; there is, for one thing, their water supply, and if their lakes and dams remain good to swim in, conservation of farmland upstream may have a lot to do with it.

It should also be pointed out that, while public use does not necessarily go with an easement, there are many opportunities for limited use. We tend to underestimate how much public recreation takes place on private land. In the course of making a movie record of the Brandywine area, I have been struck with how many people use the Brandywine and the land along it; at first sight you don't notice many people, but if you stay put in one spot only a few hours you'll bc amazed at how many canoers will pass by, how many people you'll see fishing whom you didn't spot at first. (I have also been amazed at how traveled are the back roads, particularly on weekends; and the number of picnics is awesome.) The landowners are very good about letting people go across their property, and the local sporting club, which has built "step-overs" to protect the farmers' fences, has posted the area with signs telling people to come and fish but to be sure to clean up any trash. As population mounts, landowners can't be expected to keep on providing free parks without a quid pro quo, but certainly there are ways to work out sensible agreements that will protect the landowner and compensate him for any increase in the burdens involved.

Control of sprawl. One of the great benefits of an easement program is that it provides a way of channeling metropolitan growth; it should be valuable, not just for the land it saves but also for the way it helps concentrate development in the land around. The economic benefits of this can be clearly demonstrated; the case against sprawl has been documented to a fare-thee-well, and though easements are only one of several tools that must be used, any brief for establishing the public purpose of easements should bear down heavily on sprawl.[11]

There are other points that should be made the relationship of open space to our air pollution,[12] for example, or how it can lead to a more economic spacing of highway interchanges. But in whatever order the arguments are advanced, they must be brought to focus on one simple clearly stated proposition: that open space is a public benefit in its own right. This is the critical part of any legislation, for it is the rock on which favorable court "construction" and tax decisions can be based.

The California Act does this superbly (see appendix A), but one passage deserves quotation now:

The legislature finds that the rapid growth and spread of urban development is encroaching upon, or eliminating, many open areas of varied size and character, including many having significant scenic or esthetic values, which areas and spaces, if preserved and maintained in their present open state, would constitute important physical, social, esthetic or economic assets to existing or impending urban and metropolitan development.

As if this isn't touching all bases, later, in defining open spaces, the Act goes on to say that these areas "would enhance the present or potential value of abutting or surrounding urban development, or would maintain or enhance the conservation of natural or scenic resources."

Before concluding this section on the public purpose, let us consider one other potential benefit: *the reservation of future options*. In conserving open space by easements, we may have a relatively inexpensive way of reserving land, even though we may not be sure at the time exactly what future use the community might need to make of it. In the case of a possible park, for example, the community could lose nothing by securing an easement on suitable land; if subsequently, the community decided that a park was desirable, then it would still have to pay for the land, but the easement would have insured that the land remained open and that there would be the choice to make.

This is an attractive argument, but the writer has come to believe that it can be a dangerous one too. There must, of course, be an opportunity for the public to adjust to changed conditions, and in a later section we will take up the advisability of reversionary clauses, the question of subsequent condemnation by another public body, and such. But valuable as easements might be in giving us future choices, to stress this is to stress the hypothetical and thereby to undercut the force of the major argument. To repeat, open space must be established as a benefit in its own right and a benefit *now*. For another thing, landowners might reasonably become suspicious that the authorities were using the device as a back door to make sure they'd get the land later for a park. Do they want me to keep my land open for the reason they say they do, he may well ask, or are they buying time at my expense? We should take care that the issue is not clouded by the hypothetical. Present use is the best yardstick, legally, politically, and otherwise. In selecting land, and advocating a program for doing it, the key question is not what open space might provide but what it does provide.

It should not follow from this that the land must be frozen, or that easements cannot be used to prepare for future conditions. Take, for example, the advisability of reserving land for reservoirs that may be needed in 1990 or 2000. Planners in the Delaware River basin area have just such a problem, and they are studying the applicability of the easement device. One question has been that of futurity: would the courts approve the acquisition when the needs are so far off in the future? Whatever the answer to this question, it might well be possible to justify the acquisition to the courts on the basis of present benefits. Even if the reservoirs were never built, the existence of these open areas might serve a readily perceivable public purpose in water retention, silt control, recreation, or whatnot. The wording of the California Act again comes to mind. If there's a good piece of open space which we can't find some reason for saving for the here and now, we have lost our capacity for invention.

While the matter of futurity is tangential to our main case, it should be noted that courts and legislatures have been looking with increasing favor on advance land acquisition. In seventeen states there are now statutes specifically authorizing land acquisition for possible future highway use. In most cases, the authority is granted to the state highway departments, in several instances to a specific state authority, and in one instance, to counties. In five additional states there is legislation which seems to imply that there is authority to acquire land for future highway use (North Carolina, Oregon, Tennessee, Texas, Washington). Most of the statutes run for only a relatively short time.

Even though there had not been specific legislation authorization, in at least six states the courts have sustained the acquirement of lands for future highway use (Arkansas, prior to its law, Illinois, Iowa, Kansas, Mississippi, Missouri), and the Delaware high court has approved the concept in principle. Aside from highways, acquisition for future use has been authorized or sanctioned by the courts for a series of other public needs. These have involved schools, waterworks, railroads. Some of these date back to the 1800s, so that precedent of long standing is involved.

To sum up: the cardinal requirement of an open space easement is that it provide a public benefit. It may provide future benefits not yet clear, but though the courts are becoming more liberal on this score, it is not necessary to justify open space on what it might do; we have abundant reasons to show that it is a benefit now, and it is this proposition that we must put before the public.

How do you convince the public that open land is a benefit—particularly when it remains in private hands? Many landowners and citizens ask this question, and though they say they recognize the benefit, they're still not sure the public at large will. May not the public look on the whole thing as a tax dodge?

It is true, unhappily, that people most readily recognize a benefit only when it is being taken away from them. About the time an open space is threatened—whether by a highway, a subdivision, or one of the many crews of tree cutters that seem to be everywhere these days—the public begins to get aroused. At this very moment, undoubtedly, there are scores of protest meetings over outrages to be committed—and if events run true to form, the outrages will be committed just the same.

Outrages do have their usefulness: one of the reasons why Monterey County citizens girded for action on open space was the sight of a hilltop being chopped up for a highway cloverleaf, and the smoke of burning stumps ("funeral pyres," as one citizen put it) roused many tempers to a high pitch. Question: but is there not some way to dramatize a benefit *before* it is too late? Some vigorous showmanship might accomplish a great deal.

Let me illustrate with an outrageous scheme I heard put forward. A large landowner was complaining that though the hills of his land made the view for miles around, people would begrudge him any tax concession if he gave up an easement; they took his land for granted. Someone came up with this idea: rent a large neon sign, transport it up the highest hill, then, at dusk— just as householders were contemplating their blessings over cocktails on their terraces—turn the thing on. In short order, hundreds of angry people would be on the phone. The landowner would agree with them: yes, it was a shame and he hated to do it. But, after all, he had children to educate, and he just couldn't turn down the money. "Perhaps," he might go on, "they could work out a compromise." If all the landowners who enjoyed the view would chip in enough to make up for the money the sign people would pay him, then he could afford to keep the hills open. The cost, spread among so many people, would only come to a dollar or so a year for each household. Was the view for which they built their picture windows and their terraces worth a dollar?

The suggestion was facetious, but the basic principle is there. The public has an equity in the open spaces it has long taken for granted; if it is to be persuaded to preserve this equity, the fact of it must be graphically and forcibly demonstrated.

From *The Last Landscape* (1968)

Whyte was a prominent spokesman for a growing movement to cope intelligently with the outward march of suburbia into the open spaces of rural America. *The Last Landscape* was accurately described by *The Washington Post* as "a practical handbook for all who care enough to fight for a more liveable environment." Addressed to the nonspecialist and infused with empowering optimism (as well as urgency), the book provides both compelling reasons and practical tools for preserving the nation's open spaces.

Whyte's discussion of easements, reprinted below, remains perhaps the clearest discussion of this vital conservation tool ever addressed to the lay reader. The chapter entitled "Cluster Development," also reprinted below, is based on Whyte's monograph of the same title published in 1964 by the American Conservation Association. In his introduction to that book, Whyte characterized the cluster concept as a "counter-revolutionary movement" based on an ancient idea: "It is the principle of the early New England town; it is the principle of the medieval village; it is, in fact, the basic principle of community design since we first started building several millennia ago."

"The New Towns" is a cheerful broadside against the aseptic concept of pre-planned—"suburbias without a city," which Whyte rebuts not least on the grounds that messiness and sin have been eliminated from them. "The Case for Crowding" addresses the question why so many of our high-density neighborhoods are the most sought-after. Whyte's answer—that "concentration is the genius of the city, its reason for being"—anticipates a main theme of his later writing, namely, that "what attracts people most, it would appear, is other people (page 256)."

EASEMENTS

In discussing gifts and purchases of land, we have been talking largely of the fee-simple acquisition. This is the clearest and surest way to save land, but it can take us just so far. The number of landowners who can afford to give away their land is limited, and though more should be walked up the mountain, only so many will go along. Nor can we buy up the land. There is not enough money. Even were public acquisition funds tripled, they would fetch only a fraction of the landscape. If we did have the money, furthermore, what would we do with all this land? How would we maintain it?

But we do not need to buy up the land to save it. There is a middle way. Through the ancient device of the easement, we can acquire from an owner a right in his property—the right that it remain open and undeveloped.

To understand the device, let us go back to the origin of the term "fee simple." In medieval times, a great lord would grant a man a tract of land to use in return for which the man would be obligated to perform certain services, or fees. The land with the fewest strings attached—the simplest fee, you might say—was the closest to outright ownership. But there were always strings.

There still are. The fee simple has never been absolute or indivisible, nor, laissez-faire economics to the contrary, have landowners inherited license to do anything they please with the land. What the landowner has is a bundle of rights—the right to build on the land, for example, or the right to grow timber on it, or to farm the land. Some rights he does not have: his riparian rights to a stream running through his property may not include throwing a dam across it. All of his rights, furthermore, are subject to the eminent domain of the state.

When we wish to acquire a man's property, we usually buy the whole bundle of rights from him—the fee simple. But we can buy less. To achieve a particular purpose, we may only need one or a few rights in the property. We buy these, in the form of an easement, and leave the rest of the bundle with the owner.

One class of easements is positive; that is, we acquire the right to do something with part of the man's property. A public agency may buy a right of way for a public footpath or a hiking or bicycle trail; it may buy the fishing rights so the public may use the banks of a stream. Utilities may buy a right to lay a pipeline or high-tension wires across the property, and they have not the slightest qualms about using condemnation powers to do it. Businessmen may buy rights to cut timber on the land, to graze livestock on it, or to dig minerals under it. They may buy air rights to build a structure above it, or to make sure that nobody else does. When a property is being subdivided, municipalities require the developer to give easements for sewer lines and roads. There are few properties that do not have some sort of easement on them.

The other main category of easement is negative. In this case we do not ask for physical access to the property; what we do is to buy away from the owner his right to louse it up. Through a conservation or scenic easement we acquire from the owner a guarantee that he will not put up billboards, dig away hillsides, or chop down trees; with a wetland easement, we acquire a guarantee that he will not dike or fill his marshland. Except for the restrictions, he continues to farm or use the land just as he has before; one of the main points of the easements, indeed, is to encourage him to do just that.

To understand the benefits of the easement approach, it is important to understand its limitations. One of the reasons some observers have been critical of the device is that they have asked too much of it. They have considered it as a means for sweeping control of whole regions. In this scheme of things, a public agency would acquire easements for all the open land, not merely to keep it open but to stage development; phase by phase, certain easements would be relinquished so that development would be encouraged to go where the master plan indicated it would be best to go. This would be a terribly complicated procedure, as the British found when they tried something like it after the war. But the problem is not the limitations of the easement device; it is the expansiveness of the goal.

The approach to be discussed here is a more modest one. It is to tailor easements very closely to the pattern that has been set by nature and by such man-made features as highways. They would not be applied wholesale to blanket vast areas; in many cases they would be applied only to portions of individual properties.

Let us take a stream valley as an example. It is a beautiful valley on the edge of suburbia, still unspoiled, with most of the land in farms and small estates. The meadows on either side of the stream are a flood plain; and quite properly they have been zoned against development. The rest of the valley is zoned as low-density residential, with minimum lots specified at two acres. There are no subdivisions yet and landowners are still assuring each other that they would not dream of selling out. Most of them believe it.

Obviously, the place is ripe for development. Technically speaking, the upland meadows and hills are quite suitable for housing, with excellent soil percolation characteristics for septic tanks and good drainage. We know development is going to come, whether we like it or not. But there is still some time to work with. We would like to use it to secure the key spaces in the heart of the valley, the network of streams that run down to it and, perhaps, several wooded ridges on the rim of the valley.

We have, then, three kinds of land: the flood plain that can be kept open by zoning, the highly developable land that probably cannot be kept open, and the in-between land where there is a fighting chance. Here is where the easements can be most useful. No one landowner has to give up very much. He is not asked to give an easement on all his property, but only on that part of it which falls within the conservation zone along the streams.

The community benefits in a number of ways. It preserves the heart of the open spaces of the valley without having to buy the land outright. The land remains on the local tax rolls. There is, furthermore, no maintenance burden: The owner, by continuing to farm the land, maintains the landscape, and the net result is far more pleasing than were the whole thing formally manicured and maintained in conventional parkway style.

There are considerable benefits for the owners. The most obvious is that they keep their land, and by agreeing to the easement they forestall the necessity of outright acquisition. The possibility of such action can have a persuasive influence on the landowner. This is a tricky matter for public officials to deal with, for it is easy to get landowners' backs up. But in several instances where possibility of a condemnation has been softly raised by officials, landowners have become so enthusiastic about an alternative that they have offered easements as gifts.

Landowners may get more out of easements than they give up. By agreeing not to develop the most scenic portions of their property, they may enhance the value of the portions they might develop. It would be just as well, perhaps, if they didn't want to develop at all, but it can be pointed out that if later they did wish to build, they would have a more marketable proposition than otherwise. And subdivision, let us remember, is not necessarily the highest and best use. The market for estate land and relatively modest tracts for gentlemen or part-time farmers is a very flourishing one, and the supply of such land is getting smaller. Those who take the long view in this respect may do very well for themselves in the years to come.

Another important benefit for owners is the flank protection that they get. This is an important selling point in estate country, for owners there are often nervous about the intentions of some of their neighbors, and there are few things that worry them so much as the thought that they will wake up one morning to see bulldozers hacking into one of their favorite views. Where the easement program is tailored to the natural features and thereby involves a group of landowners, all benefit. This is another reason why it is good to have the power of condemnation in reserve. It can chasten hold-outs who would exploit their neighbors.

Then there are the tax benefits. If a man gives an easement on part of his property, he can enter the value of it as a charitable deduction on his income tax. More important is the local property tax. If a man gives an easement, he will not necessarily get a reduction in his present taxes; in all likelihood, the assessor has been valuing the land only at its open-space value. What the easement does is ensure that he will keep on valuing it that way and not raise the assessment on the basis of the development potential. Some states have passed laws to that effect, but in principle they should be unnecessary. In most state constitutions, there are guarantees against assessment at more than fair market value. If a man gives an easement on certain portions of his land, the assessor should recognize this in computing market value. He cannot rightly value it as developable land if there is a binding agreement that it is not developable.

Easements are very binding indeed, and there should be no sugarcoating the fact. This is why they work. The deed forms must be explicit as to what is granted and what is not, and there can be no open-end clause by which the purchaser can make up new conditions for the landowner as time goes by. Such flexibility would appeal to administrators; it would not to the landowner or to the courts. They frown on loosely drawn easements, particularly those so loose that it is difficult to determine how much the landowner is letting himself in for and, thus, how much he is entitled to be paid.

Easements "run with the land," and their conditions apply to subsequent owners of the property. Unlike covenants, they are held by someone with a truly proprietary interest in seeing that they are enforced. (One legal complexity that some lawyers like to fondle is the matter of "gross" versus "appurtenant" easements. What this boils down to is whether or not you can acquire an easement on a man's property if you don't have property yourself nearby. Gist of opinions: Yes, you can, although it is often helpful if you have a piece of property as anchor.)

Most easements are for perpetuity. Some people blanch at the thought of such a commitment and would like to see short-term easements. But the sale of the fee simple, or of most anything else, for that matter, is for perpetuity, and there are practical reasons why easements should be too. If they are not, the landowner is likely to have trouble persuading the assessor to overlook the development potential. Nor will the landowner be able to get capital gains treatment. If the payments are for a lesser period they will be taxed as income, just as lease payments are.

Short-term easements can also create problems for the purchaser. Public agencies have found that it is as much trouble to renegotiate an easement that is about to expire as to negotiate one in perpetuity and be done with it, and agencies that used to secure short-term easements are now switching to the long term. They find that it costs them no more to do so.

And perpetuity does not last forever. In almost every easement deed there will be a reverter clause to the effect that if the purpose for which the easement was acquired is abandoned, the easement will then automatically be voided and all rights will return to the owner of the fee simple. Many of the old interurban trolley lines were laid down on easements; now that the trolleys have gone, the easements have long since reverted. The people who own the land are often unaware of this, and in many areas these ghostly traces can still be found, weedy and unused.

The device, to repeat, is an ancient one, and its application to conservation goes back many years. In 1900, Charles Eliot had easement provisions incorporated into the Massachusetts Bay Circuit Act. At the urgings of Frederick Law Olmsted, a number of scenic easements were acquired in California. In 1930, through the Capper-Cramton Act, Congress authorized easement acquisition along the streams and parkways of the national capitol area. In the 1930s, the National Park Service used scenic easements along many stretches of the Blue Ridge and Natchez Trace Parkways.[1]

But attempts were sporadic. By the late 1940s the device was almost forgotten. Conservation and park officials were not particularly interested in exploring its potentials, nor did there seem at the time a great reason to do so. The great postwar building boom was gathering force, but state and federal park acquisition was still largely in rural areas where fee-simple costs were low; anything over $150 an acre was considered very expensive land.

What prompted the new interest in easements was the outward push of suburbia, and the initiative for action came as much from land-owning groups as from public officials. The history of the open space acts is illustrative. In Monterey County, California, a number of landowners, alarmed at the threat to their magnificent coastline, warmed to the idea of giving easements on key scenic tracts to the County. There was some doubt, however, as to whether the County could accept such easements, and there was a feeling some sort of legislation would probably be necessary.

At the time, a lawyer and I had just finished drafting a model easement bill for Pennsylvania. It was not getting anywhere in Pennsylvania, a large-scale study project being then in process, and now that we look back on it, there were quite a few holes in the bill. But it was something on paper, and the Monterey people saw it as a lead. Their state senator, Fred Farr, was an ardent conservationist, and with state planner William Lipman, he worked up a bill for the California legislature. (See Appendix A.)

It was a great improvement on the Pennsylvania proposal. For one thing, it specifically authorized not only easements but the purchase of land for the purpose of selling it or leasing it subject to restrictions. Second, and perhaps more important, it greatly broadened the public purposes for which open space could be acquired, whatever the techniques, and clearly established that the purposes were by no means restricted to the traditional concept of immediate public use. It did all this, furthermore, in ringingly affirmative language. Here are the first two sections:

It is the intent of the Legislature in enacting this chapter to provide a means whereby any county or city may acquire, by purchase, gift, grant, bequest, devise, lease or otherwise, and through the expenditure of public funds, the fee or any lesser interest or right in real property in order to preserve, through limitation of their future use, open spaces and areas for public use and enjoyment.

The Legislature finds that the rapid growth and spread of urban development is encroaching upon, or eliminating, many open areas and spaces of varied size and character, including many having significant scenic or esthetic values, which areas and spaces if preserved and maintained in their present open state would constitute important physical, social, esthetic or economic assets to existing or impending urban and metropolitan development.

There were only a few days left before the legislature was to adjourn, and ordinarily such a bill would not have had a chance. Because his fellow legislators had just voted down a billboard control program Farr had sponsored, however, they were feeling somewhat contrite, and the word was passed around that the next time it would be Fred's turn.

This was the next time. The bill passed unanimously. If it had been written in Chinese, Farr says, it would have passed unanimously.

As these things often happen, the particular local cause that prompted the bill ran into snags, and it was not until several years later that the Monterey program got going. The moment the bill became an act, however, hundreds of copies were made and sent to conservationists and planners in other states. It was fine news to them, and emboldened by the unanimity of the vote, they went to work on their own legislatures. In less than a year, New York had passed a similar bill, and in short order Maryland, Connecticut, and Massachusetts did likewise. Others were to follow—and eventually, I am happy to note, Pennsylvania.

While most planners welcomed the acts, some felt they were an invitation to rash action, and a few seemed gripped with the fear that communities would start saving too much land in advance of a comprehensive plan to determine what land should be saved. They need not have worried. Lead time on these things is very slow. There was no rush to precipitate action, nor was too much open space saved.

But here and there local and state governments stuck their necks out. They were not interested in being pioneers; they were trying to solve a particular situation and found easements would be useful. The news spread. Others tried the device. More enabling legislation was passed.

Now, at last, the breakthrough has arrived. Even highway departments have come around. Just in the last few years, the highway departments of most of the big states have embarked on large-scale scenic easement programs. The momentum should pick up. There is still self-reinforcing skepticism in many park and conservation agencies but no longer do they have a dearth of precedents to complain about. The key propositions about easements have been put to the test, and most of the important questions that stilled resolve have been answered.

How much do easements cost? The greatest single obstacle to greater use of the device has been the assertion that it probably would cost as much to buy an easement as to buy the land outright. This is simply not true, but it has been repeated so often in the literature, accumulating footnotes along the way, that it has become a fact in itself. It gives officials just the discouragement they need.

Actual experience bears out what common sense would indicate. Easements are worth what the landowner is giving up. Sometimes this is a good bit; sometimes it is very little.

The rule of thumb for estimating the value of an easement is to figure the "before and after" value of the property; the difference between what the property is worth without the restrictions and what it is worth with them is the value of the easement. This depends on time and place. If you want an easement forbidding development on a piece of prime land in an area that is ripe for development, the owner is giving up a major part of the value of his property, or thinks he is, and you could pay through the nose. At the Antietam Battlefield the National Park Service has been offering landowners up to thirty percent of the fee value of their land for scenic easements, but the landowners have not been interested; they think the development of value is going to increase much more. In cases like this, it often makes more sense to buy the land outright.

In the rural areas where there is yet little development pressure, however, the cost of easements has been quite modest. A good example is the success Wisconsin has had with easements on the Great River Road along the Mississippi. Originally, the highway department was going to buy a wide right-of-way so the landscape could be kept to parkway standards. For a number of reasons, including the protests of sportsmen (who were afraid they would be sealed off from the river), the department decided to have a smaller right-of-way and protect it with scenic easements extending 350 feet from the center line on both sides of the road. Between 1951 and 1961, easements were secured along fifty-three miles of the road. Prices paid to landowners averaged $16 an acre, versus $41.29 for comparable land in fee simple. Since 1961, an additional 100 miles have been secured and though land costs in general have been soaring, prices paid for easements have risen only moderately, to an average of $21 an acre.

The Wisconsin highway people have learned a lot about keeping easement costs down. The most important factor, they emphasize, is clarity. Original costs and later enforcement costs depend very much on how well owners understand the device; violations are almost always the result of misunderstanding and ambiguity, not willful transgression. The highway people have kept such instances to a minimum by careful, and continuous, explanation of the terms of the easement. Recently, they revised the deed form to clear away the legal jargon and put into simpler English exactly what rights the landowner is yielding and what rights he is not.

As the highway people have been seeking more precision in the instrument, they have been applying it more flexibly. Instead of acquiring a uniform strip 350 feet on either side, they now tailor the easements to the contour of the view. If a nearby ridge foreshortens it, they buy no further; in other cases they may extend the easement to 700 or 900 feet. They will also zig and zag when they run up against unusual situations or very high-cost land. In areas just beyond town limits, for example, they do not try to buy all the development rights but secure an "urban scenic easement" permitting houses spaced 300 feet apart. Where there is merchantable timber, they will buy the full fee simple, and will do the same with land that is of so little use that even the fee cost is nominal. (This is one reason why comparisons between fee and easement costs can sometimes be misleading.)

There are still problems to be licked. Appraisal costs, of fee purchases as well as easements, seem to have gotten out of hand. The highway department has recently professionalized its appraisal staff and one result is such a display of zeal in survey and documentation that it frequently costs as much or more to figure out what an offer to a landowner should be as the offer amounts to itself. Condemnation has posed no great difficulties—it has been used in only about 10 percent of the acquisitions—but juries can be extremely generous at times; one recently upped a $250 award to $6000. The highway department would like the option of disengaging from the purchase when juries ask that kind of money, but under present law it has to go through with the deal.

On the whole, however, the economics have worked out as well as the aesthetics, and for the landowners as well as the public. Had there not been an easement program, many stretches of this road would long since have become rural slums. Nobody would have made much money out of it—a few dollars for leasing billboard sites, some income from a trailer camp—and everyone would have paid in future values. But the desecration has not taken place, save in stretches within town limits. Along most of this splendid road each man's property enhances his neighbors' and the whole is the greater for these parts. Landowners have not had their values diminished. A check of sale prices indicates that land covered with easements has been fetching as much as comparable land not covered by easements. Some people believe that in time the properties protected by easements might actually fetch more.[2]

The constitutionality of the program, furthermore, has been successfully tested. One group of landowners brought suit against the state, charging that the easements were only for aesthetic goals and that this was no proper public purpose since the public didn't get to use the land. In a decision of great importance to other states, Wisconsin's Supreme Court upheld the easements. They did serve a public purpose, the court held, providing "visual occupancy"; they were not imposed by the police power, but were paid for under eminent domain, and the legislature had laid down proper standards for their application (*Kamrowski v. State*, 31 Wis. 2d. 2456; 1966).

People who want to know the costs of scenic easements should study the costs of actual scenic easements—those along the Great River Road, for example. This would seem obvious enough, but there has been a persistent tendency among officials to look away from the obvious. They hypothesize what easements *might* cost, and without making clear what kind of easements they are talking about. Officials who want to stick with straight fee acquisition sometimes arrive at alarming generalizations about the cost of scenic or conservation easements by using the costs of quite another kind of easement and they sometimes forget to mention the unusual circumstances involved. They are particularly fond of cost data about flood easements. With these the public buys from landowners the right to flood private lands around reservoirs if it becomes necessary. Most of the time it is not necessary, but the landowners are obviously yielding rather considerable rights, and the easement costs are likely to run to about 80 percent of the cost of the fee. If the land is suitable for recreation the public agency would have good reason to pay the additional 20 percent to secure it outright.

It hardly follows, however, that easements in general cost 80 percent of the fee simple. There are no easements in general. Each is specific. It is one thing to ask a man to keep his land looking nice and quite another to tell him you want to put it under water, and to talk of the costs of one by using the data of another is to talk of apples and oranges.

People who want to use easements can be similarly imprecise. The most frequent error is a failure to distinguish between a scenic easement and an easement that grants public access. The two rights can be combined in an easement deed for a particular tract, but the two can't be had for the price of one. Several years ago a town conservation commission found that the owners of parcels that made up an especially attractive meadowland were quite receptive to scenic easements; most, indeed, said they would give the easements. The commission members were so encouraged by this proffer of good will that they got a little greedy and decided that for good measure they would add to the deeds a provision for public access. The landowners stiffened. Who would pick up the trash? How would the hordes be kept away? The gift offers were withdrawn; some landowners said they would be damned if they would give the easements at any price. The program was stalled for three years, and only now, on a more modest scenic-easement basis, is it at last getting underway.

Another key variable in costs, and one that is rarely noted in studies, is the man who is doing the negotiating and, sometimes more important, the man who runs the department. In tracking down scenic-easement costs I have been struck by the relationship between such presumably objective data as payments to landowners, engineering and survey costs, incidence of court appeals and the like to the attitude the officials have toward easements. In those states where officials welcomed the easement approach, costs figures have been moderate, there has been little litigation, and enforcement problems have been minor. In those states where officials didn't welcome the approach, cost figures have been notably higher, and there have been recurring maintenance and enforcement problems.

The Wisconsin experience sheds further light on this phenomenon. In 1962, Governor Gaylord Nelson proposed a $50 million conservation program, and noting the Highway Department's success with the Great River Road easements, he called for a broadened use of the device by other agencies. He said:

> In addition to scenic easements, I propose that we purchase public access rights, public hunting and fishing rights, use and alteration rights of headwaters and spring heads, wetland drainage rights, scenic overlook rights, fencerow rights for the protection of game cover, platting rights along trout streams, subdivision and timber-cutting rights along lake shorelines, and development rights to protect lands adjacent to state parks and camp grounds from the clutter of billboards, taverns, and concessions.

The state conservation department was not enthusiastic. At the hearings before the legislature, a top official said he and his colleagues yielded to no one in applauding the overall goals of the program; however, they did wonder whether this was the time for untried devices, or for a program of such magnitude. They recommended more study.

The program passed. The draftsman of the act, Harold Jordahl, was a student of administrative behavior and he had so worded it that the conservation department very well had to turn to. There were no escape clauses. The act gave each division some mandatory pioneering to do; specific sums were allocated to specific easement programs in specific areas and if the money was not spent, it would revert. For many officials it was a wrenching assignment to ponder.

I remember well a two-day clinic on easements staged for state agency people. Some were still in a state of administrative shock. Here was this damn easement business they had fought and now they were stuck with it. In an atmosphere of truculent curiosity, the reluctant pioneers learned for the first time that an easement program had been operating in Wisconsin for some years, and quite successfully. They were shown the cost figures on the Great River Road program, and learned that no, costs were not almost as high as the fee simple; they were low. Legal obstacles? The late Jacob Beuscher, an authority with a gift for direct English, assured them the statutes gave them leeway to do far more than they had yet attempted. Easements would work, went the charge, just about as well as they wanted them to work.

That is the way it has turned out. Both the overall effort and the easement programs have been successful, and it is a pleasure to read the conservation department's bulletins on its part in the pioneering work. But some of the easement programs have worked significantly better than others. Many factors are involved, but it is evident that the skill and enthusiasm of the personnel involved are probably the most important of all.

Park people, who were the least enthusiastic about easements, have only recently begun to make progress. Fish-and-game people, however, have done extremely well. They have secured easements on 200 miles of lake and river frontage and at a fraction of the fee simple cost. For each dollar they get about three and a half feet of frontage with easements; only a half foot with fee simple. They have also covered some 9000 acres with wetland and hunting easements at an average cost of $8.30 an acre. (Comparable fee-simple costs: $26.00 an acre.)

Easements can be made to appear much more expensive. It depends on how much in the way of engineering and overhead costs the particular agency decides to cram into the figures. On one series of projects it looked as though everything but the main office light bill was included; the extra costs attributed came to more than the money paid for the easements themselves; on other projects, by contrast, officials were able to achieve the same end with much more economy of effort. One particularly good negotiator has sewed up as many easements as a number of others combined, and at very reasonable costs.

Occupational bias is important. The attitude that agencies take towards easements depends a great deal on whether or not they have been used to working on a continuing basis with landowners. In most states the highway engineers want to buy land in fee and be done with it. Recreation and park officials tend to feel the same way. Forest service and fish-and-game people, by contrast, have been more used to working with landowners and tend to be receptive to any tool which helps them in this mutual relationship. They have been responsible for some of the most successful easement programs, though the news does not always seems to reach other conservation agencies down the hall in various capitals.

An excellent example is what the Fish and Wildlife Service of the Department of the Interior has been doing in the "pothole country" of

Minnesota and the Dakotas. This is the great nursery for the ducks of this country, for the thousands of little holes left by glaciers make a unique habitat for the breeding of wild fowl. For farmers, however, these wet patches have seemed a nuisance and a waste of cropland, and after World War II they began filling them in at a rapid rate.

To counteract this, Congress passed legislation by which the revenues from the sale of duck stamps could be used to conserve these wetlands. The Fish and Wildlife Service started out by negotiating twenty-year leases. It quickly found that it would be easier to obtain easements in perpetuity. Farms change hands frequently (in that area, the Service discovered, about every six to eight years on the average); owners preferred a lump sum in hand to income payments stretched into the future.

The Fish and Wildlife Service settled on a conservation program involving both acquisition of the fee simple and of easements. Where there were large wetlands it would try to buy these in fee as "nucleus areas." For the smaller wetlands it would use easements.

The easements stipulate that the farmers won't burn, fill, or drain the wetlands on their property. So far 102,000 acres of wetland have been bought outright and 500,000 acres covered by easements. Field men have done an outstanding job working with the farmers and have been getting the easements at an average price of $11.50 an acre. Enforcing them over so vast an area promised to be a problem, but the Service has solved this by aerial surveillance. Periodically, field men fly over the area; by checking previous aerial photos they can quickly spot where a farmer has filled in a hole or touched a match to the brush.

In a quietly effective way, New York State's Conservation Department has been buying fishing easements along trout streams. The easements give fishermen the use of the strip stretching thirty feet from either side of the stream. They do not have access to the rest of the property. Where parking areas are needed the state buys parcels in fee simple. Since 1950, it has secured easements along 1000 miles of stream; acquisition costs are currently running about $1000 a mile.

The negotiators, who conceive of their job as essentially a direct selling operation, spend a good bit of time casing an area. Before making the first call they will know all the local gossip about the farmers, their financial situation, the history of the properties, and the state of their titles. They go to work first on the "Elmers," the most influential of the farmers, and then work down the list. The man they have been told will give them the most trouble they leave to the last, by which time he will be feeling so left out he will be almost pathetically eager to be included. Negotiators do not haggle. They make each offer on the same price-per-foot basis as the other offers in the area, regardless of how good the land is as farmland. This saves time and money in appraisal costs, and since farmers are quick to compare notes with each other, no one feels that he has been had—a matter of particular importance in farm country.

In states that have followed New York's lead, negotiators have had similar success. In Minnesota they have been securing fishing rights from almost all of the landowners they have approached, and for the minimum consideration of one dollar per easement. In Wisconsin, fish-and-game negotiators used to lease strips along streams for twenty-year periods; they now find it more economical to secure easements in perpetuity. Since 1961, they have obtained easements along 170 miles of stream, at a cost of 30 cents per foot of frontage, as opposed to $2.38 for fee-simple acquisition.

So far I have been emphasizing the opportunities in rural areas. For a long time many people assumed that in urban areas easements might be prohibitively expensive. (So did I, and I have been chagrined to see an earlier study of mine quoted by officials on this point as justification for not inquiring further.)

On the face of it the case would seem open and shut. It rests primarily on the very high average cost of open land in urban areas. Wherever land is selling at $2000 and up an acre it is obvious that the development potential accounts for most of the cost, and, ergo, it would appear that an easement stripping this development potential would run almost as much as the fee simple.

The conclusion tends to be self-fulfilling. Several years ago, for example, one state that had just put through a program providing for easement purchase commissioned a university study to determine where, if anywhere, the state might buy easements. The man who did the study took what he called the macro-view and charted average land costs for large areas. Where the average price was over a thousand dollars—which is to say, most of the urban area of the state—the charts said No go. (For good measure the study also ruled out the areas where land value was very low, the theory being that there was so little development value there would be no point to purchasing easements.) The state's easement program died aborning.

This is the kind of result you get when you do not look at the land itself. If you do, you will find that average land costs can be highly misleading, for they mask all sorts of variations and unexpected opportunities—and it is the developers, of all people, who are now teaching us this lesson. Just in the last few years it has become apparent that in the urban areas we may find some of the best opportunities of all for less-than-fee acquisition. Here is where the pressure for more intensive land use is strongest, but it is because of this fact, not despite it, that all the ingredients for some excellent bargains are at hand.

Let us take a suburban area, where the going price for land ranges anywhere between $2000 and $10,000 an acre. As farmland, it is not worth more than $150 or $300 an acre. Thus the development value, on the average, also runs somewhere between $2000 and $10,000 an acre.

Let us take a closer look at the land. Assume a tract of 100 acres for which a developer paid $500,000. The average value was $5000 an acre. But is each acre worth $5000? This figure is only an arithmetic average, and it covers a wide variation in the value of different parts of the tract—variation assessors usually take into account as a matter of routine. It is the frontage land, the highly buildable part that the developer was after, and in some cases only a third of the tract may account for the bulk of the value. The chances are that some of the property is not worth building on at all—a patch of swamp, perhaps, a stream, or an extremely steep hill. What is the development value of these acres? They may have no development value; and if there is any value, the bulk of it will have to be realized by the developer through extensive grading, diking, filling, and such; and this costs him a great deal of money.

This marginal land may have great value as open space, and aesthetics aside, the developer is better off if he does not have to build on it. If he can concentrate his building on the buildable parts, it is to his self-interest to keep the land as an open space and recreation area, or deed it as such to a homeowners association or a special district. And this, with unexpected fervor, is just what developers are trying to do.

The open-space acts have been a help. When the original act was put through in California, the sponsors were not preoccupied with helping the developers. They were supposed to be the dirty guys. One of the first consequences of the act, however, was to make it easier for developers to give away open space. A number of them had been offering to deed large parts of their tracts as permanent open space if they could cluster their houses on the remainder. Communities, however, were suspicious. Just how permanent, they wondered, would the open space be?

The easement device, several California communities found, could resolve the impasse. Whether the developer held the open space himself or deeded it to a homeowners association, he could prove his good intentions by deeding a conservation easement on the open space to the municipality, guaranteeing that it would forever remain open. Developers liked the idea and have been helping to spread it to other states.

The new interest of developers in cluster planning has important implications for landowners, and the fact that there is a pocketbook motivation makes it all the more compelling. Until not so very long ago one had to argue hypothetically with a landowner that if he were to agree to the conservation of certain parts of his land he might not necessarily be damaging the over-all development value of the property for enlightened developers. Landowners would be skeptical. Where were these enlightened developers? As far as landowners could see, most developers wanted to develop every bit of ground they could get their hands on, and they'd pay less for a property if they couldn't. As for cluster, fine idea in principle, but it might never come about.

Now it has come about and the case for easements is no longer hypothetical. The landowner can be shown, with concrete examples, that conservation of the natural features goes hand in hand with a development layout which is not only pleasing but commercially profitable. He will not, in short, be giving up very much. Even though he may not intend to sell for development, the assurance that easements would not prevent him from doing so will make it much easier for him to take the altruistic view.

The gift potential for easements has been stronger than was generally expected, and it has turned out to be strongest in the urban areas. Again, the initiative has come as much from landowners as from public officials. In some cases the latter have been so sure that easements would be outrageously expensive that when landowners actually offered them as gifts they found it too hard to believe, and it was the landowners who had to do the arm twisting.

One of the best examples of the trickle-up effect is the evolution of the government program for the protection of the view of Mount Vernon. Back in 1959, an oil-tank farm was planned for the Maryland shore just opposite Mount Vernon. Representative Frances Bolton of Ohio was so exercised that she bought the property with some of her own funds, and with some neighboring landowners set up the Akokeek Foundation to expand the holdings. Everything went well until 1960, when the Washington Suburban Sanitary Commission announced it was going to condemn land along the shore and build a sewage plant there. This precipitated a tremendous outcry. Representative Bolton and others pressed the federal government to make a park of the area, and many of the landowners in the area pledged that they would give easements free if the federal government would act. In 1961, Congress passed a resolution authorizing the Secretary of the Interior to acquire land and interests in lands to establish a conservation area, Piscataway Park, and to receive gifts of easements from landowners in the area. He would acquire 586 acres in fee, secure easements on surrounding land.

To the considerable surprise of many government officials, the landowners made good on their pledge of easements. The owners of 167 properties pledged easements on 1215 acres. The easements specified that the land was not to be subdivided into lots of less than five acres, and strictly regulated future land uses and buildings. They also provided that no trees thirty feet or higher could be cut without permission of the Secretary of the Interior.

Officials of the county, Prince Georges, liked the easement plan and thought that it should be encouraged in other areas. To provide a carrot, the county passed an ordinance in early 1966 providing a 50 percent tax reduction on properties covered by such easements. Landowners along another scenic stretch, the Patuxent River, indicated they would like to give easements too.

But there was one important condition to all this. The Piscataway landowners who had started the whole business insisted on a *quid pro quo*. They made their easement deeds contingent on the federal government's going through with its part of the bargain. If the government purchased outright the 586 park acres within five years of the original resolution— that is, by August 1967—the easements would become perpetual; if not, the easements would expire.

It was a good thing that the landowners insisted on the proviso. The government, or to be more accurate, the House Appropriations Committee, reneged. Though Congress had authorized $937,600 for the purchases, the Committee appropriated only $213,000. This was nowhere near enough to buy the land, and over the next few years rising land prices widened the gap further. Additional appropriations were denied in 1963 and 1964. By 1967 the market values of the unbought land had gone up so much that to finish the job Congress was moved to authorize $2.7 million. In May, a subcommittee of the House Appropriations Committee struck out every penny. By thus kicking a gift horse, the Committee not only jeopardized the easements that had been given but the possibility of additional gifts. The Patuxent landowners, for example, announced they would have to rethink their easement plans.

This is the same committee that has been scolding federal agencies for not making their acquisition dollars go further. Since the Piscataway project happened to be an outstanding effort to do just that, the cut stirred vigorous protests and just before the deadline a House-Senate conference committee restored $1.5 million. This was enough to reassure the landowners and the easements were left in force.

Another important confrontation took place several miles farther upstream. The Merrywood estate, a wooded tract with a dominant position on the heights above the Potomac, was bought by developers. They applied for a zoning change so they could put up high-rise towers. There was fierce protest, for towers would change the whole character of the area, but the local authorities made the zoning change, and that seemed to be that.

Then, in one of those acts of affirmation that change everything, Secretary of Interior Udall moved in. He had his lawyers find the right statutes, invoked the right of eminent domain, and slapped a scenic easement on the property forbidding high-rise development. The situation was by no means ideal for an easement; because of the recent zoning change, development values had increased considerably, and the government had to pay $745,000.

What was gained, however, was far more than the stopping of several towers. The action was an important precedent, and it started a chain of responses. Landowners in the area offered similar easements as gifts to the government, and this in turn led to a long-awaited ruling by the Internal Revenue Service. One of the donors asked for a ruling on whether the value of the easement could be entered as a charitable deduction on the income tax return. The Internal Revenue Service said that it could and made the ruling applicable to similar gifts of easements throughout the country.

One thing does lead to another.

I do not want to overstress one device. There are other ways to achieve the same results and sometimes it might be better if they were used. For shoreline land, for example, we could use a procedure that would be the mirror image of the easement approach. We could acquire the land in fee and then sell or lease the rights to use it.

Another possibility would be "compensable regulations." Under this proposed device the police power would be used first. An area would be zoned for open-space or low-density uses. Later, when a landowner in the area sold his property he could put in a claim for compensation. If his property had suffered a loss in market value because of the restrictions imposed on it, he would be paid the amount of the loss. In effect, an easement would be retroactively purchased from him.

But technique is secondary. I have been emphasizing easements not because I think they should be the major tool but because they are probably the clearest illustration of a basic approach. What we are essentially concerned with is finding ways of working with the people who own most of the landscape so that private interest will be coupled with public interest. If officials are really interested in seeking the middle ways, they will find that there are plenty of them and that they will work if they want them to.

The point is combination. Alone, any single device is limited; together they strengthen each other. If we zone flood plains, for example, it will be much easier to buy open space in them later and the price will be more reasonable when we do; if we buy land in fee simple, it will be easier to buy easements on land that buffers them. Each step makes another easier.

To illustrate, let me conclude with a brief account of what happened along the Sudbury River. The river winds through a lovely valley on the outskirts of Boston. Along its banks lie beautiful expanses of marshlands, which from earliest times have tempered the floods, nourished wildlife, and delighted the eye. In the 1950s, developers began eyeing it, and the Massachusetts legislature passed an act envisioning their protection by a combination of state and federal action. The key wetlands were being bought in fee simple by federal Fish and Wildlife Service. The rest of the job would be up to the state.

The then Conservation Commissioner of Massachusetts, Charles Foster, did not have much money to spend for acquisition and being very much a Yankee, he wanted to see what could be done without spending any money at all. At a public meeting in the Sudbury area, he made a proposal to the local people. He said he was prepared to buy or condemn the additional wetlands in fee. But was this necessary? He noted the job that already had been done by conservation commissions and private groups in the area. (One group, the Sudbury Valley Trustees, had been buying swamps.) Foster suggested that maybe the local people could work up a scheme that would preserve all of the wetlands. He wasn't too concerned what devices they used just as long as there was a real guarantee of permanence. He would give them a year to see what could be done.

The response was almost instantaneous. Within a matter of weeks all the owners who had land along a key stretch had voluntarily given easements on the wetland portions to the local land trust.

Much has taken place since: strengthened wetland zoning, more gifts of easements and gifts of land in fee. There is such a dense mix of public and private efforts, indeed, that it is impossible to chart them clearly on a map, or to assess which have been most responsible for the saving of the area. And that is the reason it has been saved.

That is how hundreds of other areas can be saved. Officials who are really interested in exploring the possibilities with landowners will find that between zoning and outright purchase there are all sorts of middle ways, in all sorts of combinations, and that if they want them to work they will work. But they have to try them. Where they are not we should be building fires to see that they do.

CLUSTER DEVELOPMENT

We have been considering ways of saving open space. Now let us turn to the question of how to develop it. There is a conflict, to be sure, but you cannot grapple with one problem and not the other. People have to live somewhere, as it is so often said, and if there is to be any hope of having open space in the future, there is going to have to be a more efficient pattern of building. The mathematics is inexorable. The only way to house more people is either to extend the present pattern of sprawl and cover vastly more land, or, alternatively, to use less land and increase the carrying capacity of it. The latter is by far the best approach and at last we are beginning to pursue it. By whatever name it is called—"planned unit development," "open-space development," "cluster development"—it signals a reversal of the land-wasting pattern that had come to seem permanent.

In the great postwar building boom, developers froze on a pattern that used five acres to do the work of one. They had to, or they thought they had to. For one thing, it was a well-known fact that Americans had a deep psychic urge for a free-standing homestead on a large country plot, or as close a replica as possible. The assumption was self-proving, for it was built into the standards of the Federal Housing Administration and the major lending institutions. If a developer wanted mortgage money, he hewed to these standards or he did not get it.

Suburbs were similarly demanding. Most wanted no development at all, not in their area anyway, and they looked to large-lot zoning as their best defense. They reasoned that if they could force developers to provide large lots for each house, there would be fewer houses, and the grounds of those that did go up would conserve the open-space character of the community. Minimum lot sizes varied, but most suburbs pushed them as high as pride and wealth could enforce. The stiffer the minimum, they thought, the more likely the developers would be to leave them alone and go somewhere else.

The developers did go somewhere else, at first, but the respite did not help the suburbs, which soon found that they were not being penetrated so much as enveloped. Later the developers would come back; their first response to the barriers was to leap-frog over them and seek the open country where land was cheaper and the townships had not gotten around to zoning it.

So the best land was ruined first, and when developers got there, they sometimes found the locals had attended to the job already. While the gentry of the rural townships kept a wary eye out for the likes of Levitt, a motley of local builders and contractors would buy up frontage land from farmers and line it with a string of concrete bungalows on overblown lots. Very few people would be housed on a great deal of land, but since the land was along the road, the place would look filled up. The premature development also had the effect of sealing off many hundreds of acres from any kind of effective development pattern, and when the feared invasion did come, the chances for coping with it amenably were gone.

The suburbs farther back were coming under increasing pressure. Developers were filling in the spaces wherever they could and they were pressing relentlessly for variances. Where the minimums were as high as three or four acres, they attacked the ordinances themselves and complained to the courts that such minimums were not for the welfare of the public but to exclude the public that was not rich. Whatever developers' motives in saying so, this was the case, and in some instances the courts struck down ordinances as excessive and discriminatory.

The main problem, however, was not so much the relative size of lots as the uniformity with which they were laid out. With few exceptions, subdivisions homogenized the land with a pattern of curvilinear streets and equal-spaced lots that were everywhere the same, large lot or small, and in the denser areas, the pattern was compressed to the point of caricature. Even though lots were so small that houses would have only a few feet between them, the estate pattern was repeated, producing subdivisions that looked very much like toy villages with the scale out of whack.

These were the little boxes that so outraged people of sensibility and means. Photos of their rooftops and TV aerials, squeezed together—the telephoto lens again—became stock horror shots. But critics drew the wrong conclusions. What was wrong, they thought, was that the houses were too close together, when what was really wrong was that they were not close enough.

For years, planners had been arguing that if lots took up less of the land, subdivisions would be more economical to build and more pleasant to live in. Rather than divide all of a tract up into lots, they suggested, developers could group the houses in clusters, and leave the bulk of the land as open space. It was an ancient idea: It was the principle of the New England village and green, and its appeal had proved timeless. "Garden City" advocates had reapplied it in the planning of several prototype communities; most notably, Radburn, New Jersey, in the late 1920s, the green belt towns of the New Deal, Baldwin Hills in Los Angeles during the late 1930s.

Some of the utopian expectations with which these experiments were freighted were never fulfilled, but as individual communities, they were, and still are, quite successful. But they remained outside of the mainstream. Some of the features found their way into commercial developments, such as the superblock and cul-de-sac streets, but the basic cluster principle of the communities did not. Few developers even went to look at them.

By the early 1950s, however, the conventional pattern had been pushed close to the breaking point. It not only looked terrible, it was uneconomic, and for everybody concerned. Communities were forcing developers to chew up an enormous amount of land to house a given number of people and to provide an overblown network of roads and facilities to tie the sprawl together. This created havoc with the landscape, and saddled the community with a heavy servicing burden, the costs of which usually outran the tax returns.

For new residents, the open space was turning out to be a chimera. The woods and meadows that so attracted them disappeared as soon as developers got around to building on them, and if the residents wanted to find what other natural features would be next to go, they had only to check the names of the subdivisions being planned. When a developer puts a woods into the name, or a vale, heights, forest, creek, or stream, he is not conserving; he is memorializing. Subdivisions are named for that which they are about to destroy.

The open space of the resident's own lot was not much compensation. It was trouble to maintain but did not provide as much usable space as a small courtyard and nowhere near the privacy. (The open space between the houses strikes a particularly unhappy mean: big enough to mow, too small to use, and a perfect amplifier of sound.) Nor would there be much in the way of neighborhood open spaces. Most communities required developers to dedicate some part of the tract as open space, but it would be a very small space, and quite often a leftover the developer could not use for anything else.

The developers were being hurt more than anybody else. No matter how far and fast they pushed outward to the countryside, land prices kept soaring ahead of them. Contrary to public belief, most developers do not make money on land speculation; they do not have the capital to stockpile land for very long and they have to pay dearly to those who do. Such costs are usually passed on to the home buyers, but by the 1960s developers were bumping up against a market ceiling.

The price that builders had to pay for land had risen far more than the price that people would pay for their houses. Between 1951 and 1966 the cost of raw land rose 234 percent. The sale price of the average house and lot, however, rose 87 percent and most of this increase was due to the larger size of the houses; per square foot, house prices rose only 21 percent. Even before tight money hit them, developers were in a bind. They could not mark up their finished product without pricing themselves out of the market, and they had to keep on paying exorbitant prices for their land to stay in the business.

There is one good thing about high land costs. They discipline choice. Since communities would not let developers squeeze more houses onto their tracts, developers had only one way to turn: they could try squeezing the houses they were allowed onto the most buildable parts of the tract and leave the rest alone—that is, cluster, just as planners had been suggesting. The National Association of Home Builders undertook a missionary campaign and began proselytizing builders and communities to try the cluster approach.

Here and there cluster developments began to go up. In several cases developers took the initiative; they retained land planners to prepare an advanced cluster plan and then went to work to sell the community on it. Sometimes it was the other way around, with the community doing the selling. Most typically, however, the genesis would be thoroughly mixed up, marked by plans and counterplans, false starts, and controversy.

To examine the pros and cons of cluster, let us follow such a case.

A medium-size builder has purchased a 112-acre farm in a well-to-do township on the outer edge of suburbia. The tract is pleasant, gently rolling land with a stream running through the middle and a stand of woods at one end. The site has some defects—a small marsh, for one—but it should make a fine subdivision. Mill Creek Woods, the developer will call it.

The township has zoned this area for half-acre lots. The developer explores the chances of getting it rezoned for quarter-acre lots, but finds that they are poor so he proceeds to work up a standard plan. This won't

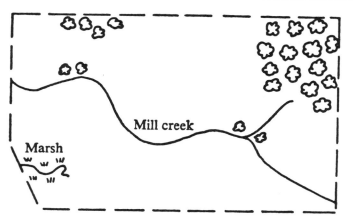

take long. He will probably work up the basic plan himself, possibly on the back of an envelope, and then later will turn it over to a civil engineer to be worked up in detail.

The plan almost draws itself. By rule of thumb, the developer knows he will have to subtract about twenty-two acres for roads. Another six acres he will have to dedicate for playgrounds. This leaves him only eighty-four acres for his half-acre lots and some of the acreage will require extensive land improvement. To squeeze in as many houses as regulations will allow, about 168, he figures to put the creek in a concrete culvert, level the wooded hill and saw down most of the trees. He would like to fill in the small marsh and develop it too, but finds the cost would be too great. He will dedicate the marsh as a park area.

Here is the tentative plan he submits:

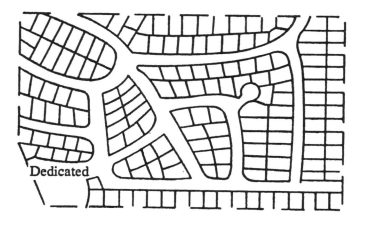

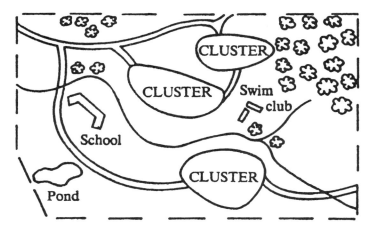

The county planner is very unhappy. He thinks it is a shame to ruin such a fine piece of land with a hack layout and he does not think it is necessary. He suggests that the developer start fresh, this time with a cluster approach. The developer is skeptical, but curious. The two go out to the tract and the planner makes a rough sketch of what could be done.

This way, the planner points out, the developer will be able to get up as many houses as before, possibly a few more, and his costs will be considerably less. Under the first plan, he would have had to spend about $4500 a lot for land improvement; under the cluster plan, he will pay about $3000. He will have to lay down only about half as much roadway, his utility runs will be shorter, and he will not have to cover the stream and chop down the wooded hill.

The developer's enthusiasm grows. He wonders, however, about the planning and zoning board, for there is as yet no cluster provision in the local ordinance. The planner thinks that if a really attractive plan is worked up the zoning boards will go along. At his urging, the developer calls in a professional site planner.

In designing the clusters, there are a number of possibilities. What both the site planner and the developer would like best is to put the 168 houses into groups of row houses and arrange them around common greens. Here is how a cluster would look:

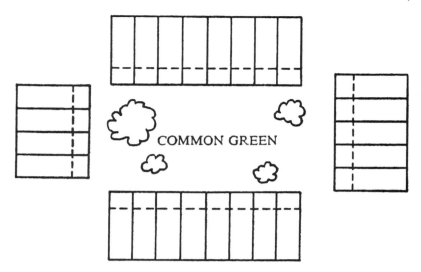

COMMON GREEN

Such an economical layout would obviously be the most profitable of all for the developer. But it would also provide a very good buy for the home-owners. Dollar for dollar they would get the most house—whatever the price range—and one easy to maintain. There would be no private open space save the backyard patio, but this would be very usable space, and with the enclosed common green, would make a functional arrangement for families with children.

But the people in this particular township wouldn't swallow so dense a pattern, and they would be dead set against row houses. They would seem too much like a garden-apartment project, and there are very few forms of housing that can arouse so much resistance among suburbanites. After taking some more soundings of local opinion, the developer decides to settle on a modified cluster layout, grouping free-standing houses on quarter-acre plots.

The developer will use stock builders' houses—ranchers and split levels that he has found successful in his other developments. This will sadden the site planner, who may be an architect also and who would like to see clean, advanced designs worthy of his site plan. The developer says he has stuck his neck out far enough as it is. He doesn't think architects know how to cost out a builder's house or design to the market, and he reasons that he is going to have enough trouble selling the cluster idea without saddling it

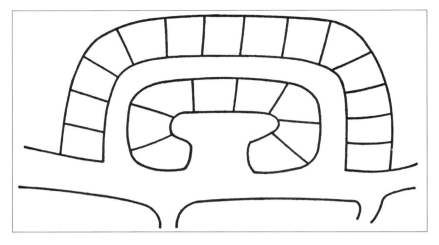

with far-out architecture. (Developers tend to be much too timid on this score, but they do have some reason for their fears. Several of the best of the first cluster proposals were disapproved by local governments, and the deciding factor was not so much the newness of the cluster idea, but of the architecture of the houses.)

The overall plan, however, remains relatively intact and it is a good one. Of the 112 acres, the house lots take 42, the streets 18, leaving some 52 acres of open space to work with. In the center of each cluster there will be a common green and playground. Midway between the clusters there will be a swimming pool, tennis courts, and a clubhouse. The rest of the tract will be treated as countryside with a minimum of landscaping. Paths and bridle trails will be laid along the stream and a few willows planted. The woods will have some of the underbrush thinned out and a small picnic and barbecue area will be fashioned but otherwise it will be left in its natural state and so will the sloping meadows. As for the troublesome marsh, the site planner finds that for the cost of an inexpensive dam it can be turned into a pond. The developer is delighted. He thinks it will be a great merchandising plus and will supply it with a covey of ducks.

The developer will deed some of the open space to the local government. The county planner has suggested that in addition to the gift of a school site, the developer should sweeten up the proposal by also giving a strip along the stream. It would lead to the community park and eventually could be linked with similar spaces in cluster developments that might be built later in the area.

The bulk of the common open space, however, will be deeded to the people who buy the houses. If it were given to the community as a public park, the homeowners would have a legitimate complaint. They are the ones, after all, who will have paid for it. For though the developer will make a big point of his generosity in giving open space, he has already built the cost of it into the purchase price of the homes. The most equitable procedure is to give each person who buys a home an undivided interest in the common open space, and make this part of the basic deed.

To maintain the common areas, a homeowners association will be set up. Each home buyer automatically becomes a member and is obligated to pay his share of the costs of maintaining the open space and operating the recreational facilities. In a cluster development like this, the assessment will probably come to about $100 a year, with the cost rising when and if the homeowners decide to add more elaborate facilities.

Homeowners associations have a good record behind them. A number of them have been working since the 1920s and 1930s—at Radburn, for example, and the Country Club developments in Kansas City. Some date back much further—Boston's Louisburg Square has been run by a homeowners association since 1840, and New York's Gramercy Park since 1831. Today there are over 350 developments with homeowners associations and with very few exceptions, they are working out well. The key requirements, experience indicates, are that the association be set up at the very beginning and that membership be mandatory.

A question that will inevitably be raised by townspeople is the possibility of a sellout. Suppose the homeowners later decide to cash in and sell off the common area for additional housing? The record is reassuring. In very few instances have such open spaces ever been converted. One of the green belt communities sold off land when the federal government relinquished ownership, but this happened only because there were no firm stipulations in the original deed. Where there are, it is virtually impossible for homeowners to divide up the common area. The local government, furthermore, can easily remove the temptations entirely. At the time the developer deeds the title to the homeowners, he can be required to deed an easement to the local government stipulating that the open space remain open.

•

Since the cluster subdivision will require a change in the local zoning ordinance, a public hearing is scheduled. It will be turbulent. Most of the members of the planning board now favor the cluster proposal, but a number of citizens do not. A vigorous antidevelopment group has been formed ("Citizens for Open Space") and thanks to its agitations and circulars, the hall is packed with non-enthusiasts for cluster. They listen restively while the planner and the developer make presentations with flipflop charts and slides. Then the questions start. If the developer is so keen on this, what's the catch? If this new type development does not sell, won't we be left holding the bag? Maybe it will sell too well, and then won't every developer for miles be swarming over us? And what kind of home buyers will be coming in? People who have recently moved into the area will be especially zealous on this point. Lower the bars, they will say, and we'll get a new kind of element we've never had before. The meeting breaks up on a note of acrimony.

But the planning board has been won over and the fact that there has been opposition gives it some extra bargaining power with the developer. It is suggested to him that community resistance might be overcome if he will make a few more concessions in the plan. The developer says absolutely not. He is feeling very put upon by this time and says he is going to chuck the whole thing and sell the land. To a convent perhaps, he adds.

It is not entirely a bluff, but he has sunk too much preliminary money into the project to give up now, and the board knows it. He is persuaded to increase the size of the school tract by two acres and to include the duck pond in the park strip deeded to the township. To lay to rest the fears expressed by the local Garden Club, he also guarantees to preserve a line of sycamores bordering the north part of the tract. The board reciprocates by letting him cut down slightly the width of one of the access roads. A few more items are negotiated, and at length the subdivision is approved.

These first, semicluster developments laid the groundwork for what was to follow. Now there were real-life examples to show skeptical planning boards and citizen groups on cluster tours. Soon a sort of critical mass had built up and by the mid-1960s, cluster communities were going up in most areas. The Federal Housing Administration was now encouraging cluster design and had revised its standards to provide developers with incentives to try it. The leading barracks builder, the Defense Department, was beginning to apply the principle to multifamily housing at military bases.

The big question mark had been the attitude of the consumer and the answer was now at hand. If they had the choice, many people would choose cluster. Conventional, detached-house development still accounted for most new housing, as it still does and will continue to for some years to come. But the test of the marketplace had been met. Most cluster developments were selling as well as conventional developments in the same areas, and in a number of places, spectacularly better.

The best selling were the most compressed. These were the "townhouse" developments, and they caught on so well that the developers themselves were somewhat stunned. In the Los Angeles area one large townhouse development sold out so quickly that developers all over the area junked plans for conventional subdivisions and so swamped the local FHA office with applications for townhouse developments that extra help had to be flown in from Washington to help with the paper work.

Townhouse developments have been such a market success that a standard all purpose layout is emerging. There are some regional variations. In the East, builders do them up as Williamsburg Squares or New England villages. In the West they are more eclectic, mixing colonial, contemporary, oriental, and the gingerbread known in the trade as Hansel and Gretel.

But the basic plans are much the same: groups of two-story row houses, the first floor featuring an open kitchen leading to a living room which in turn opens out through sliding glass doors onto a patio twenty feet square, with a cedar or redwood fence eight feet high, the gate opening onto a common area roughly 100 feet across to the patios of the next row of houses, a play yard at one end with swings, a large concrete turtle, and a sand pit. The area is lit with old-fashioned Baltimore gas street lamps.

The gimmicks are often laid on thick, especially in the lower-priced developments, and it is easy to look down one's nose at the whole because of these parts. Several corned-up but significant developments have been dismissed by architects and observers as of no consequence because of their banalities. But overemphasis on façade cuts two ways. For all the laid-on touches, these developments have fastened on a basic plan of commendable simplicity and serviceability. That is why people like them. They buy the houses not because of those gas street lamps, or diamond-shaped panes; they buy because they get more house for their monthly payment than they would elsewhere.

They also get services, and in some developments, a quite encompassing package of them. Townhouse developments not only relieve the homeowner of any mowing, they often take care of the outside of his house, including roof repairs and painting, and some throw in such services as day-time supervision of children's areas and corps of babysitters. ("The management of Pomeroy West cares for it all. The landscaping, the community center and pool, even your home. Whether it's weeding or watering, repainting or repairs, you have no maintenance worries. Everything is done for you. This gives you time for a weekend at the lake, or a month in the Orient, or just more relaxing moments in your own private gardens. There are no cares of homeownership here, only the rewards.")

It is quite a package and is especially attractive to older couples who have done their time with a regular suburban homestead. With surprising vehemence, they will talk about the lawns they left behind, and how nice it is to be rid of such tyrannies. Young couples find the service package appealing too. Because they do not have to putter around and paint and fix up, they say, they have more time to be with their children.

Recreational facilities are elaborate, and becoming more so. Almost every cluster development save the very smallest will have tennis courts and a swimming pool, and the way competition is going, Olympic-size swimming pools are becoming standard. Usually there will be a clubhouse or community center and in some instances, a separate building for teenagers.

Some of the larger developments, such as New Seabury on Cape Cod, make recreation their principal motif, and center each cluster around a particular activity—boating on one, for example, riding in another. In most large developments there will be an eighteen-hole golf course, sometimes two, and wherever there is any water, the most will be made of it. Developers will spend a great deal of money to create an artificial lake, as Robert Simon did at Reston, for these not only are good for boating and swimming—and scenery—but markedly increase the value of the encircling land. Where there is a waterway, developers will also invest heavily in marinas.

Big developments or small, recreation facilities take a lot of the developers' "front money" for they have found it vital to leave nothing to the imagination of the prospective home buyer. The first thing that most of them build, along with the model houses, is the swimming pool and the clubhouse, which will do double duty as reception center and sales office. Such complexes are often so artfully contrived that once prospects are inside the reception center, there is no way out except by following a labyrinthine trail through the models, and back through the sales cubicles.

At this stage, the developments can look oddly like a movie set. The townhouse façades have a two-dimensional quality and one almost feels surprised to find there is something real on the other side of the front door. Activity abounds. Few families may yet have moved into the development, but the swimming pool, snack bar, and cabana club appear to be going full tilt. (In one as yet uninhabited development I visited, a troupe of happy children could be seen cycling around the greens, hour after hour after hour. They dressed up the scene so effectively, I thought they might have been hired as shills. The developer said they certainly were not. But an interesting idea, he said, a very interesting idea.)

The packaging concept has been carried to its ultimate in the retirement communities. For their monthly payment, couples get a small house or apartment unit and a prodigious range of facilities and services—including, among other things, complete medical care, golf courses, minibus transportation, organized recreational and hobby activities, craft shops, social rooms, library, and central clubhouse. Whatever one may think of the concept of such enclaves, physically they have been set up with great skill; the land planning is generally of a very high order and so, often, is the architecture. The Leisure Worlds of entrepreneur Ross Cortese are an outstanding example. Mr. Cortese built so many communities so fast he ran ahead of his market and further building has been stalled for want of financing. The communities that are up, however, furnish some of the best prototypes of cluster design in the country.

Where to now? The cluster approach is opening up some wonderful opportunities, but there are some pitfalls as well. One is that developers will use cluster as a wedge for achieving unreasonably high densities. What appeals most to them is the cluster, not the open space; the doughnut and not the hole. Where they have been allowed to get away with it, some developers have compressed people to the point of claustrophobia, with mean little spaces labeled as commons largely given over to parking.

But compression is not the main problem. In the long run, higher densities are inevitable, whatever kind of layout, and the cluster approach is one of the best ways of meeting the problem with grace. There will be efforts to abuse it, but communities, not developers, lay down the ground rules, and it is up to them to say this many people and no more.

The big danger is standardization. There is a strong possibility that cluster will congeal into a form as rigid and stereotyped as the conventional postwar layout it is replacing. This is already the case with townhouse developments. The basic designs of the first ones have been good, but not so good that they ought to be frozen. They have proved so marketable, however, that developers are copying their externals, gas lamps and all, no matter what the topography or the latitude or the surrounding neighborhood.

Cluster requires a fresh approach to house design. In too few cases do developers have architects design houses for the cluster layout—or, indeed, use architects at all. They use stock designs they have been used to. In outlying areas where lot sizes are relatively large, this is not too great a problem; there the conventional detached houses can work fairly well in a cluster arrangement—even the builder's stock ranchers. As lots are compressed, however, the houses and the layout begin to work at cross-purposes. The typical one-story house is designed for a wide suburban lot and throws everything into the façade on the front side, and puts it parallel to the street, which is just the wrong axis for a cluster layout. The windows on the side of the house not only lose their function but become a disadvantage; there is nothing to see except the neighbors' window shades. The vestigial strip of side yard becomes an echo chamber. The better-designed cluster houses solve the problem by doing away with side windows altogether—in the case of townhouses, by necessity.

Exteriors require different handling also. A cluster layout magnifies faults. When detached houses are laid out in conventional fashion, the contrived individuality of the stock models is mercifully separated by enough space to obscure the trumpery; a split-level colonial can be put on the next lot to a rancher without clashing too much, and with enough buffer space and greenery, Hansel and Gretel houses can be assimilated too. Move such houses close together, however, and the result can be a polychromatic mess—an out-of-scale toy village with all the visual defects of a conventional subdivision and no camouflage to hide them.

To go well with a cluster layout, houses should have an underlying unity. This is easiest come by in townhouse developments; even in the most hoked up examples, economic necessity forces the developer to keep the basic structure fairly clean. Variations or no, the houses will be unified by consistent roof lines and setbacks, and the recurrence of certain basic dimensions, as in the height and shape of windows. What makes stereotypes of them is not the uniformity, but the way developers tack them up to disguise the uniformity.

As with the houses, so with the land. There is still too much hack site planning. One of the most difficult things to find out in studying cluster developments is who, if anybody, was responsible for the final site plan. Small developers usually do the basic planning themselves and for professional assistance they tend to favor exsurveyors or engineers whose principal expertise is an ability to squeeze in the maximum number of lots the rules will allow. The larger and more successful developers do use trained land planners, and often very good ones; whatever the aesthetic impulses of the developers, they know that they will end up with a more economical layout if they do.

But the lesson comes hard to many developers. Often they will bring in a land planner only after it has become apparent that the original hack plan is not going to work very well. Of some sixty developments that I checked, in at least twenty cases the final site plan was drafted as a rescue job. (One of the most encouraging things about studying cluster development is to see the plans that *did not* get built.)

Site plans are getting better, but the unparalleled opportunities cluster opens up for imaginative treatment of the land are still relatively unexploited. Trees are an example. Since it virtually pays developers to leave as many standing as possible, they do not resort to the practice of sawing down all the trees and starting fresh with saplings. Cluster developments will have more trees around than conventional ones. But that is about it. In a few cases, trees will be used as an element in the architecture of the housing—in some cases, squares have been built around a particularly magnificent old tree, and with striking results. But this is the exception.

The way developers handle earth is similarly uninspired. Wonderful things can be done with the spoil from excavation, especially in prairie or desert areas where there is not a hillock in sight, but efforts are few and they are usually perfunctory. Occasionally a developer will proudly show you a big pile of dirt on which he has planted grass and talk to you about the creative use of overburden. It will look just like a pile of dirt on which grass has been planted—and a convenient justification for not carting the stuff away.

Where there are hills, the potential of cluster design is great but little exploited. As the flat valley floors are being filled up, developers have been turning to the hills, and they have been learning how to do things with rocks and slopes they never did before. They have been doing away with them. They have had to; under conventional zoning and building standards, they have to lay out their subdivisions as though the land were flat and then undertake extraordinary land-grading operations to reduce the topography to fit the subdivision.

The Los Angeles area is a particular case in point. One of the most horrifying sights in the U.S. is that of platoons of giant graders and scrapers chewing into the hills along the San Fernando Valley. Small hills the developers have simply leveled out of existence; the big ones they have chopped up so they look like the side of a pyramid; and on the building "pads" they have superimposed the same kind of ranchers with which they have covered the valley floor. The result is offensive to the eye, and as periodic slides and inundations have shown, is offensive to nature as well.

The desecration is so unnecessary. By applying the cluster principle developers can work with the slopes instead of obliterating them. This saves money. It also saves the terrain, for developers can concentrate the housing on the knolls and leave the rest undisturbed. The homeowner enjoys more privacy rather than less, and because of the successive changes of elevation, a finer view than he would have in the usual large-lot subdivision.

Where slopes are very steep or rocky, the cluster approach is even more relevant. Much can be done with the cantilever principle, and as Frank Lloyd Wright demonstrated so many years ago with "Falling Water," rocks can be used as structural elements with stunning effect. Unfortunately, this kind of imagination is still restricted to expensive custom homes and "second" homes in vacation areas. It has yet to be applied in any scale to developments.

One reason it has not been is the attitude of municipal engineers. They are a conservative lot, and for hillside plans they demand that developers lay down curbs and gutters and pavements almost as if they were working with a flat piece of land, and they generally insist on streets bigger than necessary. Developers are correct in protesting that the standards are overengineered, but then they have always been saying this about standards; steep slopes or gentle, they have habitually tried to get out of laying down curbs, gutters, and pavements so they can preserve the "character of the site"—and, at $5 a lineal foot, save a lot of money. Understandably, the engineers are skeptical, and many look on the cluster approach as another device of developers to cheat on the regulations. Planners have been arguing the developers' case, and since planners can talk about the public interest with more plausibility than developers, they have had some success in getting hillside standards liberalized. But there are many fights ahead.

Overengineered standards also help explain why streams are treated so insensitively in most developments. Developers are not against streams; they put them in culverts because the regulations force them to, and one reason they like cluster planning is that they can leave the streams. But engineers like concrete. If there is the slightest danger that streams might overflow, they insist that the banks be "stabilized," and they usually mean by this that it be put in a concrete trough. Reston suffered from this: the master plan called for storm sewers in the high-density areas, but the bulk of the drainage was to be handled the way it always was, by the streams. Where banks had to be stabilized, it would be with ferns and trees. The county engineer objected strongly. He wanted concrete. After protracted negotiations, Reston won some of its streams, but it lost some.

The critical problem in cluster planning is the handling of the interior commons and the private spaces. One lesson is abundantly clear. The private space is far and away the most important. The space is usually quite small; in townhouse projects the patios average out to no more than about 20 feet by 20 feet, the dimensions being determined by the width of the houses. But these small spaces are extremely functional. They are fine places for parking infants, for naps in the sun, for the happy hour, and it is a rare one that doesn't have a well-used charcoal grill.

Patios and courtyards also have the great advantage of extending the apparent size of the inside of the house. Since the living room opens onto them through the sliding glass doors, there is a considerable visual sweep from the kitchen in the front of the house to the back of the patio. (In the perspective of developers' brochures, the expanse is so vast the patio is scarcely visible in the distance.)

The enclosed court or garden is especially suited to city living and it has been proved many times that people will pay a premium for dwellings that provide them; as a check of real estate ads for New York converted brownstones with south garden will demonstrate, the premiums sometimes reach the fantastic. But this kind of private space has generally been available only in rehabilitated housing. Until recently, designers of city developments were dead set against private spaces. They claimed they were uneconomic, raised maintenance problems, and cluttered up the picture. The projects provided plenty of open space to work with, but the designers preferred to mass the space into common areas and thereby give order and unity to the design.

Much criticism was leveled at these collectives and at length a few projects were put up that included duplex units and gardens. The mating of styles was not always felicitous and to some architects the trend seemed calamitous. I recall visiting a mixed project with one of the architects. We looked down from a tower, which he had designed, to a block of duplex houses with private gardens, which he had not. It was a warm afternoon in fall and the people were busy at one thing or another in their gardens. A pleasant scene, I ventured. A hideous compromise, he said, and with the intense moral indignation that architects can summon up in dismissing designs they do not like, explained that the gardens were an asocial, selfish use of space, and utterly ruinous to the overall unity.

But the old brutalism has been giving way, albeit slowly. The trend in new urban projects is to have both towers and two- or three-story houses and to combine common open spaces with private patios and courts. In comparison to the stark projects of the past, these new ones do tend to look a bit messy, but this defect, if such it is, is apparent only when you are look- ing down at models. In actuality, the courtyards and gardens tend to enliven the scene for the people in the towers.

The trickiest problem is the relationship between the private spaces and the common ones. In most cases there is a fairly definite separation, with brick walls or high fences enclosing the private space. This method pro- vides the maximum privacy but it does cut down the size of the interior commons and for this reason some architects prefer to treat both kinds of space as one. Save for a low hedge, or line of bricks, there is little to indi- cate where the private open space ends and the common space begins. This makes for a cleaner design and a roomier commons.

It also makes for ambiguity, and if architects had to live in their develop- ments they would not do it this way. In almost any development where peo- ple live close together there is usually a lot of neighborly contact. Where the houses focus on a commons, the amount of contact is at its greatest. There is more kaffeeklatsching, more visiting back and forth, and while this has its advantages, without fences it becomes mandatory. There is no avoid- ing it, and a good many people would like to avoid it.

But there is no redoubt, no place to draw the line. Wives complain that if they feel like stretching out on a beach chair to read or just plain rest, their siesta is sure to be interrupted. Then there is the entertaining prob- lem. When couples do their *al fresco* entertaining in full sight of everyone, neighborly relationships can be put to a severe strain. (Will they under- stand it's an out-of-town couple we haven't seen in years? Shall we ask them to come over and join us just for cocktails? Will they leave before supper?) The poet's point about good fences and good neighbors is true. All in all, experience suggests, private open spaces should be private.

There need be no antithesis between common spaces and private ones. They complement each other; even in very high density developments there should be room for both. When there is a buffer zone of private gardens, interior commons do not have to be very large; the fact they are enclosed by buildings on three or four sides makes them look larger than they actually are.[3]

The usual commons consists of a rectangle of green lawn, some hedges and trees, and a play area at one end. The result is pleasant enough, but if you have seen one you have seen a great many. Occasionally there are fresh touches—an open air pavilion with a huge fireplace, for example—but in most cases the originalities are standard: a piece or so of free form sculpture, perhaps, or a string of those gas street lamps.

As Georgian architects knew so well, the great advantage of a tight housing layout is the opportunity it affords to design the spaces for the buildings and the buildings for the spaces—at one and the same time, and not seriatim. But few aspects of cluster are so unexploited. If there is to be an interior commons, for example, why not follow through and design the buildings for real enclosure? Open space is at its most inviting when it is approached through a covered passageway, yet this ancient principle has been little applied. Neither has the crescent or the arcade or the circus.

There are many fresh approaches to explore. Do the commons, for example, have to be green? There can be too much and some of the most celebrated garden-city communities suffer from the overemphasis. Without enclosure, or a striking foreground or background, expanses of green can be quite dull, and sometimes they can be downright oppressive. (Radburn, for example, is almost smothered in foliage in summer, and to this observer, looks best in spring.)

Punctuation and contrast are needed, and one of the best ways to provide them is through the paved courtyard or small plaza. It can provide an excellent common area, and tends to heighten the effect of any greenery there is. In few settings does a large tree seem so handsome. The paved court also makes a nice transition between the private open space and the surrounding common areas, all the more so if the housing clusters are surrounded by large expanses of green. They are also the best of settings for a fountain.

The paved court, however, still strikes many people as much too revolutionary for the market. One of the best-looking designs in the country was ditched because of this bias. The site planner had set his clusters in the middle of a golf course. Since there was to be green around them, he planned the common space within each cluster as a paved courtyard. The developer lost his nerve and asked a market consultant to give his judgment. The consultant said it was too radical, and recommended that the spaces be grass and look "pretty and soft."

Such timidity is unwarranted, even by commercial standards. The court has been given a pretty good consumer test for quite a few centuries, and where it has been tried anew it seems to work as well as ever. Charles Goodman's paved courts for the River Park development in southwest Washington are a fine example. Compared to architect Chloethiel Smith's grassy spaces in the neighboring Capitol Park development, Goodman's courts seem severe, but both projects sold well, and in both, the open spaces seem to work quite well—proving, once again, that different approaches can achieve satisfying results.

In rural areas where there is a lot of space to work with, there are many more things that can be done with common areas than have been tried. Grazing, for one thing. If fields and meadows are put to this kind of productive use they look much better than any formally landscaped scene. Sheep, for example, lend just the estate flavor that developers want to promote, and there is no better way to keep the grass cut. Instead of having to pay people to maintain the land, the homeowners can get it done virtually free, and sometimes even make a little. In one Colorado vacation development, the houses are clustered on the slopes, leaving three hundred acres of meadowland as the commons. The homeowners lease it out as pasture land for cattle.

Some people have suggested going so far as to have a complete working farm as the center of a commons; one such scheme has been proposed for the development of a small valley in upstate New York. One can only wish the proponents well, but the experience of subdivisions close to farms suggests that farm activity and its attendant smells is attractive to residents for about one day. After that they raise Cain with the farmer for disturbing their peace—starting up his tractors at five A.M., using dangerous sprays, letting their children get into mischief, and such. Another idea that is likely to come a cropper is the equestrian village centered around riding stables. This was proposed in the preliminary plan for Reston but was prudently dropped. There are stables, but they are located well away from any houses. People like to ride horses, developers have found, but they do not want to live near them.

While there are many more things that can be done with the spaces within developments, perhaps the greatest challenge is to find ways to link the spaces. Not much has been done to exploit this potential; by and large, the cluster developments are planned project by project, with little relation one to the other, or to the open spaces of the community. Very large developments, or "new towns," are planned on such a scale that they provide a community open-space system themselves, but while more of these are in the offing, the bulk of future residential growth will be an aggregation of small and medium-size developments.

Yet their open spaces do not have to be a miscellany. With the proper incentives, individual developers can be led to plan their open spaces so that they will eventually fit together in an overall system. The key is for the local government to anticipate the development that is inevitable and to lay down in advance the skeleton of an open-space network to which each developer will contribute as the area is built up. This presupposes a very vigorous arm twisting of developers but there is a strong indication that if planning commissions were to take this kind of initiative, developers would go along.

Philadelphia has furnished an outstanding demonstration. In the 1950s, there still remained in its far northeast section a five thousand acre expanse of open land. It was mostly farm land, gently rolling and laced with a network of wooded creeks. It was also eminently buildable, and squarely in the path of row-house development. Mulling over the fate of this area, Philadelphia city planner Edmund Bacon figured that there was no reason why the city should leave the basic land-use pattern for this area up to the speculative builders. The city, he felt, ought to lay down a master subdivision plan. Developers could fill in the details, but the open-space and housing patterns would be so strongly outlined that the end product would be the kind of unity that is usually possible only when one large developer is doing the whole thing.

With a cluster approach, Bacon figured, the total acreage could amenably house some 68,000 people. The area would be divided into a series of neighborhood groupings, and there would be an open-space network based on the stream valleys. To obtain plat approval, a builder would have to dedicate these parts of his tract designated as green space to the city. Instead of the usual aggregation of bits and pieces, accordingly, there would be a continuous open-space system that would be highly functional for recreation, and would at once connect and define the neighborhoods.

Builders took to the idea. The master plan did go quite far in telling them what to do, but it provided them excellent densities—about nine units per acre—and considerably less street and land improvement expenses than ordinarily they would have had to bear. The first builder started work in 1959. Since then other builders have joined suit and with few variations from the original plan.

The result is not a showpiece. For so advanced a plan, what one sees on the ground is disappointingly ordinary. The houses, which are in the $11,000–$13,000 range, are basically standard row houses with a few façade variations, and they do not always sit well in the circular groupings laid down by the planners. But the plan works, and one has only to look to the conventional row-house developments a few miles back toward the city to see what a difference it has made. The houses in the cluster neighborhoods have been just as profitable for the builders, no more expensive for the homeowners, yet they are complemented by a magnificent stream-valley network that cost the city nothing and will one day be priceless. They are indeed ordinary neighborhoods, but that is the point. If this kind of amenity can be achieved in middle-income neighborhoods in a city, the potential elsewhere is tremendous.

It is the *feeling* of space we must provide. This is not the same as space; our subjective reactions are as important, and as the reader can test for himself, a few key pieces often dominate our perception of a much larger area. The Taconic Parkway, running north from New York, is a good case in point. A great many people believe it is by far the most pleasant super highway in the East, and if you asked them why, they would tell you that it is because most of it runs through open farmland. It doesn't. Check its 90 odd miles and you will find that there are only a few stretches that are bordered by farms. A far greater proportion is in the densely wooded area that many people find somewhat boring. This is the reality. What people *see*, however, is a reality too, and the more important one.

With art, then, we can link the parts of our urban landscape into a very effective whole. In gross acreage, such networks may be smaller than the large greenbelt; in effectiveness they can be far greater. They can be woven throughout the urban area, where people will see them and use them, as part of their daily life—not a relief from the environment; but *within* it.

THE NEW TOWNS

The next step, many people believe, should be the building of whole new towns. Better big subdivisions are not enough, they say; what we should do is carry the cluster concept to the ultimate; group not only homes, but industrial plants, hospitals, cultural centers, and create entirely new communities. These would not only be excellent places in their own right; together, they would be the last best chance of the metropolis.

It is a hope that at last seems nearer the threshold of reality. Developers have been moving in this direction and across the country a dozen large-scale communities have been started, each of which is meant to have an eventual population of 75,000 or more. In addition, there are some two hundred "planned communities" being built which, if smaller, claim the same basic approach. Big corporations have been getting into the business. Gulf Oil financed the start of Reston, outside of Washington, and has now taken over the whole operation; the Connecticut General Life Insurance Company is financing Columbia, outside of Baltimore. General Electric has set up a special division to assist the builders of new towns and a RAND-type think center for the planning of them.

Some of these new communities have been having their troubles. Almost all builders have been hurt lately by tight money, but those who have launched the large scale developments have been particularly vulnerable. They have to borrow huge sums of money to get such operations going, and if house sales falter, they can quickly find themselves hard put to meet the interest payments. For want of enough cash flow, a number of developers have had to stop at phase one of their communities and several have gone bankrupt.

But this is the way things often go in the industry and new town advocates remain optimistic. The credit bind, they point out, does not prove that the new town idea is faulty; what it proves is that better financing arrangements are in order, and that the federal government should lend more of a hand. The administration has declared strongly in favor of new towns but the support it has been enabled to give so far has been largely moral. Through mortgage insurance and loans for land assembly, the Department of Housing and Urban Development has been offering some incentive for communities and developers to work together on new town projects. The enabling legislation is full of bugs, however.

The administration is now proposing as an aid the "federally guaranteed cash-flow debenture." This would provide developers of new towns the wherewithal to pay the interest charges on their borrowed capital until sales were rolling sufficiently to generate some real cash for them. In return for such underwriting, the developers would have to include in their plans some housing for low- and middle-income people. The administration is also proposing additional incentives for state and local government cooperation in new town projects. Congress has not been keen on subsidies for new towns—big city mayors don't want any at all—but as time goes on it will probably authorize more aid.

But this does not mean we will get a lot of new towns. Let me define terms. I am not taking up the pros and cons of better-planned suburban developments; and this essentially is what most of the new communities that appropriate the title of new town really are. What I want to explore is the validity of the ideal new town model as planners see it. It is far more than a matter of degree. Philosophically as well as physically, the true new town is to be a *complete* community—so complete that it can exist independent of the old city, and, quite literally, help cut it down to size.

The specifications are remarkably similar to those laid down some half century ago in England by Ebenezer Howard. Like many generations of planners after him, Howard sought an antidote to the city. "There are in reality," he said, "not only, as is so constantly assumed, two alternatives—town life and country life—but a third alternative in which all the advantages of the most energetic and active town life, with all the beauty and delight of the country, may be secured in perfect combination."

He proposed a garden city in the countryside—a community of about a thousand acres set in a green belt of five thousand acres. The community would own the land and lease it to people who would build according to the plan. It would be a balanced community; in addition to residential development, there would be local industry, thriving agriculture, and in total there would be enough jobs for everyone in the town.

Howard saw this not only as good in itself but as a solution to the problems of the city. London, he thought, was monstrously big and unhealthy, and its land values inflated out of reason. If garden cities were built, they would prove so attractive that they would draw people from the city; this would depress the land values in London, thus making it possible to redevelop the city at a much lower density. The new towns, he prophesied, would "be the magnet which will produce the effect for which we are all striving—the spontaneous movement of the people from our crowded cities to the bosom of our kindly mother earth."

The language of this kindly utopian is not that of today's new town planners, but in their own more scientific way they are saying the same thing. They, too, are repelled by the city. New town proposals are generally prefaced with a sweeping indictment of the city as pretty much of a lost cause. We tried, the charge goes, but the city is a hopeless tangle. Medical analogies abound. The city is diseased, cancerous, and beyond palliatives. The future is not to be sought in it, but out beyond, where we can start afresh.

The possibility of working with a clean slate is what most excites planners and architects about new towns. Freed from the constraints of previous plans and buildings and people, the planners and architects can apply the whole range of new tools. With systems analysis, electronic data processing, game theory, and the like, it is hoped, a science of environmental design will be evolved and this will produce a far better kind of community than ever was possible before.

On the main specifications, however, there is already considerable agreement. First, the new town must be balanced. It must have people of all income groups and houses to match. Second, it must be self-contained; it will have its own industry and commerce and jobs enough for all who wish to work within the boundaries of the community. No one need commute to the city.

No one will need visit the city for culture either. The new town will be self-contained in this respect as well, with its own symphony orchestras, little theaters, junior colleges, and colleges, and the town center will have all the urbanity and services of the center city. Recreation will be built in, and close to every home will be green space, tennis courts, golf courses, hiking and riding trails.

To offer all this, a new town would really have to be a city, and lately proponents have been using the term "new city" in describing their communities. But these are not to be like cities as we have known them. There is not to be any dirty work in them. There are not to be any slums. There are not to be any ethnic concentrations, or concentrations of any kind. Housing densities will be quite low. There will be no crowded streets. Yet, it will be a city—"a whole city," one developer puts it, "with all the texture and fabric of the city." It will have everything the city has, in short, except its faults.

This is an impossible vision. Certainly there are going to be more and bigger new communities built and it is good there will be. Architecturally and otherwise, some of the ones that have been going up are excellent, and as I will take up in "The Case for Crowding" (page 217), are providing many important lessons in large-scale land assembly and development.

But this is not the same thing as building self-contained new cities, and it is the validity of this concept that I am questioning: the pure, uncompromised vision—the community we would get if all the necessary legislation were passed, all the funds needed were provided, and all of the key specifications were followed.

It would not work. The reason it would not work does not lie in the usual obstacles that are decried—fragmentation of local government, lack of trained design teams, and so on. The substance of this critique is that the trouble is in the idea itself.

As elements of the metropolis, new towns could not take care of more than a fraction of our future population growth, even under the best of circumstances; nor could they significantly change the structure of the metropolis. The English new towns have not; the Scandinavian new towns were never meant to.

As a community, the self-contained new town is a contradiction in terms. You cannot isolate the successful elements of the city and package them in tidy communities somewhere else. And if you could do it, would you be able to have only the good and none of the bad? The goal is so silly it seems profound.

I would further argue that the idea of getting people to stay put and work and live together in the same healthy place is somewhat retrogressive. Americans move too much to be thus beneficently contained. Their mobility does breed problems, but it is also a dynamic and in the oversight of this the self-contained community is irrelevant if not contradictory to the main sweep of American life.

American planners tend to overplan, even where the constraints of reality are great, and when they are given a clean slate to work with, the temptation to overplan can be irresistible. There are exceptions, but physically the most striking thing about plans for ideal new towns is their finality. Everything is in its place: There are no loose ends, no question marks, and it is this completeness of the vision, more than the particulars of it, that stirs recalcitrance. It is one thing to be beckoned down the road to a distant utopia, quite another to be shown utopia itself in metes and bounds and all of it at once.

This, the plans seem to say, is the way it jolly well is going to be. There is to be no zigging and zagging to adapt the plans to people. It is the people who are to do the adapting and if there is anything they cannot adapt to, it will be just too bad because there is no provision for changing the plans as time goes on. These designs are so ordered in their intricacy that if you changed just one element, the whole thing would be rendered inoperable.

As planners of more pragmatic leanings have noted, this fixation on the "end state" plan runs directly counter to the profession's favorite axioms about interaction, feedback, and planning as an ongoing process. "The planning is neat, rational, logical, and fixed," says one critic, Marshall Kaplan. "The range of alternatives given is quite limited. . . . That the community will change, will develop after 1980 is acknowledged by the planners but often denied by the plan. Every area is planned, with little flexibility provided in the design for unforeseen want. Obsolescence—either planned or unplanned—is not a considered input."

There is really only one plan. The kind of geometrics favored may differ, but whether linear or concentric or molecular, the plans end up looking so alike it is a wonder such large staffs are deemed necessary to draft them. Several graduate students steeped in current planning dogma could work up almost identical plans in a few weeks—they do it regularly as class projects, and how they do it is pretty close to the way the most elaborate plans are drafted. The plans come into being almost full-blown. They start with a visual concept. The approach is graphic, and for all the to-do about sociological and economic research, this is supporting documentation. The design comes first.

The designs all look the same because they spring from the same design philosophy. It is the design philosophy embedded in the standard redevelopment project, with its high-rise slabs and aseptic open space. Just at a time when it is finally being conceded that the design doesn't fit people too well ("I certainly don't agree with Jane Jacobs, but . . ."), the whole thing is about to be reincarnated in suburbia, only called something else and stretched even further.

The center of the new city is a vast expanse of mall surrounded by office and apartment towers and beyond these the various neighborhoods, or "villages," stretch off in the distance, each encircled by its own spaces. The sweep is awesome. The planners will have a great deal to say about human scale, and to make up for its absence in the plan, they supply it in the brochures with ground-level sketches of what life will be like. The sketches are now standard: people sitting at outdoor cafes, mothers with baby carriages looking at Paris-style kiosks or waiting for the monorail.[4]

But it is the same old redevelopment project, magnified. There is the same compartmentation of activities, the same insistence on order and symmetry, the same distaste for the street and its function, the same lack of interest in the surroundings.

There are no surroundings. In bird's-eye renderings of urban redevelopment projects, the grubby details of neighboring streets and buildings are customarily airbrushed away. People who sketch new towns have no such impedimenta to contend with, but even so, they give little indication of what, if anything, might lie beyond the project. They don't seem particularly interested. The background is shown as a boundless tract of undifferentiated space. It is almost as if the planners had come upon a habitable planet unmarred by previous habitation. You see no palimpsests of previous towns, factories, trailer villages, or railroad tracks. Even the greenery is indeterminate; you cannot tell whether it is farmland, forest, upland or lowland, or some algaelike growth.

The treatment of space within the boundaries is similarly grandiloquent. New towns do not squander space the way conventional large-lot subdivisions do, but this is not saying very much. New towns have especial reason to waste no space at all; the whole rationale of the accompanying wedges and green belts rests on this point; if planners are to justify setting aside such vast acreages the better to contain development, the development should be very contained indeed.

But it is not. The densest part, the core, seems extraordinarily expansive. The essence of a downtown is concentration and mixture, but the malls that are sketched in the plans are quite vast, even for a big city. Beyond the core, the densities decrease further, with the houses on the periphery set in half-acre and acre lots. This, too, begs the question of the green belts beyond. For whom are they functional? The people who live next to the green belts have already been provided with the most open space of their own. The majority of the people are put in the middle, in high-rise towers and garden apartments. These are the people who need the open space the most and yet they are the farthest away from it—in some plans, up to two miles away.

True, the people up high can always look out their windows at the green belt, and the distances are not so great that they couldn't walk there if they are of a mind to. However, if the pedestrian habits of present suburbanites are any index, even relatively short distances are a deterrent, and as these are increased, the use of open space falls off drastically.

In this best of both worlds there is to be bustle without noise, concentration without confusion, people without traffic, excitement without danger. What the planners mean to do, in short, is to isolate each of the good qualities of the city from its context and reconstitute it in suburbia without its companion disadvantages. In a word, urbanity without cities.

The good elements of the city and the bad elements, alas, are often different aspects of the same function. We should try to make the most of the good and the least of the bad, but separating them out is extraordinarily difficult. Where does the bad leave off and the good begin? One of the charms of the city, most people agree, is the cosmopolitanism of its small shops—the Irish bar, the German *Konditorei*, the Italian grocery which makes its own line of pasta, the street festivals on the saints' days. But this kind of cosmopolitanism goes hand in hand with ethnic concentrations and it is certainly not the kind of thing new town planners wish to perpetuate.

Conversely, among the obvious bad things about cities are the old, dilapidated loft buildings and the once-grand neighborhoods gone to seed. But the loft buildings are a haven for marginal enterprises and an incubator of new ones because they are dilapidated and inexpensive to rent. Similarly, slightly seedy neighborhoods are the makings of new bohemias, and eventually, as the advance guard moves on to another seedy neighborhood, high-rent areas.

It would be wonderful indeed if one could isolate the desirable qualities and export them without their context. Architects and planners have a gallery of urbane places they would like to borrow from: the hill towns of Italy and Provence, for example, are great favorites for exemplifying compact development; Venice, for the pedestrian's city. In citing the desiderata, however, the tendency is to slough over the not-so-good elements that make the good elements possible, and this is even more pronounced when planners consider what is worth copying from American cities.

Let us take the matter of urbanity. Almost all new town prospectuses make a big point of it. No typical suburban shopping center for them. Their centers are going to be highly urbane, with a full range of cultural activities, specialty shops, second-hand bookstores, craft shops, off-beat restaurants, sidewalk cafes, and a host of touches evoking the flavor of Greenwich Village and Georgetown, for which latter place a considerable number of new developments have been named.

But it never seems to work out that way. What middle-class suburbia gets are shopping centers for middle-class suburbia. The institutions that flourish here are those which do an excellent job of catering to the middle range—such as Sears Roebuck and Howard Johnson—and where there is a branch of a large downtown department store, the top and the bottom of the line are left out. The supermarket provides the same kind of choice; acres of goods lie before you but they are the same goods, and they will be the same in the other big supermarket. You can find every known brand of corn flakes, or tomato catsup, or processed cheese, but if it is something slightly special you want, like a good head of lettuce, you will roam the aisles in vain. Only small stores have this kind of variety.

Restaurants seem to be an especially vexing problem for developers. In most of the new postwar communities, the restaurants are rather bland, and residents will frequently complain quite strenuously about them. Developers never planned it that way; many of them have made special efforts to bring in a good specialty restaurant or at least a first rate operation. In one case, the developer offered generous lease terms in an unsuccessful effort to get an Italian family to set up a Greenwich Village–type restaurant in his new town center.

But the environment is not right. In the first place, the kind of restaurateur that is sought does not have the capital to wait out the lean years while the population builds up sufficiently to provide a reasonable market. Only chain operations usually have the capital for that. Secondly, well-capitalized or not, the operation must inevitably become an all-purpose one. It will be a service element—the place, for example, where the local groups will hold their meetings. The lunchtime clientele will be the people who work in the center and they are the blue-plate-special or club-sandwich crowd and not the two-martini people who provide the midday support for a city's French and Italian restaurants. The weekend business will be mainly prospective homebuyers with children in tow, and the restaurateur will have to put in a supply of high chairs. And whom does he get at nights? A few regulars in the bar, a smattering of residents, and a few visitors.

To survive, the operation will have to adapt to the median. From community to community you will find that even the best of the operations generally feature the all-American menu—shrimp cocktail, baked potato with sour cream and chives, steak, salad with Roquefort dressing, and selections from the dessert wagon. As staples go, these can be pretty good fare; nevertheless, the residents will complain that there is no decent place for eating out, and even if the food were really good, they still might complain.

The image has been fixed. At nighttime the restaurateur can put checkered cloths over the formica tables, dim the lights, put out candles in fishnet containers and add a pianist. But it just won't wash. To the residents, it is still a community-service center and in their mind irrevocably coupled with daytime shopping, children, and luncheon meetings of women's groups.

In another respect, the new towns lack self-sufficiency. There's to be no sin in them. Despite the claim that the new towns are to have all of the attractions of the city, there are no provisions for night clubs, bookie joints, or any but the mildest of vices. The new towns are to cater to the widest possible range of tastes, but there is not to be any bad taste. There will be no raffishness, no garish "strip," no honky-tonks. Some suggestions have been made about filling the void with a "fun palace," an idea bruited in England for a large factorylike structure in which, as in a free play period, people could improvise all sorts of activities. But the fun would be wholesome, and as with a similar suggestion for a permanent carnival for the town centers, one senses a monitoring and somewhat condescending presence.

The bars are to be genteel, too. In the new towns of England some of the pubs are so prim they look as though they should be called alcohol dispensaries, and the ones over here are not real bars but the cocktail lounges of adjoining restaurants, the kind with Muzak. All this is understandable enough, and new towns are not to be scorned for such wholesomeness: It's one of the reasons they would be nice places to live in. But would you want to visit them?

The affinity of such communities for the middle range is a universal phenomenon. When they planned the new town of Vallingby, the Swedish planners, who are quite city-minded, were especially anxious to have a highly urbane town center, and they went to considerable lengths to provide attractive plazas, fountains, and well-designed street furniture. But the urbane shops did not take root. To the disappointment of the planners, the shops that flourished were good average, but not much more.

The same thing is true of the English new towns. The planners have lavished fine statuary on the centers, elaborate water fountains, and so forth. Enterprises that have leased the shops, however, are of a more mundane style, some rather plebeian, and the effect of the whole is somewhat tacky. (The food in the restaurants is beyond description. It is so awful that even new town planners blanch; they much prefer to eat in old towns nearby, and will be sure to take a visitor there.)

There is not very much planners could do to change things. These centers lack the essential quality of the city—its location. Urbanity is not something that can be lacquered on; it is the quality produced by the great concentration of diverse functions and a huge market to support the diversity. The center needs a large hinterland to draw upon, but it cannot be in the hinterland; it must be in the center. This is the fundamental contradiction in the new town concept of self-containment.

The kind of self-containment that most excites new town proponents is the idea of everybody's working and living in the same place. It is not to be just another suburb. In the ideal new town the planners mean to provide as many jobs as there will be workers, and the jobs will cover the whole range of skills and occupations.

Some kinds of jobs, of course, won't be included. Plans do not call for dirty work and the kind of smoky, noisy plants that would pollute the environment. But the planners don't think there will be any imbalance, for they are sanguine that the industrial trends are going in their direction. What with automation, atomic power, computerization, they hold, industry is transforming itself into the kind of clean, white-collar, smokeless facilities for which new towns would be the ideal setting. Because of this affinity, they further argue, the new town will be a powerful vehicle for the decentralization of employment. The present pattern of industrial clusters close to the city will be loosened up, the components dispersed all over the region, and each encapsulated with its own resident work force.

The planners are misreading the trends. Suburbia is going to get more plants, just as it's going to get more people, but the two are not to be so neatly packaged together. As far as employment is concerned, I hope to demonstrate, the self-contained community is impossible to achieve and it is a very good thing that it is impossible to achieve.

To have any claim to self-containment, the new towns must provide something for export. Taking in each other's laundry can keep a lot of people busy, and almost any new community provides a considerable number of local jobs—store clerks, deliverymen, service-station attendants, doctors, lawyers, bankers. But there is a limit to the number of service jobs a community can provide, and vital as these are, they give the community no dynamic. The new town must have primary industry. It cannot have just one kind, either, for it would be simply a new version of the company town.

Significantly, the most notable communities built from scratch have been built around the industry of government—Washington, D.C., Canberra, Brasilia, Chandigarh, and Islambad. These capitals may have many admirable features but they are essentially one-function towns and they are anything but models of the complete community.

New town planners are very keen on having a "balanced" population, with a pretty complete spectrum of income, education, and skills. This is all very fine, but to match all these people with jobs would require that the planners create not only a miniature city but a miniature metropolis.

No new town comes close to these specifications. The English new towns, some of which are factory-worker communities, do provide a good number of jobs, but the range is not a broad one, and a sizable number of people journey into the towns or out of them to earn their living.

In practice, it is virtually impossible to tie jobs to homes. Even when a lot of jobs are provided in a community, the people who fill them will not necessarily be the people who live there. As a matter of fact, the chances are strong that a great many won't be. In a number of places where a large supply of close-to-home jobs has been provided, there has been a large amount of commutation and reverse commutation. Vallingby is a case in point. There are 9000 jobs there, but most of the people who work at them do not live in Vallingby. They commute to them, some 7000 people, and as they do, the bulk of the wage earners who do live in Vallingby—25,000 of 27,000—commute outward, mostly to the center of Stockholm. In varying degrees, this mixed commutation pattern is true of most new towns in any modern industrial society and it is hard to see how it could be otherwise.

The oneness concept of work and residence is at odds with our dominant growth trends. It is true enough that factories are moving outward and that certain expanding industries find outlying locations excellent for new facilities. To deduce from this that a massive decentralization of employment is taking place is quite wrong. As factories have been vacating their cramped, high-cost city locations, there has been a corresponding increase in managerial, professional and service jobs in the center city. More, not less than before, the city is headquarters. The people who service it are basic to any balanced population; any new town that is to have its share of them is going to have a lot of people who must commute, just like any other suburb.

And what, it might be asked, is so therapeutic about working close to home? There is much to say for it, and it is a beguiling thought that one could take a five-minute walk along a footpath, or a short ride on a minibus, to a campuslike office in the woods, and even perhaps return home for lunch, like French businessmen used to do. But all this propinquity is not without price. The fact is that a lot of people rather like the separation of work and home. They enjoy having as neighbors people who are not the same people they have been working with all day; they even enjoy the geographic buffer between the work place and their wives, and many of the wives do too. The commute, furthermore, is not always the ordeal it is often pictured; for many people it is the only time they ever get to do any reading, and the ride back can serve as a decompression period.

But let us suppose, for the sake of argument, that in one case the new town planners achieve their dream. They do reproduce the metropolis in miniature; they attract a broad range of people—low income, high income, blue collar, white collar—and on a one-to-one ratio, for every kind of person they provide jobs to match.

Self-containment still wouldn't work. There would be no real choice. In the aggregate there might be a lot of jobs, but for any one person there would be only a few that were suitable, and the more educated and more skilled the person, the fewer. If you were, say, a certain kind of electrical engineer, there might likely be only one job slot in the whole area for you— the one you have. You are, in effect, in a company town. If you came to dislike the job, you would have no practical alternative within the community. If you did like it, you would be in a poor bargaining position with your employer. In the tacit negotiations for raises or advancement, or, simply, having your opinions prevail, your ability to get as good or better a job, and the employer's awareness of this, is crucial. Pleasant surroundings cannot compensate for a lack of choice.

Self-containment would hurt employers as well. When residence in a certain place is packaged with a job, the employer may have some good talking points about the good life and the non-job benefits. But for all this, he is under severe disadvantage in competing for people with specialized skills. Just as the worker needs access to a wide range of jobs, the employer needs access to a wide range of people, and the further he is out on the periphery, the tougher his position. In a more central location he can compete much more effectively for prospective employees, for he does not have to persuade them to pick up stakes and move to the new town as part of the deal.

Theoretically, the accessibility problem could be solved if the new towns were linked directly with each other with a circumferential rapid transit system. Then a man might live in New Town A and journey around the circle to work in New Town B, or C, or D. Ebenezer Howard suggested something like this in his original prospectus. He proposed a circular arrangement of municipal railways that would link the new towns in a system. Much the same idea has been advanced for tying together future new towns, with the inevitable monorail sketched as a possible means. Another suggestion is creation of an additional set of belt freeways around the outer ring.

This circumlocution would be very bad transportation planning. To be economic, mass-transportation routes must tap great concentrations of high-density traffic. We are having enough trouble in getting good mass-transit systems even when they go with the region's traffic flow, which is essentially radial, with the lines converging toward the center. The capital cost of another mass-transit system cutting across the grain would be prodigious.

Highways, of course, can go where mass transit cannot. The new beltways have created a great deal of suburb-to-suburb traffic and in some areas more commercial development is being built to tap these circumferential routes than the old city to suburb axes. But only so many circles can be built. Additional freeways across suburbia would consume inordinate amounts of expensive land, and would further aggrandize the role of the car, a prospect that should be anathema to planners. In the long run, such freeway systems would be economically unfeasible for the same reasons that a similar rapid-transit system would be; high-cost facilities to serve low-density traffic.

Theoretically, the only way you could generate enough traffic to justify these systems would be to force new town people not to work in their own new town or in the city but in another town along the ring. But this would be a refutation of the new town ideal, and the worst of both possible worlds—suburbias without a city, a vision truly peripheral.

As the major answer to the growth problems of the metropolis, the new town concept is not practical. For the New York metropolitan area the Regional Plan Association has figured that to take care of the expected population growth over the next two decades via the new town route, one hundred new towns of 100,000 each would have to be built. This would take some doing and even if it were possible, the Association does not think it would be desirable. The result would be an extremely inefficient pattern, for the dispersal would rule out any effective mass-transportation system.

The Regional Plan Association believes that the heart of the growth problem is employment. The RPA is trying to encourage a concentration of industry and business in a relatively small number of centers; some would be new, some would be built on existing centers. There would be residential development around these centers, to be sure, but job and residence would not be tied together.

Access to jobs, not propinquity, is what is important. "For the same reason that people prefer to live and work in large metropolitan areas," says Stanley Tankel, RPA's planning director, "they are willing to trade a walk to work in a self-contained new town with its limited choice of jobs for a somewhat longer trip to work to a center where job choices abound. A region with deep and well-greased channels of transportation provides security of choice whether you are seeking work or workers."

In the new town scheme of things, people not only won't have to leave the town to go to work; they won't have to leave ever. The new towns are to provide total environments so encompassing, so beneficent that they will to a large extent eliminate the rootlessness and mobility of urban life.

The ultimate aim is the "life-cycle community" with a full range of accommodations, activities, and culture for every stage of life's journey. It is conceded that there would be some transients—the plans for the culture centers virtually require some staff bohemians on the premises—and undoubtedly there would be constant leakage as some people broke out of the cycle. For the bulk of the population, however, there would be no point in leaving. From cradle to grave they could progress through all phases— kindergarten, school, college, child rearing, retirement—moving within the community to the kind of housing units and neighborhoods appropriate to the particular stage of the cycle. (The planners do not pursue the logic of the progression to the conclusion, however. In no new town plan I have seen is there space allotted to a cemetery.)

The idea is a very old-fashioned one. From the time of utopian communities of the early 1800s there have been many attempts to encompass the good life within the physical boundaries of an ideal community. They have all foundered. Even in the more agrarian days of the early eighteenth century, such communities were at odds with the main currents of American life. Today they would be utterly inconsistent.

Planners are behind on their sociology. Several decades ago there was a tendency to look on mobility as a bad thing, and there was much concern over the *anomie* of rootless people and an exaggerated veneration of the psychic benefits of the structured society and the belongingness of small-town life. But this was nostalgia even then. Americans move; they always have, and though they have paid in many ways for this mobility, they move because of opportunity, and the people who move most are the managerial and professional people the new towns would like to have—such as planners, who are among the most mobile of professionals.

Characteristically, new middle-class suburbs have a relatively high rate of turnover, even the best of them. A case in point is Park Forest, south of Chicago. When developer Philip Klutznick built it shortly after the war, it was the most advanced new town in the country. In some respects it still is. Unlike most new towns, it was set up at the beginning as a self-governing political unit.

Developers are usually fearful of such an arrangement. They prefer to be benevolent on their own terms, with democracy expressed through unofficial civic organizations. They fear that if the residents had political control they would raise all sorts of mischief over zoning and taxes. But a real government also means a real community. Park Foresters did give Klutznick some rough times, but their involvement in the community was thorough and deep and the community was much the better for it. People are more attached to a place they run than one they do not.

Compared to older communities, however, Park Forest has had a fairly high turnover. Residents tend to be touchy about this, as I found when I published a study on Park Forest. I had noted that the greatest number of transients were in the rental units and that as the proportion of single family homes increased more people would be staying on. But many people bristled just the same, especially those who were staying on. Like developers and new town planners, residents want to see the stabilities emphasized and they regard talk about turnover as a reflection on the quality of the community.

But the turnover is normal. It is not a defect of new communities that they harbor transients; it is one of their great functions. No matter how "balanced" the community, it is the college-educated middle-income people who usually provide its leadership, whatever their numbers. When they leave a community, they are not necessarily rejecting it. Many leave because they have to. Their organization may be transferring them to another post or they may be moving because they are switching to another company. It is the game.

There are some people who do not have to leave but do so because the community has no housing suitable to the next rung up. As they sometimes put it, it's time they "graduated." The new town approach, by providing a broader selection of housing, would tend to cut down this kind of turnover. (This certainly was the case at Park Forest. When it was first built, the developer concentrated on rental units and houses in the $14,000–$18,000 range, and all the young people spoke warmly of the benefits of living in a "classless" community. But then time went on and incomes went up, and some people left for more expensive houses in nearby communities. The developer wisely began adding new units in higher price ranges and this allowed a considerable number of people to "trade up" within the community.)

A broad range of housing is certainly a worthy goal for new towns. Any new community which provides a range will be more adhesive than one that does not and probably a better place for people to live in. But not forever. The community is bound to have a lot of turnover and it would be a failure otherwise. The only way to have a very low turnover is to have a one-class static community. If the community is to be truly balanced, turnover is going to be a built-in feature.

Whether or not the new town ideal is impossible to achieve, as I have been arguing, the sheer effort to achieve it can have important consequences. Some of them will be good; a number of the communities that are going up under the new town banners will probably end up as excellent places to live in—even though they do not really measure up to the true new town ideal, or, rather, because of the fact that they do not.

But an equally important question is what is not going to be built. The new town movement is essentially decentralist. The physical specifications virtually dictate that the planners look away from the city to the periphery and beyond, for the large virgin sites that are called for are not to be found within the present metropolitan area.

If the new town movement could be stripped of its anticity utopianism, there would not have to be this decentralist effect. Many goals of the new town approach are excellent—the range of housing types; the mixture of industry, commerce, and homes; the weaving in of recreation and open space. They are quite applicable to the more built-up areas; indeed, as some have suggested, there is a case to be made that new towns should be in the city, or very close to it. A new town that would make a lot of sense, for example, is the one recently proposed by the State of New Jersey; it would like to create an authority to build an urban complex on the Hackensack Meadows, a boggy expanse five miles from mid-Manhattan.

Within the metropolitan areas, of course, there are tremendous problems to be surmounted. For one thing, there is apt to be a difficult tangle of governmental jurisdictions—in the case of the Hackensack Meadows proposal, some eighteen local governments would be involved. Good sites are hard to come by, they are usually irregular and they are expensive. The land would have to be much more efficiently used; the development more compact. But the communities would not necessarily be the worse for the discipline of these realities. And they would be where the need is.

But then, it can be argued, they would not be true new towns. The whole idea of new towns, advocates maintain, is not to try and rework a hopeless tangle but to get away from it and start fresh. That blank slate is crucial. Listening to some new town discussions, one gets the feeling that the end object is not a workable community so much as the untrammeled exercise of expertise in planning it. The approach must be experimental, new, uncompromised by the present. At one recent meeting, a new-town advocate was asked why there couldn't be new towns close to the city. He said: "If you try one of these ambitious and innovative projects in a situation where you are going to be forced by circumstances that are far beyond your control into all sorts of compromises, then I think you are likely to be forced to erode the vision with which you began." The city of today, then, will not do. It is a tangle of situations with circumstances.

But this fractured, messy, tangled place is where the main problems are, and to talk of seeking its redemption somewhere else is sheer escapism. Building new towns can greatly improve suburbia but as a means of saving the city the movement is somewhat off-center-rather like taking a mistress, Robert Herman has observed, to improve relations with your wife.

And is the tangle so hopeless? It is hopeless if the measuring stick is perfection; it is hopeless if we demand a solution. There is no solution to the city. It is full of circumstances; some of them are good, some of them are bad, and as soon as one bad one seems about licked, others will crop up. That is the way of cities, and of people.

THE CASE FOR CROWDING

The net of what I have been saying about landscape action is that we are going to have to work with a much tighter pattern of spaces and development, and that our environment may be the better for it. This somewhat optimistic view rests on the premise that densities are going to increase and that it is not altogether a bad thing that they do. It is a premise many would dispute. Our official land policy is dead set against higher densities. It is decentralist, like official policies in most other countries. The primary thrust of it is to move people outward; reduce densities, loosen up the metropolis, and reconstitute its parts in new enclaves on the fringe.

I do not think it is going to work out this way. Certainly, outward movement will continue, but if our population continues to grow, the best way to accommodate the growth will be by a more concentrated and efficient use of the land within the area. The big "if" is whether or not intensity of use will be coupled with efficiency of use. It may not be. But it can be. Europe is the proof of this. Many of those who ask why we cannot take care of the landscape like Europeans do fail to realize that these landscapes, both urban and rural, accommodate far more people per acre than do ours. The disparity is not due primarily to our averages being weighted by the vast open spaces of the West. Even in our most urban states the metropolitan areas average out to lower densities than their counterparts in Europe—indeed, to some entire European countries.

The case for higher densities cannot rest on a shortage of land. There is none. It is true that top-grade agricultural lands are being overrun by urban expansion, that open space in the right places is increasingly difficult to save. The fact remains, however, that if we wish to go the expansion route, there is room for it. Expand the diameter of a metropolitan area by only a few miles and enough land will be encompassed to take care of a very large population increase. This may be a poor way to do it, but the option exists.

Nor are our cities running into each other. Metropolitan areas are being linked more tightly, but this is not the same thing as collision. Consider, for example, the great belt of urban areas along the Eastern Seaboard from Boston to Norfolk. It is well that we are paying more attention to the continuities of this megalopolis, as Jean Gottman has done so well, but to call it a "strip city," as many are doing, is misleading.

There is no such city, and the proposition can be easily tested. Fly from Boston to Washington and look out the window. Here and there one suburbia flows into another—between Baltimore and Washington, for example—but the cities retain their identities. This is especially apparent at night when the lights beneath simplify the structure so vividly: the brilliantly lit downtowns, the shopping centers, the cloverleafs, the spine of freeways that connect it all. But just as striking is what is dark—the forests of Massachusetts and Connecticut, the pine barrens of New Jersey, the farmlands of the Eastern Shore, the tidewater of Virginia. For many miles along the great urban route you can look down and see only the scattered lights of farms and small towns.

Urbanized sectors in other parts of the country—excepting, always, Los Angeles—show much the same characteristics. They are systems of cities, tied by high-speed rail and road networks, but they have not yet congealed into an undifferentiated mass. There is room outside them for expansion. There is room inside them. Whichever way is best, a measure of choice is still open to us.

The choice is by no means an either-or one, for there are forces working in both directions, and there is only so much we can do by planning and public policy to shape these forces to our liking. But this margin is important. Our government programs for transportation, for new housing and urban development have a great leverage, and a shift of emphasis one way or the other could have a considerable effect on the metropolis of not too many years hence.

Decentralize or concentrate? Most of the prescriptions for the ideal metropolis opt for decentralization. Expansion of the metropolis is to continue, only this time the expansion will be orderly. Instead of a sprawl of subdivisions, new development is to be channeled into planned new communities, with rapid transit linking them and green belts separating them. Some proposals would place the new communities outside the metropolitan areas altogether.

Obviously, the limits of suburbia are going to expand some in any event, and obviously there are going to be new communities. But the main show is not going to be out on the perimeter. Outward expansion looks easiest, but it is the least efficient way of taking care of an increased population. As development moves further outward from the core, returns diminish and costs increase, and at an accelerating rate. Water distribution is an example. If you double the population within a given area, you can service it by enlarging the diameter of the present pipe system; if you try to take care of the population by doubling the area, however, you not only have to enlarge the present pipes, you have to lay down a prodigious amount of new ones, and as they poke out into the low density areas costs become progressively steeper. The new residents may be charged an extra sum to help foot these capital costs, but the rest of the community bears most of it.

The same is true with mass transit and other utilities and services. A disproportionate amount of capital investment is needed to provide urban services for people out in the low density areas out on the periphery, but because of the rate structures that usually apply to these services, the fact is masked that other people have to pay more than they should to make up the difference. The other people are the ones in the high density areas that are easiest and most profitable to serve. We have made utilities, economist

Mason Gaffney observes, "an agency for milking the center to feed the border, thus subsidizing decentralization."

Concentration provides efficiency; for the same reason it provides maximum access to what people want. This is what cities are all about. People come together in cities because this is the best way to make the most of opportunities, and the more accessible the core, the more choice of opportunities there are, the more access to skills, specialized services and goods, and to jobs. By subsidizing new freeways and peripheral beltways we can make it easier for people to move about within the outer area, but vigorous centers are not the less vital for this but the more, and a policy for dispersing their functions will fail.

Business and industry talk decentralization but while firms may be dispersing their production units, they have been centralizing their office and managerial operations more than before. As I have noted earlier, the British tried to reverse this trend by doing everything possible to stop commercial growth in London and make it go somewhere else. Despite the constraints, commercial growth expanded mightily, and an office building boom of spectacular proportions took place.

For a while we also entertained notions of a commercial exodus. Right after the war it was widely predicted that corporations would be moving their headquarters to campuslike retreats in the suburbs, and there was much favorable publicity when several firms in New York did so. Executives, it was said, would be able to think more; the office force would be closer to home, and more content; space would cost less; the surroundings would be more pleasant in every way. But the movement never quite came off, and several firms who had moved quietly repatriated. New office buildings went up, and on the highest-cost land in the center of the city. Before long, in what seemed almost a frenzy of centralization, whole blocks of big buildings on Park Avenue were being torn down to put up bigger buildings.

The center of things attracts because it is the center of things. What the decentralists would like to do is to cut down the number of things, or, rather, put them somewhere else. They are for urban renewal, but at much lower density. They want to open up the center, disperse as many of its functions as possible, and reassemble them in subcenters out in the hinterland where, in miniature, will be all the advantages of the city—art, music, commerce, universities, urban excitement—but without the disadvantages.

A dull metropolis it would be. This kind of decentralization would not only be a very inefficient way to accommodate growth, it would go against the grain of all the forces that give a metropolis its vitality. Rather than pursue this ill-conceived provincialism, we must look inward as well as outward, to the strengths of the metropolis, and seek a much more intensive and efficient use of the land already within it.

One way is to raise housing densities—both by putting more people on acres developed for housing and by bringing into use acres now wasted or underused. Densities are, of course, relative. What would be considered a very high density for suburbia—twenty people to the acre—would be low for the core, and densities will probably always tend to diminish as the distance from the city grows. At almost any point, however, there could be some increase in density without a lowering of living standards. In some cases the standards would be higher if there was an increase.

This is particularly true in the city. The decentralists who bewail its insensate concentrations talk as though cities are bad because we have been compressing more and more people into them. But we have not been. The populations of our cities have remained static or have decreased. One of the big problems of the gray areas of the cities, indeed, is that they do not have a sufficiently large or varied population to support an urban concentration of services and stores. Instead of cutting down the densities still further, it would make more sense to raise them.

In the city, English architect Theo Crosby points out, high densities are needed for a high level of amenity. Transportation, for example. "The typical planners' compromise—between 100 and 200 people per acre," says Crosby, "makes the vehicle-pedestrian dilemma insoluble. It is only at reasonably high densities (200–300 people per acre is the minimum) that the car is downgraded to the status of a luxury. At this density you can choose to use a car; you don't have to use it. Such a density also means that the network of public transport can be afforded, for it is only at high densities that rapid-transit systems make economic sense."

Density also has an important bearing on the look and feel of a neighborhood. If it is urban it ought to be urban. Most of our redevelopment projects are too loose in fabric. They would look better, as well as being more economic, if the scale were tightened up. This is true even of one of the best: the Southwest redevelopment area in Washington. Some of the architects involved believe that there would be more life and style to it if they had been able to pull the components closer together.

This does not mean putting everybody up in towers. Unfortunately, the arguments for and against high density are usually presented in terms of towers versus anything else—either spread out or go up in the air.[5] But this is a false choice. A well-knit pattern of low buildings can house a great many people, and often quite amenably. So, obviously, can towers; on any one acre, the maximum possible. But there are other acres to be counted. When towers are spaced out in rows, as in the conventional urban project, the density figures for the over-all project can be surprisingly low.

The usual redevelopment or public housing project generally houses less people per acre than the neighborhood that was torn down to make way for it. The design formulas call for lots of space, almost to a suburban scale, and a big point is made of how little ground is taken for the buildings themselves. The projects of the New York City Public Housing Authority, for example, cover some 2000 acres, an area almost a seventh the size of Manhattan Island. The Housing Authority proudly points out that only 16 percent of the area is used for buildings.

What is gained? Open space, it is said. But the open space is drab and institutional and much of it is forbidden to human trespass. The open space is for the architects, so they can have enough ground to put up towers. But to what end? The design does not pursue its logic. The towers are put up, presumably, for density's sake—to make up for the housing that was not built on the open space. But the net density remains low, and not just by slum standards. In the standard public housing project the number of people per net acre is lower than in many middle class neighborhoods of three and four story houses.

This is an inefficient use of high cost land, and if we are to continue it, we ought to have some strong social reason for doing so. The stock justification is that lower densities mean healthier living, and planners of this persuasion make much of the correlation between the number of people per acre and the rate of crime and disease in slum neighborhoods. There is a correlation. But is it cause and effect? There is a distinction to be made between overcrowding—that is, too many people per room—and a high number of people per acre. Overcrowding does make for an unhealthy environment; high density may or it may not.

A lot of nonsense is heard these days about the psychological effects of living too close together in cities, or of living in cities at all for that matter. Many of the stock criticisms are quite ancient—filing-cabinet apartments producing filing-cabinet minds, neuroses, tenseness, conformity, and so on. But now the accusations are being made more scientifically. There is a rash of studies underway designed to uncover the bad consequences of overcrowding. This is all very well as far as it goes, but it only goes in one direction. What about undercrowding? The researchers would be a lot more objective if they paid as much attention to the possible effects on people of relative isolation and lack of propinquity. Maybe some of those rats they study get lonely too.[6]

If we study the way people themselves live, we will find strong empirical evidence that they can do quite well in high-density areas. It depends on the area. Some neighborhoods with relatively low densities have high disease and crime rates. Conversely, some neighborhoods with higher densities have low disease and crime rates. Obviously, other factors are the determining ones. (Hong Kong, one of the most densely populated cities in the world, with up to 2800 people per acre, has relatively low disease and crime rates compared to congested areas in the U.S.)

Why is it, furthermore, that so many of our high-density neighborhoods are the most sought after? This is not just a matter of high-rise luxury apartments; in New York some of the tree-lined blocks of four- and five-story brownstones with interior gardens have net densities higher than nearby public housing projects. The latter average about 250 people per acre. Remodeled brownstone areas run from about 180 people to as high as 350 people per acre.

Brooklyn Heights is an example. The fine old homes there (which are about 25 feet wide by 50 feet deep, plus a 50-foot garden) have been lovingly rehabilitated into a neighborhood of outstanding charm. But densities are high. For each gross acre (including streets) there are about 13 houses, and, on the average, they provide a total of 65 units. The number of people per unit averages between three and three and a half people, giving an overall density of about 200 people per gross acre. On the basis of land use efficiency, let alone amenity, this beats many a high rise collective.

Other attractive examples can be found in Washington, Chicago, San Francisco, and many other cities; areas that by orthodox planning standards should be hopelessly congested are among the most pleasant, and sought after, in the city. Too much should not be made of the correlation, but surely something is wrong with a planning policy which calls for density standards so out of whack with the marketplace.

The standards are the legacy of a utopian concept which was never originally intended for the city. It is the garden city ideal: difficult enough to achieve in suburbia, and wholly inapplicable to the city.

In some aspects the original model was more realistic in its specifications than the current standards. Ebenezer Howard's ideal garden city called for somewhere between 70 and 100 people per acre and this was to be out in the country. For rebuilding of our cities some planning standards call for densities not much greater—about 100 people per acre for ideal neighborhoods, rarely more than 150 people.

To do away with congestion, these plans would do away with concentration. But concentration is the genius of the city, its reason for being. What it needs is not less people, but more, and if this means more density we have no need to feel guilty about it. The ultimate justification for building to higher densities is not that it is more efficient in land costs, but that it can make a better city.

THE LIVING STREET

William H. Whyte at work in New York City. (*Photo by Margaret Bemiss*)

New York and Tokyo: A Study in Crowding

From *A Comparative Study of Street Life: Tokyo, Manila, New York* (1977)

Whyte was several years into the Street Life Project when he visited Tokyo under the auspices of the Japan Society in New York and the International House, Tokyo. The resulting study is highly empirical, but certain generalizations—why some public spaces fail and others succeed, the virtues of density and bustle, etc.—are expressed with Whyte's typical clarity and verve. Many of the findings of this study later found their way into *The Social Life of Small Urban Spaces* and *City*; but Whyte's comparison of these two great cities is stated here in its purest form.

In this report I am going to make some observations on the pedestrian environments of New York and of Tokyo—how they differ, how they are alike, and what lessons might be drawn from the denominators. To venture such generalizations, I realize, is a bit foolhardy. There are enormous cultural and physical differences between the two cities, and my knowledge of one is quite limited. While my observations on New York are based on five years of research, those on Tokyo rest on only two short visits: one in the spring of 1976; the other in the spring of 1977, in connection with the conference on street life organized by Professor Hidetoshi Kato.

As we compared the aspects of street life in our respective cities it became clear that for all the outward differences we were discussing the same factors, the same kind of behavior, and the recurring patterns seemed more significant than the differences. Secondly, by our common emphasis on observation, we were encouraged to place some stock in what we could see in front of us—at the very least, to look.

Here, briefly, is what we saw and the conclusions drawn.

1. New York and Tokyo people *like* street life. Not always, to be sure, and there is a lot about it they don't like. But much of their use of the street is

strongly social and this activity is a large component of the crowding every-one so frequently deplores.

2. They are highly skilled pedestrians. They walk fast, navigate adroitly, and as a form of transportation they make very efficient use of limited spaces.

3. They have to. Their cities treat them badly in allocating space and time vis-à-vis vehicles.

4. The streets they like best are the opposite of what planning fashion now favors. Their amiable disorder should not be destroyed, but emulated.

5. In both cities modest reallocations of space could greatly improve the street environment, and without asepsis.

In the U.S. the conventional image of the high density core city is of a bad place, and bad not simply for its defects but for its essential qualities. Centrality, high density, compression—these are the factors that documen-taries on the plight of the city customarily pick on, and the stock horror shots are of people jammed on the streets of New York, tense, unhappy, unsmiling. The image, unhappily, affects the reality it misrepresents; it is widely believed in Washington, not only by rural moralists, but by progres-sives who would save the city from itself. With few exceptions federal aid programs for cities have been laden with anti-density criteria which make it difficult for center city projects to qualify.[1]

It is no frivolous matter, then, to note that many people on the streets of New York can be observed smiling, even laughing, and on the most crowded streets and at times, like the rush hours, when there might not seem much to be smiling about. New Yorkers themselves fervently deplore the city, its horrendous traffic jams, the noise and litter, the crowding. It is their favorite form of self-praise. Only the heroic, they imply, could cope. But they are often right in the middle of it all, and by choice; stopping to have a street corner chat, meeting people, arguing, making deals, watching the girls go by, eating, looking at the oddballs and the freaks.

People in Tokyo seem to enjoy themselves even more, and one of the reasons there is more crowding is the large number of them who are on the street because they want to be. The employment density in the center of Tokyo is less than in New York but there are more people on the streets throughout the day and the disparity is especially pronounced in the evening. At a time when most New York streets are nearly empty the Japanese will be out in force. Many will be in groups, a high proportion will be younger people.[2]

One is struck by the number of people to be seen smiling. Tokyo people are a street people and they see the comedy. Even during the morning rush hour, when some people break into a last minute run toward the office, there is laughter. The activity at major pedestrian crossings is similarly appreciated. The Japanese are quite serious about getting across: feet tap impatiently waiting for the green. But they also seem to look on it as a game, and the best fun is holding out to the last possible moment to make one's break.

Measurable? A smile index might be unduly solemn but there are many ways by which the social behavior of pedestrians can be recorded and compared. Let me go back to our early studies in New York. To chart the avoidance of crowding we focused a number of time-lapse cameras on several of New York's busiest street corners. We were interested to find out how far people would move out of the pedestrian traffic stream when they stopped to talk. To our surprise, we found that they didn't move out of it. Quite the contrary, they stayed there, or moved into it, and the longer the conversation the more apt it was to be in the very middle of the flow. Subsequent studies of behavior in other kinds of places reveal the same propensity. What attracts people most in an urban place is other people.

You do not see these phenomena unless you look. One of the troubles with most pedestrian surveys is that they focus almost wholly on the pedestrian as a transportation unit—and how he gets from A to B. But what he does between A and B is important too. Study the social behavior of the pedestrian and you find that a significant part of his activity is not moving, but standing, talking, and looking. Much of the congestion on busy streets is traceable to this behavior.

This seems to be just as much the case in Tokyo as New York. Here too, much of the congestion is self-congestion. At the busiest corners, at the busiest times, you can see two or more people having a conversation, and they appear not in the slightest bothered by the fact they may be blocking traffic. Sometimes there is a "traveling conversation," moving in a small orbit, back and forth, but with the center of gravity the 100% location.

The greatest incidence we saw was in Shinjuku Station. There is such a maelstrom of foot traffic there as to scarcely afford room for any kind of socializing, yet there was a great deal of it, and during the peak of the rush hours especially. Some instances: Two young women, apparently waiting for a third, move back and forth in a ten foot range, chatting animatedly. After ten minutes they see their friend and go off with her. Three young junior executive types stand four feet outboard of a pillar; one of them practicing a golf swing. Two middle age women are engaged in a prolonged goodbye; they are directly athwart the stream of people emerging from a turnstile.

Department store doorways are another habitat. They are a great place for meeting people, for conversing, and unlike New York's stores, Tokyo's do a good bit to accommodate this use. Takashimaya, for example, provides ashtrays for the people who sit on the ledges next to the doors. Matsuya has a line of twelve chairs at its side entrance.

The number one element, of course, is the heavy flow of people in and out of the store and it is in the middle of it that conversations are most apt to recur. Below, from Margaret Bemiss' log of a day of department store life, is a chart of the conversations lasting one minute or longer in front of the Mitsukoshi store between 4:55 P.M. and 5:10 P.M. For comparison is a chart of the doorway of the Alexander's store on Lexington Avenue.

Other prime actors will be people waiting for other people. During the period sketched below there would likely be anywhere from three to six individuals waiting next to or in front of the doorway. And there would be no mistaking what they were doing. Waiting is structured activity, more so than in New York. Tokyo people are punctilious, and impatient waiters; just before the hour, or half hour, there will be much glancing at watches, scanning of the crowd for the missing face; past the mark there will be signs of growing annoyance, not always suppressed when the late-comer eventually arrives.

It is an interesting activity to watch, especially for those who are themselves waiting. This is the case at the great rendezvous area around the statue of the dog Hachiko at Shibuya Station. Many of the people around it are obviously waiting and as they wait, there are scores of potential dramas to observe. Who is the unhappy girl waiting for? Is she waiting? Why has the man in blue come back? Denouements may be anticlimactic, but they are worth waiting for.

Plaza use affords another basis for comparison. There are few office building plazas in Tokyo, but one of them, that of the Mitsui Building, is one of the best anywhere. Save in one respect it has all of the elements we have found to be basic for successful plazas. It is for one thing, eminently sittable: its ledges and planters alone provide more sitting space than the minimum we recommended for the new zoning standards in New York.[3] In addition it provides tables and chairs—movable chairs—both on its central portion and the raised terrace. It has an adjoining food facility, water, trees, and while the multilevel design is a bit busy, there is a nice sense of enclosure. The street, being cut off from the plaza, does not do much for it, nor does

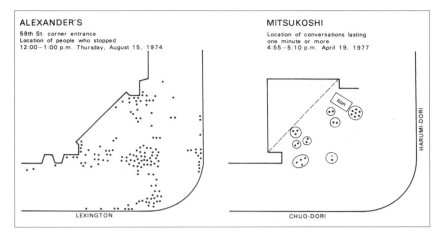

Alexander's vs. Mitsukoshi, the social life of department store doorways. These two charts are not wholly comparable. The chart of Alexander's records every person who stopped, whether alone or with others, during the hour 12:00ñ1:00. The chart of Mitsukoshi records people who stopped to talk during the fifteen-minute period of rush hour. But both show the same inclination to cluster in the middle of the pedestrian flow. At Alexander's the cumulative pattern for five hours records almost half of the people concentrated in a small area where building lines would intersect.

the plaza do much for it. The bulk of the users, however, are office workers from the building, and there is easy access for them on several levels.

The main point is that people obviously like the plaza very much. Our sightings were of lunch periods on only two days, April 14 and 15, and it was overcast and cool. But there was a good sized number each day, averaging 120 and 134 people sitting at any one time, plus fairly heavy crosscurrents of people walking. In really good weather, the usage should be very heavy indeed.

On some counts, use patterns differed from those in New York. The proportion of people in groups was markedly higher—averaging 88 percent versus about 60 percent for comparable New York plazas. The groups were larger too, with some 39 percent in groups of four to eight people. The lunch hour, we noted, was just that—an hour—and a few minutes before one o'clock a very quick exodus began. (In New York the busy time for plazas runs from noon to just before 2 P.M.)

In general, however, the place had the same amiable feel to it that good plazas do in New York. Characteristically, the most favored spots—the chairs and tables—were those in the middle of the pedestrian flow, and the prime activity was people looking at other people. While the proportion of females was low—only 28 percent by one count—there was the same elaborate inattention paid them by men in New York. Spacing patterns on ledges and planters appeared similar.

Since these comparisons are based almost wholly on observation, let me pause for a few remarks on methodology. In our research in the U.S. we have done interviewing from time to time and we have made as much use as possible of such data as subway turnstile counts, vehicle flow records, and the like. But our emphasis has been on the direct observation of what people do. We have used cameras extensively but our principal tools have been a pad of paper and a pencil, and a place to sit.

Observation is not a technique that ranks high in U.S. universities, nor, for that matter, in its elementary or secondary schools. Social science courses generally put observation on the bottom of the technological ladder and expose students to it briefly before taking them onwards to the more quantitative techniques. Because of this bias, most research tends to be once or twice removed from the reality being studied; on subjects like urban crowding, it is not apt to be of people on streets, but of data on responses to questions about people on streets. For students of street life, as a consequence, there are few counterpart studies to provide a base for comparison.

One fine exception is the work of the remarkable Mr. Wajiro Kon. Over fifty years ago he was studying the life of the streets and public places of Tokyo. Nothing seemed to have escaped his curiosity and he set down what he saw with clarity and thoroughness. He charted the flow of students, minute by minute, as they came and went from school: the flow of pedestrians at various places; their age, their dress, their apparent occupations, how many were alone (75 percent on Ginza streets), how many were in groups; the length of their trips. He even charted the location of suicides in parks.

Most interesting to us, the methodology he evolved was very much like that we worked out by trial and error for our street life research. (In charting daily pedestrian flows he cumulated counts at five minute intervals; we used six minute intervals. Aside from that techniques are identical.) I have not had an opportunity yet to read all of his analyses, but when a translation becomes available I am sure there will be many good cues in it for current research.

•

The pedestrian is a social being; he is also a transportation unit, and a remarkably efficient one. He is able to propel himself, shift speeds and direction, sense obstacles and collision courses of other pedestrians; estimate crossing angles, accelerations, decelerations and counter-moves, and all this in a split second. To produce a machine that would be his equivalent would require a computer technology and a degree of miniaturization of fantastic sophistication. Most transportation experts, however, scant the pedestrian and his potential; millions are being spent in research on new kinds of people-movers but very little on the oldest and best kind: people themselves. And nowhere is the attention more needed than in the center city.

Pedestrian speeds are a clue. It has often been observed that people in big cities walk faster than people in smaller cities. Just why they should has been a matter of conjecture. Social psychologist Stanley Milgram attributes the pace to the sensory overload on individuals; presumably so great in big cities as to induce them to speed up to secure relief. Whatever the explanations, the fact is big city people *do* walk faster. A number of comparative studies have shown a surprisingly strong statistical correlation between speeds and population, regardless of country or continent.

In any one city pedestrian speeds vary considerably according to the time of day, or the occasion, but the diurnal rhythms are quite consistent. There is the morning rush hour pace—in New York about 270 feet per minute on a clear pavement. In Tokyo the walking speed seems about the same but overall speed is higher because of the way so many people break into a run as they near the office. (In our motion picture footage, the runs recur at the moments just before the half hour and hour marks.)

Lunch hour speeds can be brisk too but there is a different quality to the pace. In New York it is upbeat. Groups on their way to lunch are apt to be smiling or laughing, as if on their way to a party. Something good, they seem to be conveying, is going to happen. For many people it is at this time of anticipation, that the cyclical peak of the day is reached. Anticlimax or no, the post-lunch pace is slower. This is the time for the interminable leave-takings, and the sidewalk conferences when someone in the group brings up the real business the lunch was supposed to have been about. It is a deceptively casual time.

With the evening rush hour pedestrian flows again reach their maximum. At key points where opposing streams of pedestrians cross each other congestion is heavy, and this is compounded by the "platooning" effect the traffic lights have on the flow. The crowd moves in pulses. Even so, where most of the people are moving in the same direction—on Park Avenue south to Grand Central Station, for example—average speeds are about 250 feet per minute. Flank speeds, of those who use or create passing lanes, go as high as 300 feet per minute.

As a New Yorker, I have taken some pride in being one of the city's pedestrians. They are an aggressive lot, incorrigible jaywalkers, and where a hesitant driver gives them a chance they will bully cars to a dead stop. With fellow pedestrians, however, they are quite cooperative, and here is where their timing and skills are most evident. We have filmed their behavior at subway entrances and key corners and through stop motion techniques have studied the various ways by which they avoid collision courses, signal intentions to oncomers, or bluff them into giving ground. The performances are impressive.

But Tokyo's pedestrians are in a class by themselves. Consider Shinjuku Station. By all accepted density standards it is a manifest impossibility. It is really a complex of stations and separate lines, confusing in its layout, interconnected with an intricate set of corridors, walkways, escalators, stairs, cul de sacs. Its concourses are a mass of cross-flows, obstructed by knots of people waiting for other people, teenagers, vendors, people saying goodbye. Even at off-peak times one has to look sharply to find a clear path; at the rush hours, when the pedestrian traffic reaches an intensity unmatched anywhere, the scene appears utter chaos.

But it isn't. Somehow, people sort themselves out and for all the density the pedestrian speeds remain quite high; indeed, it is at rush hour that one sees the most running. By rights, people should be bumping into each other all over the place. They don't seem to; our studies were informal but neither in our memories nor our film was there an observed collision. While it may be a subjective judgment, we also got the impression that a good many of the pedestrians were rather stimulated by the challenge, and perhaps a bit pleased with themselves.

With good reason. Pedestrians in cities like Tokyo and New York are fast and expert because they very well have to be. Not only are there more fellow pedestrians to contend with, there has been increasingly less space given to them. In New York pavement widths were periodically narrowed over the years to make room for vehicles. Today the imbalance is almost ludicrous.

Lexington Avenue is the clearest example. As a transportation corridor it measures 75 feet in width. Fifty of these feet are given over to cars. The remaining 25 are given to two 12-foot sidewalks. This is just about the inverse of the way people use the space. In the stretch between 57th and

58th Streets, one of the most crowded in the city, about 12,000 vehicles pass between 8:00 A.M. and 6:00 P.M. carrying a total of about 28,000 people. During the same period some 42,000 people use the sidewalks. The 12-foot widths, furthermore, are only nominal; because of obstructions such as trash containers, signs, grates, the effective width is as narrow as five feet in places. It's a feat that so many people manage to traverse the space, but it is a bad mismanagement of space that forces them to. In less extreme form, the same imbalance in space use can be found in most large U.S. cities.

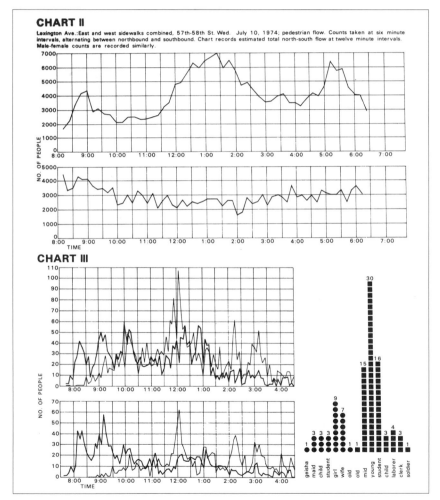

CHART II

Lexington Ave.:East and west sidewalks combined, 57th-58th St. Wed. July 10, 1974; pedestrian flow. Counts taken at six minute intervals, alternating between northbound and southbound. Chart records estimated total north-south flow at twelve minute intervals. Male-female counts are recorded similarly.

CHART III

(*A Comparative Study of Street Life*)

The pass at Lexington Avenue and 57th Street. This exasperating street had its sidewalks narrowed to twelve and a half feet. The effective walkway, however, ranges from four to six feet, depending on the placement of signs, floral displays, vendors' tables, and various impediments.

Tokyo treats its pedestrians even worse. Save a few main avenues its sidewalk widths are narrower, and ratios between vehicular space and pedestrian space are heavily weighted in favor of vehicles. The small scale of the streets parallel to the avenues is an offsetting amenity and the very narrowness of their sidewalks induces pedestrians to use the center space as their own. The fact remains, however, that in the places where the most people have to walk there is relatively little walking space. On Harumi-Dori, for example, effective walkway space on the south side by a main subway entrance is twelve feet. I counted pedestrian flows there between 4:30 and 5:30 P.M. of up to 6,000 people an hour. (In terms of people per foot of walkway width, the theoretical result should be complete stoppage.)

On major avenues pedestrian overpasses have been provided. But these are more a concession to the car than the pedestrian. Cars don't have to stop for as many lights; it is the pedestrians who do, and because of the way the lights are set, for a long while, it's notable that many people wait for a chance to cross at street level rather than mount the stairs for the overhead crossing.

Tokyo's pedestrian crossing areas are well marked, well policed, the lights and the rules clear cut. At some main intersections the pedestrians get almost a minute for their crossing (versus thirty to forty seconds in New York). But the government does seem to regard the pedestrians as children, and incipiently naughty ones. The dainty girl voice on the loudspeaker; gently, this pitchwoman for authority chides people: "From now on the pedestrian crossing is dangerous. . . . Let's cross safely at the next green light."

Tokyo does have heavy vehicle traffic to accommodate. But in good part the traffic may be heavy for the accommodating. That is the way it has been in the U.S.; but Tokyo has less reason. It has a splendid subway system and is in a far better position than most cities to shift some space away from vehicles. Not only on the grounds of amenity, but of transportation efficiency it could well gain if it did so. As a user of space the pedestrian is a far better unit than a vehicle and the space now allotted him is so minimal that even modest additions could have a high leverage effect.

Tokyo pedestrians are well disciplined and almost always wait before crossing. At this intersection, loudspeakers broadcast cautionary announcements by a little-girl voice. It's almost the end of the WALK cycle, she says, so don't be childish. At this point, the final mad rush begins.

New York is being forced to such opportunities. For air pollution control the federal government is demanding that the city sharply curb vehicle use in the central business districts. The city is aghast at the prospect; it fears that a curb on street parking will keep customers out of the stores. If our studies of parking and vehicle use are any criterion, no such result will come about, and eventually this will be recognized.[4] Willy-nilly, a lot of vehicular space is going to become redundant and the opportunities for creating pedestrian space are going to be increasingly evident. They may seem unrealistic today, but now is the time to lay the groundwork.

Both Tokyo and New York have experimented with traffic-free pedestrian streets. They have done it gingerly, and so far most of the street closings have been temporary. But they do afford an excellent basis for comparison. Fortuitously, the physical characteristics of the streets are similar and so, to a surprising degree, have been the patterns of use.

In 1972, New York designated a fifteen-block stretch of Madison Avenue for a test. Every weekday over a two-week period the avenue is a busy one of stores and office buildings, but it is canyonlike and treeless. The rudimentary benches the city was going to put out seemed a highly inadequate way to furnish the expanse. Merchants were unenthusiastic; some very hostile. They feared the absence of cars would mean less customers but many "undesirables" (i.e., bums, winos, hippies, characters, young people, very old people, teenagers, students, etc.). To find out just what the results would be we mounted time-lapse cameras and began to record the entire trial period.

Here is what we found out.

1. The number of pedestrians doubled. From, a rate of about 9,000 pedestrians per hour, the flow increased to 19,000.

2. This increase was not at the expense of pedestrian flows on the parallel avenues, Park and Fifth. Rates there were about as high as they usually were.

3. Most of the pedestrians, 60 percent of the total, stayed on the sidewalks—where the shop windows were. The street was favored by people in groups, promenading.

4. The benches, which were placed in the middle of the street, got very heavy use. No places remained empty for more than a minute.

5. Food vendors were centers of activity. Wherever they set up their carts, usually at the curb, knots of people formed.

6. Most of the people were the people who ordinarily worked or shopped

in the area. The undesirables that so obsessed merchants were seen by some merchants, but not by our cameras.

Subsequent plans for a permanent mall on Madison fell through, largely because of the objections of a merchants' group and the taxi drivers union. But other projects did go through: Sunday closings of Fifth Avenue, a permanent mall on Nassau Street in the Wall Street area; on Fulton Street in Brooklyn. New York has been less venturesome than a number of other U.S. cities but it has learned a basic lesson. With a well conceived pedestrian facility, supply creates demand. The existence of the amenity where none was before sets up new patterns of use, and new expectations.

The Ginza experience provides an interesting parallel. Beginning in 1970 a sixteen-block stretch of Chuo-Dori Avenue was closed to vehicle traffic on Sundays for a pedestrian "paradise." It was an immediate success. There was surprisingly little use of the street itself, however; as had been the case on Madison Avenue, most of the people stayed on the sidewalks. To liven things up, the department stores began putting tables and umbrellas and chairs along the center line of the street. In its dimensions, as well as in the character of its stores, Chuo-Dori resembles Fifth Avenue. From building line to building line, the right of way is about 95 feet wide on Chuo-Dori; 100 feet on Fifth. Sidewalks of both are about 22 feet. Pedestrian volumes, however, are markedly higher on Chuo-Dori. On weekdays, our counts indicated volumes at rush hour and lunch time of about 6,500 people per hour on the sidewalk alongside the Matsuya Department Store. Even during the mid-afternoon lull the rate was around 4,000. And this was just one sidewalk.[5] For both sides peak volumes ran between 10,000 and 12,000 people per hour. Fifth Avenue volume at comparable periods ranges between 7,000 to 9,000.

Chuo-Dori and Fifth Avenue are similar in the degree of congestion— or, to be more accurate, of perceived congestion. Pedestrian flows are high, very high, and by conventional standards of people per foot of walkway width, they could be very uncomfortable. But they are not.

In part this is because of the breadth of the sidewalks. You cannot equate a given flow per foot of walkway on a narrow sidewalk with the same flow on a broad one. The figure may be the same; the psychological experience is not. Another factor is the attractiveness of the street: Chuo-Dori and Fifth Avenue are both lively and attractive streets and the people on the street are among its chief attractions. At choke points, such as subway entrances, the congestion is intense and this can color one's sense of the whole area. Along most of the way, however, the weekday hustle and bustle is quite tolerable, and to many, enjoyable.

Now let us look at Sunday. On the Chuo-Dori pedestrian volumes about double. Though there is now fifty more feet of walkway to traverse, the sidewalks get more traffic than they do on weekdays. Here are comparison pedestrian flows we checked on the Chuo-Dori by the Matsuzakaya Department Store (expressed in rate of pedestrian per hour).

	Weekday—1:30 P.M.	Sunday—1:30 P.M.
East sidewalk	4,160	4,280
West sidewalk (next to store)	2,060	3,320
Street	—.	5,000
	6,320	13,100

Checks made later in the day at other spots show a consistently high level of activity; even at the northern end, by the Takashimaya Store, flows were about 8,000–10,000 an hour. These flows, let it be noted, are quite different in character than those of the weekdays: the pace is slower, there are no rush hour peaks. But it is still a very heavy flow.

About 41 percent of the activity is on the sidewalks; 38 percent on the street. That the sidewalks continue to get the main play is understandable. This is where the vendors are. It is also where the stores are and Tokyo's are much more aggressive than New York's in beating vendors at their own game. They put out displays, special promotions, fast food stands, and they hustle for the business.

The street is less used but well used. The line of tables and chairs in the center of the street has proved successful in seeding activity. As soon as they are put out, the people come. Sitting there they can watch two strands of people traffic and the watching seems the main pastime. There is plenty of room for promenading, and as in New York groups tend to spread out as they make the tour. Eccentrics do their acts: we followed one man along the Chuo-Dori as he harangued people and waved his arms, an object of much interest to the seated groups he passed by.

In Tokyo as in New York, Sunday crowds are strongly weighted with family groups and children are much in evidence. In Tokyo they appear to be setting the pace, with the parents indulgently following as the children veer this way and that. There are impromptu games, much throwing of balls. And the eating is prodigious.

•

One of the most interesting of all streets is the alleylike one in the Asakusa district leading to the Kannon Shrine. It is laid out in the traditional Japanese fashion: as a linear progression of shops, and it is narrow. The width is about seventeen feet and because of the open stalls on each side the effective walkway width is about fifteen feet. We were fortunate to be there on the day of the shrine's annual celebration and see it tested by some of the heaviest crowds of the year. The pedestrian flow was that of a downtown sidewalk—running at a rate of about 3,800–4,200 people per hour in mid-morning. The pace was slow. There was considerable self-congestion; people stopped frequently to look at the merchandise, reassemble their groups, buy something to eat. Two handbill passers stationed themselves in the middle of the flow.[6] But it was a congenial kind of crowding, quite appropriate to the time and place.

It is probably not happenstance that so many of the most popular walkways range between 15 to 20 feet in width. This is narrow by modern planning standards, but it seems to be quite functional, for both heavy and light loads. The walkway is broad enough to take care of very heavy flows; narrow enough to feel comfortably busy when there are fewer people. At peak times or slack, furthermore, the pedestrian experiences both sides of the street as he walks along. The various stores and attractions reinforce each other. It was with this in mind, Professor Kato has noted, that the merchants of Osaka developed guidelines over a proposal for a broad Ginza-type avenue. The merchants decided against it; they felt that the traditional 15–17 foot width was better for their mutual businesses.

I am not trying to suggest that the optimum width is 15–20 feet, or indeed, that there is any one optimum. Context is all-important and this has to be studied just as much as such quantitative factors as lane width and people per foot of lane width per minute. But if this were done for a cross-section of highly liked walkways, however, observation would likely reveal significant consistencies, some obvious, some not so. The range should be eclectic; in addition to the walkways chosen in our joint studies in Tokyo, New York, and Manila, there could be included such places as the Ponte Vecchio in Florence, the Burlington Arcade in London, the Stroget in Copenhagen; Jan Gehl's excellent studies of the latter furnish a fine basis of comparison. There should also be included highly liked places that are unusually expansive: the Champs-Elysées in Paris, the Galleria in Milan, Las Ramblas in Barcelona. How dispersed or concentrated are the flows in them? What are the paths? What channels them?

But we need not await further study to apply one finding already clear. The places people like most are places where there are lots of other people in a fairly contained amount of space—in a word, somewhat crowded. This is a lesson many planners and architects ignore. They over-scale, and especially so in the development of new areas. In the mega-structure approach now fashionable in the U.S., they have done away with the street almost entirely; they have buried it in vast underground concourses, dispersed it over great stretches of concrete, put it up in the air in glass-enclosed walkways. In creating pedestrian malls in smaller cities, they have often diluted what street life there was by spreading it over too much space. The vital frictions of the street are eliminated; the attractions placed too far apart to support each other. There is no critical mass of activity to seed more activity.

Tokyo provides examples too. Compare the old streets of Shinjuku with the new ones in the redevelopment area. As seems to be the case when designers are given a large blank canvas, the scale is Olympian. The streets are laid out expansively, with visual order and coherence. And they are a bore. They are far easier to negotiate than those of the older section and

New street, Shinjuku redevelopment area in front of Mitsui Plaza. As sterile as any U.S. redevelopment area.

because of the office population the pedestrian flows are heavy. But they are essentially transportation flows; along most of the streets there are no bordering stores or coffee shops to cause one to tarry. Save in the pedestrian tunnels there is no sense of enclosure. The sides of the streets are so far apart as not to belong to the other. There are some good spaces at the destination—the plaza of the Mitsui Building, especially—and as the area is unfilled, there should be more. But it all could have been so much better. In one of the liveliest sub-centers in the world, it does seem a shame that the planners were unable to replicate the factors that help make it so. This does not mean slavish copies of the picturesque, gratuitously complex street patterns. In eminently contemporary terms it should have been possible to incorporate some of the basic factors.

The most basic factor is mixture. This is the reason Tokyo's streets are consistently more interesting than New York's. Tokyo's present an amiable disorder of activities, up and down and sideways, with pachinko parlors, offices, coffee shops all mixed up together, and restaurants going up two, three, and four floors. Actually, there is a great deal of order. Tokyo's streets have long been structured as a linear succession of uses, and if they are

Akususa: street leading to Kannon Temple. This traditional shopping alley provides a pleasantly tactile hustle and bustle.

experienced that way they are eminently sensible as well as interesting. Significantly, the one area in Tokyo that is supremely dull is the one most rational by western planning standards—the single purpose Kasumigaseki government district. In its imposed order, it is like the civic center areas of many U.S. cities, and its streets have as much interest.

Some of the characteristics of Tokyo's streets may be too rooted in Japanese culture to be transferable. But in such basics as mixture of uses the U.S. has a great deal to learn from Tokyo. For years the whole impetus of our zoning has been to enforce a rigid separation of uses. Market forces have further accentuated this by pricing out marginal uses. Now office buildings are erected where once stores and cafés were. But the new rents are too high for stores and cafés, and in their stead are windows of banks. In the case of mega-structures, as Los Angeles is demonstrating, there may be no windows at all; just blank walls. (At the biggest tourist attraction in the area, Disneyland, people pay money to walk along a replica of a regular street, with sidewalks and stores.)

There have been countertrends. New York has introduced vertical zoning to encourage multiple use buildings, combining stores, office space, and apartments. In the new open space zoning, developers of office buildings qualify for floor space bonuses only if 50 percent of the frontage is given over to retailing or food.

But far more needs to done; if nothing else, there should be programs to assure mixture where there still is mixture. The areas that have a street life most like Tokyo's are the mixed use areas on the fringe of the office and residential areas—such as Lexington in the upper Fifties. Keeping them mixed is going to be no easy task.

In both New York and Tokyo more space should be given to pedestrians. One way is to create space in new construction. New York has done well in this respect. Through incentive zoning it has induced developers to provide plazas and arcades; in total more new space than in all U.S. cities put together. Many of the plazas lacked basic amenities but this is a curable defect; guidelines have recently been adopted by the city to assure that the plazas be inviting and enjoyable.

Another way is to transfer space from vehicular to pedestrian use. This can be done with little hurt to space needed for vehicular movement. It is space for non-movement—parking—that is redundant. Elimination of just one 10-foot lane along a street could free up large amounts of space and the leverage effect would be great. Five feet added to most sidewalks would more than double the effective walkway width.

So it can be with other kinds of spaces—small parks, arcades, sitting places. In high density core areas they can be a very efficient use of space. In New York the most heavily used and yet pleasant and amenable of spaces are among the smallest; the two best measure 42 by 100 feet and 65 by 100 feet, respectively. In Tokyo, similarly, the spots where people most like to tarry are small, busy places—a sidewalk with shoeshine people, the benches alongside a store, a meeting place outside a station. These are the kind of bits and pieces usually scorned in orthodox planning, with its emphasis on order and structure. But in them is the genius of the place; and with just minor reallocations of space many more can be created.

For Tokyo and New York, in sum, the opportunities are incremental, small scale, subtle—and therefore immense.

From *The Social Life of Small Urban Spaces* (1980)

This handbook was essentially a stopgap to capture some of the major findings of the Street Life Project until the full-blown version could find its way into print as *City*, which came eight years later. There is a certain amount of overlap between the two books, and in the sections reprinted below—this chapter and the next—an effort has been made to distill the essential parts from both books.

INTRODUCTION

This book is about city spaces, why some work for people, and some do not, and what the practical lessons may be. It is a by-product of first-hand observation.

In 1970, I formed a small research group, The Street Life Project, and began looking at city spaces. At that time, direct observation had long been used for the study of people in far-off lands. It had not been used to any great extent in the U.S. city. There was much concern over urban crowding, but most of the research on the issue was done somewhere other than where it supposedly occurred. The most notable studies were of crowded animals, or of students and members of institutions responding to experimental situations—often valuable research, to be sure, but somewhat vicarious.

The Street Life Project began its study by looking at New York City parks and playgrounds and such informal recreation areas as city blocks. One of the first things that struck us was the *lack* of crowding in many of these areas. A few were jammed, but more were nearer empty than full, often in neighborhoods that ranked very high in density of people. Sheer space, obviously, was not of itself attracting children. Many streets were.

It is often assumed that children play in the street because they lack playground space. But many children play in the streets because they like to. One of the best play areas we came across was a block on 101st Street in

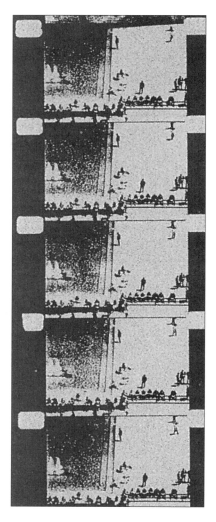

East Harlem. It had its problems, but it worked. The street itself was the play area. Adjoining stoops and fire escapes provided prime viewing across the street and were highly functional for mothers and older people. There were other factors at work, too, and, had we been more prescient, we could have saved ourselves a lot of time spent later looking at plazas. Though we did not know it then, this block had within it all the basic elements of a successful urban place.

As our studies took us nearer the center of New York, the imbalance in space use was even more apparent. Most of the crowding could be traced to a series of choke points—subway stations, in particular. In total, these spaces are only a fraction of downtown, but the number of people using them is so high, the experience so abysmal, that it colors our perception of the city around, out of all proportion to the space involved. The fact that there may be lots of empty space somewhere else little mitigates the discomfort. And there is a strong carry-over effect.

This affects researchers, too. We see what we expect to see, and have been so conditioned to see crowded spaces in center city that it is often difficult to see empty ones. But when we looked, there they were.

The amount of space, furthermore, was increasing. Since 1961, New York City has been giving incentive bonuses to builders who provided plazas. For each square foot of plaza, builders could add 10 square feet of commercial floor space over and above the amount normally permitted by zoning. So they did—without exception. Every new office building provided a plaza or comparable space: in total, by 1972, some 20 acres of the world's most expensive open space.

We discovered that some plazas, especially at lunchtime, attracted a lot of people. One, the plaza of the Seagram Building, was the place that helped give the city the idea for the plaza bonus. Built in 1958, this aus-

Ledge at Seagram's Plaza.

terely elegant area had not been planned as a people's plaza, but that is what it became. On a good day, there would be a hundred and fifty people sitting, sunbathing, picnicking, and schmoozing—idly gossiping, talking "nothing talk." People also liked 77 Water Street, known as "swingers' plaza" because of the young crowd that populated it.

But on most plazas, we didn't see many people. The plazas weren't used for much except walking across. In the middle of the lunch hour on a beautiful, sunny day the number of people sitting on plazas averaged four per 1,000 square feet of space—an extraordinarily low figure for so dense a center. The tightest-knit central business district anywhere contained a surprising amount of open space that was relatively empty and unused.

If places like Seagram's and 77 Water Street could work so well, why not the others? The city was being had. For the millions of dollars of extra space it was handing out to builders, it had every right to demand much better plazas in return.

I put the question to the chairman of the City Planning Commission, Donald Elliott. As a matter of fact, I entrapped him into spending a weekend looking at time-lapse films of plaza use and nonuse. He felt that tougher zoning was in order. If we could find out why the good plazas worked and the bad ones didn't, and come up with hard guidelines, we could have the basis of a new code. Since we could expect the proposals to be strongly contested, it would be important to document the case to a fare-thee-well.

We set to work. We began studying a cross-section of spaces—in all, sixteen plazas, three small parks, and a number of odds and ends. I will pass over the false starts, the dead ends, and the floundering arounds, save to note that there were a lot and that the research was nowhere as tidy and sequential as it can seem in the telling. Let me also note that the findings should have been staggeringly obvious to us had we thought of them in the first place. But we didn't. Opposite propositions were often what seemed obvious. We arrived at our eventual findings by a succession of busted hypotheses.

The research continued for some three years. I like to cite the figure because it sounds impressive. But it is calendar time. For all practical purposes, at the end of six months we had completed our basic research and arrived at our recommendations. The city, alas, had other concerns on its mind, and we found that communicating the findings was to take more time than arriving at them. We logged many hours in church basements and meeting rooms giving film and slide presentations to community groups, architects, planners, businessmen, developers, and real-estate people. We continued our research; we had to keep our findings up-to-date, for now we were disciplined by adversaries. But at length the City Planning Commission incorporated our recommendations in a proposed new open-space zoning code, and in May 1975 it was adopted by the city's Board of Estimate. As a consequence, there has been a salutary improvement in the design of new spaces and the rejuvenation of old ones. (Since the zoning may have useful guidelines for other cities, an abridged text is provided as appendix C.)

But zoning is certainly not the ideal way to achieve the better design of spaces. It ought to be done for its own sake. For economics alone, it makes sense. An enormous expenditure of design expertise, and of travertine and steel, went into the creation of the many really bum office-building plazas around the country. To what end? It is far easier, simpler to create spaces that work for people than those that do not—and a tremendous difference it can make to the life of a city.

THE LIFE OF PLAZAS

We started by studying how people use plazas. We mounted time-lapse cameras overlooking the plazas and recorded daily patterns. We talked to people to find where they came from, where they worked, how frequently they used the place and what they thought of it. But, mostly, we watched people to see what they did.

Most of the people who use plazas, we found, are young office workers from nearby buildings. There may be relatively few patrons from the plaza's own building; as some secretaries confide, they'd just as soon put a little distance between themselves and the boss. But commuter distances are usually short; for most plazas, the effective market radius is about three blocks. Small parks, like Paley and Greenacre in New York, tend to have more assorted patrons throughout the day—upper-income older people, people coming from a distance. But office workers still predominate, the bulk from nearby.

This uncomplicated demography underscores an elemental point about good urban spaces: supply creates demand. A good new space builds a new constituency. It stimulates people into new habits—al fresco lunches—and provides new paths to and from work, new places to pause. It does all this very quickly. In Chicago's Loop, there were no such amenities not so long ago. Now, the plaza of the First National Bank has thoroughly changed the midday way of life for thousands of people. A success like this in no way surfeits demand for spaces: it indicates how great the unrealized potential is.

53rd and Lexington: New buildings derive a sense of place from old ones—until they are demolished.

The best-used plazas are sociable places, with a higher proportion of couples than you find in less-used places, more people in groups, more people meeting people, or exchanging goodbyes. At five of the most-used plazas in New York, the proportion of people in groups runs about 45 percent; in five of the least used, 32 percent. A high proportion of people in groups is an index of selectivity. When people go to a place in twos or threes or rendezvous there, it is most often because they have decided to. Nor are these

The dull plaza that replaced trendy 53rd and Lexington.

sociable places less congenial to the individual. In absolute numbers, they attract more individuals than do less-used spaces. If you are alone, a lively place can be the best place to be.

The most-used places also tend to have a higher than average proportion of women. The male-female ratio of a plaza basically reflects the composition of the work force, which varies from area to area—in midtown New York it runs about 60 percent male, 40 percent female. Women are more discriminating than men as to where they will sit, more sensitive to annoyances, and women spend more time casting the various possibilities. If a plaza has a markedly lower than average proportion of women, something is wrong. Where there is a higher than average percentage of women, the plaza is probably a good one and has been chosen as such.

The rhythms of plaza life are much alike from place to place. In the morning hours, patronage will be sporadic. A hot dog vendor setting up his cart at the corner, elderly pedestrians pausing for a rest, a delivery messenger or two, a shoeshine man, some tourists, perhaps an odd type, like a scavenger woman with shopping bags. If there is any construction work in the vicinity, hard hats will appear shortly after 11:00 A.M. with beer cans and sandwiches. Things will start to liven up. Around noon, the main clientele begins to arrive. Soon, activity will be near peak and will stay there until a little before 2:00 P.M. Some 80 percent of the total hours of use will be con-

centrated in these two hours. In mid and late afternoon, use is again sporadic. If there's a special event, such as a jazz concert, the flow going home
will be tapped, with the people staying as late as 6:00 or 6:30 P.M.
Ordinarily, however, plazas go dead by 6:30 and stay that way until the next
morning.

During peak hours the number of people on a plaza will vary considerably according to seasons and weather. The way people distribute themselves over the space, however, will be fairly consistent, with some sectors
getting heavy use day in and day out, others much less. In our sightings we
find it easy to map every person, but the patterns are regular enough that
you could count the number in only one sector, then multiply by a given
factor, and come within a percent or so of the total number of people at the
plaza.

Off-peak use often gives the best clues to people's preferences. When a
place is jammed, a person sits where he can. This may or may not be where
he most wants to. After the main crowd has left, the choices can be significant. Some parts of the plaza become quite empty; others continue to be
used. At Seagram's, a rear ledge under the trees is moderately, but steadily,
occupied when other ledges are empty; it seems the most uncrowded of
places, but on a cumulative basis it is the best-used part of Seagram's.

Men show a tendency to take the front-row seats, and, if there is a kind
of gate, men will be the guardians of it. Women tend to favor places slightly
secluded. If there are double-sided benches parallel to a street, the inner
side will usually have a high proportion of women; the outer, of men.

Of the men up front, the most conspicuous are girl watchers. They work
at it, and so demonstratively as to suggest that their chief interest may not
really be the girls so much as the show of watching them. Generally, the
watchers line up quite close together, in groups of three to five. If they are
construction workers, they will be very demonstrative, much given to
whistling, laughing, direct salutations. This is also true of most girl watchers
in New York's financial area. In midtown, they are more inhibited, playing it
coolly, with a good bit of sniggering and smirking, as if the girls were not
measuring up. It is all machismo, however, whether uptown or downtown.
Not once have we ever seen a girl watcher pick up a girl, or attempt to.

Few others will either. Plazas are not ideal places for striking up acquain-
tances, and even on the most sociable of them, there is not much mingling.
When strangers are in proximity, the nearest thing to exchange is what
Erving Goffman has called civil inattention. If there are, say, two smashing
blondes on a ledge, the men nearby will usually put on an elaborate show of

Jean Dubuffet's *Four Trees*, on the Chase Manhattan Plaza in lower Manhattan, tames the plaza.

disregard. Watch closely, however, and you will see them give themselves away with covert glances, involuntary primping of the hair, tugs at the ear lobe.

Lovers are to be found on plazas. But not where you would expect them. When we first started interviewing, people told us we'd find lovers in the rear places (pot smokers, too). But they weren't usually there. They would be out front. The most fervent embracing we've recorded on film has usually taken place in the most visible of locations, with the couple oblivious of the crowd.

Certain locations become rendezvous points for coteries of various kinds. For a while, the south wall of Chase plaza was a gathering point for camera bugs, the kind who like to buy new lenses and talk about them. Patterns of this sort may last no more than a season—or persist for years. Some time ago, one particular spot became a gathering place for raffish younger people; since then, there have been many changeovers in personnel, but it is still a gathering place for raffish younger people.

•

What attracts people most, it would appear, is other people. If I belabor the point, it is because many urban spaces are being designed as though the opposite were true, and that what people liked best were the places that they stay away from. People often do talk along such lines; this is why their responses to questionnaires can be so misleading. How many people would say they like to sit in the middle of a crowd? Instead, they speak of getting away from it all, and use terms like "escape," "oasis," "retreat." What people *do*, however, reveals a different priority.

This was first brought home to us in a study of street conversations. When people stop to have a conversation, we wondered, how far away do they move from the main pedestrian flow? We were especially interested in finding out how much of the normally unused buffer space next to buildings would be used. So we set up time-lapse cameras overlooking several key street corners and began plotting the location of all conversations lasting a minute or longer.

People didn't move out of the main pedestrian flow. They stayed in it or moved into it, and the great bulk of the conversations were smack in the center of the flow—the 100 percent location, to use the real-estate term. The same gravitation characterized "traveling conversations"—the kind in which two men move about, alternating the roles of straight man and prin-

Schmoozers on Seventh Avenue.

cipal talker. There is a lot of apparent motion. But if you plot the orbits, you will find they are usually centered around the 100 percent spot.

Just why people behave like this, we have never been able to determine. It is understandable that conversations should originate within the main flow. Conversations are incident to pedestrian journeys; where there are the most people, the likelihood of a meeting or a leave-taking is highest. What is less explainable is people's inclination to remain in the main flow, blocking traffic, being jostled by it. This does not seem to be a matter of inertia but of choice—instinctive, perhaps, but by no means illogical. In the center of the crowd, you have the maximum choice—to break off, to continue—much as you have in the center of a cocktail party, itself a moving conversation growing ever denser and denser.

People also sit in the mainstream. At the Seagram plaza, the main pedestrian paths are on diagonals from the building entrance to the corners of the steps. These are natural junction and transfer points and there is usually a lot of activity at them. They are also a favored place for sitting and picnicking. Sometimes there will be so many people that pedestrians have to step carefully to negotiate the steps. The pedestrians rarely complain. While some will detour around the blockage, most will thread their way through it.

Standing patterns are similar. When people stop to talk on a plaza, they usually do so in the middle of the traffic stream. They also show an inclination to station themselves near objects, such as a flagpole or a statue. They like well-defined places, such as steps, or the border of a pool. What they rarely choose is the middle of a large space.

There are a number of explanations. The preference for pillars might be ascribed to some primeval instinct: you have a full view of all corners but your rear is covered. But this doesn't explain the inclination men have for lining up at the curb. Typically, they face inwards, toward the sidewalk, with their backs exposed to the dangers of the street.

Foot movements are consistent, too. They seem to be a sort of silent language. Often, in a schmoozing group no one will be saying anything. Men stand bound in amiable silence, surveying the passing scene. Then, slowly, rhythmically, one of the men rocks up and down: first on the ball of the foot, then back on the heel. He stops. Another man starts the same movement. Sometimes there are reciprocal gestures. One man makes a half-turn to the right. Then, after a rhythmic interval, another responds with a half turn to the left. Some kind of communication seems to be taking place here, but I've never broken the code.

Whatever they may mean, people's movements are one of the great spectacles of a plaza. You do not see this in architectural photographs, which typically are empty of life and are taken from a perspective few people share. It is a quite misleading one. At eye level, the scene comes alive with movement and color—people walking quickly, walking slowly, skipping up steps, weaving in and out on crossing patterns, accelerating and retarding to match the moves of others. There is a beauty that is beguiling to watch, and one senses that the players are quite aware of it themselves. You see this, too, in the way they arrange themselves on steps and ledges. They often do so with a grace that they, too, must sense. With its brown-gray monochrome, Seagram's is the best of settings—especially in the rain, when an umbrella or two spots color in the right places, like Corot's red dots.

How peculiar are such patterns to New York? Our working assumption was that behavior in other cities would probably differ little, and subsequent comparisons have proved our assumption correct. The important

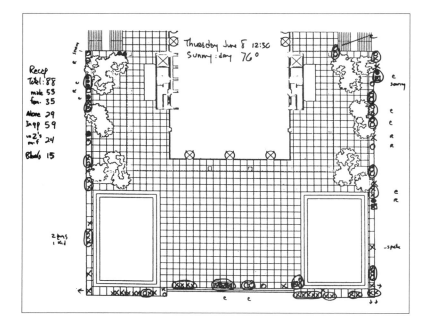

A typical sighting map can be used to plot locations of sitters almost as quickly as a simple head count. Xs and Os represent male and female sitters, respectively.

variable is city size. As I will discuss in more detail, in smaller cities, densities tend to be lower, pedestrians move at a slower pace, and there is less of the social activity characteristic of high traffic areas. In most other respects, pedestrian patterns are similar.

Observers in other countries have also noted the tendency to self-congestion. In his study of pedestrians in Copenhagen, architect Jan Gehl mapped bunching patterns almost identical to those observable here. Matthew Ciolek studied an Australian shopping center, with similar results. "Contrary to 'common sense' expectations," Ciolek notes, "the great majority of people were found to select their sites for social interaction right on or very close to the traffic lines intersecting the plaza. Relatively few people formed their gatherings away from the spaces used for navigation."

The strongest similarities are found among the world's largest cities. People in them tend to behave more like their counterparts in other world cities than like fellow nationals in smaller cities. Big-city people walk faster, for one thing, and they self-congest. After we had completed our New York study, we made a brief comparison study of Tokyo and found the proclivity to stop and talk in the middle of department-store doorways, busy corners, and the like, is just as strong in that city as in New York. For all the cultural differences, sitting patterns in parks and plazas are much the same, too. Similarly, schmoozing patterns in Milan's Galleria are remarkably like those in New York's garment center. Modest conclusion: given the basic elements of a center city—such as high pedestrian volumes, and concentration and mixture of activities—people in one place tend to act much like people in another.

INDOOR SPACES

As an alternative to plazas, builders have been turning to indoor spaces. There are many variants: atriums, galleries, courtyards, through-block arcades, indoor parks, covered pedestrian areas of one shape or another. Some are dreadful. In return for extra floors, the developers provided spaces and welshed on the amenities. But some spaces have been very successful indeed, and there is enough of a record to indicate that the denominators are much the same as with outdoor spaces. Here, briefly, are the principal needs:

1. *Sitting.* Movable chairs are best for indoor parks. Most of the popular places have had excellent experience with them; some places, like Citicorp, have been adding to the numbers. In all cases the total amount of sitting

The Crystal Court of the IDS Center in Minneapolis, designed by John Burgee and Philip Johnson, is one of the best interior spaces in the United States. Psychologically as well as visually, the Center has an excellent relationship with the street and surroundings, which are eminently visible, and this helps make pedestrian flows easy. It has been a hospital place, with plenty of seating—though a new owner bought the building and removed the open seating.

space has met or exceeded the minimum recommended for outdoor spaces—one linear foot for every 30 square feet of open space. There is a tendency, however, to overlook the potentials of ledges and planters. Too many are by inadvertence lower or higher than need be.

2. *Food.* Every successful indoor space provides food. The basic combination is snack bars and chairs and tables. Some places feature café operations as well.

3. *Retailing.* Shops are important for liveliness and the additional pedestrian flows they attract. Developers, who can often do better renting the space for banks or offices, are not always keen on including shops. They should be required to.

4. *Toilets.* If incentive zoning achieved nothing else, an increase in public toilets would justify it. Thanks to beneficent pressure, new indoor parks in New York are providing a pair or more, unisex-style as on airplanes. These facilities are modest, but their existence could have a considerable effect on the shopping patterns of many people, older ones especially.

One benefit of an indoor space is the through-block circulation it can provide for pedestrians. Planners believe this important, and developers have been allowed a lot of additional floor space in return for it. But walking space is about all that developers have provided, and it has proved no bargain. Unless there are attractions within, people don't use walkways very much, even in rainy or cold weather. At New York's Olympic Towers, which is taller by several million dollars worth of extra space for providing a through-block passage, the number of people traversing the passage is about 400 per hour at peak. On the Fifth Avenue sidewalk that parallels the passage, the flow is about 4,000 per hour.

Not so paradoxically, the walk-through function of a space is greatly enhanced if something is going on within it. Even if one does not tarry to sit or get a snack, just seeing the activity makes a walk more interesting. Conceivably, there could be conflict between uses. Planners tend to fret over this and, to ensure adequate separation, they specify wide walkways—in New York, 20 feet at the minimum. But that is more than enough. As at plazas, the places people like best for sitting are those next to the main pedestrian flow, and for many conversations the very middle of the flow. Walkers like the proximity too. It makes navigation more challenging. At places where there is a multiplicity of flows, as at the IDS Center in Minneapolis, one often gets blocked by people just standing or talking, while there are others in crossing patterns or collision courses up ahead. The processional experience is all the better for the busyness.

In an important respect, public spaces that are inside differ from public spaces that are outside. They're not as public. The look of a building, its entrances, the guards do have a filtering effect and the cross section of the public that uses the space within is somewhat skewed—with more higher-income people, fewer lower-income people, and, presumably, fewer undesirables. This, of course, is just what the building management and shop owners want. But there is a question of equity posed. Should the public underwrite such spaces? In a critique of the Citicorp Building, Suzanne Stephens argues in *Progressive Architecture* that it should not. The suburban shopping mall, she notes, is frankly an enclave and

> owes its popularity to what it keeps out as well as what it offers within. Whether this isolationism should occur in "public spaces" created through the city's incentive zoning measures should be addressed at the city planning level. . . . Open space amenities are moving from the true public domain, the street, to inner sanctums where public and private domains blur. Thus this public space is becoming increasingly privatized.

This is very much the case with most megastructures. They are exclusionary by design, and they are wrongly so. But buildings with indoor spaces can be quite hospitable if they are designed to be so, even rather large ones. The Crystal Court of the IDS Center is the best indoor space in the country, and it is used by a very wide mix of people. In mid-morning, the majority of the people sitting and talking are older people, and many of them are obviously of limited means.

Inevitably, any internal space is bound to have a screening effect; its amenities, the merchandise lines offered, the level of the entertainment— all of these help determine the people who will choose to come, and it is not necessarily a bad thing if a good many of the people are educated and well-off. But there should be other kinds of people, too, and, if there are not, the place is not truly public. Or urban.

The big problem is the street. Internal spaces with shops can dilute the attractions of the street outside, and the more successful they are, the greater the problem. How many more indoor spaces it might take to tip the scale is difficult to determine, but it is a matter the planning commissions should think very hard about. More immediate is the question of the internal space's relation to the street. If the space is underwritten by incentive zoning, it should not merely provide access to the public, it should invite it. A good internal space should not be blocked off by bland walls. It should be visible from the street; the street and its surroundings should be highly visible from it; and between the two, physically and psychologically, the connections should be easy and inviting. The Crystal Court of the IDS building is a splendid example. It is transparent. You are in the center of Minneapolis, no mistake. You see it. There is the street and the neighboring buildings, and what most catches the eye are the flows of people through doorways and walkways. It is an easy place to get in and out of.

Most places are not. Typically, building entrances are overengineered affairs centered around a set of so-called revolving doors. The doors do not of themselves revolve; you revolve them. From a standing start, this requires considerable foot-pounds of energy. As does opening the swinging doors at the sides—which you are not supposed to use anyway. These doors are for emergency use. So there is frequently a sign saying PLEASE USE REVOLVING DOOR mounted on a pedestal blocking the center of the emergency door. Sometimes, for good measure, there is a second set of doors 15 or 20 feet inside the first.

All this is necessary, engineers say, for climate control and for an air seal to prevent stack-effect drafts in the elevator shafts. Maybe so. But on occasion revolving doors are folded to an open position. If you watch the entrances then, you will notice that the building still stands and no great drafts ensue. Watch the entrances long enough, and there is something else you will notice. The one time they function well is when they are very crowded.

I first noticed this phenomenon at Place Ville Marie in Montreal. I was clocking the flow through the main concourse entrance, a set of eight swinging doors. At 8:45 A.M., when the flow was 6,000 people an hour, there was a good bit of congestion, with many people lined up one behind another. Ten minutes later the flow was up to a peak rate of 8,000 people an hour (outside Tokyo, the heaviest I've ever clocked). Oddly, there was little congestion. People were moving faster and more easily, with little queuing.

The reason lies in the impulse for the open door. Some people are natural door openers. Most are not. Where there is a choice, they will follow someone who is opening a door. Sometimes they will queue up two or three deep rather than open a door themselves. Even where there are many doors, most of the time the bulk of the traffic will be self-channeled through one or two of them. As the crowd swells, however, an additional door will be opened, then another. The pace quickens. The headway between people shortens. In transportation planning, it is axiomatic that there should be a comfortable headway between people. In doorway situations, the opposite is true. If the interval between people shortens to 1.2 seconds or less, the

The Place Ville Marie sequence shows how heavier flows can make for less con-gestion in doorways. People tend to queue up behind open doors; when there are so many people that all doors are open, everyone moves faster.

doors don't get a chance to close. All or most of the doors will be open, and instead of bunching up at one or two of them, people will distribute themselves through the whole entrance.

One way to provide a good entrance, then, is to have big enough crowds. But there is another possibility. Why not leave a door open?

This novel approach has been followed for the entrance of an indoor park. As part of the new Philip Morris building, architect Ulrich Franzen has designed an attractive space that the Whitney Museum will operate as a kind of sculpture garden. An entrance that invited people in was felt to be very important. Before the energy shortage an air door would have been the answer, and had been so specified in the zoning code for covered pedestrian areas. But this was out of the question now. So, at the other end of the scale, was the usual revolving-door barricade.

To check the potentials of an open door, I did a simple study of heavily used entrances. I filmed rush-hour flows with a digital stop watch recorded on the film, and then calculated how many people used which parts of the entrance. Happily, the weather was mild, and at several of the entrances one or two doors would be wedged open. As at Place Ville Marie, it was to the open door that most people went. This does not mean that the other doors were redundant; even if one doesn't choose to use them, having the choice to do so lessens one's sense of crowding. But for sheer efficiency, it became clear, a small space kept open is better than a wider space that is closed. At the main concourse entry to the RCA building, two open doors at one side of an eight door entrance accounted for two thirds of the people passing through during the morning rush hour. At Grand Central Station, most of those using the nine-door entrance at 42nd Street traversed open doors, and at any given time three doors accounted for the bulk of the traffic. The doors at Grand Central are old, in disrepair, and the glass is rarely cleaned. But they do work well.

Franzen's design for the entrance to the Philip Morris indoor park incorporates these simple findings. Visually, the entrance will be a stretch of glass 20 feet wide. At the center it will have a pair of automatic sliding doors. In good weather and at peak-use times, the doors will be kept open to provide a clear six-foot entry. This should be enough for the likely peak flows. For overflows, and people who like to open doors, there will be an option of swinging doors at either side. In bad weather, the sliding doors will open automatically when people approach. In effect, there will be an ever-open door. It is to be hoped that there will be many more.

•

SMALLER CITIES AND PLACES

Will the factors that make a plaza or small space successful in one city work in another? Generally, the answer is yes—with one key variable to watch. It is scale, and it is particularly important for smaller cities. For a number of reasons, it is tougher for them to create lively spaces than it is for a big city. Big cities have lots of people in their downtowns. This density poses problems but it provides a strong supply of potential users for open spaces in most parts of the central business district. Where 3,000 people an hour pass by a site, a lot of mistakes can be made in design and a place may still end up being well used.

Smaller cities are not as compressed. True, some are blessed with a tight, well-defined center, with some fine old buildings to anchor it. But many have loosened up; they have torn down old buildings and not replaced them, leaving much of the space open. Parking lots and garages become the dominant land use, often accounting for more than 50 percent of downtown. This is true also of some big cities—Houston, for one. Houston has some fine elements in its downtown, but they are so interspersed with parking lots that they don't connect very well with one another.

Many cities have diffused their downtowns by locating new "downtown" developments outside of downtown, or just far enough away that one element does not support the other. The distances need not be great. If you have to get into a car and drive, a place six blocks away might as well be a mile or more. That is precisely the kind of trouble you have in a number of cities. Kansas City's Crown Center, for example, is only 11 blocks from the central business district, but the two centers still remain more or less unconnected.

Cities in the 100,000–200,000 range are not just scaled down versions of bigger cities. Relatively speaking, the downtowns of these smaller cities cover more space than the downtowns of bigger cities. Often their streets are wider, and their pedestrian densities much lower, with fewer people in any given area of the central business district. Sidewalk counts are a good index. If the number of passersby is under a rate of 1,000 per hour around noontime, a city could pave the street with gold for all the difference it would make. Something fundamental is missing: people. More stores, more offices, more reasons for being are what the downtown must have.

Some cities have sought to revitalize their downtowns by banning cars from the main street and turning it into a pedestrian mall. Some of these malls have worked well. Some have not. Again, the problem is diffusion.

The malls may be too big for the number of people and the amount of activities. This seems to be particularly the case with the smaller cities—which tend to have the largest malls.

What such cities need to do is compress, to concentrate. Many of them were very low density to begin with; in some, most of the buildings are only two or three stories high. Spread over many downtown blocks are activities and people that might have come together in a critical mass had they been compressed into two or three. Such places are sad to see. So many hopes, so many good intentions, so many fountains and play sculptures have gone into them. Yet they are nearly empty.

Smaller cities are also highly vulnerable to the competition of suburban shopping centers—in particular, the huge centralized ones going up next to interchanges. The suburban centers that do well are more urban in their use of space than the cities they are beating out. True, they are surrounded by a vast acreage of parking space, much of which is never used save on peak days. Unlike the earlier generation of linear shopping centers, however, the new ones are highly concentrated, one-stop places. You don't have to drive here for this and there for that. You enter an enclosed pedestrian system that is, in effect, a gigantic customer-processing machine.

A model for downtown? Some cities now think so. To beat suburbia at its own game, they have been inviting developers to put up shopping centers in downtown. The developers have responded with copies of their suburban models, with very little adaptation: concrete boxes, geared to people who drive to them, that have little relationship to the sidewalks or surrounding buildings of the city. These mini-megastructures may be an efficient setting for merchandising of the middle range; in suburbia, they provide something of a social center as well. But they are not for the downtown. They are the antithesis of what downtown should be.

Cities do best when they intensify their unique strengths. Salem, Oregon, for example, at one time thought its last, best hope would be a suburban-type shopping complex, complete with a skyway or two for razzle-dazzle. But somehow it didn't seem like Salem. The city decided on an opposite approach, filling in empty spaces with buildings to the scale of the place, putting glass canopies over sidewalks, converting alleys into shopping ways, tying strong points with pedestrian spaces and sitting areas. An old opera house has been converted into a complex of stores with felicitous results, and other old structures may be recycled, too. In sum, Salem has embarked on a plan that works with the grain of the city.

It is significant that the cities doing best by their downtowns are the ones doing best at historic preservation and reuse. Fine old buildings are worthwhile in their own right, but there is a greater benefit involved. They provide discipline. Architects and planners like a blank slate. They usually do their best work, however, when they don't have one. When they have to work with impossible lot lines and bits and pieces of space, beloved old eyesores, irrational street layouts, and other such constraints, they frequently produce the best of their new designs—and the most neighborly.

From *City: Rediscovering the Center* (1988)

City is data-rich, philosophical, and stirringly eloquent: a magnum opus. It was long in coming and was greeted with widespread enthusiasm when it finally arrived. Whyte's legions of supporters included *The New York Times,* whose reviewer praised *City* as a work of "genuine brilliance [which] punctures commonplace assumptions about urban life in virtually every chapter." Indeed, the book was a harbinger of a new way of looking at cities, namely, appreciatively. Whyte's longtime friend Brendan Gill wrote a tribute to the book and its author in *The New Yorker,* in which he summarized Whyte's achievement:

> Over the past sixteen years or so, with the help of grants from several philanthropic foundations, Whyte has been at work in scores of different neighborhoods not only in this city but in other cities, throughout the country and abroad, analyzing the way people use parks, plazas, streets, street furniture, sidewalks, and even curbstones and window ledges. He has earned a high place in the ranks of learned amateurs; indeed, he cannot be pigeonholed as this or that sort of professional only because no single profession can be said to contain him.... Whyte finds much to deplore in the mutilation of our cities by blank-walled megastructures, by elevated walkways, by the rise of suburbia and its inhumanly vast shopping malls. In Whyte's view, mankind is instinctively centripetal. He believes that a desire for concentration, and not scatteration, has been characteristic of city dwellers since cities began; historically, they have always preferred the disorder of an overcrowded Athenian agora to the clinical orderliness of the broad boulevards of a Brasília.... To Whyte, there can scarcely be such a thing as urban overcrowding; in most cases, he says, our streets suffer not from having too many people on them but from having too few.

STREET PEOPLE

Many people work the street. There are the regulars: cops, postmen, sanitation men, traffic directors, doormen, bus dispatchers. There are supervisors:

transit authority people checking on bus dispatchers, traffic officials on traffic directors. There is even a man to check that the grate cleaners are doing their job.

Store owners can be street people. On a high-volume street with many small stores, some owners spend a lot of their time standing in the doorway. If a passerby stops to look in the window, they will start to sell him. There is very little they do not know about the street.

The irregulars are the most numerous: handbill passers, pushcart food vendors, merchandise vendors, messengers, entertainers, palmists, solicitors for religious causes, blood pressure takers. Then there are the odd people: Moondog, Mr. Magoo, Mr. Paranoid, Captain Horrible, Aztec Priestess, Gracious Lady, Tambourine Woman. Whatever the fantasies they have been acting out they make a beneficent presence on the street. Since the mid-1970s, however, their ranks have been swelled by scores of disturbed people released from institutions. There has been no outpatient support for these people and a number are on the streets who ought not to be. The bag ladies are a special category. They antedated the wave of released patients and endanger no one save themselves. They remain fiercely independent. There appears to be more of them on the street than before.

The underlife of the street has a rich cast too. There are the beggars, the phony pitchmen for causes, the three-card-monte players and their shills, the whores and their pimps, the male prostitutes and the Murphy Men, the dope dealers, and worst of all, the muggers in their white sneakers.

Bad or good, the variety of street people is astonishingly wide. To appreciate this, stand still. If you stay in one spot long enough, you will begin to see how many different kinds of people there are; how regular are their ways; and how many seem to know each other, even the ones you would assume to be adversaries.

If you stand in one spot long enough you will also become aware that they are noticing you. They have reason. You are not part of the routine of the block. You have no obvious business being there. If you write things down on a pad of paper they are more curious yet. Before long someone will come up to you and ask what you are up to. If you establish yourself as OK the word will get around. You will be accepted. People will say hello to you.[1]

There is one regular you will find puzzling. He is the familiar stranger. You recognize him—you've seen him often. But you don't know who he is. He knows you. He nods to you. But who *is* he? He is out of context. He is not in uniform. He is not in the surroundings you usually see him in. Is he the assistant manager at Gristede's? The bartender at Gianni's? You need to *place* him.

The process works both ways. The barber next door has been cutting my hair for fifteen years. But he always calls me Doctor. He thinks I'm a surgeon at the hospital down the block. I'm not going to tell him I'm not. It's too late. And it would not be fair to him. Calling me a doctor is part of our relationship and it is best let be.

Let us now take a closer look at the principal kinds of street people. Without drawing lines too fine we will go from good to bad.

Vendors

Street vendors sell everything. There are perennial staples: junk jewelry, watches, umbrellas, plastic raincoats, toys. But the vendors are always trying out new items and occasionally most of them will be riding one fad, or whatever the jobbers are loaded up with. Several years ago it was leather belts. So many vendors took to selling them that it looked like the point of saturation had surely been reached. But supply created demand, and the sight of all those leather belts on the sidewalks drove people to buy more leather belts. They are still buying them.

The vendors have been growing in number. They have been broadening the range of the merchandise sold. To the aggravation of merchants, they have also been staking out more of the sidewalk space, that in front of stores especially. They have been doing more selling in winter and more night selling. Some illumine their racks and tables with battery-powered fluorescent lamps.

Whatever the merchandise, the pitch is much the same. It's cheaper on the street. Ten dollars inside. One dollar here. Why pay more? The pitch is often made in a furtive manner, as if the deal were shady. Many vendors look shady. Many try to. It is to their advantage. There is a widespread assumption among knowing New Yorkers that much of the merchandise is stolen. Vendors do nothing to discourage this idea. As in a con game, the latent dishonesty of the customer is all for the good. He *wants* the goods to be stolen. That explains why he is going to snare a bargain. In actual fact, very little of the goods sold by vendors is stolen. They pick up their stuff from the jobbers in the Broadway–Thirtieth Street area who specialize in novelty merchandise. But if you ask the vendors where the goods came from, they may look at you slyly and wink.

Virtually all street vending is illegal. Under the statutes, food and merchandise vendors can be licensed, but that does not exempt them from all sorts of restrictions. Merchandise vendors are banned from the business districts; from areas zoned light commercial; from sidewalks less than twelve feet wide; from crosswalks; from bus stops; from places within ten feet of a driveway, or twenty feet of the entrance to a building. In other words, banned from almost anywhere.

The police do go after the vendors. But not very hard. Cops arresting vendors is one of the standard dramas of the street. Both parties know their parts and they play them cooperatively. When a cop comes up to a vendor and pulls out his summons book, he may say, I got a complaint—that is, this is not his idea. If any customers are still looking at the vendor's merchandise the cop may tell them it's OK to buy; it's going to take him some time to fill out the summons. The vendor won't be happy, but he knows that most judges think it is a to-do about little and will lay a fine of only a few dollars.

Confiscation of the goods is the ultimate sanction, and the police dislike it as much as the vendors do. Periodically the police will make a sweep, arriving on the scene with one or more vans into which they proceed to pack the vendors' stuff. These confrontations draw a crowd—from which come boos—and newspaper publicity. And that, to the chagrin of the Fifth Avenue Association, will be that.

Individually, some cops do go after vendors. One I used to see would sneak up on the traffic side of a line of parked trucks and then suddenly pounce on the unalerted vendors. A real mean bastard, they told me, not like the regular cops, who would approach them from the sidewalk.

There is another reason why vendors are not too unhappy about the police. The police thin out the competition. While vendors are fairly cooperative with one another—the regulars, that is—they don't like to be crowded in with a lot of amateurs. In a contest with the police, the amateurs have nowhere near the survival powers of the regulars.

Vendors are very adept at quick dispersal. This is particularly evident on blockfronts where a group of vendors has lined up. They will maintain one or two lookouts, usually a kid standing on a box at the street corner. Lately some groups have taken to using walkie-talkies. They are prepared for the getaway. They have determined which doorway they will use, which subway entrance, which parked van. Their displays are instantly collapsible and the merchandise can be thrown into one or two cartons. The racks they use for leather goods have wheels on the bottom and can be raced away.

The vendors also know the precinct lines. If a Midtown North patrol car is coming up, the vendors rush to the south side of Fifty-ninth Street. Now they're in the Seventeenth Precinct, and to hell with you, bud. If a car from the Seventeenth is spotted they rush right back again.

If the police do descend on them in force there will be shouts and whistles, and vendors racing this way and that. It takes about twenty to thirty seconds—I have timed these flurries—and then there will be no one except the police, and perhaps one hapless vendor who has been a bit too slow. Half an hour later the vendors will all be back. Teamwork is important in such situations. So is having a helper. They function not only as lookouts, but as extra salesmen and relief persons.[2]

Many vendors, probably a majority, are recent immigrants. Until recently, Middle Easterners dominated merchandise vending, as Greeks did food vending. But ethnic patterns are shifting. Since 1983 there has been a strong influx of young men from Senegal, a former French colony on the west coast of Africa. From generation to generation street selling has been an honored tradition in Senegal. In recent years Senegalese vendors have become a fixture on the streets of Paris and from there they have spread to other European cities. Now they are in New York, over six hundred at latest estimate, and their numbers are increasing rapidly.

They are different from other vendors. They are polite, for one thing, even the police who arrest them note this. They speak little English, but they speak it with a soft French accent. They sell everything, but they are partial to gold trinkets and watches. Like other vendors, they buy from the jobbers.

They do not hawk their wares; they just stand silently behind their trays of goods. If they do address a customer, it is with a whispered question. Gold watches? Gold watches? Their serenity is disarming.

Other new arrivals are the book vendors. Some sell new books; some sell used ones. A few specialize in comic books. The most venturesome sell large-format art books and coffee-table gift books, usually at a discount from their high list prices. Spread out on the sidewalk, the large books make an attractive display and induce many a passerby to pause and look.

Unlike so many other vendors, the book vendors do not keep looking over their shoulders for cops. They are on to a secret. The cops can't arrest them. The selling of books comes under the protection of the First Amendment and cannot be prohibited by local ordinances.

Food vendors have been the caterers of the outdoor life of the city and their numbers are growing: from 3,400 licensed in 1978 to 4,300 in 1988. The bill of fare has broadened too. It used to be hot dogs, soft pretzels, soda, ice cream, and chestnuts. They are still the staples but to them have been added a host of dishes, many of them foreign, many cooked on the spot: souvlaki, falafel (with or without pita), Greek sausage, Italian sausage, bratwurst, omelets to order, Chinese beef, tacos, chili, quiche, stuffed Rock Cornish game hen. Another specialty is the juice squeezed to order from chilled fresh oranges.

The fare is surprisingly good. Is it safe as well? Merchants and officials are forever fretting over the possibility of contaminated food, airborne bacteria, and other such dangers. The record appears to have been quite good. Requirements for food carts in which cooking is done are strict; they must have hot and cold water, provisions for chilling as well as cooking, and hoods with filters and exhaust fans. The Health Department says there has never been a case of food poisoning traced to a food vendor.

Vendors can do very well. A good one with a good location can make as much as $40,000 a year. Consistency is important. The ones with the best clientele are the ones who are always in the same spot. One buys from them not just for the food, but to check in. There is Gus, for example, at the northeast corner of Fifty-second and Park. He has had his hot dog cart there for over fifteen years—every day, no matter what the weather. In winter he moves his cart directly over the cover of a steam manhole and traps the warmth with an awning. He is not very talkative but people like to stop by and say hello. He has put a son through college and graduate school from his earnings.

Food vendors are clearly functional and people appreciate this. Dealings with merchandise vendors tend to be adversary; with food vendors, agreeable.

Merchants will keep up the fight against vendors—all kinds—but victory will continue to be elusive. It always has been. Over the years vendor regulations have fluctuated in degree of severity, sometimes leaning toward permissiveness. But these shifts do not make much practical difference. Even at their most liberal, the regulations are so full of nullifying stipulations that were they enforced to the letter there could be no more vendors at any place at any time. And this is not tenable.

Over time you cannot enforce a law that is against something people like. There is a parallel here to Prohibition. Authority is being refuted by the marketplace. People are told that food vending is bad for downtown business, bad for traffic, bad for them and their health. But people do not believe this. They like eating out-of-doors. They like the choices. They like the prices. They prefer a hot dog and a soda they can afford ($1.65) to a fuller lunch they cannot. So they buy. The vendors are providing what the established order is not.

There is a vacuum and it is of the city's own making. Take New York's Sixth Avenue. Once it was lined with places to eat: delis, cafeterias, Irish bars, coffee shops. New office building construction, spurred by incentive zoning, did away with these places. In their stead were plazas and bank windows. But no food. Not even a snack. Then vendors came. Then more. Today the sidewalks are full of them, lined up sometimes six to eight in a row. The revenge of the street.

Entertainers

Probably the finest street entertainer of our time is Philippe Petit. I was lucky enough to catch one of his first performances after he arrived from Paris. It was on upper Fifth Avenue at the Pulitzer Fountain. A gamin-like fellow with a battered high hat was stringing a tightrope between two trees. As a crowd began to gather, he got on a unicycle and pedaled around, simultaneously juggling some balls. He was obviously a master of the use of props.

The prop that he was to use best was a policeman. For the climax of his act, Petit got up on the tightrope, lit three batons, and proceeded to juggle them as he went across. The crowd applauded vigorously. Petit dismounted and made the rounds of the crowd with outstretched hat. At this point a friendly black cop who had been enjoying the show from the rear came forward. Petit looked stricken. He recoiled as if hit. "Don't hit him," someone shouted. The crowd was angry. Outraged at this display of police brutality, people pressed additional contributions on Petit, who had sufficiently recovered from his terror to make another round. As the bemused cop looked on, Petit mounted his unicycle, doffed his hat, and made his getaway.

Several weeks later, at seven-thirty in the morning, people around the World Trade Center looked up in amazement. On a wire between the two towers, 1,150 feet in the air, a figure was walking back and forth with a balancing rod. With an accomplice, Petit had gained access to a tower the night before and, with a crossbow, shot a rope and then pulled a metal cable across to the other tower. "When I see two oranges, I want to juggle. When I see two towers, I want to go across."

By quarter of eight a tremendous crowd had gathered. Traffic was stopped dead. For thirty minutes Petit performed. He would get down on one knee, get up, go back and forth; once he almost teetered into a fall. If there had been people on the street collecting for him, the take would have been a fortune. "I was happy," Petit recalled. "I was dying with happiness."

Petit was arrested. But the city government was rather pleased with the kind of publicity he generated. Petit was sentenced to give a special public performance. At street level.

Few street entertainers are in a class with Petit, but there are many talented ones. Some of them are professional; most are part-time students, unemployed actors. One of the best ventriloquists in New York one summer was a Princeton philosophy major. The largest single category is "music students"; to judge by the signs, a large part of the street population is working its way through Juilliard. There are many musical groups, some pickup and some semipermanent—for example, the Fly-by-Night String Band, the Illusionary Free Lunch Band.

One way or another they all make a pitch for money. They pass the hat, they have someone pass it, or they have an empty instrument case or box in front of them. Propped up on it may be a hand-lettered sign with an admonition. People are very curious to see what it says.

"No credit cards please."

"Be a patron of the arts."

"Support live music."

"Send this weird boy to camp."

One black saxophonist had a sign that said "Send me back to Africa." He had done very well with it. "The blacks chip in because they want me to see their roots," he said. "The whites wish we'd all go back and figure it might as well start with me."

The donation and receiving of money is part of the performance. As with beggars, there is a strong domino effect; if two or more people stop to put in money there will likely be a rapid succession of givers. The entertainers usually acknowledge the donations with a smile and a thank-you. A musician may salute with a few high notes. The accepting, in sum, is done with grace. Rarely do entertainers express discourtesy to those who do not give.

Entertainers are a temperamental lot, many with large egos. But there is a good bit of occupational camaraderie among them. They are cooperative in settling territorial problems. On a busy afternoon they will work out a loose agreement as to who will play when at a key public space. At the steps of the Metropolitan Museum of Art, for example, there may be four or five acts waiting to go on but none will encroach on the one that is playing.

While they are waiting, they serve as a volunteer claque and vigorously applaud the others' acts.

The same is true at London's Covent Garden and of the *ateliers* at Centre Pompidou in Paris. At both places there appears to be a tacit understanding that acts stay within a ten-to-fifteen-minute period. Both places have enough space to accommodate a number of concurrent acts, but entertainers dislike this kind of competition.

The size of the space is not the important factor for entertainers. They would as soon squeeze people in as not. What entertainers most look for is a place with a strong *flow*—a constantly self-renewing audience of regulars, such as office workers, and of tourists. Among the best places in midtown New York are the steps of the New York Public Library, the steps of St. Thomas Church, Grand Army Plaza, the mall in Central Park. Street corners can work very well. One of the very best is Fifty-ninth and Fifth. For individual musicians it is the closest thing to playing the Palace. *The New York Times*'s William Geist tells of listening to an excellent saxophonist there, Ray Peters. A woman put fifty cents in his case. "You're an exceptionally gifted young man," she said. "You'll make the big time someday."

"Madam," he called after her, "this *is* the big time."

In Boston the best space is in the Common at the Park Street station. In San Francisco one of the best places is Ghirardelli Square. It is so popular that entertainers must be auditioned by the managements before they can play there.

How do they like street performing? They are of several minds. Some say they do not like it; they feel that it is degrading, that there is no future in it. But most of them say that they enjoy it, the good parts at least. "It's terribly insecure," says one, "but I like the insecurity of it." Entertainers speak of free choice, the give-and-take with people, the honing of one's skills, the immediacy of the audience.

They also speak of what it is like when there is no audience, and of the humiliation of performing when no one stops to look or listen.

"I haven't yet hardened myself to the rejection and in this line of work there is rejection right and left," says a ventriloquist. Sometimes he talks to his dummy on a park bench for as much as twenty or thirty minutes—alone. It is a bitter wait. But then someone stops and listens, and then another stops. Soon there will be an audience.

Entertainers praise the toughness of street audiences and say that of all audiences, New Yorkers are the toughest. But also the most appreciative. If you can collect from them, they say, you've got to be good, which is to say that they are pretty good themselves.

It is interesting to watch people as they chance upon an entertainer. So often they will smile. A string quartet. Here at Forty-fourth! Their smile is like that of a child. For these moments they seem utterly at ease, their shoulders relaxed. People enjoy programmed entertainment, too, but not the same way. It is the unexpected that seems to delight them most.

Street entertainers can have a strong binding effect on people This is particularly the case when the entertainer is skillful in involving members of the audience in the act—like magician Jeff Sheridan, who borrows a businessman's coat and then appears to burn a hole in it; who gets a pretty girl to take off her straw hat, from which he produces a bottle of beer. How did he do it? Watch his left hand, someone says. No, it was up his sleeve, says another.

Sheridan is very skillful. But even a bad performer can unify a crowd. There is one magician who has a perfectly dreadful act and his patter is so corny that one almost has to say something about it. But he does get people involved and his inept performance provides a connection between them.

There is a communal sense to these gatherings and though it may be fleeting, it is the city at its best. I remember especially the end of a mime's act in front of Pulitzer Fountain at Fifty-ninth Street. The mime was making fun of people. He walked up to two junior executives and drew a square in the air over them. Everyone laughed, even the junior executives. Then a cop walked across the plaza with a side-to-side swinging gait. The mime walked behind with the same side-to-side swinging gait. The cop saw people laughing, looked over his shoulder at the mime, laughed, and then turned to the mime and shook his hand. The crowd applauded. It was a splendid moment, a very city kind of moment.

Historically, the police have warred against street entertainers, or, to be more accurate, have been made to war. Left to their own judgment, cops usually take a live-and-let-live stance. When one does move against an entertainer he may tell him he's sorry, but the captain has been on his back. And he has been so because the merchants have been on his back.

Merchants have been the main force against street entertaining, and it has been largely on their say-so that city councils have passed repressive ordinances against it. One feature of such ordinances is a prohibition against soliciting money. The vehemence of the phrasing in New York's old hurdy-gurdy law well conveys authority's attitude: "It is unlawful to solicit, ask, or request money in any way, shape or manner, directly or indirectly." The old statute was repealed in 1970 but the spirit lives on. Street entertaining is legal, but only if

1. not much noise is made.
2. the sidewalk is not obstructed.
3. there is no solicitation for money.

It is odd that people who champion the free market are against such a pure expression of it. What is so wrong about solicitation? The passersby are under no duress. They don't even have to stop. If they do stop they don't have to give. If they give, the amount is entirely up to them and their judgment of the worth of the entertainer. It is the latter who has taken the entrepreneurial risk. He should be entitled to some reward.

Merchants say that the entertainers have hurt their business and future inundations would make matters far worse. Michael Grosso, head of the Fifth Avenue Association, puts it this way: "If you allow one musician or peddler in, then you have to let them all in and they would take over the whole midtown area."

I wish I could say that our research proved that street entertaining is good for the merchants' stores. I think it is, but our research does not prove this. What it does prove is that there is a high degree of compatibility between a strong retail street and a lively street life. Merchants do not see this. They do not like much about street life anyway, except for customers coming in the door. Entertainers block them, the merchants complain, and block everybody else, to the point of endangerment. It is on this basis, pedestrian safety and amenity, that the merchants have mounted their legislative assaults on the entertainers.

There have been two federal cases. Both of them, fortunately, deal with physical situations that almost spectacularly belie the ordinances.

The first was *Davenport v. City of Alexandria*. Lee Davenport was a music teacher who played his bagpipes on the streets of Alexandria. The city forbade him to do this. At the behest of merchants the city enacted an ordinance that banned street entertainers from performing on any of the sixty-one blocks of the central district and restricted them to certain designated park areas. Davenport did not want to play in the designated park areas. There were not enough people there. He wanted to play on the sidewalk, in particular the sidewalks of the two most attractive blocks of King Street. He sued to have the ordinance struck down. The case went to the U.S. District Court.

The city's case was based largely on assertion. Some merchants had been reported to observe instances of sidewalk blocking. The city manager said that once he had seen people pour out onto the street because of an entertainer. A check of the actual facts belied the claims of congestion. As a witness for Davenport, I was able to point out that the city's own counts and the measurement of the sidewalk showed there was an excellent balance between sidewalk space and pedestrian flows. In this respect, indeed, Alexandria was outstandingly well provided—not only the two blocks in question but the whole central district.

Judge Albert V. Bryan struck down the ordinance. Here are some of the reasons he cited:

> The court is unpersuaded that there is any actual safety endangerment, any real impediment of pedestrian traffic or any substantial interference with patrons of businesses even in the affected area . . . Furthermore, more persuasive testimony satisfies the court that, overall, pedestrian traffic is not congested—no more than 2.8 persons per foot per minute of passing pedestrians, a pedestrian "ease" level well below the standard for pedestrian comfort.

As to the designated park areas, the judge held that they were not an adequate alternative to the sidewalk:

> The exponent of the First Amendment expression is entitled to be "encountered" by those he wishes to receive his or her message. The sidewalk is a traditional place for such expression. Pedestrian flow and turnover is the "life blood" of the street performer.

The city appealed. The U.S. Court of Appeals reversed Judge Bryan's decision in part. It found that the ordinance was a reasonable regulation. It was not sure, however, that it was drawn "as narrowly as possible to maximize speech while securing the city's interest in public safety." It sent the matter back to the District Court, asking Judge Bryan to make explicit the factual reasons for holding the ordinance unnecessarily broad. How wide were the streets? What were the pedestrian flows? There was ample documentation on these points. By making them explicit, Judge Bryan re-established his original finding. There was plenty of room.

The second federal case was in Chicago. For quite a while the city had been hospitable to street entertainers. In the summer of 1979 Mayor Jane Byrne had the city hire a corps of young entertainers to perform at bus stops and transit stations during the summer. (Pay: ten dollars an hour.) People were delighted. STREET ARTISTS HELP CITY SPARKLE, said an editorial in the Chicago *Sun-Times*.

But the merchants did not like street entertainers, anywhere. In 1982, they prevailed on the city council to pass an ordinance that would effectively ban them from the upper Michigan Avenue area—that is, the place most suited for them.

Guitarist Wally Friedrich initiated a class action suit against the city, and the American Civil Liberties Union joined in support. I served as expert witness on the pedestrian aspect.

The city's contention was that congestion on the sidewalk had reached drastic levels, and that entertainers added sorely to this congestion and should be banned, providing more room for pedestrian safety and amenity.

It was an extraordinary complaint. Of all the avenues in the United States, they could not have picked one with broader sidewalks than upper Michigan Avenue. They range between thirty and thirty-five feet in width. Pedestrian volumes were strong but did not tax them. My sampling counts and the city's counts jibed. The amount of space per pedestrian was very generous and provided a level of service that rated an A by anybody's computation.

There was, indeed, almost a surfeit of space. The city itself had judged there was so much space it had encouraged the withdrawal of large chunks of sidewalk space for roped-off planting beds. Were these grassy expanses converted back to sidewalk space, the level of service would be higher yet.

In *Friedrich v. City of Chicago* the court upheld the ordinance in part and denied it in part. The court found that the city was within its rights to curb street entertaining when it endangered the public safety. It also found that the ban was much broader than necessary. On Michigan Avenue all performances were banned on Saturdays and Sundays, and on weekdays from 11 A.M. to 2 P.M. and from 4 P.M. to 11 P.M. The court observed that the city had not done any homework to support these sweeping restrictions, and that its own records indicated that pedestrian flows diminished dramatically after 7 P.M. Rush Street was another matter. It is the city's disco, tavern, and caf(strip and gets lots of pedestrian traffic after dark, especially on Friday and Saturday nights. But this did not justify a ban starting at 3 P.M., the court found, nor one on Wednesday nights.

The most interesting part of Judge Marven E. Aspen's decision concerns break dancing. As in New York, so in Chicago break dancing surfaced as a fad in 1983. Everywhere one looked, it seemed, young blacks were staking out large swaths of sidewalk and doing acrobatics. Some were terrible—a few people jumping up and down to a portable tape player. But some were really quite talented and put on a show that attracted large crowds. It was these crowds, Judge Aspen noted, that caused most of the mischief.

But break dancing peaked in 1984 and is now performed only sporadically. This raises a question. If break dancing was the only major threat to public safety and if it has largely disappeared, why then the ordinance? In a section that could be subtitled "Much Ado About Break Dancing" Judge Aspen tackles the question:

> If it is true that breakdancing has gone the way of the hula hoop and is a faded fad, then perhaps the frequency of large audiences has substantially fallen . . . Thus, if the City chooses to renew the ordinance next year, it would be well advised to consider the passing of the breakdancing phenomenon in its evaluation. If it has passed, and if—as the evidence showed— most other performers attract only small crowds, the constitutional underpinnings of the ordinance may have vanished for future years.[3]

Handbill Passers

For all the differences in people, times, and places, the rhythms of handbill passing and taking are surprisingly regular. If the passer makes any effort at all—that is, stands near the center of the sidewalk and actually offers handbills to passersby—the completion rate will run at least 30 percent or three out of every ten persons. The rate will vary according to pedestrian flow, character of flow, and time of day, but by far the most important factor will be the handbill passer himself and the assertiveness of his technique. Somewhat like the staccato patterns of donations to beggars, the taking of handbills tends to occur in bunches. In part this is due to the follow-the-leader tendency of the people who take handbills. But close analysis of the film record of these occurrences shows that they are primarily due to the handbill passers. Success emboldens them. Their stance becomes more commanding, their thrust more firm. The passing and the taking become an end in themselves.

The best passer I've come across is Frank. With a face off an Etruscan coin, he works through persistence and a kind of genial intimidation. He uses a direct address; he will look at you straight in the eye with a look of amused disdain, often with a comment. I saved this for you. Here's one for you, honey. Sometimes a person will take a card, look at it disgustedly, and then hand it back. Frank will hand it to them again and this time it often sticks.

Frank seeks to dominate the encounter, and like most who do, he is responsive to the reception given him. At midday one August, from a fifth-floor window at Bloomingdale's, I filmed him at work. It was hot and muggy and people were moving more sluggishly than usual. Frank was doing all right, but there were some lulls. After two or three turndowns in a row, Frank would just stop and not offer handbills to anyone. In a minute or so, however, he would be at it again. In the half hour he spent, he averaged 50 percent completion to handbills offered.

I spoke to Frank later and told him about our midday count and how high his rate had been. He was pleased but said it was not a good time. We should get him when he's hot. Five o'clock. Rush hour. In front of the subway steps.

He was right. At five the southeast corner was a mass of people and in the middle, dominant, was Frank. The people were scarcely moving as they edged toward the curb or the subway stairs. But Frank was moving, making his own space. He was turning, first one way and then the other, and as the crowd swelled he worked faster and faster. Now he was giving a sharp flick to the cards at the end of the thrust. He was not smiling. He was staring intently, almost belligerently. There was no easy badinage now. He was giving commands. Take it, he would say, take it. And they did. It was six out of ten now. Frank was hot.

The only ones I've seen to match him were in Tokyo. Two young men were working the crowded alley leading to the Kannon Shrine. They were got up in ancient costume. One worked about twelve feet in front of the other and jiggled a sign up and down that told people to be sure to read the interesting message that was about to be given. The other handed out the message with a rate of completion similar to Frank's, about 55 percent. The message was for an eel restaurant several blocks away.

Handbills are a very important medium for places people pass by but do not see: places up alleys or up on a third or fourth floor. One of Frank's best customers is Sister Lane, a spiritual adviser and palm reader who has a third-floor room on the east side of Lexington. She has a neon sign in the window but is out of the pedestrian's line of sight. Handbills are a necessity for her.

Frank sometimes subcontracts. To handle some of the bill passing for Sister Lane he took on a young rascal named Eddie Leet. Eddie turned out to be almost as skillful as Frank; a film sequence I have of his hand motions and leering grin shows a master of insinuation.

Eddie broke with Frank and began dealing directly with Sister Lane. At the same time he took on bill passing for Mrs. Williams, another spiritual adviser, who had an upstairs room on the west side of Lexington. Eddie liked to work both sides of the street.

Another group of handbill passers was organized by Louis, the owner of a second-floor haircutting establishment on Lexington. He hired several personable young Puerto Ricans and showed them how to walk alongside women, give a quick spiel, and ask them to sign up for a 50-percent rebate on a hairdo. Right upstairs, they were to say as they drew abreast of the doorway.

It was a very effective technique. "A real bunch of hustlers," Louis told me. "And I really psych them up." But their interest flagged. What they liked to do most was to sit on the hoods of the cars parked out front and chat with their friends, of whom there seemed to be an ever increasing number. Louis would look down on them, like Fagin watching his brood, and rap sharply on the window to snap them to. At length he fired them. They went to work, carrying Louis's technique with them, for another haircutting establishment. Louis hired three of their friends as replacements. He said they worked harder and better than the others. A real hustle crew, he told me.

Eventually they were fired too. But they stuck around, joining that informal network of handbill passers, errand runners, vendors, lookouts, and the like that staffed that stretch of Lexington. They all seemed to know each other. One or two could usually be seen cruising from Fifty-seventh to Sixtieth and back, stopping to check in with a friend.

Let us turn to the handbill takers. Whether or not people accept a handbill has very little to do with content. People usually have no idea what is on them until after they have taken one. But people do read them. Some then immediately throw them away. But most hang on to them for a while. Some twist them. Some crumple them. Before they throw them away, some will walk a block or so clutching them, as if they were a kind of talisman.

Whatever the message, it will rarely be written with any style. The artwork will be bad. So will the paper and the printing. Advertising agencies, it would appear, would not touch the medium. And quite literally it is trash. No other activity generates so much of it or is harder to curb.

All this being the case, it would be fitting to say that the medium is also very inefficient. But it is not. For all the crudity of the form, it is an effective way of getting across a basic message—for example, come on up—and doing it close to the potential point of sale. And audiences can be targeted: some handbills for women only; some for men only. Costs are moderate, the labor supply inexhaustible. With a handbill-passing rate of no more than 40 percent, the cost per completed transaction will range between a half mill and several mills. There is a potential here that has not been touched. Thank heavens.

Mr. Magoo

The most compelling character on the streets of New York is Mr. Magoo. He is a man in his seventies, stocky, red-faced, and with a perpetually choleric expression. He dresses nattily, always with a flower in his buttonhole. In winter he wears a chesterfield and a black homburg.

Mr. Magoo directs traffic. On Fifth Avenue, his favorite, he will station himself in the middle of the intersection and with eloquent arm gestures direct the cars. Keep it moving is his idea. Taxis making slow right turns infuriate him. Taxis picking up people ten feet out from the curb infuriate him. He will go over and slam his hand on the hood. The drivers will curse. He will curse. A crowd will gather.

Mr. Magoo talks to the traffic, car by car. He calls their license plates. A woman in a car with Virginia plates is driving very slowly. "You're not in Virginia, honey," says Mr. Magoo, "you're in New York. Move! Move! Move!" The woman speeds up. To a white-haired lady who is jaywalking

Mr. Magoo on Fifth Avenue.

across the street: "Who in the hell do you think you are? Selfish bag, that's what you are." She is nonplussed.

All this delights the spectators, of whom quite a few will have gathered at the corners. Mr. Magoo plays directly to the gallery. He points to a New Jersey car making a poor turn. "New Jersey drivers: they're the worst," he says. The crowd laughs. "No, doctors are the worst," he says. More laughs. "No, no, New Jersey *doctors*—aye-yi-yi."

At the top of his form he is quite majestic. His gestures become more imperious. He stands taller. Cars are obeying him. The traffic is moving well—and it really does when he directs. People are listening to him and some are doing what he tells them to do. If it is a fantasy, it is a pretty good one to act out. And he is in charge.

He certainly gets people talking to each other. If you are at a corner watching him, someone is likely to ask you who in the world that guy is out there. Or tell you: that he's an ex-cop; that he scalps tickets at the Metropolitan Opera. One day a lady turned to me and in a confidential tone said that Mr. Magoo had made her day but that she wasn't sure why. We exchanged thoughts on this. Was it his arrogation of municipal authority, the individual against the system? No. He is strong for law and system. Should one feel sympathy for him? Hardly. Mr. Magoo is not a nice person. He's rude, a bit of a bully, and while he's funny about it he does treat people the way we'd like to but do not.

Let me add a methodological note. In filming street characters such as Mr. Magoo and the Witch, they are fully aware of the camera and I cannot say that is unobtrusive research. But there are usually other cameras pointed in their direction too, and they are obviously pleased to be photographed. The whole point of their performance is to be noticed.

Mr. Magoo affects great annoyance when he sees me filming with a camera. "You again," he says disgustedly and waves me away. I keep on filming, as he knows I will, and sometimes he sneaks a glance to see if I am.

Mr. Paranoid

There is a man who stands on street corners on Fifth Avenue. He wears a felt hat creased in the college style of the late 1940s. He stands at the curb, facing inward, and to no one in particular talks in a conversational tone of voice. If you pass by, you may hear the key words he keeps repeating: "FBI," "police," "IRS." What he is saying is that they're out to get him, the whole damn bunch of them. And they're out to get you too, he says, if you don't watch out. He is deranged, of course.

Tambourine Woman

She is a spare, middle-aged woman with frizzy gray hair. She walks quietly down the street until she comes to a prominent place, such as church steps or a department store entrance. She stops, takes a tambourine out of an airline bag she has been carrying, bangs it three times, and then begins a harangue. A crowd gathers.

What is she saying? It is hard to tell. As is so often the case with odd people, any one sentence is quite plausible. It is the lack of connections that is confusing. "I was Franklin D. Roosevelt's little girlfriend," she shouts, then goes on to say that Zionism is a plot. Suddenly, in midsentence, she stops, puts the tambourine back into the airline bag, and walks away, leaving the puzzled onlookers behind.

Knapsack Man

He was a handsome man who walked with a curious up-and-down loping gait. He wore a trenchcoat, no matter what the weather, and on his back was a knapsack. Fastened to it was a photograph of him and a card with a hand-lettered statement. It read ONLY MY FAMILY HAS THE RIGHT TO ASSAULT ME. IF YOU ARE NOT A MEMBER OF MY FAMILY PLEASE DO NOT HIT ME.

Passersby were fascinated by the sign and would fall in behind him, peering intently at the sign. But the up-and-down movement made the reading of it difficult. Sometimes there would be several people trying to read it and they would jostle each other for position. At street corners he would stop and then stand immobile with hands folded as if in prayer. The people who had been following him could now read the sign and soon would disperse.

The last time I saw Knapsack Man he still wore a trenchcoat but there was no knapsack or picture and he walked with a normal gait.

The Witch

She is a woman who looks like a witch. She has a long, pointed nose, black hair, eyes very far apart and one moving differently from the other. She dresses in black and usually has a folded *Wall Street Journal* under her arm. She hurls insults in a loud, rasping voice. Her targets are most often dignified people. At a St. Patrick's Day parade I watched her taunt a priest who was in charge of a parochial-school girls' band. She said she knew what he wanted, and then did a lewd bump and grind. The girls fell to giggling. The priest went up to a cop and bade him stop this terrible woman. "Sorry, Father," the cop said, "but she isn't breaking any law."

But she does spit at people she doesn't like. Children, for example. I have a splendid film sequence of her as a nice little boy and his mother walk by. The Witch rears back. "F___ you, you little bastard," she says, sending a cascade of spit hurtling his way. She is deplorable, but so are the onlookers. They exchange horrified glances. "Did you see that woman spit at that little boy!" But they are smiling, almost as though they are on her side.

The Witch plays the role of witch so convincingly and looks so much like a witch that quite likely she would have been burnt as a witch in earlier times. Many were, with far less fearsome appearance. But in these times she is good fun to watch, with vicarious malevolence, and she is pleased to have the audience. And I think she rather likes me. Whenever we pass on the street, she winks.

Shopping Bag Ladies

The toughest, hardiest of all the street people are the shopping bag ladies. They are disheveled and dirty, and their legs are often swollen. Their clothing is usually tattered. They carry two or three shopping bags—see-through plastic, mostly, filled with trash and bits of rags. Some wheel them in supermarket shopping carts. There are also a few shopping bag men. One, Cellophane Man, wraps himself in many layers of clear plastic.

Shopping bag people are very regular in their routes and stations. They tend to sleep in the same doorways or the same spots in Grand Central Station. According to the time of day, one shopping bag lady can be found at the southeast corner of Seagram Plaza, a doorway on Fifty-third Street, and the ledge of the Citicorp Plaza.

Where do they come from? Social workers find them baffling. Most shopping bag ladies are sustained by a grand fantasy of some kind, such as that they are very rich but the city is hiding their money. Another bag lady, whose beat is outside the Public Library, is working on a book that will save the world. One fancies she is still a pretty, coquettish woman and is grotesquely rouged. Most of these people come from a middle-class background. Some are well educated. There is one who is a Barnard graduate, was a Powers model with several magazine covers to her credit, and, completing the ideal of the All American Girl, was a top-seeded tennis player in the Middle Atlantic Conference thirty years ago. I know this to be so because my wife roomed with her.

What they all have in common now is a fierce independence. In the city there are many homeless people temporarily out of the social service system; they may have lost their welfare check or have just been evicted from their apartment. But shopping bag ladies are different. They are totally outside of the system. What's more, they resist efforts to get them into it. If they are taken to an institution they are so confused, frightened, and upset at the intervention that they cannot meet the institutional rules for being helped. They won't say what their name is. They have no address to give. They refuse to take showers or be otherwise cleaned up. They cannot, in sum, qualify for the aid that would put them in shape to qualify.

The problems appear to be getting greater, not just for shopping bag ladies, but for disturbed people of all kinds. With their misplaced reliance on stabilizing drugs, New York State's mental hospitals put some fifty thousand people on the streets. There is much to be said for getting them out of hospitals, but the outpatient therapy that was supposed to be part of the plan has not been provided on any scale. For many people the result has been the worst of both worlds. The institutional experience conditioned them to a highly structured environment; for such people the freedom of the city can be a frightening experience. For some the only refuge is the single-room-occupancy hotel. But they are afraid of that too, and the people who might prey on them.

One of their few pleasures is sitting in the sun on the benches in the middle of upper Broadway. Older people of all kinds come there: some talkative, some rigidly silent. There may be a head-nodding junkie or two as well. But they are reasonably safe places and there is lots of life to see.

Beggars

Like handbill passers and entertainers, successful beggars are marked by centrality and movement. The best examples I have seen are the professional blind beggars who work Fifth Avenue. They are very consistent. They stay in one spot and it is almost always in the center of the sidewalk. At their side is a dog (not a true guide dog, but it looks like one). They wear a small sign that says something like "God bless the cheerful giver." They hold the traditional tin cup.

They move. One moves his body back and forth in a walklike motion while his feet stand still. All move the cup back and forth, occasionally giving it a sharp rattle. The fact of movement seems to be important. I found this out when one day by chance we had the equivalent of a controlled experiment. We had been filming time-lapse coverage of the beggar who usually stationed himself in front of St. Thomas Church. He was getting donations at his customary rate. Then another blind beggar appeared. He must have been truly blind, for he positioned himself about fifteen feet behind the first beggar. And he did not move. All he did was hold out the cup. He did not shake it. He just stood there, waiting for donations. There were not many. During a twenty-seven-minute period, the moving beggar received four times as many donations as the stationary one.

There is a pronounced domino effect in the giving of money. Donations tend to come in bunches—three or four in a row, quickly—and it is understandable that they do. Potential givers usually slow up about twenty feet away from the beggar and start fishing for a coin. This appears to trigger any latent impulses to give in the people behind them. If they give too, there may be some congestion, and this may slow others and provide additional time to consider giving.

One hears stories about beggars being driven by chauffeurs in Rolls-Royces. I did see, on several occasions, one of the blind beggars being dropped off by a car at the Fiftieth Street entrance of Saks. It was an ordinary car. But they do not do badly. To get an idea of their take I charted the frequency of donations over considerable periods of time. The median interval between donations was twenty seconds. But because of the staccato nature of many donations and the slack periods, the average was one donation for every fifty seconds, or seventy-two an hour. The size of the donations, however, I could not determine. The beggars are always emptying small coins from the cup and leaving the big ones in. Assuming an average of 25 cents, their take would be about $18 an hour. Most of the professional blind beggars work about six hours a day. At the least they should average $100 to $150 a day—in all probability a good bit more.

These beggars are the regulars—same spot, same time, same props. Like members of a guild, their numbers have not increased materially. But begging in general most certainly has. I have taken no census, but I would estimate that the number of people begging on the streets of midtown has doubled since 1980. Much of this increase is due to the rise in homelessness. As a matter of fact, some of the most successful soliciting is for donations to the homeless. There is also a good bit of occasional and part-time begging, much of it by younger people, and with considerable aggressiveness. The Bowery bums who cleaned your windshield have been supplanted by teenagers who clean your windshield and are quite intimidating about being compensated for it. Some surprisingly well-dressed young women beg, usually for "fare money." One has a flaxen-haired baby with her and, whether rented or not, it draws very well. Most of the beggars, however, are without skill or stratagem. They are mostly winos and derelicts, too dazed to beg effectively or to defend themselves against predators. That there are so many of them at this time of apparent prosperity is not a good augur.

Pitchmen for Causes

Groups making pitches for religious causes range from the naive to the fraudulent. Some, such as the Hare Krishna, are true believers in whatever they believe in. They may seem foolish, but so have a lot of groups over the years. And while their music and their saffron robes make an odd sight, it has been a friendly one. They are not to be seen so much anymore and many people rather miss them.

A group that is not missed is a rock group of young men and women who dressed in black monks' robes and hoods and spoke as if they had all gone to Harvard. They looked like some kind of satanic cult but they said they were in the fight against drugs. They were ambulatory operators, like Louis's handbill passers, and while walking along with you would invite you to purchase their publication and make a donation. They made a point of saying they accepted checks. An odious bunch.

A jaunty fellow with a tweed cap stands beside a small table. On it is a clipboard and writing pad. A sign fixed to the table says SAVE THE PORPOISE! As people go by he says to them, please join the fight and sign the petition for the porpoises. Many people stop. Just sign here, he says, extending a pen. As they sign up he suggests that a small donation would help. Overhead. Printing expenses. He is giving his time free. Most of those who stop, sign, and most of those who sign, give.

He came upon this modus operandi some years ago. I first saw him when his sign read SAVE GRAND CENTRAL. This was in 1975, when many citizens were quick to give for this estimable cause. The Municipal Art Society was most upset to have an impostor siphon away contributions, and it went to the police.

SAVE THE WHALES, the sign next read. A picture next to it showed small whales being clubbed to death. This appeal must have proved very lucrative, for he continued with it until the early eighties, when he switched to the porpoise.

Pickpockets and Other Crooks

Pickpockets usually work in pairs. They like crowds. If there is a street crowd watching an act, the pickpockets will work the "tip" of the crowd: they will be on the outer rank, looking in at the marks, and with a clear field behind them for the exit.

Pickpockets especially like crowds in confined places. Buses are ideal. I know, for I have been an easy mark. On two recent occasions I was fleeced while standing near the rear exit door. An older man standing near me dropped a package on the floor. I leaned down to help him pick it up. A younger man who had been standing next to me quickly lifted my wallet from my right rear pocket and vanished out the door. I looked around for the older man. He had gone out the front.

This was a standard operation, two top pickpocket detectives told me later. And I had been virtually asking for it, they added. There are many variants, but the crux is the quick, disconcerting move. Whether it is a shove, a jostle, a slight collision, it is a matter of only a few seconds and the two are off. My most recent encounter, again on a bus, was with a man who unfortunately got his hand mixed up with mine as we held on to the overhead straps. This time I was more alert. I disentangled and told him to cut it out. But he was gone, and so was my wallet. From my right rear pocket, unbuttoned.

You have to spot them beforehand, the detectives told me. Some of them they knew on sight; indeed, they had an almost friendly relationship with them. In most cases, however, it was a matter of observation.

I walked with them as they went back and forth over several crowded shopping blocks. I asked them what made them suspicious. Suspicious-looking people, they said. They were not being facetious. Pickpockets and other crooks are paranoid about the police, they explained, and are forever looking over their shoulder and darting their glance this way and that. When they spot a man doing this they can be sure they are on to something.

There is another thing to watch for, they said. Watch out for the guy who is moving around a lot but is not going anywhere. He keeps coming back, circling, like the predator he is. If he also is a teenager, black, and is wearing white tennis shoes he is likely to be taken as a mugger. This is not very fair to white tennis shoes, or teenagers, or blacks. While it may be true that most muggers wear white tennis shoes, most people who wear white tennis shoes are not muggers.

The key advice, to repeat, is to watch out for the guy who is moving but not going anywhere. And if he starts circling, move.

Three-Card-Monte Players

Three-card-monte players provide some of the best street theater —and a demonstration of the lengths people will go to be gulled. They should be suspicious from the start. Two raffish young men, usually black, put a carton down on the sidewalk and play begins. The dealer shuffles three cards: two of them black, one red. Periodically he shows the red card face up. He taunts the player to bet which one it is. He has a chant:

Red you win
  Black you lose
It all depends
  On the card you choose.

The two are arguing very loudly. This attracts people and soon a crowd has formed. A second shill will join the crowd. He will probably be an older person, occasionally a woman, but in any event will be in disguise as an ordinary citizen.

The game is obviously rigged. The shill should be easy to spot. He wins. But on the players come. There is a lot of ego here. The active players have a knowing look. They're on to this crook. He's met his match. As they win some small bets the dealer is visibly upset; he almost cowers. The player moves in for the kill and triples his bet.

In more cases than not, however, the dealer will be hostile and menacing and the game becomes an exercise in intimidation. The dealer shouts at the player. He glares malevolently at him. Put down the twenty dollars, he says. Put it down. Put it *down*. Why anyone should obey is a puzzle, but they do.

Sleight of hand and the law of averages are enough to assure that the dealer will win. And so he does, invariably. But to win big he has another tool. In the classic gambit of the con game, he uses the player's own taste for larceny. The sequence goes like this. A shill shouts "cop." The dealer goes off to investigate, leaving the cards lying on the carton. One of the onlookers picks up the red card; with a wink at the audience he slightly crimps one corner of the card and puts it back on the carton. The dealer returns. The onlooker puts a big bet on the crimped card. It comes up red. He wins. He bets again and wins. The dealer is furious. He tells the onlooker he can't play anymore. Leave. Onlooker does.

Now people are jostling each other to be first to get a big bet down on the crimped card. One man comes up with two hundred dollars and lays it on the card. The dealer turns it over. It is black.

Red you win
  Black you lose
It all depends
  On the card you choose.

Dope Dealers, Whores, and Pimps

I did a study on loitering for the police department and the Fund for the City of New York. The place was the West Forty-second Street area in front of the Top Bar and the store and boxing club in the building next to it. They were the key hangouts for the pimps and dope dealers of the area. What the police wanted to find out was the effect of the police presence on the activity. Were frequent sweeps better than fewer, longer ones? Were the usual two-man patrols a better use of manpower than three- and four-man patrols?

In a room on the fourth floor of an abandoned hotel across the street, I set up a 16mm camera and two Super 8 time-lapse cameras. As with most observational studies of a place, the first step was to find out what normal was. In the case of the Top Bar normal was a heavy flow in and out of the entrance and a forming and re-forming of groups on the wide sidewalk outside. Loitering, one might call it, but there was more purpose to it than that. Discussions were animated; there were greetings, with much hand clasping. Some of the groups were ambulatory, ranging from the bar area all the way to the corner of Broadway and back. The cast had many regulars, and they were easy to identify because they usually wore what they had been wearing before.

A recurrent event was the arrival of a red two-door sedan in midafternoon. After parking directly in front of the bar, the driver would open the hood and then unlock the trunk. He would be joined by several people. After about ten minutes of activity the driver would get back in the car and leave. This routine would take place two more times in late afternoon.

However illegal, the goings-on were satisfyingly regular. On a hot summer night the first test came. At 7:03 three cops walked up to the lamp pole in front of the bar. During the previous hour there had been five group sessions of about six to eight minutes. At exactly two minutes before the arrival of the cops the last group broke up. For the ensuing thirty minutes the cops remained by the light pole—loitering, you might say—and at one point were joined by a fourth.

At 7:33 the cops began to move east. At almost the same time, three of the regulars materialized. By 7:34 the cops moved out of the picture. We are back to normal again. The group activity continued unabated the rest of the evening. On subsequent occasions also we found that the activity that ceases with the appearance of the cops resumes within a few seconds of their departure.

We did a similar study of the loitering patterns around the Aristo Hotel, a squalid old hotel in the Times Square area. Prostitution and dope peddling appeared to be its principal activities. As was the case around the Top Bar, the area of activity embraced the street corner and a half-block stretch beyond. There were usually four to five whores; they stood in doorways most of the time, spaced twenty to forty feet apart. If they walked it would be only as far as the next doorway or so and back. Customer behavior was equally regular. Potential johns would look in a shop window or just stand there for a while before approaching a whore. Another predictable occurrence would be the arrival of a big fat woman about every four hours to check on the whores. She would chat briefly, accept what appeared to be money, and go on to the next one. Late in the afternoon a pink Cadillac convertible would stop, and out would get a tall black man in a long fur coat. He was so much the archetypal pimp that one suspected he might be an undercover cop.

There were several other common denominators. There was a loose network of people and it included some street regulars. A guard at a nearby bank moonlighted on and off as a sort of messenger. There was a cooperative lookout system. We noticed that every once in a while a window shade on the third-floor front would be yanked up and down. Invariably, it signaled the approach of a police car.

Around Forty-second Street and Times Square it is hardly surprising to see people who look like criminals. Go down to the subway world underneath and there are many more—tough, mean, and dangerous. This is the national cesspool, and when people from other cities start talking about their undesirables the New Yorker has to laugh. They should see ours. Here are the real undesirables.

In view of this great concentration, what is remarkable is how safe is the adjoining business district. I have been keeping reasonably abreast of activity on its plazas and small parks, and as far as assaults on one's person are concerned, they have been largely trouble free. This needs some qualifying, of course: no street is safe at 2 A.M.; certain fringe locations are best avoided; white-collar drug traffic, while not dangerous, continues to be a problem. Similarly, prostitution waxes and wanes as a street phenomenon. In the 1970s there were a lot of whores on the street, Lexington in particular; they have been less visible since but there are indications streetwalking is picking up again.

There is plenty of sin, in short, but not so much danger. Perceptions, however, are otherwise. In many cities the perception of crime in the center is considerably greater than the actuality. In Dallas, a poll of citizens indicated that most agreed that crime in downtown was a serious problem; quite a few added, however, that personally they had had no trouble. Statistics bear out the qualification. Of all the parts of Greater Dallas, the one with the lowest incidence of reported crime has been downtown.

So in other cities, the central business districts are among the safest of places during the hours that people use them. Conversely, among the most dangerous are the parking lots of suburban shopping malls.

But the image of crime is itself a force. Corporations seeking sanctuary in suburbia invariably cite crime on the streets as a reason for their move. It may, in fact, be a minor one. But the corporations are worried enough by the image that they build their new headquarters like fortresses.

I don't wish to be Pollyanna. There are dangerous places in the city, and dangerous times. There are dangerous people. But it is important to differentiate between kinds of people—between the mugger, say, and the vendor. Many businessmen and civic leaders do not differentiate. Being themselves insulated from the life of the street, they lump all its people as undesirable, and some leaders would be quite happy if they were eliminated altogether, a result that their policies in some cities are calculated to bring about.

They should be working in the other direction. The time to worry is when street people begin to leave a place. Like canaries in a coal mine, street people are an index of the health of a place.

This is not reflected in the kind of city rankings lately so popular: the ten best quality-of-life cities in the U.S., the twenty happiest communities, and so on. Cities like New York go at the bottom, the top going to communities that could also qualify as the highest on any blandness index. While one would not wish to add yet another spurious statistical exercise, it might be in order to come up with a city index of enjoyability—the number of street entertainers, food vendors, people in conversation, the number smiling. A silly index, perhaps, but there is a simple point to be made. Street people are not just a problem; they are the heart of the street life of the center. Its liveliness is the test of the city itself.

Good performers and good audiences. These are the stuff of a good street life. Its vigor is a test of the vigor of the city itself.

THE SENSORY STREET

The street I have spent the most time on is New York's Lexington Avenue—specifically, the four-block stretch from Fifty-seventh to Sixty-first Street. The sidewalks are narrow and crowded; their pavements are cracked, full of holes and subway gratings; they are obstructed by a host of badly designed light standards, parking signs, mailboxes, trash containers; and much of the surface is in permanent use for temporary storage of crates, newspapers, displays of merchants, signs, and whatnot. Further obstructing the flow is a host of street operators: handbill passers, demonstrators, hustlers for second-floor establishments, pitchmen for stores, pushcart food vendors, knickknack vendors, beggars. There are all sorts of noises—the cries of the vendors, the blare of transistor radios. From food counters come smells—of pizza, knishes, hot dogs. At the sides and above is a miscellany of awnings, rickety marquees, flags, neon signs.[4]

Why do people persist in using this street? Many have to; it's to and from a major subway station and their way to work. But if you track pedestrians, you will find that many of them could use less tacky or crowded routes if they wished. You will also find that on Lexington Avenue the side of the street with the most obstructions and slowest going is the side that attracts the most people. People love to hate Lexington, and they have terrible things to say about it. Some actually do avoid it, but it does appear that many of the people on Lexington are there because they want to be.

One reason is messiness. Wherever you are in the area, you seem to be on the edge of something else. There are no clear boundaries. On one side are the office buildings of the central business district; on the other, the apartment buildings and brownstones of the residential East Side. In between are department stores, savings banks, restaurants, bars, small shops. It is highly local, and a succession of service facilities such as cleaners, liquor stores, and delicatessens keeps repeating itself. The place is, in sum, a mishmash of activities—the kind that zoning was originally set up to prevent.

There are many shifts: commuters on their way to work, early shoppers, office workers going to lunch. The five o'clock crowds: late shoppers (Bloomingdale's open till nine), people lining up at the movies, people going to dinner. Most important of all, especially at night, are the people who live there. More than anybody else, they keep it alive.

On Saturdays, Lexington becomes a recreation area. You will see many family groups, with children perched on the fathers' shoulders. It is a time for shopping, browsing, eating, and looking at the crazies. The crowding reaches its peak in early afternoon, and it is of a different character from the weekday rush. The pace is slower, more amiable, and there is a lot of cruising back and forth. Puerto Rican teenagers come down from the Bronx and East Harlem to catch the action—and if you stay in one spot long enough, you'll repeatedly see the same ones passing up and down the street and across, stopping to greet friends, sitting on car hoods to watch the goings-on.

Many blind people know Lexington well. That admirable institution, The Lighthouse, has its headquarters a half block from Lexington and conducts its mobility training for the blind there. Because it is so congested, Lexington Avenue is an extraordinarily difficult challenge for the blind, but it is unusually rich in sensory cues. One who reads them with accuracy is Jerry, a young man recently blinded but with a great deal of self-confidence. Unlike the congenitally blind, he has a visual memory of the place, and he has learned to reconstruct it from touch and smell and sound. Approaching Lexington, he explains that the newsstand up at the corner is a smell cue. Newspapers have a very identifiable odor to him. Another cue is the voice of Bob, the man who runs the newsstand and who is always saying something to somebody. Ten feet further on, there is the smell of the hot pretzels of the vendor at the corner.

Now Jerry is on Lexington itself. There are many cues: the sound of water dripping from the leaky air conditioner over the door of the pet shop; the touch and smell of the flowers at Rialto Florist; the rush of warm or cool air in front of Alexander's doorway; the smell of beer from Clancy's Bar. (The smell of incense at the head shop had been a strong cue, but it was closed up.)

Lexington has so many cues, and some are so strong as to blot out others. The loudest is the loudspeaker at the record shop, playing rock. This kind of sound masks others that can be more helpful—such as the change in the pitch and reverberation of street noise as it is bounced off a building wall or canopy. For good reason Jerry keeps moving his cane from side to side, constantly testing.

Even Lexington's disadvantages can be helpful. The wretched topography of its pavement is a map to be read. Jerry knows every hillock and depression, the cracks and puddles, and he can tell from the angle of the pavement's slant exactly where he is. As Lighthouse instructors explain, Lexington is not a place for a "subtle traveler." Its cues are gross and blatant.

Second Storiness

Another reason Lexington works is its second storiness. There is still a good supply of brownstones along it, and in most cases the second story as well as the first is used for stores or restaurants. Along a three-block stretch one finds the following:

Dance studio
Palmist
Haircutting parlor
Doll hospital
Karate academy
Chinese restaurant
Nail studio
Mattress store
Record shop
Clock repair shop

Together they make a lively sight, especially at dusk and after. When the balance of light shifts to the interior, there is much movement silhouetted or spotlighted: dancing couples, hairdressers and customers, couples eating at window tables. The scenes are an excellent argument for bringing back the double-decker bus.

The second storiness has a pronounced effect on the street level. Being a flight up, the proprietors must work hard to gain the attention of passersby. So they put out banners and flags—the haircutting establishments, which are fiercely competitive, are especially given to these. At the bottom of the stairs, signs are put out on the sidewalk. Sometimes a proprietor will station a pitchman there or send out a handbill passer. (One flight up, check us out.)

Madison Avenue, between 69th and 70th: a fine example of second storiness.

An outstanding example of second storiness is Madison Avenue in the Sixties and Seventies. It is now probably the finest specialty-shop street in the world, yet its basic elements are quite ordinary. The basic module is the five-story brownstone, twenty feet wide, ten brownstones to a block; and, while quite a few have been replaced by newer and higher buildings, the brownstone still sets the form and character of the street. With few exceptions, their first and second stories are used for stores, and the same is true with a number of the newer buildings that adjoin them.

It is not a good-taste street—not as a whole, at any rate. There is no uniform cornice line; the façades are a jumble of styles; so is the signage. But the scale is right for the pedestrian's-eye view; the ensemble is pleasing. Manifestly, the place works, and the rents bear witness. In the Lower Sixties, stores rent for about $300 a square foot, and half to a third of that on second floors.

What we have here is a double-loaded street—and a format almost the reverse of that of the suburban shopping mall. The latter also has two levels of shopping, often three. But it provides walkways for each level—and quite generously sized ones, too, some twenty to thirty feet across. Madison, by contrast, loads its two levels onto only one walkway, thirteen feet wide. This is squeezing things more than they should be—five more feet would help—but the sidewalk does work well. On Madison the load is still building. Cafés and delis have been putting out chairs and tables on the sidewalk, and on Saturday, Vanity Fair day, one has to thread one's way with care.

Window Shopping

In many cities window shopping would appear to be a dying activity. There are, for one thing, fewer windows to shop. More department stores have been closing downtown than opening up, and the new ones that have been built feature few windows at street level, if any, and none at all on their upper levels. Furthermore, that former adjunct to the window, the door, may be on its way out, too. Increasingly, access is from within the buildings, sometimes along replicas of shopping streets.

But the real thing still works. Where there are display windows, people window-shop, and the stores that have them enjoy a competitive edge greater than before. With an attractive window, even a small, twenty-foot-wide store can draw up to three hundred window shoppers an hour. How many become buyers is harder to tell, but the number of lookers and buyers does correlate with the number of pedestrians—with which figure, to the chagrin of retailers, rents correlate, too.

Window shopping is highly selective. As our tracking studies show, pedestrians tend to slow down or stop in certain places; they skip past others and speed up as they do. Most window shoppers are women and they are quite professional about it. The serious window shopper takes in the whole window in a kind of visual sweep and then looks down at any placard that might be there. If there are two women together, usually they will exchange comments. But it's all done very quickly. The median elapsed time is somewhere between forty and sixty seconds. There are many conversations that last longer and these are important in attracting more people, but the great bulk of window shopping is done with dispatch.

People on the inboard side walking to the right tend to look at the windows more than those outboard. But the close-up view has its drawbacks and the people on the outboard part of the sidewalk frequently get a better view of the displays. Many window displays appear to have been composed as though they were to be viewed from a perspective about twenty feet out in the middle of the street—somewhat like architectural renderings showing a façade from a point of view nobody could share because a building is in the way.

Window shoppers tend to come in bunches. Partly this is due to the fact that the pedestrian flow itself comes in bunches. The traffic light at the corner is a key factor but there are other reasons for bunching. Window shoppers attract window shoppers. One person stops, another stops, then a couple. They attract others. The domino effect is short lived, to be sure, and it may be followed by several minutes of nobody stopping at all. Then someone stops again.

Pauses lead to successive pauses. When a person has stopped to look at one attraction, he is likely to be more responsive to other stimuli in the same vicinity. The behavior of passersby at the Rialto Florist is an example. Almost always, there is a stand of forsythia, or pussy willow, or the like out on the street. As people pass by, some will brush up against the flowers; others will stop to touch them. These momentary stoppages may trigger similar touching by the people following behind—in much the same way that people putting money in a beggar's cup induces others to do the same.

This is good for the business of the florist; some of the touchers will go into the shop and buy something. But the stoppage is also very beneficial to the store next door. This is a store that features T-shirts with decals on them. People who come to a full stop because of the flowers get a much better view of the T-shirt store than do other passersby, and they are more likely to look at the windows. This in turn prompts a number to go on in through the door.

Stoppages are so effective at inducing spillover traffic that merchants might well consider it worthwhile to deliberately create them. One who did was Mr. Kadescu, a former Romanian musical comedy star who ran a fruit juice stand on Lexington. He used to stick a street sign out on the sidewalk advertising discount cigarettes; he was anxious to preempt business from a discount cigarette store two doors north. He soon saw that the really valuable function of the sign was obstruction. It reduced the effective walkway to about six feet and so constrained pedestrian traffic as to divert more of it to his counter. He began moving it farther out onto the sidewalk. Occasionally somebody would angrily move the sign back to the counter. But Mr. Kadescu would keep pushing it farther onto the sidewalk. I have a film sequence of him pushing it so far as to reduce the walkway to only four feet. It was bad of him and I certainly don't want to advocate such brigandage. As an example of the manipulation of space, however, it certainly was effective.

What draws people? The merchandise itself, of course, is the key. On Lexington Avenue women's novelty fashions and accessories are prime draws. Price is part of the attraction, and almost all of the pitches you hear emphasize the incredible bargain being offered, and how fleeting it will be. Today only. Everything half price. Today only.

But the very expensive attracts too. One display that we studied was of manikins in very elegant skirts made from Chinese court robes. Though the prices were out of reach for all but a very tiny fraction of passersby, the particular window drew many more people than the location usually does, and many of the lookers were low-income people.

In this case, we found the display led to a significant number of sales. Ordinarily it is difficult to figure what correlation there may be between lookers and eventual sales. Some high-drawing displays do indeed induce many sales—some clearly do not. But one must not apply too immediate a yardstick. Whatever else it is, window shopping is entertainment. It sells the store and it sells the environs.

The merchandise that attracts most is the merchandise that is out front, on the street, where you can pick it up, feel it. Wherever store owners have put a display on the street there is a marked increase in the numbers of lookers and stoppers; the Argosy Book Store, with its inset entry and piles of secondhand books, is one of the best such places. Oranges, apples, junk jewelry, even a pile of remnants will draw a crowd. Watching them, one gets the feeling that the fingering of the goods is an end in itself.

So is the back-and-forth chatter. Among the reasons outdoor merchandise pulls well is that the merchant or one of his staff will usually be out there, too. If he is at all aggressive, the merchant is physically in the ideal spot to turn a looker into a buyer.

Movement attracts. Day in, day out, the best drawing display on Lexington Avenue is a pet shop with a window full of puppies and kittens. Live people do well too. Bloomingdale's windows often draw best when the window dressers are themselves the show, fussing around with manikins and lights. A whole party of people can be better yet. One time Bloomingdale's staged a disco dance in a corner window and kept sending in relays of pretty girls and junior executive types to dance away. The crowds outside got so big that traffic came to a halt.

Around the corner is Fiorucci, a woman's specialty shop that frequently features live people in its windows—girls having their legs painted with tattoolike designs, for example, or a live person done up as a mime who's affecting not to be live.

But one of the biggest draws I ever saw was when a store displayed nothingness. Bonwit Teller covered several of its windows with brown wrapping paper and cut small eyeholes in it at tiptoe height. This drove people crazy. Before long they were queuing up to get a crack at the peepholes. There was nothing much to see when they looked, but this amused them, too, and they stuck around to see how others would react.

Light attracts. The raunchiest block on Lexington (Fifty-seventh to Fifty-eighth, west side) was notable for its lighting effects. One store, Icarus, featured blinking strobe lights and neon. The effect was so chaotic one would think that the adjoining store owners would object. They did not. They did not even object to the combination of displays and light at the Lexington Rap Club. A sign on the sidewalk said "Come rap with one of our six lovely conversationalists." At the bottom of the stairs leading up to the club a pitchman stood. Over one doorway, two red lights revolved slowly.

Sound attracts. Selling streets are noisy. On Lexington the pizza man rattles a cowbell when he sees a platoon of people approaching. With bullhorn or loudspeakers, salespeople shout at passersby that a sale is on. Everything half price! Check us out! Then there is the rock. Alan, the young man who ran a music shop, had a loudspeaker canted at just the angle to catch people full blast as they went by. He played the same hard-rock selection time after time before he changed to another tested favorite. Again, neighboring store owners were surprisingly tolerant. The police were not. Alan was hauled into court a number of times and fined one hundred dollars each time. He has since moved on, unrepentant.

•

Food and the eating of it is Lexington's major activity and most of it takes place right on the street. Many of the shops have open counters: the fruit juice and pizza places, for example; the soft ice cream shop, which for good measure pushes the freezer out onto the sidewalk in fair weather. Some food shops have folding fronts; when they are folded back it is hard to tell where the sidewalk ends and the shop begins, a distinction further blurred when the proprietors put out tables and chairs.

All of this, mind you, takes place on sidewalks twelve and a half feet wide. It is a use of public space that is either illegal or, in the view of municipal officials, should be. Most cities ban such a sidewalk purveyance of food; some go so far as to prohibit citizens from the eating of it. Necessary for public safety, you will be told, for sanitation reasons—for decent appearances.

But the marketplace is stubborn. Witness what happened to the Avenue of the Americas in New York. When it was Sixth Avenue and had the El running along it, it was full of food places—restaurants, Irish bars, cafeterias, coffee shops, delis, mom-and-pop soda canteens. Then it was redeveloped. The El went; so did the old buildings, and the shops and bars. In their stead went up a series of towers and plazas and windows of banks.

Then, slowly, the street took its revenge. A few food vendors came to fill the vacuum, then a few more. Business boomed. Today the sidewalk in front of the Exxon Building, the liveliest sidewalk on the avenue, is in good weather jammed with as many as two dozen vendors and their customers.

But one element is missing. There is no drinking fountain on the avenue. There are none on Lexington. There are none on any major avenue in the city. There are few in most other cities.

An exception is the fine system of Portland, Oregon. It goes back to civic leader Simon Benson. Many loggers and seamen used to come to town, and Benson thought it would be a good idea to make water so available they would be less tempted to other drink. He gave a citywide system of fountains. There are 140 operating today.

This is no small achievement. In these technically advanced times, we seem to have lost the capability of repairing the simple faucet. To their shame, most American cities not only have failed to provide new fountains for their streets but have failed to maintain the few that still exist. (Worst example: New York's Lincoln Center. Its one outdoor drinking fountain went out of order in 1980. Since then the city financed a renovation of the open spaces at a cost of over $1 million. The repair of the drinking fountain was not included, however, and as of this writing it is still out of order.)

Trash

One corollary of food on the street, unhappily, is trash on the street. There is certainly a great deal on Lexington. We spent some time studying where it comes from, where it goes, and, by time-lapse, just what happens, minute by minute, in the daily life of a trash container.

We found, among other things, that trash containers are badly designed; that they are badly sited, being spotted in the same proportion on blocks with high trash loads as on blocks with low loads; that the containers are very functional for a number of nontrash uses.

We also found that the citizen is maligned. The gist of public service advertising sermons directed to him is to stop being such a slob. But he is not, usually. He is good about litter *if* there is a place to put it. The problem is that too often there isn't.

We rarely saw anyone deliberately throw trash on the street. Indeed, when we followed people who had taken handbills, we were struck by how far they would carry the handbills to find a place to dispose of them. We were similarly impressed by people's behavior on plazas. Since there are usually a lot of food vendors alongside, there is a heavy load of trash generated. There are rarely enough containers to take care of it. Initially, people will be very good about carrying their trash to a container, even if it involves quite a walk. Once the containers start to overflow, however, discipline vanishes and some citizens become the slobs they are accused of being. The conventional wisdom is right: In a place that is tidy, people are tidy. In a place that is messy, they make it messier.

The clear thing we found was that the trash container can be a very useful piece of street furniture. When we did our study, New York was in the process of shifting from one kind of container to another. The standard wire basket had worked well, but so many of them were being stolen that the sanitation department decided to switch to something that would be too heavy to cart away. It settled on a concrete container weighing some 470 pounds. It was about three feet high and on top of it was a hinged metal lid with an opening for the trash. The sanitation people liked it so much they didn't bother to have a trial run. A complete supply was ordered all at once and the switchover was made.

It was a very bad trash container. The opening at the top was so small that much of the trash aimed at it fell on the lid, from which it would soon be redistributed to the street by the slightest breeze. Because of the small opening, furthermore, the trash that did get inside was not compacted the way it usually is, and a relatively small volume of trash would be enough to clog the opening. All subsequent trash people would place on the lid, now functioning as a litter dispenser.

Scavengers made the containers work better. Most scavengers follow a regular route, and in the course of a day they will call at many containers. On the average, we found, containers get about one scavenger visit per hour. With the concrete kind, the scavenger would reach under the lid, pull the release lever, lay back the lid, and then stick a hand down and start rummaging through the trash for something of value. As they did so, the trash was distributed more evenly, air pockets were eliminated, and the trash was reduced in volume. Scavengers would not take very much out—they are quite choosy—but when they were through, the container's capacity to receive more trash was considerably increased.

Passersby scavenge also. It is surprising how many well-dressed people can be seen rummaging through trash containers, and not surreptitiously, either. Newspapers are especially sought, and in our time-lapse studies of trash containers, we have run across instances of the same newspapers being transferred back and forth from one container to another in a small area.

As we watched people using these trash containers we began to appreciate how very useful they were. They were not very good for trash, to be sure, but they were highly functional in other ways. They were used for so many different purposes that they served as an indicator of what's missing in our street furniture.

There are two basic reasons for their utility. First, whatever their shape and size, they are objects, and objects attract people. Second, they are placed at street corners, adjacent to the 100 percent locations.

Here are some of the ways they served:

As a shelf for rearranging packages or sorting through handbags or briefcases.
As a table for sandwiches and fast-food snacks. (We once saw a group of four having lunch on one container.)
As a desk for documents for street conferences. (On two occasions we observed secretaries resting steno pads on the container while they took dictation.)
As a stand for vendors' merchandise trays.
As a footrest for people sitting on nearby car hoods.
As an object for schmoozers to lean against.

•

The shelf function seems to be the most important. The flat expanse that made it so useful in this respect is what made it bad as a trash container. But there are a number of models that could be modified to handle trash and still have shelf functions. Another thing designers might want to think about is a molding on the side of the container at a height suitable for tying shoelaces—twelve inches is about right.

Elements of a Good Street

Let me recapitulate the elements of the good street. They are as follows:

Buildings flush to the sidewalk.

Stores along the frontage.

Doors and windows on the street.

So far, not very novel. The description applies to many existing streets. But not all cities appreciate what they have in this inheritance. Nor do all plan-

Bookstalls on Fifth Avenue: They do busy up a sidewalk, but it is an amiable kind of congestion.

ners and architects. A whole new generation has come of age for whom the norm is the suburban mall. To commend to them the basic street form, it is best to present it in entirely new terms. Speak of the multiple-access block, the continuous fenestration, the rhythmic repetition of entry points. The homely street will sound like a wonderfully fresh concept.

To continue with the list:

Second-story activity—with windows, so you can see it.

A good sidewalk. (It should be just broad enough so it's slightly crowded at peak. On side streets, fifteen feet should be ample; on main streets and major avenues, twenty-five feet.)

Trees. Big trees.

Seating and simple amenities.

Too many pedestrian malls and redone streets are over-designed. There's too much unified signage, too many award-winning light standards—too much good taste in general, or the pretension of it, and since many designers have the same good taste, the result is a bland conformity.

What's needed are simple benches, placed in relation to use; such basic amenities as clocks and drinking fountains, and trash containers that work. The Japanese are much more thoughtful than we are about such possibilities. In the spaces just outside department stores they are likely to provide such amenities as benches, large ashtrays, pay phones, and sculpture to meet at.

Some of the best spaces are accidental ones. My favorite has been the indented ledges of the Chase Bank at Madison and Fifty-seventh Street. They can be sat upon, albeit they're a bit high. They provide some wind protection and they still get some sun. There is usually a food cart at the corner and a good flow of passersby. The bank recently put spikes on the ledges. This has curtailed the sitting but has made the ledges more serviceable for vendors of books and pictures; they prop them up against the spikes.

Similarly, some of the most useful items of street furniture function more out of inadvertence than design. Trash receptacles with flat tops, for example, do not work well as trash receptacles but do work well as small tables. Fire standpipes are often the only sitting available on a block. Most such amenities are unintended. Why not intend them? They would cost little or nothing—a few lines on a plan—and if it's early in the game, they might be had for the asking. Here are some possibilities:

Most ledges are inherently sittable. With ingenuity and additional work, they can be made unsittable. The ledges in front of the General Motors Building, below, have a fussy little railing that catches you right in the small of the back.

- A sitting ledge—about a foot deep, sixteen to twenty inches high.
- A shelf ledge for rearranging packages and sorting papers.
- Glass or steel walls—useful to women as mirrors for checking makeup, to men for checking trouser lengths.
- A ledge low enough to tie one's shoelaces on. Don't laugh. Watch how men use a fire hydrant.
- Chiming poles. People love to touch or rap on objects as they pass by, and if this makes an unusual sound, so much the better.

THE UNDESIRABLES

The biggest single obstacle to the provision of better spaces is the undesirables problem. They are themselves not too much of a problem. It is the actions taken to combat them that is the problem. Out of an almost obsessive fear of their presence, civic leaders worry that if a place is made attractive to people it will be attractive to undesirable people. So it is made defensive. There is to be no loitering—what a Calvinist sermon is in those words—and there is to be no eating, no sleeping. So it is that benches are made too short to sleep on, that spikes are put on ledges, that many needed spaces are not provided and the plans for them scuttled.

One of the problems in dealing with undesirables is a failure to differentiate. For most businessmen, curiously, it is not muggers, dope dealers, or truly dangerous people that obsess them. It is the winos, derelicts, men who drink out of half-pint bottles in paper bags—the most vulnerable of the city's marginal people, but a symbol, perhaps, of the man one might become but for the grace of fate. When some people speak of these men they smile as if they were telling a dirty joke.

For retailers, the list of undesirables is more inclusive. There are the bag women, bag men, people who talk out loud in buses, teenagers, older people, street musicians, street vendors.[5]

The preoccupation with undesirables is a symptom of another problem. Many corporation executives who make key decisions about the city have surprisingly little acquaintance with the life of its streets and open spaces. From the station they may have to walk only a few blocks to their office building, but once inside, some do not venture out again until it is time to head back to the station. So circumscribed is their territory that many spend a decade or so without straying more than a few blocks off their set pathways. If their office building has a plaza, they are likely to have seen it every day but not to have ever used it themselves. I showed a film to the brass of a large corporation on the life of their plaza. The plaza happened to be a successful one and the executives were fascinated by it—as if it were a far-off island place. They had never known it.

If it is a defensive plaza, few other people will have used it either. Places designed in distrust get what was anticipated and it is in them, ironically, that you will most likely find a wino. You will find winos elsewhere, but it is the empty places they prefer. It is in them that they look conspicuous— almost as if the design had been contrived to make them so.

Fear proves itself. Highly elaborate defensive measures are an advance indicator that the corporation may clear out of the city entirely. Long before Union Carbide announced it was leaving New York City for outer suburbia, its building said that it would. Save for an exhibit area, the building was sealed off from the city, with policelike guards with black uniforms and walkie-talkies. Outside were large expanses of paving and not a place to sit.

There still is not a place. Manufacturers Hanover Trust, which got the building for a song, put long, black, marble objects on the spaces with the name of the bank on them. But you cannot sit there; the sides are so steeply canted you slide off.

The best way to handle the problem of undesirables is to make a place attractive to everyone else. The record is overwhelmingly positive on this score. With few exceptions, center city plazas and small parks are safe places.

They mirror expectations. Seagram management is pleased people like its plaza and is quite relaxed about what they do on it. It lets them stick their feet in the pools; it tolerates oddballs and even allows them to sleep the night on the ledges. The sun rises the next morning.

Good places are largely self-policing. Paley Park is an excellent example. It is courtly to people. Jackson Carithers and Jasper Green, the guards, are amiable hosts and rarely have to do much admonishing. If it is necessary— somebody throwing trash on the ground, for example—other guests are likely to do the admonishing. With its movable chairs and tables the park should be highly vulnerable to vandalism. But it is not. Here is the record of security infractions since the park opened in 1967:

1969	One of the flower units on the sidewalk was stolen by two men in a van.
1970	The "Refreshments" sign was taken from the wall.
1971	A small table was taken.

1972	A man tried to carve his initials on one of the trees.
1974	One of the brass lights at the entrance was removed.
1980	Snack bar broken into; new door required.
1983	Small refuse fire on sidewalk; probably accidental.
1967–1986	In entire period no movable chairs have been stolen.

In the sixteen years that I have been studying New York plazas and small parks, there has been real trouble in only three, all three of them badly designed and managed. In well-used places there has been no trouble.

Places that are designed primarily for security worsen it. For one thing, they feature walls. The idea is to keep out bad people. The effect can be the opposite. About ten years ago a corporation with a well-used small park was alarmed to note that some dope dealers were working the place at lunchtime. The management panicked. It took away half the benches. Then it had steel-bar fences put up along the two open sides of the park. These moves sharply cut down the number of people using the park—much to the delight of the dope dealers, who now had the place much more to themselves and their customers. Management decided to reverse course. Applying the recommendations of the Project for Public Spaces, it redid the park: it put in new food kiosks and chairs and tables and scheduled a series of musical events. The park has been doing well ever since.[6]

The most striking example of a walled enclave is New York's Bryant Park. It should be one of the greatest of center-city parks. It is spacious—some nine acres—and it is in the very heart of midtown, just west of the Public Library at Fifth Avenue and Forty-second Street. And for over fifty years it has been a troubled place.

In the early 1930s there was a design competition for a major redo of the park. The winning scheme was rooted in a firm philosophic premise. The park was to be a refuge from the city, free from the hustle and bustle of pedestrians. To that end, it was physically removed from the surrounding streets. It was elevated about four feet above street level, lined with an iron fence, and then, for good measure, given an additional separation from the street in the form of dense shrubbery. There were relatively few entrances into the park. Once there, one could not cut across the park. The idea was to discourage through pedestrian flows, not invite them, and beelines and shortcuts were blocked by continuous balustrades.

The intentions were the best. The basic design, however, rested on a fallacy. People may say they want to get away from the city, avoid the hustle and bustle of people, and the like. But they do not. They stayed away from

Bryant Park. On fine summer days they would use the great lawn. In relation to its size and central location, however, the park remained very much underused.

Except by undesirables. A succession of various kinds dominated the park during the off-hours, culminating in the virtual rule of it by drug dealers in the late 1970s. They even had people standing at the entrances, and when they walked down the pathways they walked in the middle. This was their place.

A coalition of civic groups and neighboring corporations has launched a large-scale effort to redeem the park. There are many elements in its program—a glassed-in grand café, for example; food kiosks, bookstalls, and the like. But the key aim is to open the park up to the street. Several new entrances are to be added; the labyrinthine internal layout is to be simplified to encourage through pedestrian flows. The shrubbery has already gone. Landscape architects Robert Hanna and Laurie Olin are dealing with a certified landmark and have had to be respectful of the original design. They have been adroitly so, however, and the result is a plan that looks very much like the old one but in function is the opposite of it.

Most well-used places have a "mayor" of sorts. He may be a building guard, a newsstand operator, or a food vendor. Throughout the day you will notice people checking in with him—a cop, perhaps, a bus dispatcher, various street professionals, and office workers and shoppers who stop by briefly for a hello or bit of banter. The mayors are great communication centers, and they are quick to spot any departure from the normal life of the place. Such as us. When we start observing at a place—unobtrusively, we like to think—the regulars spot us very quickly. We're not moving, for one thing. Before long, the mayor will drift over and try to find out just what we're up to.

One of the best mayors I've ever seen is Joe Hardy of the Exxon Building of Rockefeller Center. He is an actor as well as a guard and was originally hired to play Santa Claus, whom he resembles. Ordinarily, guards are not supposed to initiate conversations, but Joe is gregarious and curious and has a nice sense of situations. There may be an older couple looking somewhat confused. He will anticipate their questions and go up to them. Are they, by chance, looking for a reasonable place to eat? Well yes, that's what they were going to ask him. On another occasion there might be two girls taking turns photographing each other. Joe suggests maybe they'd like him to take a picture of the two of them. Yes, they would.

Joe is tolerant of winos and odd people, as long as they don't bother anyone. He is very quick, however, to spot incipient trouble. Groups of teenagers are an especial challenge. They like to test a place. The volume knob on stereo "blasters" is a favored weapon. Joe says you have to nip this kind of thing early or you've lost. One tactic he uses is to go up to the toughest-looking member of the group and ask his help in keeping things cool.[7]

Another fine mayor is Debbie Day of the Portland, Oregon, Pioneer Courthouse Square. A young woman with a theater arts background, she was out of work when the square was opening up and applied for a job as guard. She has been a beneficent presence there ever since. A smiling, friendly person, she enjoys talking to people, such as the older people who come so regularly. She is especially good with teenagers. "If they have a problem with someone, they appreciate having me here," she says. "That's what I'm here for—to make people feel comfortable being here."

Guards are an underused asset. At most places they don't do much except stand. For want of anything to do, they tend to develop occupational tics. One might wave his arms rhythmically to and fro or rock up and down on his heels. Another may bend his knees at periodic intervals. If you watch him you'll get mesmerized trying to figure when the next knee bend will come.

The guard's job ought to be upgraded. The more one has to do, the better he does it, and the better the place functions. The two mayors at Paley are a case in point. It was originally expected that special security guards would be needed, in addition to several people to keep the place tidy and do painting and repairs. The two mayors were able to do all the jobs, and in a notably relaxed way.

There are antimayors. At one of our largest civic institutions, the head of the militia is a mean-looking fat man in a black uniform who cruises about in a golf cart. I have never seen him actually hit anybody, but he comes so close and at such speed you feel he really wants to. The guards under him are an agreeable lot, but the jobs are so dull they are bored to death. It is little wonder they sneak off to a nearby street to smoke pot.

The most bedeviling problem of access is the public rest room. Its numbers have been declining, and now, with the recent increase in the homeless, it is on the brink of disappearance. Failure to deal with one problem rationalizes the other. Provide rest rooms, it is said, and they will be overrun by the homeless. This would attract yet more undesirables and stop downtown's revival.

This is very much like the argument for spikes on ledges. It is not just the homeless who need rest rooms. Older people, shoppers, visitors to the city, and people in general need them too, and a policy that withholds an amenity from all of them to withhold it from the homeless is a mean one indeed. The city has an obligation to provide such facilities, and in providing them it may find that it is also acting in its larger self-interest. Paris has come to this conclusion with its new unisex toilets.[8] So has Portland, Oregon. Its park department has been putting individual unisex toilets in park areas and now has six in the heart of downtown.

For any major downtown project in which zoning incentives are involved—which is to say, most projects—provision of public rest rooms should be required and so should their maintenance. What catastrophes would result? Precedents suggest none. At the Citicorp atrium there are separate rest rooms for men and for women, and they are well looked after. At the Whitney sculpture garden in the Philip Morris Building a unisex toilet and lavatory is provided. It is tucked away by the espresso counter, and you have to ask for it to find it. But it's there.

In the gallery of the IBM Building there are attractive rest rooms scrupulously maintained. There is also a checkroom for coats and hats, with service on the house. Such internal spaces do not solve the problem of the homeless—they are basically upscale in their clientele. But they do meet a need and they demonstrate that it is practical to press for more of them.[9]

But there must be more public rest rooms in truly public places. There used to be. There should be again. The rehabilitation of Bryant Park may prove an indicator. One problem has been what to do with the rather ornate structures that were originally provided as rest rooms—one on the one side for men, another on the other side for women. This use having been out of the question for some time, the structures have been used as storage and tool sheds. Now a radical proposal is being considered. Use them as rest rooms. If they work in Bryant Park, it will be remarked, they will work anywhere. And there is a very good chance they will work.

There is another problem with rest rooms and it is quite pervasive. At the very least, women's rooms should be half again as large as men's. But they are not. The dimensions of women's rooms tend to be the mirror image of men's rooms. The amount of space is the same in each. The difference is in the fixtures: sometimes the women get an extra toilet; sometimes not. The supply-and-demand factor is all out of whack, a fact that is painfully evident when the facilities are taxed with peak crowds. Intermission time at the theater is a case in point. When the bell rings for the curtain, there still may be a queue of women outside the rest room, but no queue of men outside theirs. Space has been symmetrical; function has not been.[10]

Cities have an opportunity to seize. Philadelphia is one. Through a design competition it has been canvassing ideas for the revitalization of the public spaces in and around City Hall. The basic aim is to make City Hall a meeting place for the workers and shoppers of downtown. There have been many excellent ideas: outdoor cafés, waterworks, laser beams, and such. But probably the best amenity of all would be good clean restrooms, for women especially, and for that overlooked constituency, women with children in tow. Such provisions would be much appreciated and all the more for the lack of them most anywhere else in downtown. And they are lacking in most every downtown.

There is a related question. How public are the public spaces? On many plazas you will see a small bronze plaque that reads something like this: PRIVATE PROPERTY. CROSS AT THE RISK OF THE USER AND WITH REVOCABLE PERMISSION OF THE OWNER. It seems clear enough. It means that the plaza is the owner's and he has the right to revoke any right you fancy you may have to use it. Whether or not a floor-area bonus was given, most building managements take it for granted that they can bar any activity they find undesirable. Their concept of this, furthermore, goes beyond anti-social or dangerous behavior. Some are quite persnickety. When I used a rule to measure the front ledges at the General Motors Building, the security people rushed up in great consternation. This was not permitted, even though I was on the public sidewalk. If I wanted to measure I would have to secure written permission from the public relations department.

This is not a matter to go to the Supreme Court on, perhaps, but there is a principle of some importance involved. The space was provided by the public through its zoning and planning machinery. And the owner went along with the deal. It is true that the space falls within the property line of the owner, and it is equally true that he is responsible for the maintenance of it. But the legislation enabling the floor-area bonuses for such spaces unequivocally states that the space "must be accessible to the public at all times."

What does "accessible" mean? A commonsense interpretation would be that the public could use the space in the same manner that it uses any public space, with the same freedoms and the same constraints. Many building managements have been operating with a much narrower concept of access. They shoo away entertainers and people who distribute leaflets or give speeches. Apartment building managements often shoo away every-body except residents. This is a flagrant violation of the zoning intent, but to date no one has gone to court on it.

The public's right in urban plazas would seem clear. Not only are plazas used as public spaces; in most cases the owner has been specifically, and richly, rewarded for providing them. He has not been given license to allow only those public activities he happens to approve of. He may assume that he has license, and some owners have been operating on this basis with impunity. But that is because nobody has challenged them. A stiff, clarifying test is in order.

BLANK WALLS

The dominant feature of the townscape of U.S. cities is coming to be the blank wall. I first noticed this in the late 1970s. When I was sorting out the slides I had taken on my travels, it struck me that I had been favoring pictures of buildings with blank walls. Megastructures were the showiest examples, but there were many others, and they were all surprisingly photogenic: crisp verticals, clean horizontals, no fussy detailing to busy up the expanses. Just pure white space, like the kind in architectural models.

Since then I have been cataloging the many different kinds of blank walls, tracing their origins and, where possible, their effect on downtowns. I will not feign neutrality. I think the blank walls are bad for the city. But I must confess that I take a perverse pleasure in coming across newer and bigger blank walls—big not only in absolute dimensions, but in relation to what's left of the streetscape.

I have toyed with the idea of calculating a blank-wall index. It would be based on the percentage of blockfront up to the thirty-foot level that was blank. Compute this for all of the blockfronts of a downtown and you would have an objective rating applicable to all U.S. cities. Too much work. And it is not necessary. It is already clear which cities belong at the top of the list.

The blank walls here discussed are not inadvertent—the kind that are uncovered by the demolition of adjacent buildings. They are, rather, walls that were meant to be blank from the very beginning. And they have a message. They are a declaration of distrust of the city and its streets and the undesirables who might be on them.[11]

Small and medium-sized cities are the most susceptible. Big cities do have blank walls: New York, for example, has the biggest blank wall in the world;

The world's tallest blank wall: AT&T's Long Lines building in New York City.

San Francisco, one of the most boorish. If one were to construct a blank-wall index, however, the highest readings would be found in smaller cities. They have been the most immediately hurt by the regional malls, and the most prone to throw in the towel and take an if-you-can't-beat-'em-join-'em attitude. The civic leadership is likely to be almost wholly suburban, in place of residence if not in spirit; the oncoming generation even more so. There will be few who have any memory of what a thriving downtown was like. The nearest thing to a center they have experienced is the atrium of a suburban shopping mall. This is often as true of architects as of their patrons.

•

The primary model is the suburban shopping mall. Out by the freeway interchanges the blank wall is functional. It provides more shelf space, and the absence of display windows is no problem. People already made the decision to enter the store when they drove their cars there. There is no need to beckon passersby. There are no passersby.

Now the mall is being transplanted to downtown. Here there are passersby and adjacent buildings and streets. But the form is little changed. Everything is internalized, as it was out in suburbia, with few or no windows. The one major difference is the parking; instead of being spread over acres of asphalt, the parking is concentrated in multilevel structures. Some add yet more blank wall, but a number have good, simple geometries and are better to look at than the complexes they serve.

Another contributor is the convention center. They are big in big cities; they are big in smaller cities as well—great hulks of concrete stretching two or three blocks with scarcely a window in them. Convention center experts say that this sealed-box format is the way it has to be. Otherwise there would be "leakage," or "contamination"—that is, natives without badges mixing it up with the others. Thus the tight seal. Some experts would lock up the convention goers for the whole day.

The separation works. I've charted pedestrian activity on civic spaces adjoining some of these centers and found surprisingly little relationship between what's going on inside and what isn't outside. Within, there might be four thousand ophthalmologists, but on the sidewalk and benches of the adjoining spaces only a handful of people.

In some places the separation is so pronounced there are two cities: regular city and convention city. In the latter, the conventioneers follow an almost closed circuit: by shuttle bus from the convention hotels to the center and back. Spouses do get to shop, but they're segregated too, and on the whole there is little intermingling between the conventioneers and the natives. At night the separation is complete. The streets are deserted. Most restaurants have closed. The office work force has gone home. The only life is in the atriums of the hotels, conventioneers with other conventioneers.

The ultimate expression of the blank wall is the megastructure. The blank wall is ideologically necessary to it. The megastructure must acknowledge the dangers of the city around it and promise security from them. It must offer delights within but keep them carefully shielded from external view. A blank wall does all this, and the bigger and more declarative it is, the purer its expression of function.

But for whom? As it happens, most of the big megastructures have not been doing well at all. The marketing premise that people who come to the city want to be walled from it has been emphatically disproven. But suppose, for the moment, that the megastructures had been doing well financially. There would still be a larger question to be answered. How well have they been functioning for their neighbors, and for downtown in general?

They have been deadening it. Walk past one of these brutal hulks. Whatever is going on inside, there will be little going on outside. There will be few people on the sidewalks alongside and few on the blocks beyond. The blank walls, the lack of stores and activity have killed off the life that might have been.

Institutions like blank walls. Almost always there is a technical explanation: the wall space is needed for the stacks, for climate control for the computers, for lighting unvaried by natural light. But these are not the real reason. Blank walls are an end in themselves. They proclaim the power of the institution, the inconsequence of the individual, whom they are clearly meant to put down, if not intimidate. Stand by the new FBI headquarters in Washington. You feel guilty just looking at it. It is a truly menacing presence, yet, ironically, it is itself vulnerable, full of the kind of lurking spaces and dead ends and niches the wise person avoids.

Power and fear are conjoined. To judge by their design, one would gather that the institutions feel themselves under siege. TV surveillance cameras are everywhere. Signs abound telling you, redundantly, not to do this or do that. THESE STALLS FOR GOVERNMENT CARS ONLY. NO ADMITTANCE AFTER 3:30. KEEP OUT.

Utilities go for blank walls, the elements of the Bell system especially. Even when they are in the heart of a downtown, they usually turn a blank face to the street. The outstanding example is AT&T's Long Lines Building in the Wall Street area. The expanse is absolutely breathtaking—about forty-plus stories of solid brick, surely the biggest blank wall in all the world. And at its base is a very small sign. It says NO BALL OR FRISBEE PLAYING.

What to do with blank walls? The one good thing that can be said of them is that they are so awful anything else looks good by contrast—against a background of opaque black glass, for example, a chromium fire standpipe looks rather elegant. These walls fairly cry for something to set them off—some enlightened graffiti, a "Kilroy was here," a touch of the vulgar. But this cannot be. These buildings are utterly without humor.

Regional variation? With my collection of slides of hundreds of blank walls across the country, I have tested people's perception of place. As part of a presentation on the blank wall, I show about sixty slides in rapid succession. They are arranged not geographically but in order of the number of saplings. For some reason audiences find this amusing, but on the matter of location they draw a blank. Regional cues? There are none. Nobody, myself included, has ever been able to discern any regional variation, or, indeed, any real variation of any kind. Close up, to be sure, you can see some differences—concrete striated horizontally on one wall, vertically on another. But from afar the differences in the walls disappear. They look like, well, blank walls.

The best thing to do with blank walls is to do away with them, or, at the very least, to prevent their recurrence. The way to do this is to fill the vacuum, or replace nothing with something—most particularly, street-level retailing.

The people of the city have an equity in this. An owner who lines his frontage with a blank wall not only deadens his part of the street; he breaks the continuity that is so vital for the rest of the street. Stores thrive on the propinquity of other stores and the traffic they generate. Seal off a blockfront, interrupt a sequence of stores, and part of the line of the street is lost.

This was especially evident along the Avenue of the Americas. Where once there had been delicatessens and bars and shops, there were now plazas fronting on expanses of glass behind which were bankers sitting at desks. One of these buildings was bad enough; whole stretches of them, blockfront after blockfront, were stupefyingly dull. There was a true loss of amenity. These buildings took away far more in food facilities than they provided anew, and much of this was buried in off-street concourses.

Left to their own devices, developers would prefer to rent their ground-floor space to corporations—more rent, less trouble. But for providing these dull plazas, they had been getting very handsome floor-area bonuses. It seemed only fair that they liven up their frontages as a quid pro quo. We supported a provision requiring that at least 50 percent of the buildings' ground-floor fronts be devoted to retail uses. There were so many other provisions in the plaza legislation that this one went through with no fuss at all.

For the next five years there was no fuss. To repeat an observation: developers are a pragmatic lot, and once something is on the statute books, that tends to be that. Developers routinely provided the retail frontage, and the retail rents were apparently quite high enough not to be a hardship to them. When the midtown zoning code came up for a major overhaul, it seemed in order to raise the requirements to 100 percent of the frontages (less the entrance). This provision, furthermore, would be divorced from incentive zoning. Bonus or no bonus, it would be mandatory. Two other conditions had to be met: the stores would have to be accessible from the street; the glass fronts would have to be of see-through glass.

The legislation has worked unobtrusively and well. Some of the stores were wider than the planners had hoped they would be; they would like to see a greater number of the smaller frontages—twenty to twenty-five feet—so characteristic of good specialty-shopping streets. But in general the results have been good. The streets are certainly the livelier for the stores—and for the blank walls that were not put up but might have been.[12]

Other cities are following suit. Bellevue, Washington, now requires ground-level retailing on designated streets. San Francisco does not specifically mandate stores in retail areas, but twists developers' arms to the same effect in project review. For its Sixteenth Street Mall, Denver gives incentive bonuses of extra floor space to developers for providing ground-level retailing. Shops must be directly accessible from the street and shopfronts be of see-through glass. No city has banned blank walls per se; it seems more effective to require positive uses. (For the text of the New York statute, see appendix C.)

Cities would do well to have the discipline of a good statute. This is especially the case with smaller and medium-sized cities where the developers of downtown have lately arrived from suburban mall projects. In one recent center-city project the developer ruled out street-level stores, save a token or two. His leasing agent, he explained, told him that that kind of retailing wouldn't go in that location. And it most definitely will not, the design precluding it and a supine planning commission acquiescing.

Blank walls are tough to fight because no one is for them. There are no civic debates whether to have them or not. There is often no recognition that they have become a problem at all. Their growth is too incremental. They are the by-product of other causes, many seemingly good—separation of vehicular and pedestrian traffic, off-street circulation, and such. Given current momentums, the blank walls will continue to spread, even in the most exemplary of cities.

Such as St. Paul, Minnesota. It is the blank-wall capital of the United States. You would not expect it to be. It is a most habitable, attractive, and friendly city; it has one of the most resourceful and effective mayors in the country; its Lowertown redevelopment is of an eminently human scale and has a fine street presence. St. Paul also has one of the most complete sky-

Architect John Portman's definitive statement on the U.S. Street: Bonaventure Hotel, Los Angeles. Here we have a megastructure—the ultimate development in the flight from the street. Their distinguishing characteristic is self-containment. Their enclosing walls are blank, windowless, and to the street they turn an almost solid face of concrete or brick. They are a wretched model for the future of the city.

way systems in the country, and it is probably the best designed of all of them.

It is paying a steep price. In a striking example of the Gresham effect, skyway level has led to the blanking-out of street level. The result is as drastic as if shop fronts and windows had been decreed illegal. There are few to see. The experience is so dull that to walk at street level is to do penance for not using upper level. Block after block, it is blank wall. Occasionally there is a break to indicate what might have been—like the trompe l'oeil windows on the wall of a parking lot.

It is not entirely farfetched to prophesy that one day St. Paul might embark on a rediscovery project to uncover its buried street level. Atlanta made a tourist attraction of its old underground streets; so did Seattle of its Skid Row. But prime shopping streets are a much greater treasure, and the fact that they have been concealed should make their reappearance all the more dramatic. Disneyland merchandises a simulation of a street. But cities have something even better: actual streets. Right under their noses.

THE CORPORATE EXODUS

The out-migration started slowly. The first to move was General Foods, to White Plains in 1954. Ten years later IBM moved out, to Armonk. Then Olin, to Stamford. In 1970, the momentum picked up. A few corporations headed for the Sunbelt. Most headed for the suburbs, to Connecticut's Fairfield County in particular. By 1976, over thirty major corporations had moved out of New York City, and more were leaving—including one of the biggest, Union Carbide. Office vacancy rates were climbing. With the city on the edge of bankruptcy, it looked as if a full-fledged rout was in the making.

High time, many people said. Even New Yorkers joined in the reprehension. Couldn't blame Union Carbide, *The New York Times* editorialized; the city had let it down. Dr. George Sternlieb, director of Rutgers' Center for Urban Policy Research, who had been prophesying such events, fairly chortled at their arrival. "It takes a man who's been shot in the head a while to realize he's dead," Sternlieb observed. "New York may not realize it, but if you look at the numbers it's clear that New York is dead."

But the rout did not come off. The bad news about New York had been so bad that a classic bottom was being formed. Any corporation that had not yet decided to leave probably would not leave. The ones who had left had long before signaled their intentions. In our research on public spaces we had found an early warning indicator. It was the corporation's own building. Often it would give an advance tip that the corporation was not long for the city.

Union Carbide's headquarters on Park Avenue was one such. This sleek black building was one of Skidmore, Owings, and Merrill's best, and it was superbly located. In operation, however, it bristled with distrust of the city.

Large strips of empty space bordered its sides and fronts, and with nary a bench or a ledge for anyone to sit on. Guarding entry was a corps of guards. It should have come as no surprise when the company announced in 1976 that it was forswearing the city and would move to Danbury, Connecticut.

Union Carbide's timing was not very good. The mass exodus was just about over. Preposterous as it may have seemed then, the bad news was peaking just as the city's competitive position took some decided turns for the better. Overseas business had become a great stimulant; there was an influx of foreign firms, especially in finance. International divisions of corporations were expanding and it was in New York that they were doing it. A number of firms that had earlier contemplated leaving the city had second thoughts. Philip Morris announced it would stay. So did Pfizer. New York's troubles were by no means over, but there was to be a respite, and time for mulling over some lessons.

One thing had become clear. While the relocations were touted as economic measures, they were in fact very costly, and for more parties than the corporations. Let us follow the Union Carbide case. At 270 Park Avenue it had a fifty-three-story building with 1.2 million square feet. It sold it for $110 million, or $92 a square foot—a fire-sale price for such a building at such a location, and a great coup for the buyer, Manufacturers Hanover Trust Company. It sold its previous headquarters, a smaller building, for $161 million, or $333 a square foot.

Union Carbide's new headquarters would be slightly larger than the old one: 1.3 million square feet. It would cost $190 million. To link up with the highway system, a freeway section and cloverleaf had to be constructed, the cost to be borne by federal taxpayers.

The design, by Kevin Roche and John Dinkeloo, was a handsome one and in horizontal terms matched the highly centralized management structure of the company. Some observers were surprised. They thought the company would take advantage of the move to shift to a looser, more contemporary organizational setup, with more autonomy for the divisions. But it did not, thereby producing, in the words of one critic, a monument to the 1950s.

In any event, it was far away: some ninety miles from New York and in an area not well served by mass transportation. Relocation costs were heavy: $40 million. Of thirty-two hundred employees, about seven hundred lived close enough to the new site not to have to move. About twelve hundred did have to move and find new homes and schools, and the company subsidized their moves. About twelve hundred people refused to move and left the company.

At the time of the move housing was in short supply in the Danbury area—in particular, housing affordable by middle-income people. The move itself put housing further out of reach for people who would work there. So they made do. They commuted, and for a number, the commutes were long indeed.

In varying degrees other office growth areas have suffered similar imbalances. Housing is not where the office jobs are, and vice versa, and the newtown ideal of one's working within walking distance of one's home was never further from reality. In the fox-hunt country of New Jersey's Morris and Somerset counties, new office complexes are bringing many white-collar clerical workers to a beautiful countryside. But for daytime use only. Not to live there. Physically, there is plenty of room for new housing, and eventually most of the remaining farms and estates will go, and there will be housing. But it will be long in coming and probably very dear. Arcadia will ever be receding.

In the meantime another steep price is being paid. Traffic. It is the prime problem that the office growth areas face and it is hard to see how there can be any substantial relief for years to come. The highways were laid out for other settlement patterns, other kinds of journeys, and they do not match with the mixed, all-directions traffic spawned by office centers. Wherever you want to go in these areas, there never seems to be a direct route. You zig and you zag, stop for interminable lights, turn right for one route, left for another. The freeways aren't so bad; it's the mishmash between them that is awful.

Engineers cannot solve this problem. It is essentially governmental. How many more access points to allow on a given stretch of highway? Should developers be assessed the cost of overpasses? Should there be overpasses? Should there, for that matter, be more projects? In whose township? There are few regional bodies with teeth to make the tough decisions. Until there are, stay on I-95. Leave it and you are in trouble.

In the downtowns as in the countryside, companies are befouling the surcease they sought. Greenwich, Connecticut, now has over 2 million square feet of office space, much of it in the downtown area. For most employees, however, there is no mass transit that is practical for them. They must drive, and via a street system that was laid out in the 1700s. Five o'clock can be a memorable experience. For the executives the geography is fine; some have homes only a few miles away. Those who head north to the woods and the estates have only a few miles more. But most employees do not live in Greenwich. They head south—for Exit 5 of the New England Thruway and, after they get on it, some of the densest traffic on the Eastern Seaboard.

In both Greenwich and Stamford the stations are only a few blocks away from many of the headquarters. But only a minority of employees appear to use them. Possibly because of the need for a car trip at the other end of the line, the majority make the whole trip by car.

Is it for such factors that companies have moved? They cite transportation as one; they cite tax differentials; they site office costs, availability of trained people, and other tangible factors. Sometimes, as at Pfizer, the various factors have been ranked by computer studies and then given weightings by each of the executives. Location consultants, such as The Fantus Co., have been retained by companies to advise them whether they should move or not, and if so, to where. Detailed comparisons have been drawn up to measure the relative merits of locations A, B, and C.

Such studies have been impressive. The boilerplate alone has sometimes been as thick as a phone book. But what the studies have mainly proved is that tangible factors have little to do with the moves.

It is the intangibles that have been the key. "Environment" is the umbrella term. Shorn of euphemism, here is what executives mean by it: (1) The center city is a bad place: crime, dirt, noise, blacks, Puerto Ricans, and so on. (2) Even if it isn't a bad place, middle Americans think it is and they don't want to be transferred here. (3) To attract and hold good people we have to give them a better environment. (4) We have to move to suburbia. Thus Union Carbide, concluding a two-year study: "The long term quality-of-life needs of our headquarters employees" were the overriding factors.

Self-serving piety has been characteristic of the moves. Not for the brass; not for the company; it has been for their people that they have moved, and for their lifestyle needs.

It's a wonder executives keep a straight face. Lifestyle needs of employees? Companies don't have to spend all that money researching them. They don't have to compare area A with area B and area C. All they have to do is look in the phone directory. Where does the boss live? That is where the company is going.

And that is where they went. During the height of the exodus I made a location study. I plotted the moves of all the major corporations that had moved from New York to the suburbs and beyond over the previous ten years. By checking old phone directories, street maps, and registers of executives, I plotted the home locations of the chief executive officer and his fellow top executives at the time the decision was made to move. Then I plotted the location the company moved to.

The correlation: of thirty-eight corporations, thirty-one moved to a place close to the top man's home. Average distance: about eight miles by road.

The geographic concentration was extraordinary. The heartland was in Greenwich—specifically, in a circle about four miles in diameter, bounded on the east by the Burning Tree Country Club and on the west by the Fairfield Country Club. Within it were no fewer than twelve chief executive officers.

And where did most of their companies move to? Greenwich and environs.

This was hardly a chance distribution. As a check I plotted the home locations of the top executives of ninety-five corporations that had not moved from New York. Rather than being concentrated in a few spots, they were widely distributed over the metropolitan area, with about a quarter in New York City itself.

Companies say the top man's preference becomes a factor only after the basic decision to move has been made. The facts suggest the reverse: that it is a prime motivating factor from the beginning. The coincidence is too great to be rationalized otherwise. Obviously something other than objective analysis had been at work in the Greenwich cases. Peers had been at work. The place was rife with chief executive officers, and it was in the locker rooms of those golf clubs that the most important location research may have taken place.

If executives wanted to take their people to the suburbs, that was their prerogative. But would it be good for the company? Very much so, said the executives, and they had glowing stories to back them up. Certainly not, said urban loyalists, and they had stories, too. The test, of course, would be performance. Later, some astonishing data would become available, but at the time there was not too much to go on. I made year-to-year earnings comparisons but most of the moves had been too recent for firm conclusions to be drawn.

Several points were clear, however. Some kind of cyclical process had been at work. A number of companies had shown a predisposition to move and this appeared to have been linked to the company's stage of life. Move-out companies tended to be big companies, near the top of the Fortune 500. They tended to be technically oriented, with a high quota of engineers in management. The companies were heavily capitalized and self-sufficient enough not to need banks as much as they did earlier. Most started out in small cities or towns elsewhere, moved to New York, and were now moving once again, away from the city.

Whatever the impulses for the moves, most executives seem to be pleased with them. They have a strong psychic investment in being pleased, of course, but most of the middle management people appear to be pleased also. They like the pleasant surroundings and the time saved in commuting—which has generally been used for more time at the office than at home. (The usual arrival hour is nearer 8 A.M. than 9.) As for the hustle and bustle of the city, people who have just moved out may miss it at first; after a while they do not. Whatever they are missing, they are happily unaware of what it is.

And there may be the rub. Migrations are a self-proving proposition, and if executives are happy, it is in part because the moves tend to screen out people who would not be. Some people, among them the most able and aggressive, refuse to go out, and they join other companies. Some who do go out find the atmosphere deadening and leave.

Most people adapt. The rural environment is easy to adapt to. Physically, there is much space, pleasantly arranged. Individual offices and worksta-tions tend to be larger than their counterparts in the city—vastly so in the case of some top executives' offices. There are attractive common areas. Outdoors there may be shaded walks and picnic areas.

These places are quiet places. What one notices at first is the stillness. Outside, the loudest noise heard is the swish of the water sprinklers on the lawn, the muffled hum of the traffic on the nearby parkway. Except at 8 and 5, not many people are to be seen coming and going. At outlying campuses some executives may stroll around the buildings. At General Electric there are "one-turn" men and "two-turn" men. Most of the time, however, there is little activity outdoors.

The pace is slow, visibly so. Both migrants and visitors remark on how much more slowly people seem to move. To some this is a healthy lack of hassle—a relaxed, low-stress atmosphere that is good for clear thinking. To others, it is torpor.

"They walk slower," says a nonmigrant executive. "They talk slower. They think slower." The charge is expressed in other ways—"dry rot," "gone to seed." It is a biased charge, to be sure, but it is one that companies should hear. "It's not right for guys to have such big offices," says an executive whose office size is disciplined by city costs. "It gets to a person after a while. They're big frogs out there and they're getting out of touch." Executives of migrant firms sometimes wonder themselves. It's not that they themselves will go slack, they say; they had their formative years in a tougher clime. But what about the younger men? "They're the ones I worry about," says one senior executive. "There's just too damn much contentment. Over the long run the move is going to be bad for this company."

These are subjective matters. One aspect that is not is self-containment. Headquarters, even those in the center of towns, have little connection with their surroundings. They are elements of a car culture: one arrives by car and leaves by car, and there is not much interchange with the outside world in between. Within the headquarters a range of services makes the outside unnecessary. These are particularly bountiful in outlying campuses. At Beneficial Management's corporate village in Peapack, New Jersey, a pleasant grouping of low buildings is arranged around a courtyard and bell tower. There are outdoor dining areas, dining rooms within, shops, health facilities; the garage is laid out so that one drives to an underground space and takes an elevator to within a few feet of his office.

Even in downtown locations, headquarters are self-sufficient. In Stamford there is a broad boulevard lined with them. But it is not much walked upon. There appears to be little human traffic between the separate headquarters. Employees do visit the huge shopping mall across the way, but not so many that the sidewalks are ever too busy. Or that the traffic lights have to be timed to give the pedestrian a break. He has to press a button to get on the waiting list.

What Stamford has made is an architectural park. The buildings, by some of the country's most noted architects, form a series of detached exhibits, several mounted on podiums. Only one has a street-level presence: Champion International's, designed by Ulrich Franzen—it has an outdoor plaza and a branch of the Whitney Museum on the ground floor. A number of the others do not have any pedestrian access at street level at all; their entry points are up above, on the upper levels over the parking garages.

Campus location or downtown, headquarters people share a similar problem. People do not go out to see them very much. Traffic at checkpoints, such as gatehouses and security desks, is light; so is the parking in the area reserved for visitors, the provision of which clearly anticipated far more of them than have been turning up.

Executives of companies contemplating a move are wary on this point. They have heard about the low visitor rates. But they believe they have enough clout that people will go out to see them. So people will: people with something to sell to the company; people with accounts to service; people who are less important than whomever they are going to see. Nobody drops in. The visits are planned visits, and as the companies' how-to-get-there booklets indicate, these can take some effort. ("After exiting from the Merritt at #38, turn right onto Middle Ridge Road and continue to the third stoplight . . .")

Some would-be visitors balk, and they are apt to be the important ones. "They even sent a limousine in for me," recalls a top antitrust lawyer. "They said I should prepare the case out in White Plains. One visit was enough. I said no, they could send the executives in to me. We'd rent a suite at the Barclay and go over the case there. And that's what we did."

The problem is not just the infrequency of the visits but the character of them. When senior executives have to travel out to see senior executives of an outlying company, they can be keenly aware that a measure of coercion is involved. They don't like this. One executive told me of a journey he and two fellow executives had to make to a company with a New Jersey campus. They went out because they had to; the New Jersey company had a process they badly wanted to license. "We had to go out twice," he said. "They really stuck it to us. There they were in the big chairs. It was like a court and we were serfs. We felt silly, frankly. It was a bad place to do any negotiating in."

Another man's home territory is not the best place to bargain with him, especially when the trip out is itself an obeisance. Truly critical negotiations are best done informally, on common meeting grounds equally accessible to both parties. These the city has in abundance—clubs, restaurants, building lobbies, street corners. These places are the heart of the city's intelligence networks, and a company that cuts itself off from them loses something that no electronic system can ever provide.

Some companies have tried to compensate for the isolation by using consultants more. Many experts have been earning their per diems by traveling out to brief company people and shoot ideas back and forth with them. One executive summed it up in a word. What, I had asked him, gesturing to the empty visitors' parking lot, did they do about visitors? "We hire them," he said.

Executives of outlying companies do go back into town periodically, and the companies would like to have them see more people when they do. "We encourage them to schedule their contacts more tightly," says one executive. "No wasted time on purely social stuff; no long lunches with old college buddies." Which is to say, no surprises: no chance encounters, no unexpected points of view.

There has been some relocation work back to town. Companies are quite touchy on the matter, but many of their people are commuting to the city for their key work: keeping in touch. This is especially the case with people in communications. You can't work the room if you are not there. Some of the intown offices that companies have kept are now more crowded than they were before. General Electric's former headquarters building on Lexington Avenue has more GE people working in it than when it was headquarters. Some companies that kept no space have reestablished their presence with "regional" offices and with hotel or apartment suites.

In some respects, the moves to suburbia have spurred contact. Plane travel to company outposts has been rising—some companies have been enlarging their private fleets—and executives have been spending as much if not more time on the road than before. Within the new headquarters, furthermore, some of the predominantly horizontal layouts have led to more interchange than in the vertical structures of the city. This is especially noticeable around lunchtime, as people congregate in the dining rooms and common areas.

But these are internal contacts, company people talking to company people. There is a price to pay for this inbreeding and the farther away from the mainstream a company goes, the more vulnerable it is to it. Every large organization has within it tendencies to turn inward on itself. Moving to suburbia intensifies these tendencies.

The moves are acts of withdrawal and the buildings convey it. Many of the new structures are curiously defensive in design, as if the problem were too many outsiders trying to get in rather than too few. A number of companies are sited on steep hillsides, like forts. One, then American Can, had a sort of Goldfinger's castle with an entrance that opened for executives' cars, like a portcullis. General Electric has a gatehouse for screening people before they drive on to the headquarters itself, where a designated employee will receive them.

No bag ladies, no winos, no oddballs assault their landscaped ramparts, yet the companies seem every bit as obsessed with the threat of them as

they were back in the city. Guards are all over the place. There are elaborate TV surveillance systems. With their long, white cameras, slowly rotating, they are as much to be seen as to see. So too the master consoles in the
lobby, with their banks of small TV screens and blinking lights. They are
the most impressive design element of many lobbies and the spiritual cen-
terpiece of them.

The companies say they want people to come. Their buildings say no.

After the 1976 departures the outward movement slowed to a trickle, averaging about two firms a year. Then, in 1986, the pace picked up: four moved
out and several others announced they were going to: Exxon, J. C. Penney,
Mobil, AT&T. As in the mid-1970s, the news thoroughly alarmed the city.
This time, many said, the city really had had it.

There was a widespread disposition to see the move-outs' side, and to see
their departure as a damning indictment of the city: its high taxes, crime,
and stress and strain. The moves had been preceded by exhaustive study of
all factors, the firms emphasized, and certainly this must have included the
experience of the previous move-outs. It was generally assumed that they
had done very well in their suburban campuses, and in financial as well as
environmental terms.

But had they? When I did my 1976 study, not enough time had elapsed
to draw valid conclusions. But now ten years had gone by and there was
hard data. To follow up, I tracked the performance of the 38 companies that
had moved out and 36 that had not, and by that most hard-boiled of measures, the valuation of the marketplace.[13]

The first discovery was that seventeen of the thirty-eight move-out firms
had lost their identity. They had been bought out, raided, or merged, and in
no case as the dominant partner. That left twenty-two companies. For each
I traced the stock valuation for the eleven-year period December 31, 1976,
to December 31, 1987. The average increase was 107 percent—somewhat
better than the 93 percent increase of the Dow Jones Industrial Average.

What about the companies that had stayed in New York? The results
were downright startling. For the thirty-six major corporations that stayed
the average increase was 277 percent—over two and half times the increase
of the move-outs.

Assigning cause and effect is difficult. There are just too many variables.
It could be that the sojourn in suburbia did dull reflexes, as some prophesied it would. But it could also be argued that the companies were the better for having moved and would have fared worse had they not moved.

I think the die was cast well before the companies moved out. The impulse seems to have been internal, the consequence of cyclical changes within the companies, and independent of the city and its problems. In a word, they were not doing very well. Some had grown old and fat and slow. Several had identity problems. (American Can got out of the can business entirely, changed its name to Primerica, and went into finance.) To paraphrase Dr. Johnson, if a company is tired of New York, it is tired.

Understandably, companies that were unhappy became unhappy with the city. Frequently they telegraphed their intentions by citing somebody else's complaints; the recalcitrant yokel was a favorite. When the companies finally did announce, it was with a vengeance. The leave-takings were acts of renunciation, a turning of the back to the past. The sheer mechanics of the migration, the planning studies, and the design work promised to be a shot in the arm. And so it was—for the top management group, at any rate, if not for the underlings who were unable to pick up roots and join the move. Sorry about that.

Another study revealed a wide disparity between the performance of move-outs and that of stayers. In a 1980 assessment for the Regional Plan Association, Regina Belz Armstrong analyzed three kinds of firms: those that stayed in New York City; those that moved to the suburbs; those that moved out of the region entirely. The factors she checked were productivity, profitability, and growth.

Of the twenty-three companies that had moved to the suburbs in the period 1972–75, the majority had profitability lower than average for companies in their industry in the region, and the growth rate was only a half that of the others. The twenty firms that had moved out of the region had performances moderately below average for their group.

As in my study, firms that remained in New York City did very well, some spectacularly well. The average value of output and profit per dollar of labor input increased much faster than both the regional and national average, and faster yet than the average of the move-out firms.

Costs? Both studies are illuminating on this score. At the top of the list of reasons advanced for moving out has been the cost of New York. They are indeed high, and for a range of things: for a house, anywhere; for commutation; for schooling. High too are costs of office space, it being more expensive to be at the crossroads than up a back road.

But costs are relative. What is the payoff? What is the profit earned from the lower costs? The expenditures for housekeeping are far less important to a balance sheet than profitability and performance. On this score, both studies speak loudly. The lower costs enjoyed by the move-out companies did not correlate with excellent performance. The higher costs of the New York companies did.

There will probably be more move-outs. More companies will be growing older and fatter, and as a normal consequence they will leave. This will be painful for the cities they leave, especially when the moves come in bunches, as they seem to do from time to time.

They too are losing back-office work to their suburban office parks, and sometimes they lose headquarters as well. When firms move South and Southwest, furthermore, they will not necessarily move to a downtown. J. C. Penney did not. To the discomfiture of Dallas it moved all the way from New York, not to Dallas, but to the town of Plano. Some Dallas leaders were incredulous. Plano?

On balance, the center city is competing rather well. The office jobs that it has been losing have been mostly in the big, aging companies—the ones most likely to head for suburbia and to bomb when they do. The new-job increases have been mostly in newer, smaller firms. They are local companies, most of them, but as Jane Jacobs has observed, local economies are where it all starts. The small companies need access to a wide range of specialized services and people. They cannot have this in-house. They are not big enough. They cannot have this out in some isolated location. They need to be in the center—or as close to it as rents and space will permit.

Turnover is brisk. Many will fold, but here and there some of the companies will become big companies. Eventually, some of them may defect to the suburbs, but in their dynamic years they will thrive in the city. So, at least, our comparison study would indicate. As a group, the companies that competed in the city proved to be tougher and more profitable than the companies that did not—and by an impressive margin. The crossroads, it would appear, is a very good place to be.

THE CASE FOR GENTRIFICATION

What our center cities have needed most is more people living in the center. If only, the hope has been voiced, younger people would come back to the old neighborhoods and fix them up, what a boon it would be. Here and there a few heartening precedents could be spotted. When I worked on the *Fortune* series on "The Exploding Metropolis" in 1957 we were able to run a portfolio of attractive blocks in various cities. These were mostly upper-income places, however, and from the market studies we did it was hard to see any substantial shift back to the center city.

One large reason was the kind of housing offered. The kind most in demand were the row houses of Georgetown and Brooklyn Heights. These were clearly out of reach for most people but they did provide strong cues for design and marketing of new housing. They were not heeded. The federal Title I urban redevelopment projects were just getting under way, and in scale and spirit they were the diametric opposite of the old blocks. With little variation from city to city the process was the same; not only were blocks razed, but streets as well, and huge superblock projects grouped colonies of high-rise towers in abstract green space.

A terrible mistake was being made. These bleak new utopias were not bleak because they had to be. They were the concrete manifestation—and how literally—of a deep misunderstanding of the function of the city.

By such measures as tenant satisfaction, crime rates, and maintenance it should have been evident that the high-rise towers were proving much less suitable for families with children than low-rise units. But the momentum was unstoppable. In New York City the project format became so imbedded in the rules that it was difficult to build any public housing that departed from it. And it was a photogenic format. What on the ground looked like dirty, gray concrete gleamed white against cloud-filled skies in architectural photographs. Particularly attractive were the photos of the Pruitt-Igoe project in St. Louis.

But cities—older cities especially—had a great asset: a plentiful supply of old housing. The houses were not of the quality of the red-brick Federal houses of Georgetown or Brooklyn Heights. They were ugly, many of them: brownstones, for example, the felicities of which took a lot of time to appreciate. Most of the housing was in bad shape, much of it foreclosed. But this proved a blessing. Some sites actively promoted their rehabilitation. Baltimore, for one, set up a "homesteading" program with its stock of tax-foreclosed properties; to buyers who would pledge to fix them up the city would sell the houses for a nominal sum. The result has been some very attractive neighborhoods. One, the Otterbein houses, is a very Baltimore place and with front steps as white as any in the city.

Pittsburgh is another city that has had homesteading programs. It started with a "Great House Sale," in which it put fifty-eight city-owned houses up for sale at one hundred dollars apiece to people who would rehabilitate them. Since then prices have gone up; it has been selling abandoned properties to homesteaders for three hundred dollars apiece.

By and large, however, the people who have been rehabilitating old neighborhoods have been doing it without much help from government—sometimes despite government. The federal government subsidized suburbia with FHA-guaranteed mortgages but offered no such help for rehabilitating city houses. The Department of Housing and Urban Development did have some demonstration programs, including one for "new towns in town." It was, if anything, too well meant. It was thoroughly suburban in its assumptions and was so laden with antidensity, anticity provisions that it was bound to founder.

Banks and insurance companies were not much help either. Banks would withhold mortgage financing from areas being rehabilitated until the rehabilitation was largely completed and financing no longer needed. Then they would lend. Insurance companies were often so chary of older neighborhoods that obtaining adequate fire and liability policies was extremely difficult and costly.

Cash was the big problem. When banks did offer mortgage financing there was a sizable gap to fill. The home buyer usually had to put up about 30 percent of the purchase price in cash, and raising it took some doing. Money for the actual renovation was hard to come by too. Rates on second mortgages were astronomical and the terms too short.

Despite the difficulties, the rehabilitation movement gained force. There was common sense to it. The neighborhoods might have looked shabby with their Perma-Stone facades, broken windows, and vacant lots. But with them went an infrastructure of streets and utilities and urban services substantially intact. For a fraction of any pro rata replacement cost, the home buyer was acquiring a share of this urban base.

In the eyes of these beholders the old houses acquired a beauty that had not been so discernible before. There was, for example, a considerable shift in aesthetic judgments on the brownstones. They used to be drab, dark, and monotonous—indeed, ugly. But then, with no physical change to speak of, they changed. They became fine examples of the Italianate style, their stoops a graceful evocation of the urban rhythm. To paint over the brown, as remodelers did earlier, was sacrilege. If, as in Park Slope, the brownstones were twenty-four feet or more wide, had parquet floors and stained glass, they became objects of veneration. Even the basic eighteen-footers—the tract houses of their day—commanded respect. And rising prices. People who bought them thought they were getting a tremendous bargain. As the real estate market was subsequently to demonstrate, they were indeed.

Good news? You would think so. But many people do not think so.

Invoking that dread term of urban affairs, they say it is "gentrification," and those who hailed the possibility of a middle-class revival of neighborhoods are unhappy now it has become a reality. They say that it is elitist; that it has been at the expense of the poor; that the displacement of them by middle-class people has broken up once stable neighborhoods and ethnic groups. There is not a conference on city problems that does not ring with protestations of guilt over gentrification. Shame on us for what we have done.

The gentrification charge has had an inhibiting effect on government support. Let me go back to one of the first cases. In the 1969 *Plan for New York City*, the planning commission hailed the brownstones revival with enthusiasm. "If brownstones have done what they have done in the face of major difficulties," the plan said, "it is staggering to think of what could be done if the difficulties were removed." To that end, it proposed

- municipal loans or mortgage guarantees for one- and two-family homes.
- a revolving fund to bridge the gap between the price of the house and a conventional mortgage.
- long-term loans for renovation work.
- municipal second mortgages for twenty years at regular mortgage rates.
- temporary tax abatement on house improvements.

The proposals were not supported. They were criticized, and by many of the civic activists that had been expected to support them. Elitism, they charged. The great reservoir of brownstones was in Brooklyn—many square miles of it—but to judge from the criticism, the brownstone movement was something fomented by a small coterie of smart-aleck Manhattan liberals and quiche eaters. (This was before the term "yuppies" was invented.)

What displacement? And when? The gentrification charge is very misleading. Check the year-by-year changes in neighborhood households and you will find very few cases of direct displacement; that is, a renter going out the door as a homeowner comes in. Low-income renters are frequent movers; 40 percent of the renters in a city neighborhood will move. Of all moves, the Department of Housing and Urban Development has estimated, only 4 percent are caused by displacement. When there is displacement, furthermore, it comes early in the game, usually well before the home buyers arrive.

What causes it? The implicit assumption of the gentrification concept is that the chief threat to housing for the poor is the improvement of neighborhoods. The problem is the opposite. The chief threat is the deterioration of neighborhoods. The poor are not being hurt by middle-class invest-ment. They are being hurt by disinvestment—by landlords and owners who let buildings go to rot, who walk away from them, who torch them. More units have been lost through abandonment in the Bronx alone than have been provided by brownstone rehabilitation in all of New York City.

The worst case of disinvestment is the federal government public hous-ing program. The number of units constructed each year has been falling precipitously: from 68,500 in 1978 to 1,426 in 1985. The condition of units is worsening; by law the rent cannot be more than 30 percent of the fam-ily's income, but local housing authorities are having trouble holding the line. Maintenance has suffered—and lately to such an extent that more units are being lost than built. Our public housing program needs an over-haul in policy and design. What it needs most, however, is a fair amount of money.

Rehabilitation programs are proceeding well and they are doing it with-out displacement. As part of its "Landmark Rehabilitation" program, Savannah, Georgia, is restoring 1,200 units in its Victorian district and will rent 600 of them to low-income blacks. In Kansas City the Quality Hill redevelopment is restoring what is left of a former gold coast by rehabilitat-ing old structures and infilling with new three-story row housing. During the staged construction the project has been able to house most of the peo-ple who were on the site earlier.

Harlem might one day be an example. It has already suffered disinvest-ment and displacement. It is, in fact, underpopulated, having lost almost a third of its population since 1970. Much of the tenement housing is burnt out. But Harlem has great advantages. It is well served with mass transit; it has broad, tree-lined avenues and excellent access to parks. There are many cleared sites for new housing; there is a fine stock of brownstones, some blocks of which, such as Striver's Row, have been kept in excellent shape.

In the country as a whole, let it be noted, the market for rehabilitated center-city housing is a small one. Most of the data available indicate that the prime prospects are people already living in the city. Next are people who normally would go to the suburbs but who have elected to stay in the city for one reason or another. This is probably the swing sector and could be enlarged were the supply of units increased and the cost not. About a third are people who have been living in suburbia; a considerable propor-tion of them are empty nesters, whose children have grown up and moved away. All in all, it has been estimated, house sales in rehabilitated city neighborhoods number no more than 100,000 units a year.

These few people, however, can have a profound impact on the center city and the perception of it by others. Since the base is so small, a relatively small addition can carry a lot of leverage. In Denver, for example, another twenty-seven hundred people would double the downtown resident population. Such additions will not jam the bars and put hordes on the streets at night. Like their counterparts in suburbia, city residents are homebodies. But their presence does make a difference, and a very healthy one. In Charlotte, North Carolina, the NCNB bank sponsored a town house development that is only five blocks from the center of downtown. People *walk* to work from it. They also agitate for more retailing and services, more activity at night. Of such steps is a center revitalized.

Cities-within-cities, alas, are still being built. They are usually very large—often on clear tracts, such as obsolete freight yards, that give architects and developers the blank slate they would be better off for not having. The projects are sufficient unto themselves; the surrounding neighborhoods are not in the province of their planning. For urban services the projects provide bits and pieces within: a gourmet food shop, a simulation of a raffish pub. A recent example is Presidential Towers, a middle-class development in Chicago. Writing in *Inland Architect*, Catharine Ingraham hails it as ersatz city. "The idea that one can imitate the diversity of cities in isolated developments by bringing together desirable pieces of the urban fabric has taken hold of city planning. Paradoxically, the more one imitates, or extracts things from the vernacular city, the more artificial the results seem. The development stands as a bulwark against the very diversity that it capitalizes on."

But there are some good prototypes. There have been for some time, which makes the bad ones all the less understandable. Here and there, year after year, residential projects have been built that are of reasonably high density, eminently economical, of pleasing scale, and thoroughly urban. They do not date.

One of the best contemporary models is St. Francis Square in San Francisco. With its town-house groupings, interior open spaces, and private patios, it is one of the pleasantest neighborhoods you will see anywhere. It was built for low- and middle-income people twenty-five years ago. To repeat a point: a design that is well conceived for a time and place tends to be timeless. We should not have to search hard for such lost lessons. They are all about us.

APPENDICES

Appendix A
From the California Easement Act, 1959

PURCHASE OF INTERESTS AND RIGHTS IN REAL PROPERTY
(STATE OF CALIFORNIA)

Chapter 1658, Statutes, 1959

An act to add Chapter 12 (commencing at Section 6950) to Division 7 of Title I of the Government Code, relating to the purchase of interests in real property by counties and cities and to the preservation of open spaces and areas for public use and enjoyment.

The people of the State of California do enact as follows:

Section 1. Chapter 12 (commencing at Section 6950) is added to Division 7 of Title 1 of the Government Code, to read:

CHAPTER 12. PURCHASE OF INTERESTS AND RIGHTS IN REAL PROPERTY

6950. It is the intent of the Legislature in enacting this chapter to provide a means whereby any county or city may acquire, by purchase, gift, grant, bequest, devise, lease or otherwise, and through the expenditure of public funds, the fee or any lesser interest or right in real property in order to preserve, through limitation of their future use, open spaces and areas for public use and enjoyment.

6951. The Legislature finds that the rapid growth and spread of urban development is encroaching upon, or eliminating, many open areas and spaces of varied size and character, including many having significant scenic or esthetic values, which areas and spaces if preserved and maintained in their present open state would constitute important physical, social, esthetic or economic assets to existing or impending urban and metropolitan development.

6952. The Legislature hereby declares that it is necessary for sound and proper urban and metropolitan development, and in the public interest of the people of this State for any county or city to expend or advance public

funds for, or to accept by purchase, gift, grant, bequest, devise, lease or otherwise, the fee or any lesser interest or right in real property to acquire,
maintain, improve, protect, limit the future use of or otherwise conserve
open spaces and areas within their respective jurisdictions.

6953 The Legislature further declares that the acquisition of interests or
rights in real property for the preservation of open spaces and areas constitutes a public purpose for which public funds may be expended or advanced,
and that any county or city may acquire, by purchase, gift, grant, bequest,
devise, lease or otherwise, the fee or any lesser interest, development right,
easement, covenant or other contractual right necessary to achieve the purposes of this chapter. Any county or city may also acquire the fee to any
property for the purpose of conveying or leasing said property back to its
original owner or other person under such covenants or other contractual
arrangements as will limit the future use of property in accordance with the
purposes of this chapter.

6954. For the purpose of this chapter an "open space" or "open area" is
any space or area characterized by (1) great natural scenic beauty or (2)
whose existing openness, natural condition, or present state of use, if
retained, would enhance the present or potential value of abutting or surrounding urban development, or would maintain or enhance the conservation of natural or scenic resources.

Appendix B
Sample Scenic Easement Deed, State of California, 1946

*Approved as to form by Attorney General, October 23, 1946

THIS INDENTURE, made this _____ day of _____, 194___, by and between _____ as Grantors and State of California, Grantee, WITNESSETH:

WHEREAS, the said Grantors are the owners in fee of the real property, hereinafter described, situate in Tuolumne County, California, in the Town of Columbia, and within the boundaries of the proposed Town of Columbia State Park; and

WHEREAS, the said State of California owns certain real property adjoining the said property of the said Grantors, or adjacent thereto, which property constitutes a portion of Town of Columbia State Park, and which park is a part of the State Park System of the State of California; and

WHEREAS, the State Park Commission of California has determined that the greatest use and benefit to be derived from said State Park by the people of the State of California is through the maintenance and preservation of said State Park and the surrounding area in its present natural state of scenic and historical attractiveness; and

WHEREAS, the said land of said Grantors likewise has certain attractive scenic features; and

WHEREAS, it has been determined by the said State Park Commission of California that the preservation and conservation of the scenic and historical area adjacent to lands owned by the State in the park and the securing, by the State, of a scenic easement, over, across and upon the said lands of the said Grantors is necessary to the extension and development of said State Park System; and

WHEREAS, the said Grantors are willing, for the consideration hereinafter named, to grant to the State of California the scenic use as hereinafter expressed of their said land and thereby the protection to the present scenic attractiveness of said area which will result in the restricted use and enjoyment by the Grantors of their said property because of the imposition of the conditions in connection therewith hereinafter expressed;

NOW THEREFORE, for and in consideration of the premises and the sum of One Dollar to the Grantors in hand paid, the receipt whereof is hereby acknowledged, said Grantors do hereby grant and convey unto the State of California, an estate, interest and scenic easement in said real estate of said Grantors, of the nature and character and to the extent hereinafter expressed to be and to constitute a servitude upon said real estate of the Grantors, which estate, interest, easement and servitude will result from the restrictions hereby imposed upon the use of said property of said Grantors, and to that end and for the purpose of accomplishing the intent of the parties hereto said Grantors covenant on behalf of themselves, their heirs, successors and assigns, with the said Grantee, its successors and assigns to do and refrain from doing, severally and collectively, upon the Grantor's said property, the various acts hereinafter mentioned it being hereby agreed and expressed that the doing and the refraining from said acts, and each thereof, upon said property is and will be for the benefit of the said State Park hereinbefore mentioned, of the State of California, and will help preserve the Town of Columbia as a Historic Site.

The restrictions hereby impose upon the use of said property of the Grantors, and the acts which said Grantors so covenant to do and refrain from doing upon their said property in connection therewith are and shall be as follows:

1. That no structures of any kind will be placed or erected upon said described premises until application therefor, with plans and specifications of such structures, together with a statement of the purpose for which the structure will be used, has been filed with and written approval obtained from the said State Park Commission;

2. That no advertising of any kind or nature shall be located on or within said property without written approval being first obtained from the State Park Commission;

3. That no painting or exterior surfacing which, in the opinion and judgment of the said State Park Commission, are inharmonious with the landscape and general surroundings, shall be used on the exterior of any structures now located on such property, or which may, as hereinbefore provided be constructed thereon;

4. That no structural changes or additions shall be made to any of the buildings on said property until an application therefor has been made to

and written approval thereof obtained from said State Park Commission;

5. That all new plantings by the Grantors shall be confined to native plants characteristic of the Columbia State Park region, except flowers, vegetables, berries, fruit trees and farm crops;

6. That the general topography of the landscape shall be maintained in its present condition and that no excavation or topographic changes shall be made without the written approval of the State Park Commission;

7. That no use of said described property, which in the opinion and judgment of said State Park Commission, will or does materially alter the landscape or other attractive scenic features of said land, or will be inconsistent with State Park rules and regulations, or with the proper operation of a State Park, other than those specified above shall be done or suffered without the written consent of the said State Park Commission.

8. The land of the Grantors, hereinabove referred to and to which the provisions of this instrument apply, is situate in the County of Tuolumne, State of California, and is particularly described as follows, to-wit:

EXCEPTING AND RESERVING TO THE GRANTOR:

a. The right to maintain all of the buildings now existing and if all or any of them shall be destroyed or damaged by fire, storm, or other casualty, to restore the same in conformity with the design and type of building of the historic period which the State Park has been established to commemorate; the plans to be submitted and approved by the State Park Commission as provided in Paragraph 1 hereof;

b. Nothing in this instrument shall be construed to affect the right of the Grantors to construct on said premises wells, cistern, cellars, and septic tanks necessary to the maintenance of the property now being constructed or may hereafter be approved for construction by the State Park Commission.

c. If at any time the State of California shall abandon the Town of Columbia State Park, then on the happening of such event all the rights and privileges and easements by this instrument granted and given to the State shall cease and determine to the same effect as though this instrument had never been executed by the Grantors.

TO HAVE AND TO HOLD unto the said State of California, its successors and assigns forever. This grant shall be binding upon the heirs and assigns of the said Grantors and shall constitute a servitude upon the above described land.

IN WITNESS WHEREOF the Grantors have hereunto set their hands the day and year in this instrument first above mentioned.

Appendix C
Digest of Open-Space Zoning Provisions, New York City, 1975

In 1961 New York City enacted a zoning resolution that gave developers a floor-area bonus for providing plaza space. For each square foot of plaza space, the builder was allowed 10 feet of additional commercial floor area. The requirement of the plazas was that they be accessible to the public at all times. That, as it turned out, was about all they were.

The 1975 amendments required that plazas be *amenable* to the public as well, and laid down specific guidelines for insuring that they would be. The guidelines are presented here in slightly abridged form.

1975 ZONING AMENDMENTS

Seating

There shall be a minimum of 1 linear foot of seating for each 30 square feet of urban plaza area, except that for urban plazas fronting upon a street having a grade change of at least 2.25 feet in 100 feet or for through-block urban plazas, there shall be a minimum of 1 linear foot of seating for each 40 square feet of urban plaza area.

Seating shall have a minimum depth of 16 inches. Seating with backs at least 12 inches high shall have a minimum depth of 14 inches. Seating 30 inches or more in depth shall count double provided there is access to both sides.

Seating higher than 36 inches and lower than 12 inches above the level of the adjacent walking surface shall not count toward meeting seating requirements.

The tops of walls including but not limited to those which bound planting beds, fountains, and pools may be counted as seating when they conform to the dimensional standards above.

Movable seating or chairs, excluding seating of open air cafés, may be credited as 30 inches of linear seating per chair.

No more than 50 percent of the credited linear seating capacity may be movable seats which may be stored between the hours of 7 P.M. and 7 A.M.

Steps, seats in outdoor amphitheaters, and seating of open air cafés do not count toward the seating requirements.

For the benefit of handicapped persons, a minimum of 5 percent of the required seating shall have backs.

Planting and Trees

At least one tree of 3.5 inches caliper or more shall be planted for each 25 feet of the entire street frontage of the zoning lot. They shall be planted with gratings flush to grade in at least 200 cubic feet of soil per tree, with a depth of soil at least 3 feet 6 inches.

Trees within an urban open space: For an urban plaza 1,500 square feet or more in area, 4 trees are required. For an urban plaza 5,000 square feet or more in area, 6 trees are required. For an urban plaza 12,000 square feet or more in area, 1 tree is required for every 2,000 square feet, or fraction thereof, of urban plaza area. Where trees are planted within an urban open space, they shall measure at least 3.5 inches in caliper at the time of planting. They shall be planted in at least 200 cubic feet of soil with a depth of soil of at least 3 feet 6 inches and be planted either with gratings flush to grade, or in a planting bed with a continuous area of at least 75 square feet exclusive of bounding wall, and at a maximum spacing of 25 feet apart.

Planting: When planting beds are provided, they shall have a soil depth of at least 2 feet for grass or other ground cover, and 3 feet for shrubs.

Retail Frontage

Except for that portion of a sidewalk widening along a narrow street, at least 50 percent of the total frontage of building walls of the development fronting on an urban open space, or fronting on an arcade adjoining an urban open space, exclusive of such frontage occupied by vertical circulation elements, building lobbies, and frontage used for subway access, shall be allocated for occupancy by retail or service establishments permitted by the applicable district regulations, but not including banks, loan offices, travel agencies, or airline offices. In addition, libraries, museums, and art galleries shall be permitted. All such uses shall be directly accessible from the urban open space or adjoining arcade.

Lighting

Urban open spaces shall be illuminated throughout with an overall minimum average level of illumination of not less than 2 horizontal foot candles (lumens per foot). Such level of illumination shall be maintained throughout the hours of darkness. Electrical power shall be supplied by 1 or more outlets furnishing a total of 1,200 watts of power for every 4,000 square feet, or fraction thereof, of an urban open space area, except for a sidewalk widening.

Circulation and Access

An urban plaza shall be open to use by the public at all times, with direct access from an adjoining public sidewalk or sidewalk widening along at least 50 percent of its total length of frontage. Along the remaining length of frontage, in order to allow maximum visibility from the street to the urban plaza, no wall may be constructed averaging higher than 36 inches above nor at any point higher than 5 feet above curb level of the nearest adjoining street.

The level of an urban plaza shall not at any point be more than 3 feet above nor 3 feet below the curb level of the nearest adjoining street.

Where there is a grade change of at least 2.25 feet in 100 along a portion of a street fronted upon for a distance of at least 75 feet by an urban plaza with an area of 10,000 square feet or more, the level of such urban plaza may be at any elevation which is not more than either 5 feet above or below curb level of the nearest adjoining street. Along the length of frontage not required for access, no wall higher than 36 inches above the level of the urban plaza may be constructed.

Where an entry to a subway station exists in the sidewalk area of a street on which an urban plaza fronts and such entry is not replaced within the urban plaza itself, the urban plaza shall be developed at the same elevation as the adjacent sidewalk for a distance of at least 15 feet in all directions from the entry superstructure. Such urban plaza area around a subway station entry shall be free of all obstructions.

Where an entry to a subway station is provided within the urban plaza itself, stairs shall have a minimum width of 10 feet.

An urban plaza or portion of an urban plaza extending through the block and connecting 2 streets which are parallel or within 45 degrees of being parallel to each other shall have a minimum width of 40 feet.

Any portion of a building wall adjoining such urban plaza for a length greater than 125 feet shall be limited to a maximum height of 85 feet above the urban plaza level, and above such height the building shall be set back not less than 15 feet from the urban plaza boundary, provided that such restriction shall not apply to any building wall adjoining an urban plaza which urban plaza has a minimum width of 75 feet.

Access for the Physically Disabled

There shall be at least one path of travel to each of the following:

- the major portion of the urban open space
- any building lobby accessible to the urban open space
- any use that may be present on, or adjacent to, the urban open space

Such paths shall have a minimum width of 5 feet, except where specific provisions require a greater width, free and clear of all obstructions.

Ramps are to be provided alongside any stairs or steps for such paths. Ramps shall have a minimum width of 36 inches, a slope of not greater than 1 in 12, a nonskid surface, and, for open-edged ramps, a 2-inch-high safety curb. At each end of a ramp there shall be a level area, which may be public sidewalk, at least 5 feet long.

All stairs or ramps within such paths shall provide handrails. Handrails shall be 32 inches high, have a midrail 22 inches high, and shall extend at least 18 inches beyond the stair or ramp ends.

Where stairs are used to effect changes of grade for such paths, they shall have closed risers, no projecting nosings, a maximum riser height of 7.5 inches, and a minimum tread width of 11 inches.

Food Facilities; Permitted Obstructions

Urban open space shall be unobstructed from its lowest level to the sky except for the following obstructions, which are permitted only in urban plazas and open air concourses, but not permitted in sidewalk widenings: any features, equipment, and appurtenances normally found in public parks and playgrounds, such as fountains and reflecting pools, waterfalls, sculptures and other works of art, arbors, trellises, benches, seats, trees, planting beds, litter receptacles, drinking fountains, and bicycle racks; open air cafes; kiosks; outdoor furniture; lights and lighting stanchions; flag poles; public telephones; temporary exhibitions; awnings; canopies; bollards; and subway station entrances which may include escalators. Kiosks, open air cafes, and open air amphitheaters and ice-skating rinks which charge admission may be placed within the area of an urban open space upon certification by the

Chairman of the City Planning Commission and the Board of Estimate to the Commissioner of Buildings.

Where a kiosk is provided, it shall be a one-story structure, predominantly of light materials, such as metal, glass, plastic, or fabric which does not exceed 150 square feet in area.

Where an open air café is provided it shall be a permanently unenclosed eating or drinking place, permitted by applicable district regulations, which may have waiter or table service, and is open to the sky except that it may have a temporary fabric roof in conformance with Building Code.

An open air café must be accessible from all sides where there is a boundary with the remainder of the urban open space.

An open air café may occupy an aggregate area not more than 20 percent of the total area of the urban open space.

No kitchen equipment shall be installed within an open air café. Kitchen equipment may be contained in a kiosk adjoining the open air café.

An open air café qualifying as a permitted obstruction shall be excluded from the definition of floor area.

Outdoor eating services or uses occupying kiosks may serve customers on urban open space through open windows.

For wheelchair users, where drinking fountains are placed in an urban open space, at least one fountain shall be 30 inches high, be hand and foot operated, and display the International Symbol of Access.

Maintenance

The building owner shall be responsible for the maintenance of the urban open space including, but not limited to, the confinement of permitted obstructions, litter control, and the care and replacement of vegetation within the zoning lot and in the street sidewalk area adjacent to the zoning lot.

Performance Bond

Prior to obtaining any certificate of occupancy from the Department of Buildings, the building owner shall provide to the Comptroller of the City of New York, a performance bond or the City securities to ensure the mandatory tree planting, movable seating and the litter-free maintenance of the urban open space including the replacement of such trees and movable furniture during the life of the development.

In the event of a failure in the required performance, the Chairman of the City Planning Commission shall notify the building owner in writing of such failure and shall stipulate the period of time in which the building owner has to correct the failure. If the failure is not corrected in the stipulated time the Chairman may declare the building owner in default in the required performance, and the City may enforce the obligation by whatever means may be appropriate to the situation, including letting contracts for doing any required planting, installation or maintenance and paying all labor, material and other costs connected with such work from the bond or City securities the building owner is required to provide.

Plaque

A plaque or other permanent sign shall be displayed in a prominent location on any urban open space for which a bonus is granted. Such sign shall indicate number of trees, and number of movable chairs, and any other features whose listing may be required by the City Planning Commission, the name of the owner and whomever he has designated to maintain the urban open space.

Existing Plazas

For plazas built prior to this amendment, kiosks and cafés may be placed within the area of the plaza upon certification by the Chairman of the City Planning Commission and the Board of Estimate that such uses would promote public use and enjoyment, stabilize desirable uses in the surrounding area, are part of a general improvement including more seating and landscaping, and that the uses will be maintained by the owner.

Other Provisions

Location and orientation: southern exposure is required wherever possible. To protect the continuity of the street wall, the frontage a plaza can occupy is restricted when there are other large spaces nearby.

Proportional restrictions: to discourage strip plazas, width of plazas must not be less than a third of the length.

Open-air concourses: these apply to spaces adjacent to subway stations and were written with the proposed Second Avenue subway in mind. They call for a sunken plaza at mezzanine level of no less than 4,000 square feet nor more than 8,000. At street level there should be walkways at least 20 feet wide, and, space permitting, a street-level plaza.

UNITED STATES DISTRICT COURT,

SOUTHERN DISTRICT OF NEW YORK

ROBERT TURLEY, Plaintiff,

against NEW YORK CITY POLICE DEPARTMENT and NEW YORK CITY DEPARTMENT OF PARKS AND RECREATION, RAYMOND W. KELLY, in his official capacity, and BETSY GOTBAUM, WILLIAM F. DALTON, ALEXANDER R. BRASH, MICHAEL FOX, KEVIN DOUGHERTY, and RAYMOND SPINELLA, in their individual and official capacities, Defendants.

COUNTY OF NEW YORK,

STATE OF NEW YORK

WILLIAM H. WHYTE, being duly sworn, deposes and says:

1. I am a writer, urban planning consultant, and long-time resident of New York City. My most recently published book, entitled *City: Rediscovering the Center* (1988), resulted from 16 years spent studying the street life of New York City and other major cities. I make this affidavit in support of plaintiff Robert Turley's motion for a preliminary injunction. I have received no remuneration for making this affidavit.

2. Many people work the streets of New York City. They fall into several categories: the regulars, the irregulars, the odd people and the underlife. The regulars include police officers, mail carriers, sanitation workers, doormen, and store owners, some of whom spend a lot of time standing in their doorways. The irregulars, who outnumber the regulars, include handbill passers, book vendors, merchandise vendors, pushcart food vendors, and, of course, street entertainers. Then there are the odd people acting out their fantasies on the streets such as Mr. Magoo, the stocky, red-faced, nattily dressed man in his seventies who directs traffic. The underlife has a rich

cast too, including beggars, the pitchmen for phony causes, and three-card-monte players.

3. New York City has the greatest street life in the world, due in no small part to its street entertainers. The City has a long tradition of talented street entertainers, including many street musicians. Twenty years ago, I wrote about the "fantastic collection of street entertainers" observed along a stretch of Fifth Avenue: "steel drum player at 60th Street; flutist at 59th; mime at 58th; two girl folk-singers at 54th; the Krishnas at 53rd; a trio playing Bach at 49th. There are acrobats, musicians, one-man bands, violinists, karate groups, animal acts." (Whyte, "The Best Street Life in the World: Why Schmoozing, Smooching, Noshing, Ogling Are Getting Better All the Time," *New York*, July 15, 1974, at 26, 27.)

4. One way or another, all street entertainers make a pitch for money. They make the rounds of the crowd passing the hat, they have someone pass it, or they have an empty instrument case or box in front of them. Propped up on it may be a hand-lettered sign with an admonition that may read: "No credit cards please" or "Support live music." The solicitation and donation of money is an integral part of every street entertainer's performance. Street entertainers usually acknowledge audience donations with a smile and a thank-you. A street musician may salute with a few high notes. The accepting, in sum, is done with grace. Rarely do entertainers express any discourtesy to those who do not give. There is never any coercion or threats in street entertainers' solicitations of donations from their audiences.

5. Street entertainers are a temperamental lot, many with large egos. But there is a good bit of occupational camaraderie among them. They are cooperative in settling territorial problems. On a busy afternoon they will work out a loose agreement as to who will play when at a key public space. They all recognize that no single street entertainer should be allowed to monopolize a choice location. At the steps of the Metropolitan Museum of Art, for example, there may be four or five acts waiting to go on but none will encroach on the one that is playing. While they are waiting, they serve as a volunteer claque and vigorously applaud the others' acts.

6. The size of the space is not the important factor for street entertainers. What most look for is *not* a place where they will draw a large crowd for a single show *but rather* a place with a strong flow-a constantly self-renewing audience of regulars, such as office workers, and of tourists. Street entertainers' complete shows seldom last more than 20 or 30 minutes, because their audiences are on their way to some destination, such as back to the

office, where they must be by a certain time.

7. Why does someone choose to become a street entertainer? Some do so primarily for the money. But most street entertainers truly enjoy performing on the streets. They speak of free choice, the give-and-take with people, the honing of one's skills, and the immediacy of the audience. They also speak of what it is like when there is no audience, and of the humiliation of performing when no one stops to look or listen. Street entertainers praise the toughness of street audiences in New York City and say of all audiences, New Yorkers are the toughest. But also the most appreciative. If you collect from them, they say, you've got to be good, which is to say they are pretty good themselves. By contrast, if you're not very good, you won't attract audiences and collect donations. The marketplace of the street thus limits the ranks of street entertainers without government intervention.

8. It is interesting to watch people as they chance upon a street entertainer. So often they will smile at the spontaneous entertainment. A string quartet. Here at Forty-fourth! Their smile is like that of a child. For a few moments, they seem utterly at ease, their shoulders relaxed, temporarily forgetting the realities of daily life. People enjoy programmed entertainment, too, but not the same way. It is the unexpected that seems to delight them most.

9. Street entertainers can have a strong binding effect on people. There is a communal sense to these gatherings and though it may be fleeting, it is the city at its best. I remember especially the end of a mime's act in front of the Pulitzer Foundation at Fifty-ninth Street. The mime was making fun of people. He walked up to two junior executives and drew a square in the air over them. Everybody laughed, even the junior executives. Then a police officer walked across the plaza with a side-to-side swinging gait. The mime followed behind him with the same side-to-side swinging gait. The police officer saw people laughing, looked over his shoulder at the mime, laughed, turned to the mime, and shook his hand. The crowd applauded. It was a splendid moment, a very city kind of moment.

10. Historically, the police have warred against street entertainers, or, to be more accurate, have been made to war. Left to their own judgments, police officers usually take a live-and-let-live stance, though a few officers may take out their own frustrations on street entertainers. When a police officer does move against a street entertainer, he may tell him he's sorry, but the captain has been on his back. And the captain has been on the officer's back because the merchants have been on the captain's back. The end result of the merchants' concern is that police officers on the beat may—

rightly or wrongly—charge street entertainers with making unreasonable noise, obstructing the sidewalk, or soliciting money.

11. Merchants have been the main force against street entertainers. It is odd that people who champion the free market are against such a pure expression of it. What is so wrong about street entertainers' solicitation of voluntary donations from their audiences? Passersby are under no duress whatsoever. They don't even have to stop. If they do stop, they don't have to give. If they give, the amount entirely depends upon their judgment of the worth of the street entertainment. It is the street entertainer who takes the entrepreneurial risk. He or she should be entitled to some reward. The donations received by street entertainers are not charity but rather hard-earned wages for providing public entertainment.

12. Similarly, merchants' complaints that many street entertainers obstruct city sidewalks to the point of endangerment are clearly unfounded, as I demonstrated in two federal court lawsuits brought by street musicians in which I testified as an expert witness. The first lawsuit involved a challenge to an ordinance adopted by the City of Alexandria, Virginia, in 1981, at the behest of merchants, which banned street entertainers from performing anywhere in the central business district and restricted them to certain designated park areas. Some merchants had reportedly observed instances of sidewalk blocking, and the city manager had said that he once saw people pour out on the street because of an entertainer. I showed, however, that the city's own pedestrian traffic counts and sidewalk measurements demonstrated an excellent balance between sidewalk space and pedestrian flows-no more than 2.8 persons per foot per minute of passing pedestrians, a pedestrian "ease" level well below the standard for pedestrian comfort. The federal courts agreed, declaring the ban on street entertainers in the central business district invalid. See *Davenport v. City of Alexandria*, No. 81-709-A (E.D. Va. Nov. 16, 1983), *aff'd*, 748 F. 2d 208 (4th Cir. 1984).

13. I also testified on behalf of street entertainers in Chicago, when they challenged a city ordinance, again adopted at the behest of merchants, that effectively banned them from performing in the upper Michigan Avenue area. The city contended that sidewalk congestion in that area had reached drastic levels, and that street entertainers added sorely to this congestion and should be banned, providing more room for pedestrian safety and comfort. It was an extraordinary complaint. Of all the avenues in the United States, few have broader sidewalks than upper Michigan Avenue, which range between 30 and 35 feet in width. Pedestrian volumes were strong but did not tax these sidewalks. The amount of space per pedestrian was very

generous and provided a level of service that rated an "A" by anybody's computation. Although recognizing that street entertainment could be curbed when it threatened public safety, the federal court found that a complete ban on street entertainment in the upper Michigan area was substantially broader than necessary because pedestrian flows diminished at certain times and on certain days. While upholding the ban on street entertainment in the upper Michigan Avenue area during some periods, the court made clear that the justification for even that partial ban would disappear if breakdancing, which tended to draw the largest crowds, proved to be merely a fad: "If it has passed, and if—as the evidence showed—*most other performers attract only small crowds*, the constitutional underpinnings of the ordinance may have vanished for future years." See *Freidrich v. City of Chicago*, 619 F. Supp. 1129, 1144 (N.D. Ill. 1985) (emphasis added).

14. In sum, street entertainers greatly enhance the quality of life on New York City streets, temporarily relieving people's tensions and creating a sense of community through spontaneous entertainment. Their solicitations are entirely appropriate, non-coercive requests to be paid for their entertainment. They rarely obstruct pedestrian traffic and generally accommodate competing uses of public spaces, including other street entertainment. Their ranks will always be limited by the marketplace because street entertainers who are not very good will have a difficult time collecting donations from the tough audiences in New York City.

WILLIAM H. WHYTE
October 7, 1994

Notes

THE TRANSIENTS

1. William Miller, ed., *Men in Business*, a publication of the Research Center in Entrepreneurial History, Harvard University, 1952.

HOW THE NEW SUBURBIA SOCIALIZES

1. In a detailed study of a housing project for married M.I.T. students, the importance of centrality has been well documented. In building after building, couples located near the routes of greatest traffic tended to have many more social contacts than those on the edges. (Leon Festinger, Stanley Schachter, and Kurt Back, *Social Pressures in Informal Groups* [New York: Harper, 1950].)

2. Bridge scores are another case in point. In bridge groups in traditional communities there is usually a pronounced ranking of the players. A performance chart of the number of times members of two particular Park Forest bridge clubs have won prizes shows an opposite result; per number of games, everyone wins about as many times as everyone else.

FROM *THE ORGANIZATION MAN*

1. Similar tendencies have been noticed among German youth. In *Der Junge Arbeiter von Heute*, Karl Bednarik, a former leader in the socialist youth movement, has commented on the "bourgeoisification" of younger workers as a response to the postwar situation.

THE CASE FOR THE UNIVERSAL CARD

1. Most pictures now used are too simple to bring out more than one latent psychosis. Our idea is to include cues in the picture that could bring out every possible syndrome. Thus, in addition to the customary man staring out of a window, there would be a picture on the wall of a white-haired woman (to trigger any Oedipus complex the subject may have). Similarly, we could work in father symbols, etc.

2. Cardholders would no longer have reason to carry credit cards and eventually, through the cooperation of state governments, the card would serve as operator's

license and car-registration certificate. Since the Universal Card would in effect have then become one's passport to society—what if you lost it on a trip? Conceivably you could find yourself stranded without access to lodging or food. We would overcome the danger this way: if you lost your card you would go to the office of the nearest member corporation. They would teletype the central headquarters where your master card would be checked and a coded description of the fingerprint wired back. As soon as the fingerprint was verified by matching, the member organization would issue you a temporary pass.

URBAN SPRAWL

1. Round table participants: Government and Law: Charles Abrams, chairman, N.Y. State Commission against Discrimination; Edmund Bacon, AIA director, Philadelphia City Planning Commission; Karl Belser, director, Santa Clara, Calif., Planning Department; Luther Gulick, president, Institute of Public Administration; Charles Haar, Harvard Law School; Bernard Hillenbrand, director, National Association of County Officials; Development: James Scheuer, chairman, City & Suburban Homes Co.; Stuart Walsh, director, Industrial Planning Associates; Taxation: Mabel Walker, executive director, Tax Institute; Economics and Planning: Edward A. Ackerman, Resources for the Future; Catherine Bauer, University of California; Charles W. Eliot, Harvard University Graduate School of Design; Henry Fagin, planning director, Regional Plan Association; Carl Feiss, AIA, planning consultant; Joseph Intermaggio, Committee on Urban Research, National Academy of Science; Paul B. Sears, Yale Conservation Program; Recreation: Joseph Prendergast, executive director, National Recreation Association; Transportation: David R. Levin, U.S. Bureau of Public Roads; Wilfred Owen, Brookings Institution; Presiding: Douglas Haskell, editor, Architectural Forum and William H. Whyte Jr., assistant managing editor, *Fortune*.

FROM *SECURING OPEN SPACE FOR URBAN AMERICA*

1. The standard work is *The Law of Eminent Domain,* by Philip Nichols, originally published in 1909 by Matthew Bender & Co., N.Y. It has since been extensively annotated by J. L. Sachman and R. D. van Brunt (See third edition, Bender, 1950), and the footnotes bringing it up to date have swelled it to many heavy volumes. Nichols's original running text, however, stands up admirably; even a layman can understand it, for Nichols had an inclination to plain English.
2. The law of easements in the United States is virtually identical with English law (and was borrowed by us, it might be added, several centuries before the English Town and Country Planning legislation). Here, as in England, the essential features of an easement are (1) that it is an incorporeal right, a right to the use and enjoyment of land—not to the land itself; (2) that it is imposed on corporeal property; (3) that it is a right without profit; (4) that it requires two distinct tenements: the dominant, which enjoys the right; the servient, which submits to it.

(E.g., a park commission which purchases a scenic easement would be the "dominant tenement." The owner of the property to which it applies would be the "servient tenement"—not just the owner who agreed to the purchase, but also subsequent ones, since the easement "runs with the land.")

3. *Requirements and Procedure to Govern the Acquisition of Land for National Parkways* (Washington, D.C.: National Park Service).

4. Earl A. Disque, "Land Use Treatment as Related to Maintenance" (Washington, D.C.: Highway Research Board, 1959).

5. Dudley C. Bayliss, "Planning Our National Park Roads and Our National Parkways" (Washington, D.C.: National Park Service, 1957).

6. *Madisonville Traction Co. v. St. Bernard Mining Co.*, 196 U.S. 239, 25 Sup. Ct., 251 (1905).

7. Nichols, Ch IV. Sec. 48. "If the use for which land is taken by eminent domain is public, the taking is not invalid merely because an incidental benefit will inure to individuals."

8. "That the public gets no physical use of the premises is clear. It cannot travel upon or occupy them. The use acquired, so far as the general public is concerned, is rather negative in character, except, perhaps, that its sense of the appropriate and harmonious will not be offended by the erection in the condemned district of proscribed buildings. The condemnation does not take any part of the ground away from the owner; the taking consists in restricting its use. He is compensated for the restrictions imposed." State ex rel. *Twin City Building & Investment Co. v. Houghton*, 144 Minn. 1, 176 N.W. 159 (1920).

9. Even the Pennsylvania courts. They have had rather a bad reputation with planners, but though some of their decisions on zoning have been highly conservative, they have kept up with the trend to a liberal construction of the eminent domain power. In *Oliver v. City of Clairton*, 374 Pa. 333, 98 Atl. 2d 47 (1953), land 90 percent vacant and unimproved was declared to be blighted land and condemned so that it could be redeveloped for industry. The courts supported the city on this.

10. By the same token, farmers can lament that planners don't pay much attention to farming. "Today we planners," writes one, "have done almost nothing for agriculture, because, I fear, we know so little about its needs. Even when we believe that it should be preserved, we don't know enough about the specific criteria of crop growth and land use relationships to do anything positive about it. In fact, by and large we tend to consider agriculture as a single entity without distinguishing between its vastly differing varieties and their respective characteristics and needs. How many land use maps and master plans lump all agriculture into one classification? Practically all do. From our study we believe that we must have at our fingertips such a sufficient command of basic agricultural information that we may distinguish floriculture from dairy or from poultry, as we would distinguish commercial, industrial, and residential land uses." From a letter from Leonard C. Moffit, Alameda County Planning Commission, May 20, 1959.

11. For up-to-date documentation, aerial photos can be very compelling. For people on the Eastern Seaboard, it should be noted that Aero Service Corp. at 210 E. Courtland St., Philadelphia, Pa., in the summer of 1959 made a photographic flight with a new type camera which yields picture enlargements of extraordinary detail. The photos diagram vividly the interstices of the urban area.

12. For supporting data see: Proceedings, National Conference on Air Pollution, Nov. 18–20, 1958. U.S. Department of Health, Education and Welfare.

FROM *THE LAST LANDSCAPE*

1. This was a pioneering program without enough pioneers. The National Park Service laid down excellent specifications for the rights-of-way, but the actual job of acquiring them was up to state highway departments, with the result that many of the easements were negotiated by people who did not much believe in easements. The variance in attitudes showed up in the costs: in Mississippi, for example, easements averaged only 3 to 10 percent of fee simple costs; in Virginia, 40 percent. Negotiators did not follow a standard practice for appraisal and when farmers later compared prices with each other a number got mad because they felt they had been out-dickered. Exposition of the device was spotty. When the National Park Service took over the parkways, it found that many landowners had been given no clear idea as to what they could and could not do on the easement land. This caused enforcement problems, particularly with woodland. Over the years, the parkways have proved out very well indeed, but for quite some time these early easement problems were widely cited as reason for experimenting no further.

2. Experience along the earlier Blue Ridge Parkway has not been as satisfactory. In the *Appraisal Journal* of January 1968, Howard L. Williams and W. D. Davis report that a study of land sales along the parkway in one county in North Carolina indicate that portions of property covered by scenic easements fetched appreciably less on the market than comparable land without easements. They also found, however, that owners did not suffer any loss of value, or "severance damages," on the remainder of their properties.

3. An old, but very excellent case in point is Macdougal Gardens in New York's Greenwich Village. This is a block of old houses in which the rear portions of the backyards were combined into a commons. It is an extremely pleasant place and because of the old trees and the adjoining gardens of the houses, the space seems quite large. But it isn't. The width of the commons itself is only thirty-five feet.

4. Planning brochures and promotional literature for new towns have become so standardized in their themes and illustrations that much effort could be spared if one all-purpose brochure were worked up. It would include the following: (a) aerial picture of farmland taken in 1945; (b) aerial picture of same area ten years later, covered with subdivisions; (c) photo of massed rooftops and TV aerials; (d) photo of neon signs, gas stations, and pizza stands on commercial highway; (e) photo of cars in traffic jam; (f) sign at entrance to state park saying "filled";

(g) bulldozer hacking at hillside. Next come the good things: (a) photo of new town center at Stevenage or Vallingby or Tapiola; (b) the Tivoli gardens in Copenhagen; (c) impressionistic drawing of U.S. new town center, with a group of children holding balloons; (d) picture of intelligent-looking people around a table looking at a planner pointing to a map; (e) flow chart of proper planning steps. Either at the front or at the back there will be one or two mood pictures. A special favorite is a photo of two children walking hand in hand through a woods.

5. Philosophically, the most influential exponent of low-density housing has been Britain's Town and Country Planning Association. It equates high-density housing with standard high-rise projects. It detests them, with good reason, and has been berating the authorities for continuing to build them. People do not like living in them as well as in low-rise housing, the Association argues, and they especially miss having private gardens of their own. This is a strong case, but in arguing it the Association gives short shrift to the possibility of designing the more human scale low-rise housing to higher densities. To do so, it warns, would be to court the delusion that "skill can create a new Utopia by cleverer compression." This polarizes the case much too much. Utopia, no, but surely there is a middle ground between high-density towers and low-density garden towns. People who want to build only towers like to have the argument thus polarized. Just goes to prove, they say, that they have no reasonable alternative.

6. One phenomenon they might look into is the way people often jam up in groups when they do not have to. Cocktail parties, for example. People who go to them habitually complain about the crowding, the noise, and the smoke. But notice how they behave. They do not like too much room. They bunch together and toward the end of the party they will have themselves all jammed into one corner of an otherwise empty room. The way people behave in the out-of-doors is not totally dissimilar. In a trenchant study of national parks, Noel Eichorn and Frank Fraser Darling comment on the curious psychology of the campground: "To some of us [it is] a quite baffling phenomenon. Mr. Lon Garrison told us of his study in Yosemite in the 1930s when he found that many people apparently like being crowded in camp grounds. At least, when the density of occupation of camp grounds decreased after Labor Day, there was a general movement from the outliers to the center, where the density consequently remained high." (*Man and Nature in the National Parks* [Washington, D.C.: The Conservation Foundation, 1967])

NEW YORK AND TOKYO

1. One example is the urban open-space grant program. When it was enacted in 1961 a provision was stuck in disqualifying any open-space project fewer than 25 acres. This was to prevent cities from squandering the money on "bits and pieces" of space—i.e., about the only kind that center cities could acquire. The provision has been lifted; but thanks to other constraints, the great bulk of open-space grant funds disbursed through federal programs had gone to suburban and rural areas.

2. In spot checks of pedestrians in 1929, Mr. Kon found that in the Ginza area 64 percent were younger people; in Shinjuku, 59 percent. This tendency still seems to be true today.

3. To earn the plaza bonus of extra floor space, developers must provide at least one linear foot of sitting space per 30 square feet of open space. We did not measure the Mitsui Plaza's sitting space, but cursory estimates indicated it would far surpass these minimums.

4. One result will be that store owners won't hog the spaces the way they have been; or diplomats or doctors or policemen or the special privilege parkers who have accounted for the bulk of the center's parking, legal or otherwise. The idea that parking meters encourage bulk turnover by shoppers is a myth. Spaces are dominated by long-haul parkers—such as store owners.

5. Pedestrian counts are generally given as a total figure for both sidewalks. In many cases, however, there can be a substantial difference between one side and the other, especially when there is a traffic generator as important as a department store on one side.

6. The handbill passers were as efficient as any we have studied. The best we've checked in New York is Handbill Frank: his completion rate averages about 50 percent acceptances to offers, rising to 58 percent at rush hour, when he works best. The two at Asakusa were averaging 63 percent. They had, it should be noted, a superior routine. Both were dressed in ancient garb. One worked as advance man, holding aloft a sign counseling people to take the interesting card that would be given them. The other gave out cards. (They were for a nearby restaurant featuring eels.) As in New York, most of the people who took handbills read them. Unhappily for the litter problem, handbills are a very effective form of advertising.

FROM CITY

1. It is in order to be as unobtrusive as possible, but in studying a particular place—such as Lexington Avenue in the Upper Fifties—the regulars spot you very quickly. If you are frank with them and explain what you are up to, they can be quite helpful. On Lexington we ended up knowing a larger number of regulars than we expected to be there: proprietors of small stores; haircutting establishments, and their hawkers and handbill passers; bus dispatchers, traffic people, various shills and messengers—even several of the "six lovely conversationalists" who used to lean out the third-floor window of the Lexington Rap Club. Street vendors could be a problem. They tend to be very suspicious, particularly of people with cameras. Dope dealers are the worst. You never can be sure who is a dope dealer and who isn't. In some areas, if you film in any direction you are quite likely to film a dope transaction, whether you realize it or not. The dealers do not like this at all. In Bryant Park, which they long regarded as their territory, it was risky to even carry a camera.

A salute is in order. When we started observing people on the streets of Tokyo, we found that an avid observer had been doing the same thing fifty years before. He was Wajiro Kon, a noted ethnologist of indefatigable curiosity. He charted the daily flows of students as they went to school and back; he charted the character of the crowds at various places, with a detailed breakdown of their dress, apparent age, and occupation. He noted how many people were in groups (75 percent on Ginza streets), and how far they walked. He even plotted the locations of suicides in Hibaya Park. (Wajiro Kon, *Kogengaku: Studies of the Past and Present* [1930; reprint, Tokyo: Domesu, 1971]. In it Kon used the word "modernologio," or studies in modernology, to describe his work.)

2. The importance to street vendors of helpers and allies is noted in Randolph David's fine study of Manila's street life: "In addition to the police the practical problems of vending are the simple problems of surviving a particularly slow and boring day without falling asleep, of getting a quick meal, or using the toilet while one's wares continue to be on display. For all these needs, a companion is needed. And, indeed, it seems standard policy for vendors to go at least in pairs. Unavoidably, a number of vendors will not be able to bring a companion. In such cases, fellow vendors tend to assume the responsibility for assisting one another. We have observed that, for instance, ambulant vendors effectively play the role of companion to many of their static and semi-static counterparts."

3. *Friedrich v. City of Chicago*, 619 F. Supp. 1129 (N.D. Ill. 1985), *vacated* F 2d, (7th Cir. November 25. 1986) Judge Marvin E. Aspen.

4. To study Lexington is to realize how significant can be the *nonmovement* of pedestrians. Most pedestrian studies scant this, being primarily concerned with the journey from A to B. They do not tell us much about what happens between A and B—or the fact that sometimes the pedestrian never gets to B at all. To chart the incidents of the journey, we made a series of tracking shots of people walking north on a Lexington blockfront. Here is what happened to ninety-five of them: sixteen went into one of the stores on the block; one turned around and walked back south; two stopped for a midblock conversation lasting five minutes; seventy-six completed the journey, with an average elapsed time of fifty-eight seconds—slow compared to speeds on duller, less busy streets. What the pedestrian walks by can materially affect this pace. As they passed the florist's stand, some people slowed, then made up for lost time by accelerating as they came to the dull façade of the Manufacturers Hanover Trust.

The vexations of city officials in keeping order are much like those of their counterparts in medieval England. In his book *Street Life in Medieval England* (Oxford, 1939), G. T. Salusbury-Jones tells how earnestly they tried to keep traffic moving on the main streets. They were frustrated by the narrowness of them, the encroachments, such as pens and stalls, and they were especially annoyed by the shod cart and its metallic banging. They also had a problem with pigs; they liked the street because it was so full of refuse. Streets were very noisy: there were bells of all kinds constantly ringing; the crying of wares; the sound of wooden galoshes, craftsmen banging away in their stalls, which were open to the street; the clatter of shod cart wheels. Not until noon, at the "schenche," or noon-drink, was there a respite.

5. "Undesirables" were one of the reasons the proposed Madison Avenue mall was beaten down. During the two-week trial of it our cameras recorded what went on. The film showed clearly that the people who used the mall were the people who worked and shopped in the area. But some retailers saw "undesirables." If the place had been overrun with angels they would have seen undesirables. While I was talking to one shop owner, she noted two young women in blue jeans writing things on pads. "There they are!" said the shop owner, pointing to two of our observers.

6. The Project for Public Spaces has used direct observation and time-lapse photography for a series of studies of key open spaces, ranging from Harlem's 125th Street to visitor centers of the National Park Service. It has been most effective in retrofitting problem spaces. One was the Exxon Minipark in New York City. A twelve-minute video is available on this study and reports on a range of studies. Project for Public Spaces, 153 Waverly Place, New York, NY 10014.

7. For a perceptive study of teenage "undesirables" see Nancy Linday, "Drawing Socio-economic Lines in Central Park: An Analysis of New York's Cultural Clashes," *Landscape Architecture* (November 1977). Back in 1973 we were asked by then Park Commissioner Richard Clurman to undertake a study of the troubles at Bethesda Fountain. It had become the central rendezvous for Hispanic teenagers, and there were problems with dope and vandalism. One of our best observers, Nancy Linday, spent a summer there as part of the scene. She found that the place was one of the few where the teenagers were welcome, and most of them were making good use of it, however raucous they might seem to the tourists who came to gawk at them. Among her recommendations: enlist the teenagers in programming and maintenance; make more use of their leaders as "mayors."

8. Paris, birthplace of the *vespasienne,* is trying out a new style of comfort station. Instead of the traditional cylindrical structure for men, there is an oval-shaped, fully enclosed structure and it is for either men or women. It contains a washbasin and toilet. When the patron closes the door on leaving, a self-cleaning and disinfecting process is automatically started.

9. An oddity in the plans for some office buildings are the plans for the equipment floors. The equipment is mostly for air-conditioning and heating; otherwise the floors are empty and thus do not count as part of the developer's quota of allowable commercial space. On one plan I saw recently there was a full-size men's room and a full-size women's room. Since no one save a few engineers would ever visit the floor, the provision did seem wasteful. But was it? Someday, perhaps, the developer might find that he didn't really need that equipment floor. Maybe it could be used for offices. With rest rooms already in place.

10. In an excellent study for the upgrading of Lincoln Center's concourse center and shops, consultant Paco Underhill made special note of the ladies' room. It was the

same size as the men's room and, like most ladies' rooms in public places, had a line outside it at peak times. He recommended that it be at least doubled in size, a preferable ratio being $2^1/_2$ to 1. This has not yet been done. (Paco Underhill, "Vive la Difference," *Express* [1984].)

11. A notable blank wall is the one recently built for the Los Angeles County Museum of Art. It takes the wicked pen of Manuela Hoelterhoff to do it justice. Writing in *The Wall Street Journal* (December 15, 1987), she says, "The original complex by William Periera, recently deceased and rarely admired, featured pavilions leading off from an open, stepped and elevated courtyard on Wilshire Boulevard. These pavilions wouldn't have won a beauty contest but in their own leprous little way made friendly gestures to the park behind and the sky above . . . A simply immense wall has been put up along Wilshire. It hides the Periera complex and new building, but it is also about as inviting as Lenin's tomb. This sepulchral expanse is penetrated by a very steep ceremonial staircase, and you might feel rewarded in your effort if the embalmed remains of the chiefs of Atlantic Richfield, the building's biggest sponsor, were there to greet you at the top."

12. Further requirements for street-level retailing are being incorporated into the zoning for the theater district. Developers will have to have retailing on their side-street frontage as well as their avenue frontage. Stores will have to take up at least half of the side-street frontage and be no more than forty feet wide. The planners hope this will spur more theater-related uses, such as instrument shops. costume shops, and the like. San Francisco's planning department puts strong emphasis on retail continuity. For commercial districts it provides that retail uses be the primary uses of the ground floor. "Space fronting on pedestrian rights-of-way should be principally devoted to windows, display space and other uses which are of interest to pedestrians, except for required door entries. Blank walls should be allowed only if circumstances indicate no feasible alternative."

An example of citizen concern over blank walls was the reaction to one aspect of the plans for Toronto's Eaton Centre. It promised to be a handsome atrium complex with lots of glass. But along one side, on Yonge Street, it was going to present a largely blank wall. Yonge Street had become raunchy but it remained high in the affection of many citizens. The architect was asked to open up more access to Yonge Street and get some storefronts on the street. He did so. The Centre has been a popular success, and while the Yonge Street part is somewhat tacky, it is a lot better than a blank wall.

13. The comparison study is based on two groups: (1) major industrial firms that had left New York City for a suburban headquarters location prior to 1977; (2) major industrial firms that had their headquarters in New York City prior to 1977 and stayed there. Period of comparison: December 31, 1976, to December 31, 1987.

Initially, the suburban group numbered thirty-nine firms. There was a rather severe attrition, however, with seventeen of the firms being dropped because they had lost their identity through merger or acquisition.

The New York City group was more stable. Of the initial thirty-nine, only two were dropped because of merger or acquisition.

Earlier in the research on this book I had computed the relative performances for the decade 1976–86. As time went on—and the market suffered a crash—I extended the study to include 1987. It did not make much difference. For the ten-year period, the suburban firms averaged an increase of 107 percent; the city firms, 303 percent. For eleven years the respective averages were 107 percent and 277 percent.

Selected Works by William H. Whyte

BOOKS

Is Anybody Listening? How and Why U.S. Business Fumbles When It Talks With Human Beings. With the editors of Fortune. New York: Simon & Schuster, 1952.

The Organization Man. New York: Simon & Schuster, 1956.

The Exploding Metropolis. Editor. New York: Doubleday, 1957.

Securing Open Space for Urban America: Conservation Easements. Washington, D.C.: Urban Land Institute (Technical Bulletin 36), 1959.

Open Space Action: A Report to the Outdoor Recreation Resources Review Commission. Washington, D.C.: U.S. Government Printing Office (ORRRC Study Report 15), 1962.

Cluster Development. New York: American Conservation Association, 1964.

The Last Landscape. New York: Doubleday, 1968.

The Social Life of Small Urban Spaces. Washington, D.C.: The Conservation Foundation, 1980.

City: Rediscovering the Center. New York: Doubleday, 1988.

A Time of War: Remembering Guadalcanal, A Battle Without Maps. New York: Fordham University Press, 2000.

ARTICLES

The Class of '49. Fortune (June 1949), 84+.

The Transients. Fortune (June 1949), 113+.

The Future, c/o Park Forest. Fortune (June 1953), 126+.

The Outgoing Life. Fortune (July 1953), 84+.

How the New Suburbia Socializes. Fortune (August 1953), 120+.

You, Too, Can Write the Casual Style. Harper's (October 1953), 87–89.

The Executives' Problem: The Executive. Fortune (January 1954), 79.

The Fallacies of "Personality" Testing. Fortune (September 1954), 117–21.

The Web of Word of Mouth. Fortune (November 1954), 140+.

The Case for the Universal Card. Fortune (April 1955), 137+. (Published under the pseudonym of Otis Binet Stanford.)

"Give the Devils No Mercy." *Fortune* (December 1955), 146–48.

Urban Sprawl. *Fortune* (January 1958), 102–9. (Reprinted in *The Exploding Metropolis*.)

The City Eviscerated. *Encounter* 61 (October 1958), 32–58.

Plan to Save Vanishing U.S. Countryside. *Life* (August 17, 1959), 88–90. (Reprinted as "Vanishing Countryside" in *Reader's Digest* [November 1959], 198–200.)

Please, Just a Nice Place to Sit. *The New York Times Magazine* (December 3, 1972), 20+.

The Best Street Life in the World: Why Schmoozing, Smooching, Noshing, Ogling Are Getting Better All the Time. *New York* (July 15, 1974), 26+.

New York and Tokyo: A Study in Crowding. In *A Comparative Study of Street Life: Tokyo, Manila, New York*, ed. Hidetoshi Kato, William H. Whyte, Randolph David, Margaret Bemiss, and Rebecca Erwin. Tokyo: Research Institute for Oriental Cultures, Gakushuin University, 1977.

How to Back into a *Fortune* Story. In *Writing for* Fortune: *Nineteen Authors Remember Life on the Staff of a Remarkable Magazine*. New York: Time Inc., 1980.

How to Make Downtown More Livable. *New York* (March 9, 1981), p. 24+.

Permissions Acknowledgments

Index